DATE DUE			

FOURTH EDITION

Nursing &The Law

Ann M. Rhodes, R.N., M.A., J.D.
Robert D. Miller, J.D., M.S.Hyg.

AN ASPEN PUBLICATION®
Aspen Systems Corporation
Rockville, Maryland
Royal Tunbridge Wells
1984

This publication is designed to provide accurate and authoritative information in regard to the subject matter covered. It is sold with the understanding that the publisher is not engaged in rendering legal, accounting, or other professional service. If legal advice or other expert assistance is required, the services of a competent professional person should be sought. *(From a Declaration of Principles jointly adopted by a Committee of the American Bar Association and a Committee of Publishers and Associations.)*

Library of Congress Cataloging in Publication Data

Rhodes, Ann M. (Ann Marie)
Nursing & the Law.

Rev. ed. of: Nursing & the law/Mary W. Cazalas.
3rd ed. c1978.
Includes bibliographies and index.
1. Nursing—Law and legislation—United States. I. Miller, Robert D. (Robert Desle), 1947- . II. Cazalas, Mary W. III. Title. IV. Nursing and the law.
KF2915.N8R46   1984   344.730414   84-21639
ISBN 0-89443-566-3   347.304414

Publisher: John R. Marozsan
Associate Publisher: Jack W. Knowles, Jr.
Editorial Director: Darlene Como
Executive Managing Editor: Margot G. Raphael
Managing Editor: M. Eileen Higgins
Editorial Services: Ruth McKendry
Printing and Manufacturing: Debbie Collins

Library of Congress Catalog Card Number: 84-21639
ISBN: 0-89443-566-3

Printed in the United States of America

1 2 3 4 5

Table of Contents

Preface

During the past several years, there has been an increasing emphasis placed on the effect of law on nurses and nursing practice. As nursing has developed as a profession, some of the legal principles traditionally applied to nursing have become outdated, and as nursing has changed, so has the impact of court cases and regulations on practicing nurses. As nurses have gained independence and responsibility for independent actions and judgments, the risks of liability have changed. Law, like nursing, changes in response to changing needs, roles, and relationships in society. As nursing practice has changed, the scope of applicable law has enlarged considerably.

It is with the recognition that nursing has expanded that the fourth edition of *Nursing and the Law* was developed. Nurses practice in any number of nontraditional places: the role, body of knowledge, scope of practice, accountability, and legal risks of nurses have all expanded, making a working knowledge of many areas of the law essential for the practicing nurse. *Nursing and the Law* is aimed at giving nurses an introduction to the laws that affect nursing practice, an analysis of legal risks in nursing practice, and an overview of several specific areas of law that affect nurses, their practice settings, and their clients.

The philosophy behind the selection of topics for the fourth edition of *Nursing and the Law* is that the rapid advances in nursing technology and practice require that nurses be aware of a number of new and developing areas of law. Three specific considerations affected the choice of topics. First, each nurse should be aware of the basics of nursing practice, liability, and legal questions that directly affect the nurse's interactions with clients. Second, independent practice by nurses is becoming more common, and topics relative to independent practice should be discussed. Finally, the nurse is frequently not only part of a team, but part of a health care institution.

Numerous financial, regulatory, and other pressures are being brought to bear on health care institutions, and nurses, as a critical element of health care delivery, should understand the significance of the institution and these initiatives.

Nursing and the Law begins with an introduction to law and the American legal system. Chapter 2 describes the significance of licensure and certification and discusses issues related to the nurse's scope of practice.

Chapters 3 and 4 provide the nurse with an overview of statutes, regulations, and case law that affect an employing institution and the nurse as employee or supervisor. Chapter 5 discusses issues related to the nurse who practices as an independent contractor.

Chapters 6 and 7 address nursing liability. Chapter 6 provides an overview of the legal bases for finding a nurse liable for intentional or negligent torts. Chapter 7 gives examples of tort liability involving nurses. Chapter 7 is organized into two major sections. The first section discusses nursing liability as it can arise at different points in the nursing process. The second provides specific examples of liability involving nurses in nonhospital or independent practice settings.

Chapter 8 focuses on the legal issues associated with the nurse–patient relationship: when it begins and ends, and what duties are inherent in that relationship.

The role of the nurse as a client advocate and a source of information for clients is the basis for the material provided in Chapters 9 through 13. Nurses need to be aware of the developments in such controversial areas as consent to treatment (Chapter 9), withholding and withdrawing treatment from the dying patients (Chapter 10), patient access to information (Chapter 11), reproductive issues (Chapter 12), and legal aspects of death (Chapter 13). Each of these areas can affect a nurse's communication with patients, and the nurse should have a fundamental understanding of the issues.

Nurses, as members of a dynamic and developing profession, and as the critical link between clients and the health care system, need to know the law that affects the client, the system, and the nurses' relationship with both.

Acknowledgments

There are several individuals whose contributions during the preparation of this book contributed significantly to its development and completion. I would like to thank Rachel Nicola for valuable research assistance, and Jolene Van Waus and Mary Mielnik for manuscript preparation.

I would like to acknowledge several colleagues for their support and encouragement: Deborah Berry Albrecht, Kay Broman, Nancy Emmons, William Hesson, and Sally Mathis.

Finally, I would like to thank my family for their ongoing assistance during the preparation of this book: first and foremost, my husband Steve Miller, my sisters Elizabeth Knipp and Teresa McGee, my brother Nickolas Rhodes, and my mother Kathleen Kennedy Rhodes (St. Mary's Hospital School of Nursing, Class of 1944), to whom my contributions to this book are dedicated.

Ann M. Rhodes

Chapter 1

Introduction to Law

Many of the decisions that nurses make in the course of their practice are affected by legal principles and have potential legal consequences. Since it is impossible to obtain legal advice before each decision, nurses must develop an understanding of the laws that regulate and affect their practice. With the expansion of nursing into independent practice, administration, expanded roles, and increased responsibility for decision making, a knowledge of fundamental legal principles becomes essential, for two reasons: (1) to ensure that decisions are consistent with applicable legal principles and (2) to protect the nurse from liability. This chapter provides basic information about law, the legal system, and the roles of the branches of government in creating, administering, and enforcing the law.

THE NATURE OF LAW

Law has been defined in a variety of ways. The essence of most definitions is that law is a system of principles and processes by which people who live in a society attempt to control human conduct in an effort to minimize the use of force as a means of resolving conflicting interests. Through law, society specifies standards of behavior, the means to enforce those standards, and a system for resolving conflicts.

Law is not an exact science. Lawyers frequently are unable to provide a precise answer to a legal question or to predict with accuracy the outcome of a legal conflict. Much of the law is uncertain. Some questions have never been precisely addressed by the legal system. Even when questions have been answered, the legal system may change the laws in response to changing conditions, or the answer may not be generally applicable.

There are many areas of legal uncertainty in nursing practice, resulting in part from the rapid increase in technology and the development of nursing as a profession. When dealing with a system as complicated as the law and with a profession that has as many facets as nursing, uncertainty is inevitable. A lawyer's advice still is valuable, however, because the attorney can apply knowledge of how the law has addressed similar questions and thus predict the most probable answer. After a dispute has arisen, a lawyer is essential in assuring that the dispute resolution mechanisms of the law are used to the client's advantage.

Laws govern the relationships of private individuals with each other and with government. The body of law that deals with the relationships between private individuals is called private law, while that involving relationships between private individuals and the government is termed public law.

Private law involves the recognition and enforcement of rights and duties of private individuals and organizations. It can be divided into contract law and tort law. Contract law involves the enforcement of certain agreements among private individuals or the payment of compensation for failing to fulfill those agreements. Tort law is concerned with the definition and enforcement of duties and rights among private individuals that are not based on contractual agreements.

Public law defines, regulates, and enforces the relationships of individuals with government and governmental agencies. One important segment of public law is criminal law, which proscribes conduct deemed injurious to the public order and provides for punishment of those found to have engaged in such conduct. Public law also includes an enormous variety of regulations designed to enhance societal objectives by requiring private individuals and organizations to follow specified courses of action in connection with their activities. While noncompliance with these regulations can lead to criminal penalties, the basic thrust of public law is to obtain compliance and attain the goals of the law, not to punish offenders.

The law serves as a guide to conduct, since most disputes or controversies between persons or organizations are resolved without lawyers or courts. The existence of the legal system is a stimulus to orderly private resolution of disputes. Familiarity with applicable legal principles serves as a reinforcement to compromises reached. The likelihood of success in court affects the willingness of persons to negotiate private settlements. Knowledge of the sources and application of the law, therefore, is important for those who may become involved in disputes or controversies, even if those disputes are unlikely to go to court.

GOVERNMENTAL ORGANIZATION AND FUNCTION

This section focuses on the structure of the three branches of government—legislative, executive, and judicial; how the functions of one branch relate to those of the two others; and the effect of each on nursing practice. Put succinctly, the legislature makes the laws, the executive enforces the laws, and the judiciary interprets the laws. Frequently, the functions of the branches overlap in practice.

A vital concept in the constitutional framework of the United States government and of the state governments is that of separation of powers. This means that no one of the three branches is clearly dominant over the two others; however, in the exercise of its functions, each may affect and limit the activities, functions, and powers of the others.

The concept of separation of powers—the system of controlling the dispersion of powers, or system of checks and balances—is illustrated in the relationships among the three branches in regard to legislation. On the federal level, Congress enacts a statute but until the president signs it or it is passed over his veto by a two-thirds vote of each house in Congress, it does not become law, except when he allows it to become law without taking any action while Congress is in session. Thus, by his veto, the president can prevent a bill from becoming law temporarily, and possibly prevent it from becoming law at all. At the same time, the president can suggest or promote a course of action by Congress but cannot compel such action. A bill that has become law ultimately may be declared valid or invalid by the United States Supreme Court, the top entity in the judicial branch of the government, because the Court decides that the law is not (or is) in violation of the Constitution.

Individuals nominated by the president for appointment to the federal judiciary, including the Supreme Court, must be approved by the Senate. Thus, over time, both the executive and legislative branches can affect the composition of the judicial branch of government. In addition, while a Supreme Court decision may be final with regard to the specific controversy before the Court, Congress and the president may generate revised legislation to replace the law that was held unconstitutional. The processes for amending the Constitution are complex and lengthy but they too can serve as a method of offsetting or overriding a Supreme Court decision.

Functions of the Legislative Branch

Each of the three branches of government has a different primary function. The function of the legislative branch (Congress or state legislatures) is to enact laws that may amend or repeal existing statutes or may be entirely new legislation. The legislature determines the nature and extent of the need for new laws and for changes in existing ones. Congress and legislatures use a committee system under which proposed bills are assigned or referred for study to committees with described areas of concern or interest. The committees conduct investigations and hold hearings, at which persons may present their views, to obtain information to assist their members in considering the bills. Some bills eventually reach the full legislative body where, after consideration and debate, they are either approved or rejected. Congress and every state legislature consists of two houses except Nebraska, which has a unicameral body—only one house. Both houses must pass identical versions of a bill before it can go to the chief executive. Differences usually are resolved by a joint conference committee.

Functions of the Executive Branch

The primary function of the executive branch of government is to enforce and administer the law. The chief executive, either the governor of a state or the president of the United States, has a role in the creation of law through the power to approve or veto a legislative proposal, except in North Carolina, where the governor has no veto power. If the chief executive accepts a bill through the constitutionally established process, it becomes a statute, a part of the enacted law. If the chief executive vetoes the bill, it can become law only if the legislature overrides the veto.

The executive branch is organized on a departmental basis in which each department is responsible for a different area of public concern and each enforces the law within its area of responsibility. Most federal law pertaining to nursing is administered by the Department of Health and Human Services (formerly the Department of Health, Education, and Welfare). In the states, regulation of nursing practice is delegated to the state board of nursing. Most states also have separate departments for health and welfare matters that administer and enforce most state laws pertaining to health care. It should be noted, however, that other departments and agencies of government also affect nursing care and practice. On the federal level, for example, laws relating to wages and hours of employment are enforced by the Department of Labor.

Functions of the Judicial Branch

The function of the judicial branch is adjudication, the resolution of disputes in accordance with law. When a patient brings a suit against a hospital or health care professional seeking compensation for harm allegedly suffered as the result of wrongful conduct, the suit is decided by the courts. Many other types of disputes involving hospitals come before the courts, as well.

For example, hospitals resort to the courts to challenge exercises of authority by government agencies and departments, to dispute legislation affecting hospitals, to collect unpaid hospital bills, and to enforce contracts. While news of litigation brought by patients or the government against hospitals receives the greatest attention from the public, very often the hospital initiates a suit to enforce a right or protect a legally recognized interest.

Many disputes and controversies are resolved without resort to the courts, such as by arbitration or informal means. In many situations, however, there is no way to end a controversy without submitting it to the adjudicatory process of the courts. A dispute brought before a court is decided in accordance with applicable law. This application of the law to dispute resolution is the essence of the judicial process.

SOURCES OF LAW

Each of the branches of government produces a source of law that directly or indirectly affects nursing practice. In addition, the Constitution, which creates the distribution of power and authority to enact laws, affects nursing practice. The four primary sources of law are constitutions, statutes, decisions and rules of administrative agencies, and decisions of courts.

Constitutions

The Constitution of the United States is the supreme law of the land. It establishes the general organization of the federal government, grants certain powers to it, and places certain limits on what federal and state governments may do. The Constitution establishes and grants certain powers to the three branches of the federal government—and creates the separation of powers described earlier.

The Constitution is a grant of power from the states to the federal government. The federal government has only the power granted to it by the Constitution. These powers are both express and implied. The express powers include, for example, the power to collect taxes, declare war, and regulate interstate commerce. The Constitution also grants the federal government broad implied powers to enact laws "necessary and proper" for exercising its other powers. When the federal government establishes a law, within the scope of its powers, that law takes precedence over all state and local laws; all conflicting state and local laws are invalid.

The Constitution also places certain limits on what the federal and state governments may do. The best-known limits on federal power are the first ten amendments of the Constitution, the Bill of Rights. The Bill of Rights protects the right to free speech; free exercise of religion; freedom from unreasonable searches and seizures; trial by jury; and the right not to be deprived of life, liberty, or property without due process of law. The most famous limits on state power appear in the Fourteenth Amendment: ". . . nor shall any state deprive any person of life, liberty, or property, without due process of law; nor deny to any person within its jurisdiction the equal protection of the laws." These frequently are referred to as the due process clause and the equal protection clause.

Each state also has its own constitution, which similarly establishes the organization of the state government, grants it certain powers, and places certain limits on what it may do.

Due Process of Law

The due process clause restricts state action, not private action. Actions by state and local governmental agencies, including public hospitals, are considered state actions and must comply with due process requirements. Actions by private individuals at the behest of the state also can be subject to the requirements. In the past, private hospitals sometimes were considered to be engaged in state action when they were regulated or partially funded by government agencies.

The due process clause applies to state actions that deprive a person of "life, liberty, or property." This is interpreted to include such liberty and property interests as a physician's appointment to the medical staff of a public hospital and a hospital's institutional licensure from the state. Thus, in some situations public hospitals must provide due process, and in other situations hospitals are protected by the requirement that state and local governmental agencies provide due process.

The process that is due varies somewhat, depending on the situation. Its two primary elements are: (1) the rules being applied must be reasonable and not vague and (2) fair procedures must be followed in enforcing the rules. Rules that are too arbitrary or vague violate the due process clause and are not enforceable. The primary procedural protections that must be offered are notice of the proposed action and an opportunity to present information on why the action should not be taken. The phrase "due process" in the Fourteenth Amendment also has been interpreted by the Supreme Court to include nearly all of the rights in the Bill of Rights. Thus, state governments may not infringe on those rights.

Equal Protection of the Laws

The equal protection clause also restricts state, not private, action. Equal protection means that like persons must be dealt with in a like fashion. The equal protection clause is concerned with the justifiability of the classifications used to distinguish persons for various legal purposes. The determination of whether a particular difference between persons can justify a particular difference in rules or procedures can be difficult.

In general, courts require that a government agency justify a difference with a "rational reason." The major exception to this standard is the strict scrutiny courts apply to distinctions based on "suspect classifications," such as race.

State Constitutions

Each state has its own constitution. That document, as noted, establishes the organization of the state government, grants certain powers to it, and places certain limits on what it may do.

Statutes

Another major source of law is statutory law—measures that are enacted by a legislature. Legislative bodies include the United States Congress, state legislatures, and local legislative bodies such as city councils or county boards of supervisors. Congress has only the powers delegated to it by the Constitution, but those powers have been interpreted broadly. State legislatures have all powers not denied by the United States Constitution, by federal laws enacted under the authority of the federal government, or by the state constitution. Local legislative bodies have only those powers granted by the state.

When there is a conflict between federal and state law, valid federal law supersedes. In some cases, federal law may preempt an entire area of law so that state law is superseded even if it is not in direct conflict. For example, in some areas, such as antitrust and bankruptcy, Congress explicitly preempts dual state regulation.

When there is a conflict between state and local government, state law supersedes. In some cases state law may preempt an entire area of law so that local law is superseded even if it is not in direct conflict. For example, the highest court in New York ruled that that state had preempted the regulation of abortions[1] so additional regulation by local authorities was prohibited.

The regulation of nursing practice is a function of state law. Consequently, the state legislature has the authority to pass the statutes that define and regulate nursing. The state's nurse practice act, to be valid, must be consistent with applicable constitutional and federal provisions.

Administrative Agencies: Decisions and Rules

The decisions and rules of administrative agencies are another source of law. Legislatures have delegated the responsibility and power to implement various laws to numerous administrative agencies. The example of the relationship between the legislature and the administrative agency that is most familiar to nurses is the state board of nursing, which implements and enforces the state's nurse practice act. The powers of an administrative agency include the quasi-legislative power to adopt regulations and the quasi-judicial power to decide how the statutes and regulations apply to individual cases.

The legislature has delegated these powers because it does not have the time or the expertise to address the complex issues involved in many areas that it believes need to be regulated. Administrative agencies that have been delegated such powers include, on the federal level, the Department of Health and Human Services and its agencies, the Food and Drug Administration, the National Labor Relations Board (NLRB), and the Internal Revenue Service. On the state level, administrative agencies oversee the practice of the professions and regulate various aspects of commerce and public welfare.

All of these agencies have the power to promulgate regulations and apply these to individual cases within their area of expertise. Many administrative agencies, such as the NLRB, seek to achieve some consistency in their decisions by following the position they adopted in previous cases involving similar matters. This is similar to the way courts develop the common law (discussed later in this chapter).

Administrative rules and regulations are valid only to the extent that they are within the scope of the authority granted by the legislature to the agency that has promulgated them. There are constitutional limits to the extent to which the legislature can delegate to administrative agencies. The legislature must retain ultimate responsibility and authority by specifying what regulations the administrative body may make. In the past, the courts often declared delegations unconstitutional unless there was considerable specificity. Today the courts interpret the Constitution to permit much broader delegation but the general areas of law still must be specified.

Congress and many state legislatures have passed administrative procedure acts. These specify the procedures that administrative agencies must follow in promulgating rules or reaching decisions in contested cases, unless another law specifies different procedures. Generally, these laws provide that most proposed rules must be published to allow an opportunity for public comment before they are finalized. Many federal agencies must publish both proposed and final rules in the *Federal Register* and many states have comparable publications.

Court Decisions

Judicial decisions are the fourth source of law. These are the result of the court's role in dispute resolution. In deciding cases, the courts interpret statutes and regulations, determine their validity under the appropriate constitution, and create the common law when deciding cases that are not controlled by statutes, regulations, or a constitution.

There frequently is disagreement over the application of statutes or regulations to specific situations. In some cases an administrative agency has the initial authority to decide how they shall be applied; its decision usually can be appealed to the courts. Courts generally defer to such agencies in discretionary matters, limiting their review to whether the delegation of power to the entity was constitutional and whether it acted within its authority, followed proper procedures, had a substantial basis for its decision, and acted without arbitrariness or discrimination.

Whether or not an administrative agency is involved, the court still may have to interpret a statute or regulation or decide which of two or more conflicting ones apply. Courts have developed rules for interpretation of statutes. In some states a statute specifies rules of interpretation that are designed to help determine the intent of the legislature in passing the law.

The courts also determine whether specific statutes or regulations violate the Constitution. All legislation and regulations must be consistent with the Constitution. The case of *Marbury v. Madison*[2] in 1803 established the power of the courts to declare legislation invalid when it is unconstitutional.

Many of the legal principles and rules applied by the courts in the United States are the product of the common law developed in England and, subsequently, in this country. The term common law is applied to the body of principles that evolves from court decisions resolving controversies. Common law is continually being adapted and expanded. During the colonial period, English common law applied uniformly. After the Revolution, each state provided for the adoption of part or all of the then existing English common law. All subsequent common law in the United States has been developed on a state basis, so on specific subjects it may differ from state to state. Statutory laws are enacted to restate many legal rules and principles that initially were established by the courts as part of the common law. Many issues, particularly those pertaining to disputes in private law areas, still are decided according to common law rules. A state may change these rules by legislation modifying such principles or by later court decisions that establish new and different common law rules.

In deciding specific controversies, courts for the most part adhere to the doctrine of *stare decisis,* literally, "to stand by things decided," but usually called "following precedent" (see later section on *stare decisis*). Applying the same rules and principles as in similar cases decided previously, the court arrives at the same ruling in the current case. However, slight differences in the situation presented may provide a basis for recognizing distinctions between precedent and a current case. Even when such factual distinctions are absent, a court may conclude that a particular common-law rule no longer is in accord with the needs of society and may depart from the precedent.

One clear example of this departure from precedent in health care law was the reconsideration and elimination in nearly every state of the principle of charitable immunity, which had provided nonprofit hospitals with virtual freedom from liability for harm to patients resulting from wrongful conduct. In state after state over 30 years, courts found bases to overrule precedents that had provided immunity and, thereby, allowed suits against nonprofit hospitals.

Another doctrine that courts follow to avoid duplicative litigation and conflicting decisions is *res judicata,* which means "a thing or matter settled by judgment." When a legal controversy has been decided by a court and no more appeals are available, those involved in the suit may not take the same matters to court again. This is different from *stare decisis* in that *res judicata* applies only to those involved in the prior suit and the issues decided in it. The application of *res judicata* can be complicated by disagreements over whether specific matters actually were decided in the prior case.

ORGANIZATION OF THE COURT SYSTEM

To understand the effect of court decisions as precedents, it is necessary to understand the structure of the court system. There are more than 50 court systems in the United States, including the systems of the federal government, each state, the District of Columbia, Puerto Rico, and the territories. These courts do not all reach the same decisions on specific issues. Frequently, there are a majority approach and several minority opinions on each issue. Thus, careful review is necessary to determine which court's decisions apply to any area of controversy and, if no decisions apply specifically, to predict which approach is likely to be adopted.

The federal and many state court systems have three levels—trial courts, intermediate courts of appeal, and a supreme court. Some states do not have intermediate courts of appeals.

State Court System

The trial courts in some states are divided into special courts that deal with specific issues, such as family, juvenile, probate, and limited ones that deal only with lesser crimes, such as misdemeanors, or with civil cases involving limited amounts of money. Each state has trial courts of general jurisdiction that may decide all disputes not assigned to other courts or barred from them by state or federal law.

At the trial court level, applicable law is determined and the evidence is assessed to determine what the "facts" are. The applicable law then is applied to those facts. It is the judge's role to determine what the law is. If there is a jury, the judge instructs the jury as to what the law is, and the jury determines what the facts are and applies the law. If there is no jury, the judge also determines what the facts are. In either case, the determination of the facts must be based on the evidence properly admitted during the trial, so the "facts" are not necessarily what actually happened.

In some cases, everyone agrees on the facts and the only issues presented to the court concern what the law is. In other cases, everyone agrees what the law is but there is disagreement over the facts. To determine the facts for purposes of deciding the case, the credibility of the witnesses and the weight to be given other evidence must be determined. Many cases involve both questions of law and questions of fact. The judge has significant control over the trial even when a jury is involved. If the judge finds that insufficient evidence has been presented to establish a factual issue for the jury to resolve, the judge can dismiss the case or, in civil cases, direct the jury to decide the case a specific way. In civil cases, even after the jury has decided, the judge can decide in favor of the other side.

Most state court systems have an intermediate appellate court. Usually, this court decides only appeals from trial court decisions. In some states, a few issues can be taken directly to the intermediate appellate court. When an appellate court is deciding appeals, it does not accept additional evidence but makes its decisions based on the evidence presented at the trial court and preserved in that record.

Appellate courts almost invariably accept the determination of the facts by the jury or judge in the trial court because they saw the witnesses and can better judge their credibility. Appellate courts usually base their decisions on whether proper procedures were followed in the trial court and whether it interpreted the law properly. However, an appellate court occasionally will find that a jury verdict is so clearly contrary to the evidence that it will either reverse the decision or order a new trial.

Each state has a single court at the highest level, usually called the supreme court (although in New York the highest state level is the Court of Appeals), while trial courts are called supreme courts. The highest court in each state decides appeals from the intermediate appellate courts or, in states without the intermediate level, from trial courts. The highest court frequently has other duties, including adopting rules of procedure for the state court system and determining who may practice law in the state, which includes disciplining lawyers for improper conduct.

Federal Court System

The federal court system has a structure similar to the states. The trial courts are the United States District Courts and special-purpose courts, such as the Court of Claims, which determines certain claims against the United States. Federal trial courts are fundamentally different from those in the states because they have limited jurisdiction. To be heard in federal court, a suit must either present a federal question or must be between citizens of different states. In many types of cases, the controversy must involve at least $10,000. Federal questions include cases on the application of federal statutes and regulations involving possible violations of rights under the Constitution.

When a federal trial court decides a controversy between citizens of different states, it is acting under what is called its "diversity jurisdiction," using federal procedures but applying the law of the applicable state. Sometimes federal courts will decline to decide state law questions until they have been decided by a state court. This is called abstention. It is aimed at leaving state issues to state courts, to avoid rehearing of the same questions in different courts and to minimize the workload of the federal courts. Federal courts generally will not abstain when there also are important federal questions not affected by the state law. Some states have procedures by which federal courts can directly ask a state court to decide a particular question of state law when it is important to the decision of a case before the federal court.

Appeals from the federal trial courts go to a United States Court of Appeals. The United States is divided into 12 areas, called circuits, numbered one through 11, plus the District of Columbia Circuit.

The highest level is the United States Supreme Court. It decides appeals from the United States Courts of Appeals and from the highest state courts if they involve federal laws or the Constitution. Sometimes when the highest state courts or the courts of appeals decline to review a lower court decision, it can be appealed directly to the United States Supreme Court.

Generally, cases involving issues of nursing practice are not appealed to the Supreme Court because these issues emerge in actions involving either torts or licensing sanctions. Both of those types of cases fall under state law and usually do not involve constitutional principles.

The United States Supreme Court has the authority to decline to review most cases and accepts only a small percentage of those presented. With only a few exceptions, a request for review is made by filing a petition for a writ of certiorari ("cert.," as it is called). If the writ of certiorari is granted, the record of the lower court decision is transmitted to the Supreme Court for review. In most cases, the Supreme Court denies the writ for certiorari, which is indicated by *"cert. denied,* [vol.] U.S. [page] ([year])" at the end of the case citation. Denial of a writ of certiorari does not indicate approval of the lower court decision; it merely means the Supreme Court declines to review that decision.

Stare Decisis

The preceding description illustrates the complexity of the court system in the United States. When a court is confronted with an issue, it is bound by the doctrine of *stare decisis* to follow the precedents of higher courts in the same system that have jurisdiction over the geographic area where the court is located. Each appellate court, including the highest court, is generally also bound to follow the precedents of its own decisions unless it decides to overrule the precedent because of changing conditions. Thus, decisions from equal or lower courts or from courts in other systems do not have to be followed.

A second exception occurs when a federal court is deciding a controversy between citizens of different states; it must follow the state law as determined by the highest court of the state in which the court sits. In another exception, a state court deciding a controversy involving a federal law or constitutional question must follow decisions of the United States Supreme Court. In still another situation that may force a court to alter its prior position, the applicable statutes or regulations may be changed by the legislature or an administrative agency.

When a court is confronted with a question that is not answered by applicable statutes or regulations and has not been addressed by its court system, or when it wants to reexamine its decision on a subject it has addressed, it usually will examine the solutions reached in the other systems to help decide the new issue. There is a general tendency toward consistency. A clear trend in decisions across the country can form a basis for a reasonable legal assessment of how to act even when the courts in a particular jurisdiction have not yet decided the issue. However, a court is not bound by decisions from other systems and may reach a different conclusion.

While nearly all states require informed consent to medical procedures, some states determine the information that must be provided to patients by reference to what the patient needs to know, others refer to what other physicians would disclose, and a few states have not decided which reference to use.

Differences in statutes and regulations may force courts in different states to reach different conclusions on certain questions. Some decisions, therefore, are so specific to the statutory or regulatory law of the state that they would not be considered by other courts facing the same issue.

In summary, while it is important to be aware of trends in court decisions across the country, legal advice should be sought before taking actions based on decisions from court systems that do not have jurisdiction over the geographic area in which the controversy arises.

ANATOMY OF A TRIAL

As mentioned previously, court decisions emerge from the resolution of disputes through a lawsuit that is tried in court. The goal of a trial is to reach an orderly resolution of a dispute between two or more parties who have differing interests. The procedure is designed to ascertain facts by hearing evidence, determine which facts are relevant, apply the appropriate principles of law, and pass judgment based on the facts and the applicable law. The many procedural steps in a lawsuit can be divided into six major steps: commencement, pleading, pretrial, trial, appeal, and execution of judgment.

Commencement of the Action

Lawsuits must be brought within a certain time limit that has been prescribed by law in a statute of limitations—a time span that varies with the cause of action. For example, in some states, a suit to recover damages for personal injury caused by negligence must be brought within two years of the injury. If a case is not brought within the prescribed time, the action is barred.

The first necessary element in the trial process is a person who believes a cause of action exists against another person. The first person, called the plaintiff, brings the action and makes the complaint; the defendant is the person against whom the suit is brought. Many cases have multiple plaintiffs and defendants, such as in personal injury actions where the patient and family members bring suit against the hospital and several employees. Additional plaintiffs and defendants may be added as the lawsuit progresses.

The first step is to determine what kind of legal action may be instituted. If the controversy involves the performance of a contract, the proper action is for breach of contract, whereas if a person claims to have been injured by the negligent conduct of another, the correct action would be for negligence. The second step leading to trial is to determine where the suit will be filed. The choice depends upon two factors: (1) which court has jurisdiction over the subject of the controversy and (2) which geographic district includes the area where one of the parties resides or where the alleged injury occurred. For example, a person claiming damages for negligent injury could not file suit in a court that is authorized to hear only family law matters.

There are two major methods by which a lawsuit may be begun. First, in some courts an action is commenced by filing an order with the court clerk to issue a paper, called a writ or summons, to the sheriff (or other designated official). This orders the sheriff to inform the defendants that they must appear before the court on a particular date. In the second method, used in many states and in federal courts, suits are begun by filing and delivery of the complaint itself, which is called *service*.

Upon service of the summons or complaint, the defendants should promptly notify their attorneys or insurance companies. Their attorneys will investigate, decide on a strategy, and respond to the complaint. Prompt notice by the defendant to the insurance company also may be required by the policy as a prerequisite to coverage.

Pleading

Once the action is commenced, each party must present a statement of facts, or pleadings, to the court. The modern system of pleading requires a setting forth of the facts, which serves to notify the other party of the basis for the legal claim. The first pleading is the complaint, in which the plaintiff outlines the factual basis for the claim.

A copy then is served on the defendant, who must reply within a specified time period, usually 15 or 20 days. If the defendant fails to answer within that time, the plaintiff will win by default and a judgment will be entered against the defendant. In certain instances a default judgment will be set aside if the defendant can demonstrate valid reasons for failing to respond.

Upon receiving a copy of the complaint, the defendant also has the right to file preliminary objections before answering the complaint. In these objections, the defendant cites possible errors that would defeat the plaintiff's case. For example, the defendant may object that the summons or complaint was improperly served, that the action was brought in the wrong county, or that there was something technically wrong in the document. The court may permit the plaintiff to correct the errors by filing a new or amended complaint; however, in some instances, the defects may be so significant that the case is dismissed.

The defendant also may present a motion to dismiss the action, alleging that the plaintiff's complaint does not set forth a claim or cause of action recognized by law. If the case is dismissed, the plaintiff has the right to amend the complaint or appeal the lower court's action to an appellate court. On the other hand, if the court declines to dismiss the case, the defendant then is required to file an answer to the complaint.

In some cases, the defendant may have a claim against the plaintiff and will file a counterclaim. For example, the plaintiff may have sued a hospital for personal injuries and property damage caused by a collision with the hospital's ambulance. The hospital may file a counterclaim on the ground that its driver was careful and that it was the plaintiff who was responsible for the accident and should be liable to the hospital for damages.

When the defendant has filed an answer, the plaintiff generally can file preliminary objections to that answer. The plaintiff may assert that the counterclaim is legally insufficient, the form of the answer is defective, or the counterclaim cannot be asserted in the court in which the case is pending. These objectives are addressed by the court.

The pleading may raise questions of both law and fact. As noted earlier, if only questions of law are involved, the judge will decide the case on the pleadings alone. If questions of fact are involved, there must be a trial to determine the facts. When questions of both law and fact are involved and the trial is before a jury, the jury will determine the facts after the judge decides questions of law and instructs the jury concerning the law to be applied. The right to a jury trial may be waived; in such cases, the judge will determine questions of fact and law.

Pretrial Procedures

After the pleadings are completed, many states permit either party to move for a judgment based on the pleadings. The court then will examine the entire case and decide whether to enter judgment according to the merits of the case as indicated in the pleadings. In some states the moving party is permitted to introduce sworn statements, called affidavits, showing that a claim or defense is false. This procedure cannot be used when there is substantial dispute concerning the matters presented by the affidavits.

In federal courts, as well as in most state courts, the parties have the right to discovery—the examination of witnesses before trial. It is during this process of discovery, which can last from several weeks to several years, that the nurse is most likely to become involved in the case, as either a witness or an expert witness. The usual manner of conducting the discovery is to present questions to the opposing parties and witnesses.

Interrogatories are questionnaires that are answered under oath, usually in writing, concerning the facts of the case. When the interrogatories are presented orally by an examiner, the answers, also given under oath, are called a deposition. Either party may obtain a court order permitting the examination and reproduction of books and records, such as medical records. A court order may be obtained to allow the physical or mental examination of a party when that condition is important to the case.

In certain instances it may be desirable to record witnesses' testimony outside the court before the trial. In such a case one party, after giving proper notice to the other and to the prospective witness, may require the witness to answer questions and submit to cross-examining under oath. The testimony is recorded and filed with the court and is entered in evidence if the witness is unavailable at the trial. This procedure may be used when a witness is aged or infirm and may die or be too ill to testify at the trial.

During the process of discovery, both sides determine the facts that will be presented at trial and the witnesses who will be called to attest to each fact.

In many states a pretrial conference will be ordered at the judge's discretion or upon the request of one of the parties. This is an informal discussion in which the judge and the attorneys for both sides eliminate matters that are not in dispute, agree on the issues, and settle procedural matters related to the trial. Although the purpose of the pretrial conference is not to compel the parties to settle, that often occurs at this point.

The Trial

At the trial, as noted earlier, the facts of the case are determined through evidence presented, the principles of law relating to those facts are applied, and a conclusion is reached. Evidence presented consists of witnesses' answers to questions on direct examination or cross-examination; it also may include equipment, instruments, devices, and other tangible items that have a bearing on the case.

Generally, witnesses are persons who have a direct connection with some part of the case. A witness may have seen certain events take place or heard one of the parties say something. In highly technical cases, where the ordinary layman is not qualified to appreciate or properly evaluate the significance of the facts, witnesses who qualify as experts in their particular field are called. This is typical in cases involving negligence claims in nursing or medical care. The expert witnesses state opinions in answer to hypothetical or theoretical questions.

At the start of the trial, a jury (if there is to be one) is selected. A number of apparently qualified people are selected as a panel, from which the jury is chosen and sworn. The attorneys then make opening statements. This practice may vary slightly from state to state, but usually the statement indicates what each side intends to prove.

The plaintiff's attorney then calls the first witness for that side and direct examination begins. When the direct examination is completed, the opposing attorney may cross-examine the witness in an effort to challenge or disprove the testimony. The plaintiff's attorney then may ask the witness additional questions in an effort to overcome the effect of the cross-examination. Subsequently, the plaintiff's other witnesses are questioned. The plaintiff's attorney also introduces other evidence such as documents and tangible items.

After the plaintiff's entire case has been presented, the defendant may move for a directed verdict in its favor on the ground that the plaintiff has failed to present sufficient facts to prove the case or that the evidence does not supply a legal basis for a verdict in the plaintiff's favor. If the motion is overruled, the defendant's case is presented in the same manner as the plaintiff's.

Either party then may ask the judge to rule that the claim has not been proved or that a defense has not been established and direct the jury to render a verdict to that effect. If these motions are overruled, the attorneys make oral arguments to the jury and the judge instructs the jury on the appropriate law. This practice varies greatly from state to state and even from judge to judge. Some judges summarize the facts, integrate them with the applicable legal principles, and comment on the evidence as well. Other judges merely state the controlling legal principles. The jury then retires to a separate place to deliberate and reach a verdict; when it has done so, it reports to the judge, who then renders a judgment based on the verdict.

At the time the judgment is rendered, the losing party has an opportunity to move for a new trial. If a new trial is granted, the entire process is repeated; if not, the judgment becomes final, subject to a review of the trial record by an appellate court if the losing side appeals.

Appeals

An appellate court reviews a case on the basis of the trial record as well as written summaries of the applicable legal principles and short oral arguments by the attorneys. The court then takes the case under advisement while the judges consider it and agree upon a decision. They then issue an opinion explaining their reasons. Appellate court decisions and opinions are published and are a source of continuing legal information for lawyers, who, relying in part on *stare decisis,* can prepare themselves by referring to earlier similar cases.

When a case is decided by the highest appellate court in the state, a final judgment results and the matter is ended. Under some circumstances, that ruling may be appealed to the United States Supreme Court, but this is rare because the case must involve a federal or constitutional issue, or the interpretation or application of a statute enacted by Congress. Since most negligence actions arise under state law, it is unlikely that such cases will reach the Supreme Court.

Execution of Judgments

In lawsuits naming hospitals, physicians, and nurses as defendants, a party generally will seek to recover money damages. Other forms of relief are available, such as an order or an injunction requiring the defendant to perform or refrain from performing an act. The jury decides the amount of damages, subject to review by a higher court.

If, after the trial and final appeal, the defendant does not comply with the judgment in the suit, the plaintiff may cause the judgment to be executed. This. means that if the defendant ignores an order to perform or refrain from performing an act, the failure to obey will be regarded as contempt of court and will result in a fine or imprisonment. If the judgment is for payment of money, the plaintiff may cause the sheriff or other judicial officer to sell as much of the defendant's property as is necessary to pay the judgment and court costs.

THE EXPERT WITNESS

In court, the general rule is that witnesses must testify only to facts—their opinions and conclusions are inadmissible. However, it is obvious that some cases may involve information of a technical nature that is outside the knowledge and experience of laymen. In such cases, an expert witness who has special knowledge, skill, experience, or training is called upon to submit an opinion.

In negligence actions, expert testimony falls into two categories: (1) on the extent of damage and (2) on the standard of care. Both areas require specialized knowledge and experience for a witness to render an opinion. The question of how much and what type of training and experience qualifies a person to be an expert witness is a difficult one. The American Law Institute suggests the following definition:

> A witness is an expert witness and qualified to give expert testimony if the judge finds that to perceive, know or understand the matter concerning which the witness is to testify requires special knowledge, skill, experience or training, and that the witness has the requisite special knowledge, skill, experience or training.

In practice, when it becomes evident that expert testimony is required, the attorneys for each side will obtain the services of experts. When testifying, the experts' training, experience, and special qualifications are explained to the jury. The experts then are asked to give an opinion on hypothetical questions based on the facts of the case. It is up to the jury to decide which expert opinion to accept.

Increasingly, questions arise in malpractice litigation that involve both the appropriate scope of nursing practice and the standard of care. Expert testimony is used to clarify these issues for the jury. Nurses, especially those with specialized, supervisory, or teaching experience, may be asked to testify as experts. Supervisory nurses may be asked to describe the standard of nursing care when another nurse is being sued for negligence. This provides the jury with a standard against which to measure the conduct of the defendant nurse. The actual conduct will be established by documentary and testimonial evidence. In many of the early malpractice actions involving nursing practice or the standard of care, physicians were called as the expert witnesses on nursing care. Increasingly, however, nurses are being used as experts in their own field.

After answering questions for the party that called the expert, the individual may be questioned and challenged by the opposing attorney. The attorney who called the expert is expected to object to improper questions by the other attorney. In the event of an objection, the witness refrains from answering until the judge upholds or denies the objection and directs that the witness answer or the attorney withdraw the question.

CONCLUSION

This chapter has described the nature and sources of law, the structure of the court system, and the anatomy of a trial and discussed briefly some of the ways in which nurses are likely to have contact with the legal system. Most commonly, a nurse will be involved in possible or pending litigation as a witness. The nurse may have been involved in or observed some incident or behavior that gives rise to a cause of action or may have provided care to the patient before or after the incident took place. The nurse may be contacted by one or both sides early in the process of discovery. If this occurs, it is advisable that the employed nurse contact the employer's attorney before discussing the case with either party.

If the case proceeds to a trial, expert testimony on the standard of nursing care will be required. Nurses with specialized education or extensive experience may be contacted to provide such testimony.

Another way a nurse may have contact with the legal system is by committing prohibited acts. This can subject the nurse to criminal liability under the state's criminal code, civil liability, or licensing sanctions. These sanctions are described more thoroughly in Chapter 2.

NOTES

1. *Robin v. Incorporated Villege of Hempstead,* 285 N.E.2d 585 (N.Y. 1972).
2. 5. U.S. (1 Cranch 137) (1803).

BIBLIOGRAPHY

Brown, Sharon. "Expert Witness." *Nursing Management* 15, no. 5 (May 1984):14.

Bullough, Bonnie. THE LAW AND THE EXPANDING NURSING ROLE. 2nd ed. New York: Appleton-Century-Crofts, Inc., 1980.

Foote, E. "The Role of Law (and Lawyers) in Medicine." *Pharos* (April 1976):53.

Furrow, Barry. "Iatrogenesis and Medical Error: The Case for Medical Malpractice Litigation." *Law, Medicine, and Health Care* 9, no. 4 (October 1981):4.

Gibson, J.M., and Schwartz, R.L. "Physicians and Lawyers: Science, Art, and Conflict." *American Journal of Law and Medicine* 6, no. 2 (1980):173.

Regan, William. "Legally Speaking: The Nurse as Expert Witness." *RN* 45, no. 4 (April 1982):75.

Chapter 2

Licensure, Certification, and Scope of Practice

A complex system of licensing and credentialing has developed in an attempt to assure that qualified people are engaged in the practice of the health care professions. All states require licensure for individuals who wish to practice nursing and most have instituted licensing mechanisms for advanced or specialized nursing practice. The primary purpose of licensure and credentialing is to protect the public health by helping identify qualified providers and by prohibiting unqualified ones from engaging in practices that require expertise.

There are many public and private credentialing methods. The public method is individual licensure—the method used to ensure at least minimal competence in nursing practice in all states. Private methods include accreditation of educational programs, certification of individuals, and credentialing by institutions.

INDIVIDUAL LICENSURE

Licensure can be defined as the process by which a legal authority grants permission to a qualified individual or entity to perform certain activities that are declared to be illegal without a license. In the context of health care delivery, licensure is the process by which state-authorized licensing agencies grant the legal right to practice a health profession, such as nursing, to individuals who meet predetermined standards.

Licensure can be either mandatory or permissive. A mandatory law requires that an individual obtain a license before practicing within the scope of practice reserved for those with a license, unless the individual is eligible under one of the exceptions provided in the law. A permissive licensure law usually regulates the use of titles: an individual cannot use the title without a license but can perform many or all of the same functions. Nearly all licensing laws include certain educational qualifications and require the passage of an examination. Specified personal qualifications such as good moral character usually are required.

States have discretion to determine which professions to license. In 1889 the Supreme Court upheld mandatory licensure of physicians.[1] The Court said:

> The power of the state to provide for the general welfare of its people authorizes it to prescribe all such regulations as in its judgment will secure or tend to secure them against the consequences of ignorance and incapacity as well as deception and fraud. . . . The nature and extent of the qualifications required must depend primarily upon the judgment of the state as to their necessity.

There is considerable variation in the occupations licensed by each state, but nurses are licensed in all states. In many states, physicians and dentists were the first health professionals to be licensed, with nursing generally next. Pharmacists also are licensed in all states. Many other professionals and technicians are licensed in many states, including physical therapists, psychologists, audiologists, emergency medical technicians, and radiologic technicians. In some states, staff members of hospitals or certain types of hospitals are exempt from some licensure requirements.

Most nurse practice acts provide for the imposition of a penalty for practicing without a license, including a fine and/or imprisonment. Failure to obtain a license does not usually make the nurse automatically liable to patients for all injuries they suffer while being treated by the nurse. The plaintiff usually must prove injury resulting from the unlicensed practitioner's negligence or lack of skill. However, a licensed practical nurse was held to be liable for negligence in administering an injection because she was not licensed at the time the incident occurred.[2]

The term ''scope of practice'' refers to the legally permissible boundaries of practice for the health care provider and is defined in each state by statute, rule, or a combination of the two. Mandatory licensure laws reserve a certain scope of practice for those who obtain a license. The definition and evolution of the scope of practice for nurses have been controversial, focusing on two broad issues: (1) Who may make the judgment that certain procedures may be performed? (2) Who may perform the procedures?

In general, medical diagnosis and the ordering of most diagnostic and therapeutic procedures are reserved for the physician. The nurse generally determines what nursing care is required by the patient's status and condition and when care is insufficient so that medical attention or instructions must be sought. The concept of nursing diagnosis is gaining recognition. Some states permit nurses to make some judgments traditionally reserved for physicians when acting under standing orders or established protocols.

The issue of diagnosis and its role in nursing practice is complex. Most medical procedures are restricted to physicians when they are first introduced. As the procedures are performed more frequently and become better defined, there has been a tendency for nurses and other groups (such as technicians) to begin performing the procedures. This evolution has varied from state to state and has been officially recognized in several different ways:

- The legislature in some states has changed licensing statutes to list the new procedures permitted.
- The attorney general's office in other states has issued an opinion stating that certain practices are permitted or prohibited.
- The medical and/or nursing licensing board has issued rules or statements concerning the permitted scope of practice.
- The state nurses' association, the medical society, and other private professional organizations have issued joint statements on these issues.
- Judicial decisions have defined the roles.

Thus, many sources must be examined to determine the accepted scope of practice in a particular state. The issue of the scope of nursing practice is increasingly complex as specialties develop and professional and licensing agencies strive to provide guidance for practitioners and institutions.

Some of the specific practices addressed for nurses have been administering anesthesia, injections, starting intravenous (IV) fluids and medications, and insertion of various tubes. In nearly all states, these issues have been resolved for registered nurses and some, especially starting IVs, are being addressed for licensed practical nurses.

Some states have given physicians broad authority to delegate functions to nurses. For example, Michigan permits physicians to delegate tasks or functions under proper supervision if permitted by standards of acceptable and prevailing practice.[3] This has been interpreted by the Michigan attorney general to permit delegating to nurses the authority to prescribe any drugs except controlled substances as long as the name of the supervising physician is identified on the prescription.[4]

Other states have given the licensing boards broad authority to expand the role of nurses by rule when the expanded roles are recognized by the medical and nursing professions.[5] In a 1983 case,[6] the Missouri Supreme Court found that the Nurse Practice Act permitted nurses to assume responsibilities consistent with their specialized education, judgment, and skill. (This case is discussed more fully in Chapter 5.)

It is important to be aware of restrictions on scope of practice because licensed professionals who act outside that scope are unlicensed practitioners when performing those acts, with potential adverse consequences for the professionals and their employers.

Definition of Nursing Practice

The entry of physicians' assistants and nurse practitioners into the health field, advances in nursing education, and the changing role of the nurse in performing functions previously considered the practice of medicine have stimulated revision of nurse and medical practice acts. Nursing and medical associations have been updating the definition of professional nursing in nurse practice acts. Additional legislative changes granting authority to nursing specialists to perform functions previously restricted to physicians are likely.

Historical definitions illustrate that nurses' orientation is to the promotion of the well-being of the people being served, whether that involves care of the sick or promotion of health. A 1980 definition that incorporates the concept of care for persons at all levels of wellness is: "Nursing is the diagnosis and treatment of human responses to actual or potential health problems." This definition appears in the American Nurses Association *Social Policy Statement*.[7] In 1955, the ANA adopted the following definition, which has become the basis for many states' nurse practice acts:

> The term "practice of professional nursing" means the performance, for compensation, of any acts in the observation, care, and counsel of the ill, injured, or infirm, or in the maintenance of health or prevention of illness in others or in the supervision and teaching of other personnel, or the administration of medications and treatments prescribed by a licensed physician or dentist, requiring substantial specialized judgment and skill and based on knowledge and application of the principles of biological, physical, and social science.[8]

There are three general approaches to the statutory definition of nursing. The first, or traditional, approach is based on that 1955 model definition. The traditional definition of nursing does not encompass diagnosis, prescription, or treatment. Generally, this approach is used in states that have not addressed the issue of scope of practice for advanced or expanded practitioners. The limitations are becoming less common as more states adopt statutes or rules regulating advanced practice. The second approach authorizes nurses to perform additional acts beyond the traditional definition and typically allows them to practice under standing orders or under the supervision of the physician. A few states have corresponding "delegatory amendments" to the medical practice act that authorize nurses to perform delegated medical tasks under the physician's supervision. The third approach, which the majority of states use, is administrative. This includes a definition of nursing that expands upon the ANA statement and allows nurses to perform such additional acts as may be authorized by appropriate state regulatory agencies.

Nurse practitioners and nurses practicing in expanded roles are regulated by the nurse practice act in each state or by rules adopted by the state licensing agency. Many statutes specifically prohibit nurses from performing "medical" acts, such as medical diagnosis and prescription of treatment, but there is a growing trend toward amending the laws to permit the performance of "medical acts" or "additional acts" recognized as proper by the medical and nursing professions. These amendments generally grant authority to the state board of nursing to promulgate regulations as to requirements for nurse practitioners and what tasks they may perform. The regulations then are administered and enforced by the board of nursing.

The Board of Nursing

Each nurse practice act creates a regulatory agency, usually called the board of nursing. The legislature delegates to that board the authority to implement and enforce the statute. The board is responsible for determining eligibility for initial licensing and relicensing, approval and supervision of educational institutions, enforcing the statute, and promulgating rules that regulate nursing practice. The board must follow the procedures specified by state law.

The governor of the state generally appoints the board members. Since they are expected to have expertise in nursing, the selections usually are made from a list of names submitted by professional nursing organizations. Some statutes require this advisory input from the professional organizations but most governors solicit such recommendations even when not statutorily required to do so.

The number of board members ranges from three to 20, although the majority have no more than ten. Members usually are selected to represent some area or specialty in nursing and have a direct interest in those fields. The statute often stipulates that members must have practiced nursing in the state for a minimum number of years. Boards in some states also include one or more nonprofessional members.

The nursing licensing board, like other administrative agencies, exercises several types of authority: (1) legislative, by developing rules and regulations that govern nursing practice and are binding on all licensees; (2) quasi-judicial, to hear and decide cases involving violations of professional standards or rules; (3) licensure control.

NURSING LICENSURE

The objectives of licensing laws are to limit and control admission into the health occupations and to protect the public from unqualified practitioners by promulgating and enforcing standards of practice within the professions. Nursing, along with other groups aspiring to professional status at the end of the nineteenth century, viewed licensure as a means of gaining control over the membership of the emerging profession.[9] There now is less public support for limiting the size of professions through law, so most licensing laws must be justified on the basis of public protection. All states regulate nursing practice.

Requirements for Licensure

Since the goal of licensure is to ensure the competence of practitioners, requirements generally focus on the characteristics that are thought to assure that the applicant is at least minimally competent. These characteristics include academic and clinical training, satisfactory performance on a licensing examination, and personal attributes.

Formal vocational training is necessary for nursing licensure in all states. Course requirements vary, but all courses must be completed at board-approved schools or institutions. Although many state boards still adhere to their own standards for accreditation, an increasing number (such as the National Association of Pediatric Nurse Associates and Practitioners, and the American College of Nurse Midwives) now accept standards established by national accrediting agencies. This trend has tended to standardize the instruction program at nursing schools.

Each state requires that the applicant pass an examination for nurse licensure. The examinations usually are written and administered twice a year. The board of nursing may formulate the examination, but it is more common to use material prepared by professional examination services or national examining boards. The licensing statutes also typically specify certain personal qualifications such as a minimum age, good moral character, and citizenship or an appropriate visa.

Special Licensing Procedures

Because each state has its own act, boards have had to address the issue of licensing nurses who have qualified in other states. There are four methods by which boards license such nurses: reciprocity, endorsement, examination, and waiver.

Reciprocity is a formal or informal agreement between two states that the board of each agrees to recognize licenses of the other. The initial licensing requirements of such states usually are essentially equivalent. The concept of reciprocity also is recognized in licensing sanctions. For example, in 1983 a Pennsylvania court upheld the state board's revocation of a nurse's license based on the fact that her license had been revoked in Florida under a provision similar to Pennsylvania law.[10]

Under endorsement, boards issue a license to a nurse licensed in another state if the individual's qualifications were equivalent to their own state's requirements at the time of the original licensure. As a condition for endorsement, many states require that the qualifying examination taken in the other state be comparable to their own. As with reciprocity, endorsement becomes much easier where uniform qualifications are required by the different states. The trend toward national nursing examinations and national standards for schools of nursing has simplified licensure by both endorsement and reciprocity.

Examination and waiver are much less common than licensing by reciprocity and endorsement. Some states will not recognize prior licensure by another state and require all applicants to pass the regular examination as well as fulfill the other requirements for initial licensure. On the other hand, when applicants do not meet all the requirements for licensure but have equivalent qualifications, some of the specific educational, experience, or examination requirements may be waived.

Most states grant temporary licenses while an application for a regular license is processed or to nurses in other states who intend to be in the state for a limited time. Most commonly, temporary licenses are granted to new graduate nurses pending the outcome of the state licensing examination.

Rulemaking

Boards generally have broad authority to regulate the professions they license. This authority is exercised through rulemaking—the process by which rules and regulations are promulgated to regulate and define the practice of nursing. When developing and approving rules, the board must follow the procedures specified by state law. Generally, the proposed rule must be published, and members of the profession and others must be given an opportunity to comment. Rules are valid only if they are within the authority granted to licensing boards by the legislature.

Some rules have been challenged on the ground that they are beyond the authority of the board. For example, the Washington State Nurses Association challenged a regulation of the Board of Medical Examiners that authorized physician's assistants to issue prescriptions and write medical orders for patient care. In 1980, the Washington court upheld the regulation and found that it did not exceed the board's statutory authority.[11] Some controversial rules have been found to exceed the scope of the regulatory agency's authority and have been held to be invalid on that basis. It is important for nurses to be familiar with the current positions of the board of nursing in states where they practice.

Discipline and Due Process

Licensing boards have broad authority to discipline professionals who violate the standards specified in the law or the board's rules. The discipline may be suspension or revocation of the license or a probationary period during which certain conditions must be met. Most licensing boards have been given the authority to impose various conditions, including prohibiting certain types of practice or requiring substance abuse rehabilitation efforts, consultation or supervision for various procedures, or satisfactory completion of special education programs.

Disciplinary proceedings against a nurse can be initiated in several ways, described in each state's statutes or rules. Typically, a written complaint to the board of nursing is required, setting forth the basis for the disciplinary action. The complaint can be made by anyone, including physicians, patients, and other nurses. In some states nurses are required to report actions of other nurses that could lead to discipline.[12] Occasionally the board of nursing initiates a complaint. Complaints are screened by the board and, if appropriate, an investigation is instituted.

The board has the authority to determine which charges to pursue and investigate. For example, in one case a patient filed a complaint demanding the revocation of the licenses of several nurses. The board said the evidence did not warrant disciplinary action. On appeal a Pennsylvania court held that the action of the board in determining not to pursue the charges was a valid exercise of the agency's prosecutorial discretion.[13]

In disciplinary proceedings, the board's authority is limited to the areas defined by statute. In 1981, the Tennessee Court of Appeals held that the board of nursing had no jurisdiction over a licensed nurse who provided services as a lay midwife. Noting that the Tennessee Nurse Practice Act did not deal with midwifery and that midwifery was excluded from the statutory definition of medicine, the court found that the board had acted beyond the scope of its authority in revoking the nurse's license.[14]

Before imposing disciplinary sanctions, the licensing board must provide due process to the professional, including at least notice of the alleged wrongful conduct and an opportunity to present information regarding the allegations. Many states impose stricter requirements that must be followed for the board's action to be valid. Failure by the board to comply with the requirements of due process or state law can result in a court decision reversing the board's action. For example, the Colorado Supreme Court ordered a nurse's license reinstated, in part because the statute required the full licensing board to attend the hearing concerning the revocation of her license and the full board had not done so.[15] Most laws do not require the full board to be present, but if that is the law, it must be followed. Typically, a quorum of the board must either attend the hearing or review the testimony.

Another element of due process is that the licensed professional must have adequate notice that the questioned conduct is prohibited. The courts usually rule that a prohibition of "unprofessional conduct" gives adequate notice that a wide range of inappropriate behavior is forbidden. It is not considered too vague as long as it is applied to conduct that is widely recognized as unprofessional. The Oregon Supreme Court upheld the revocation of a nurse's license for "conduct derogatory to the standards of professional nursing."[16] She had instructed, recommended, and permitted her daughter to serve as a registered nurse, knowing that the daughter was not licensed as a nurse.

However, "unprofessional conduct" is not adequate notice for all possible violations. An Idaho nurse challenged a six-month suspension of her license for unprofessional conduct. The Board of Nursing had found that she had discussed laetrile treatment in a hospital with a leukemia patient on chemotherapy without the approval of the physician, interfering with the physician-patient relationship. The board considered this unprofessional conduct. The Idaho Supreme Court ruled that the board could have prohibited this conduct by rule but that a prohibition of unprofessional conduct did not give the nurse adequate warning that this conduct was prohibited. The court ordered the reinstatement of the nurse's license.[17]

On the other hand, a Texas court in 1983 upheld a one-year suspension of a nurse's license for "unprofessional and dishonorable conduct . . . likely to deceive, defraud or injure patients."[18] The nurse had failed to check the vital signs of a patient with obvious cardiac distress and instructed the person to go to a hospital 24 miles away. The patient died en route. The court found that the nurse's behavior violated both the statute and a rule of the Texas Board of Nursing. Many licensing boards are now specifying by rule more detailed grounds for disciplinary action. Nurses should monitor these efforts closely and participate in the rulemaking process to assure that the rules do not inadvertently prohibit appropriate existing practices.

State law generally sets forth the basic grounds for disciplinary action against nurses: fraud in obtaining a license; unprofessional, illegal, dishonorable or immoral conduct; performance of specific actions prohibited by the act; conviction of a felony or crime of moral turpitude; and drug or alcohol addiction rendering the individual incapable of performing duties. Many recent licensing cases involve drug-related offenses committed by nurses, often involving the theft or use of controlled substances from their place of employment.

The statutory authority for disciplinary action in these cases usually is found in the prohibition of "unprofessional conduct" in most nurse practice acts. Many courts have held that "unprofessional conduct" gives legally adequate notice to professionals as to what conduct is prohibited. A Minnesota court defined unprofessional conduct as "conduct which violates those standards of professional behavior which . . . have become established by the consensus of the expert opinion of the members as reasonably necessary for the protection of the public interest."[19]

The grounds for disciplinary action vary widely from state to state, so nurses must inform themselves of the general basis for license suspension or revocation in the states in which they practice. Many state boards also have developed rules to define what behavior is subject to disciplinary action. Some statutes specifically authorize judicial review of board proceedings. This right may be limited to a review of the fairness and legality of the board's action, or it may permit a complete new hearing, depending on the jurisdiction.

Most courts defer to the determination of the nursing board in disciplinary proceedings. If the board acted within the scope of its statutory authority, the action was supported by the evidence presented, and the decision does not appear to be arbitrary, capricious, or unreasonable, it will be upheld. Appellate courts have criticized trial courts for substituting their judgment for that of the board.

However, in some cases courts have found that the evidence did not justify the disciplinary action that the board imposed. A Pennsylvania court reversed the board's action in reprimanding a nurse for allegedly slapping a patient.[20] The court, after examining the evidence, said that the evidence clearly showed that the nurse "tapped" the patient's arm to induce him to let go of her hand, that other means had been used to persuade the patient to release her, and that the patient was in danger of falling when the nurse tapped his hand. The court also said that the violation was not a "willful or repeated" violation as required by the Pennsylvania statute to justify a reprimand.

Usually, the nurse practice act designates which state court may hear appeals of nursing board actions. If the statute does not specifically authorize judicial review, this right is presumed. All opportunities for administrative appeals must be exhausted before a case can go to court.

Disciplinary proceedings before an administrative board differ substantially from those in court. Differences include the level of formality of the hearing, the type and scope of evidence that is acceptable, and the level of proof that is required to impose a punishment on the licensee. Nurses and other professionals involved in disciplinary proceedings before licensing boards do not receive the same procedural protections as are available to defendants in court.

PRIVATE CREDENTIALING

A wide variety of private credentialing methods has been developed. Educational programs are accredited, individuals are certified, and hospitals and other institutions investigate the credentials of prospective staff members before permitting them to practice in the institution.

Accreditation of Educational Programs

Private professional organizations sponsor programs that establish criteria to evaluate educational programs in their disciplines. For nursing, the National League for Nursing (NLN) assumes this role. Periodically, the NLN sends an individual or a team to investigate educational programs that have applied for accreditation; it then accredits programs that meet its criteria. Although accreditation is voluntary, most educational programs make a significant effort to obtain and retain accreditation from established bodies. Graduates from accredited programs find it easier to obtain permission to take licensing examinations or to be admitted for advanced study because their degrees generally are accepted without additional proof of the quality of their educational program. The NLN also has assumed a role in the establishment and upgrading of standards of nursing practice through the promotion of a national standard for educational programs as well as of research, consultation, and publication.

The Council on Postsecondary Accreditation recognizes, monitors, and coordinates bodies that accredit institutions and programs in health and other fields. The secretary of education recognizes national accrediting bodies with the advice of the Advisory Committee on Accreditation and Institutional Eligibility, using published criteria.[21]

Certification

Private professional organizations sponsor programs to certify that individuals meet certain criteria and are prepared to practice in the discipline. Certification provides the same benefits to the individual as completion of an accredited educational program, plus the benefit of being individually certified as having met additional criteria (such as passing a test) related to performance. Certification recognizes the attainment of advanced, specialized knowledge and skills beyond what is required for safe practice. Some forms of certification, especially by medical specialty boards, have become so widely accepted that it may be difficult to practice without certification.

The development of certification standards in nursing has focused primarily on practice in expanded roles. Controversy has surrounded efforts to develop certification programs within the specialty areas of nursing. A majority of the states mandate completion of a formal nursing educational program of specified length that is approved by the respective boards. Some states require certification for expanded practice licenses by a national certifying agency such as the American Association of Nurse Anesthetists, the American College of Nurse Midwives, the National Association of Pediatric Nurse Associates and Practitioners, or the American Nurses' Association. The trend is toward the development of state requirements for expanded practice, often based on certification by a professional organization, and adopted by rule.

Institutional Credentialing

Hospitals have a responsibility to evaluate the credentials of all persons working in the hospital and to delineate what they may do. For most hospital staff members, this responsibility is fulfilled through the hiring process, hospital or department rules concerning practice patterns, the continuing supervisory system, performance evaluation, and verification of relicensure. In the hiring process, the qualifications of the individual must be checked, including verification of licensure or other credentials. This is important not only to determine professional competence but also to make a reasonable effort to detect other problems that could interfere with safe patient care.

A Georgia court ruled that a hospital could be liable for the molesting of an infant by an orderly because the hospital had not checked his past, which would have disclosed a criminal conviction for being a "peeping Tom."[22] A Texas court upheld the liability of a hospital to a patient who was injured when an orderly attempted to remove a catheter from the patient's bladder without first deflating a bulb that held it in place.[23] The court upheld an additional assessment against the hospital, called punitive damages, because the hospital had failed to check the employment and personal references of the orderly before hiring him. A check would have indicated that he had been expelled from Naval Medical Corps School with a serious drug problem and criminal record.

After staff members are hired, their practice is delineated by hospital and departmental rules and the continuing supervisory system. When licensure is required for particular positions, there should be a system for assuring that staff members have maintained their licensure by appropriate renewals.

Hospitals that desire accreditation by the Joint Commission on Accreditation of Hospitals (JCAH) are required to have a formal statement adopted by the medical staff delineating the "qualifications, status, clinical duties, and responsibilities of specified professional personnel."[24] The JCAH *Accreditation Manual for Hospitals* does not specify which personnel fall into this category, but its surveyors have focused on clinical psychologists, nurse anesthetists, and physician's assistants. The JCAH does not require individual review of these professionals by the medical staff. However, the hospital should have a method for assuring that the qualifications are met.

Some nursing specialists and other professionals are seeking authorization to practice in some hospitals on an independent or quasi-independent basis without being hospital employees. These groups include nurse anesthetists and other nurse practitioners. In nearly all states, hospitals have the authority to establish whether these services will be provided in the facility and, if so, whether they may be provided by nonemployees. A hospital that decides, or is required, to permit nonemployees to practice in the facility, adopts a procedure for verifying their qualifications, obtaining their commitment to abide by all applicable hospital and department rules, defining their scope of practice, assuring appropriate supervision and evaluation of their performance, and providing for terminating their permission to practice if warranted.

NURSING SPECIALTIES

Since the mid-1960s, the development of numerous nursing specialties has led to greater emphasis on collegiate and graduate-level preparation, the uneven availability of medical services, and the escalation in health care costs. Nurses with specialized training have begun to provide primary care services such as assessment, diagnosis, and treatment to identified patient groups. The emergence of nurse practitioners as a growing body of providers has raised many legal issues, including scope of practice and liability.

Many legislatures have enacted laws that recognize nurse practitioners and define and permit their practice. As of mid-1984, nurse practitioners were practicing in at least 35 states. They have sought statutory authorization for more independence in function and decision making. Many states have opened the door to expanded delegation of medical functions but have not clearly defined the limits of permissible delegation. Many require physicians to supervise and be legally responsible for nurse practitioners' activities.

The nursing specialties most commonly recognized include nurse anesthetists, pediatric nurse practitioners, nurse midwives, and family nurse practitioners. Specialties recognized to a more limited extent include geriatric nurse practitioners, school nurse practitioners, mental health specialists, community health practitioners, and occupational health specialists.

NOTES

1. *Dent v. West Virginia*, 129 U.S. 114 (1889).
2. *Barber v. Reinking*, 68 Wash. 139, 411 P.2d 861 (1966).
3. MICH. COMP. LAWS, §§ 333.16215(1) (1979).
4. Op. Mich. Atty. Gen. 5630 (January 22, 1980).
5. *E.g.* IOWA CODE, §§ 152.1(2)(d) (1983).
6. *Sermchief v. Gonzales*, 600 S.W.2d 683 (*Mo. en banc* 1983).
7. American Nurses' Association, NURSING, A SOCIAL POLICY STATEMENT (1980).
8. "ANA Board Approves a Definition of Nursing Practice," 55 *Am. J. Nursing* 1474 (1955).
9. Shannon, "Our First Licensing Laws," 75 *Am. J. Nursing* 1327 (1975).
10. *Schoenhair v. Pennsylvania*, 459 A.2d 877 (Pa. 1983).
11. *Washington State Nurses Ass'n v. Board of Medical Examiners*, 93 Wash. 117, 605 P.2d 1269 (1980).
12. *E.g.* IOWA CODE § 258A.9(2) (1983).
13. *Frawley v. Downing*, 364 A.2d 748 (Pa. Commw. Ct. 1976).
14. *Leggett v. Tennessee Bd. of Nursing*, 612 S.W.2d 476 (Tenn. 1981).
15. *Colorado State Bd. of Nursing v. Hohu*, 129 Colo. 195, 268 P.2d 401 (1954).
16. *Ward v. Oregon State Bd. of Nursing*, 226 Or. 128, 510 P.2d 554 (1973).

17. *Tuma v. Board of Nursing*, 593 P.2d 711 (Idaho 1979).
18. *Lunsford v. Board of Nursing Examiners*, 648 S.W.2d 391 (Tex. Civ. App. 3rd Dist. 1983).
19. *Rayburn v. Minnesota State Bd. of Optometry*, 247 Minn. 520, 78 N.W.2d 351 (1956).
20. *Leukhardt v. Pennsylvania*, 44 Pa. Commw. Ct. 318, 403 A.2d 645 (1979).
21. 45 C.F.R. §§ 603.1-603.6 (1983).
22. *Hipp v. Hospital Auth. of Marietta, Ga.*, 104 Ga. App. 174, 121 S.E.2d 273 (1961).
23. *Wilson N. Jones Memorial Hosp. v. Davis*, 553 S.W.2d 180 (Tex. Civ. App. 1977).
24. Joint Commission on Accreditation of Hospitals, ACCREDITATION MANUAL FOR HOSPITALS, 1984 ed., 93.

BIBLIOGRAPHY

Bruce, Joan, and Snyder, Marie. "The Right and Responsibility to Diagnose." *American Journal of Nursing* 82, no. 4 (April 1982):645.

Cohn, Sarah. "Revocation of Nurses' Licenses: How Does It Happen?" *Law, Medicine, and Health Care* 11, no. 1 (February 1983):22.

Stultz, Harry, et al. "Nurse Practitioners: A Decade of Change, pt. 1." *Nursing Outlook* 31, no. 3 (May/June 1983):155.

————. "Nurse Practitioners: A Decade of Change, pt. 2." *Nursing Outlook* 31, no. 4 (July/August 1983):216.

————. "Nurse Practitioners: A Decade of Change, pt. 3." *Nursing Outlook* 31, no. 5 (September/October 1983):266.

Tom, Sally. "Nurse-Midwifery: A Developing Profession." *Law, Medicine, and Health Care* 10, no. 6 (December 1982):262.

Wolff, Michael. "Court Upholds Expanded Practice Role for Nurses." *Law, Medicine, and Health Care* 12, no. 1 (February 1984):26.

Chapter 3

The Nurse as Manager

This chapter is designed to provide nurses with a basic understanding of the organization and regulation of health care institutions. A substantial portion of the professional practice of most nurses is in an institutional setting, most frequently a hospital. Some may ask why many of the areas addressed in this chapter are included in a book for nurses since nurses do not have an apparent role in or responsibility for many of the areas. As nurses become more involved in the management decisions of health care institutions, a broad understanding of the context in which the decisions are made will assist them to be effective.

When seeking changes in programs, policies, allocation of resources and other matters that may affect other aspects of the institution, nurses can be more effective advocates for their patients, themselves, and the entire health care delivery system if they understand (1) the roles of those they are attempting to convince to approve the changes and (2) forces and constraints that may limit what and when changes can be made. This chapter discusses the legal basis and governance of health care institutions and licensure, health planning, financing, and medical staff issues.

LEGAL BASIS AND GOVERNANCE OF HEALTH CARE INSTITUTIONS

A health care institution is a legal entity that derives its powers and many of the limitations on its powers from its legal basis. Familiarity with an institution's legal basis is essential to an understanding of its organization and powers. This section focuses primarily on hospitals.

The organization of most hospitals, regardless of type, includes a governing body often called a board of trustees or directors, an administrator, and an organized medical staff. The governing body (which will be referred to as the board in this chapter) has the ultimate responsibility and authority to establish goals and policies, select the administrator, and appoint the members of the medical staff. The administrator is delegated the responsibility and authority to manage the day-to-day business of the hospital within the policies established by the board. The organized medical staff is delegated the responsibility and authority to maintain the quality of medical services delivered in the hospital, subject to the ultimate responsibility of the board.

The hospital is a unique organization in that many of the decisions concerning the use of its staff, equipment, and supplies are made by physicians who are not its employees or agents. Physicians usually are legally independent of the hospital and accountable primarily through the organized medical staff.

LEGAL BASIS

The powers of the hospital and its governance structure are derived from its legal basis, which also imposes limitations on those powers. The hospital can be a governmental entity, a corporation (nonprofit or proprietary), a partnership, or sole proprietorship. Each form of organization has its own implications for the governance of the hospital. While the institution's powers cannot be expanded without changing its underlying legal basis, many additional limitations may be imposed by contract, by restrictions in gifts or bequests that the hospital accepts, or by government.

Governmental Hospitals

The legal basis of governmental hospitals (such as state, county, city, or veterans' hospitals) is found in state or federal statutes. Governmental hospitals are not corporations in most states. They are created either directly by a special statute or by a governmental unit pursuant to its statutory authority.

Corporations

A corporation is a separate legal entity under the law, distinct from the individuals who own and/or control it. One of the legal benefits of incorporation is that it limits the liability exposure of the owners to their investment in the corporation. They cannot be individually liable beyond their investment except for their personal acts or omissions. The corporation itself is liable from its own resources, which include the investments of its owners. Another legal benefit is that the corporation has perpetual life, so it does not legally depend on the lives of individual owners for its continuity. Unless a corporation is tax exempt or elects another special tax status, it must pay taxes on its earnings but in most situations its owners do not have to pay personal income tax on the corporation's earnings until the earnings are distributed to them.

Corporations may be proprietary or nonprofit. A proprietary corporation is operated with the intention of earning a profit that may be distributed to its owners. The earnings of a nonprofit corporation may not be distributed for the benefit of individuals. A nonprofit facility sometimes is called a charitable hospital.

The powers of the corporation are limited to those granted either expressly or by implication in its articles of incorporation. Some articles limit the type of business the corporation may conduct. Some may find it necessary to amend their articles of incorporation before they can substantially change their scope of business.

Any business corporation derives its authority to act from the state that creates it. The articles of incorporation set forth the purposes of its existence and the powers it is authorized to exercise to carry out its purposes. Acts performed within the scope of this express authority are clearly proper. In addition to powers expressly conferred by the articles of incorporation, there generally is implied authority to perform any acts necessary to exercise the express authority and to accomplish the purposes for which it was created. Performance of acts expressly prohibited is clearly improper.

Even when a corporation has authority to begin an activity, many other factors must be considered. For example, if the hospital has exemption from property or income taxes, it must be determined whether the new activity will risk loss of this exemption. There are regulatory constraints such as zoning laws that limit the uses of land or licensing and certificate-of-need laws that require permission before certain activities can be started. Business judgment needs to be applied to decide whether it is prudent to engage in the activity.

An act outside of the corporation's authority is called an *ultra vires* act. In some states, an *ultra vires* contract cannot be enforced. The courts will not require the parties to complete what they have agreed to do nor will they order one party to pay the other for its injuries when the contract is not fulfilled. Some states permit these contracts to be enforced. The members of the corporation or the state have the right to obtain an injunction to prevent the performance of an *ultra vires* act. For example, a California court ruled in 1977 that the articles of incorporation of Queen of Angels Hospital required the corporation to continue operating a hospital. Therefore, the board could not lease the hospital and use the rent to operate clinics.[1] If an *ultra vires* act already has been completed, courts normally will permit it to stand unless the state intervenes.

Articles of incorporation and bylaws are changed for many reasons: (1) to permit expansion into new activities; (2) to reorganize the corporation, frequently in an effort to shelter activities from various regulations; and (3) to adapt to other changes in the environment. Changing corporate documents usually is possible as long as the proper legal procedures are followed and all members of the corporation are treated fairly.[2] In addition, the legislature that creates the corporation reserves the power to amend the law and the articles of incorporation even if a corporation or its members do not want the change.[3]

Partnerships

A business can be organized as a partnership of several individuals or organizations. One benefit of a partnership is that income tax is paid only by the partners; the partnership itself pays no separate income tax. However, there is no limitation on the partners' potential liability and it is more difficult to arrange its affairs to survive the death or withdrawal of a partner. The potential liability of some of the partners can be limited through what is called a limited partnership, but there must be at least one partner—called a general partner—whose liability is not limited.

Sole Proprietorships

A business also can be organized as a sole proprietorship, which means it is owned by one individual who has not incorporated the business. All of the income of the business is taxed as the personal income of the owner, and there is no limitation on the owner's potential liability.

GOVERNANCE

The organization of most hospitals includes a governing body, an administrator, and an organized medical staff.

Governing Board

The legal responsibility for the operation of a hospital rests ultimately on the governing board. In the past, members of boards of many community hospitals did not take an active role in hospital governance. They viewed their position as honorary and delegated operations to the administration and medical staff. They became involved only to resolve internal disagreements. Today, active involvement of the members is essential as communities, governmental agencies, and the courts increasingly hold the board accountable for the hospital's activities. The members have a duty to act as a reasonably prudent person would under similar circumstances faced with a similar problem.

Duty to Act with Due Care

Board members have the duty to exercise reasonable care and skill in the management of corporate affairs and to act at all times in good faith and with complete loyalty to the corporation. This general duty applies for all governmental, charitable, and proprietary hospitals.

The general duty of due care requires that any individual who accepts membership on a board personally fulfill the specified functions, including attending meetings and participating in the consideration of matters before it. All board members assume responsibilty for decisions it makes that they did not oppose.[4]

The general duty to act with due care and loyalty includes taking appropriate steps to preserve the hospital's assets from injury, destruction, and loss. The manner in which this duty may be satisfied varies with the circumstances. It obviously is not always possible to preserve specific property. Sometimes the cost of preservation may exceed the value of the property to the hospital. The law does not expect the impossible but instead recognizes that judgment must be applied in deciding how prudently to provide for the preservation of property. The duty to preserve property includes protection against liability losses.

Basic Management Functions

The board has general authority to manage the hospital's business, and this authority is absolute as long as it acts within the law. Courts usually leave questions of policy and the internal management of the corporation wholly to the board's discretion. However, where departure from the board's duties is clear, the courts will intervene.

The board's basic management functions include (1) selection of corporate officers and agents, (2) general control of the compensation of such agents, (3) delegation of authority to the administrator and subordinates, (4) fixing of policies, and (5) supervision and vigilance over the welfare of the whole corporation.

Specific management duties peculiar to hospitals include (1) determining hospital policies in connection with community health needs, (2) maintaining proper professional standards, (3) assuming general responsibility for adequate patient care throughout the institution, and (4) providing adequate financing of patient care and assuming businesslike control of expenditures.

This authority, within limits, may be delegated to the administrator or to committees. In practice, much of this authority is delegated expressly or implicitly although the board is under no obligation to do so and it can revoke any delegation at any time. Since there is no obligation to delegate any part of the function, there is no obligation to continue a delegation once made. The governing body may not abdicate its authority; it must have some mechanism to retain accountability.

Inherent in the management function is the board's authority to fix policies for the hospital. The board may exercise its policy-making authority directly by adopting rules and regulations or it may delegate the authority. Hospital administrators, subordinates, or committees may be permitted to make policies or formulate rules and regulations, subject to board review. Thus, the director of nursing or nursing committees may be delegated the authority to formulate rules and regulations concerning nursing practice.

One example of the governing body's policy-making power is a 1974 Montana case in which the court upheld a rule forbidding fathers to be present in the delivery room.[5] Another example is a 1978 Georgia court decision that upheld a rule requiring that all computerized tomography (CT) scans of the hospital's patients be performed with the hospital's machine, not one outside of the hospital.[6]

Duty to Provide Satisfactory Patient Care

The duty to provide satisfactory patient care is one of the most important elements of the board's general duty to operate the hospital with due care and diligence. It is only through the fulfillment of this duty that the hospital's basic purpose will be accomplished. The elements of this duty range from the purchase of suitable equipment for patient treatment (subject to the facility's financial ability) to the hiring of competent employees. Two important elements are the board's duty to (1) maintain a satisfactory standard of patient care by reviewing the performance of the medical, nursing, and other professional staff and (2) select and supervise a competent administrator.

The board has a duty to exercise due care in selecting and reviewing the performance of members of the medical staff. In *Darling v. Charleston Community Memorial Hospital,* the Illinois Supreme Court held that it is the board's duty to establish mechanisms for the medical staff to evaluate, advise, and, where necessary, take action when an unreasonable risk of harm to a patient arises from the treatment being provided by the patient's physician.[7] In the *Darling* case the hospital was found liable when a patient's leg had to be amputated because no one intervened to correct inappropriate treatment by a physician. One of the reasons for the hospital's liability was the failure of the nurses to inform administration of the inappropriate treatment. This issue is discussed in more detail in the communication section of Chapter 7. In a Wisconsin case, a hospital was found liable for failing to exercise due care in evaluating and checking the claimed credentials of an applicant for medical staff membership.[8] Hospitals must have appropriate mechanisms for evaluating the competency of candidates for staff appointments and for determining the privileges to be given to physicians. (The responsibilities of the hospital and the rights of physicians concerning medical staff matters are discussed later in this chapter.)

As noted, the board has a responsibility to assure that appropriate policies and procedures are adopted to promote the provision of satisfactory patient care. Often these are developed and proposed by committees or individual administrators or staff members. In some areas, committees may be delegated the authority to approve and implement procedures consistent with broader institutional policies.

Committees may be convened by hospital administrators, medical staff officers, or departmental administrators, including nursing administrators. Committees are increasingly multidisciplinary to assure that the recommendations take into account the perspectives and needs of all groups whose cooperation is necessary. When the policies are developed by individuals, they usually consult with representatives of the disciplines affected.

Nurses can assure that nursing policies and procedures are understood and implemented if they consult with other affected disciplines during the development. Nurses can optimize their roles by responding promptly to requests for input, participating actively on committees when requested, volunteering information to those serving on committees, and keeping nursing administration informed of any current efforts to develop policies and procedures.

Duty of Loyalty

The board's duty of loyalty to the hospital can be violated by board members' seizing corporate opportunities for their own benefit, self-dealing, and undisclosed conflicts of interest.

A board member who becomes aware of an opportunity for the corporation has a duty not to seize that opportunity for private gain unless the corporation elects not to pursue it.[9]

Self-dealing is a contract between the corporation and an entity in which a board member has a financial interest. Some states specifically forbid some types of self-dealing transactions. However, forbidding all self-dealing may sometimes be disadvantageous to the hospital. There are occasions when the most advantageous contract would be with a board member or with a company in which a member has an interest.

Unless there is a statutory prohibition, most hospitals permit a contract between corporation and board members if it is fair and the member did not speak or vote in favor of the contract and made full disclosure of all important facts concerning this interest. The courts have the power to void any self-dealing contract. If the fairness of the contract is questioned, the burden of establishing fairness falls upon the member with the financial interest.[10]

Conflict of interest is closely akin to self-dealing. While no actual self-dealing may be involved, nondisclosure of conflicting interests may result in sanctions. Most boards have a policy requiring periodic disclosure of all potentially conflicting interests.

Selection of Board Members

Board members are selected in several ways. In many hospitals, the board is self-perpetuating. When there is a vacancy, the remaining members select the replacement. Another mechanism is for the stockholders or members of the corporation to elect the board members. In governmental hospitals, board members frequently are elected by a vote of the people in the governmental subdivision that owns the hospital. In some states, the boards of certain governmental hospitals are appointed by elected officials.

Terms of office usually are staggered so that all members are not replaced at the same time. This assures that there will be experienced members on the board who can provide continuity to governance of the hospital.

If members are not selected in accord with applicable laws, the articles of incorporation, and the bylaws, courts may declare the board actions void.

THE ADMINISTRATOR

The administrator is the executive officer directly in charge of the hospital and is appointed by and responsible to the board. The administrator is the general supervisor of all hospital operations and is delegated powers by the board to fulfill this responsibility. The administrator has only those duties delegated expressly or by implication by the board and may redelegate specific areas of responsibility to subordinates while retaining primary responsibility. Under the following examples of the general and specific duties often delegated by the board, the administrator:

- Has the general duty to oversee every activity in the hospital and make periodic reports to the board.
- Implements board policies, including obtaining required legal approvals from regulatory agencies.
- Transmits and interprets the board's policies to the medical, nursing, and other professional staff and other personnel and is responsible for informing them as well as patients and visitors, vendors, and others of hospital rules.
- Takes appropriate disciplinary action when noncompliance with hospital rules occurs, except in cases where the board has retained disciplinary authority or has delegated it to others.

Normally, administrators are authorized to select or recommend selection of administrative department heads, including the head of the nursing department. Some administrators delegate to department heads the authority to select their assistants, while reserving the authority to coordinate the overall operation of the departments. In addition, the administrator normally is responsible for employment in the hospital and, within budgetary limits, for setting salaries and wages.

Administrators generally are responsible for the care of patients. While they should not usurp the functions of the medical, nursing, and other professional staff, they must make sure that proper admission and discharge procedures are formulated and carried out. They must cooperate with the professional staff in maintaining patient care standards and see to it that hospital departments work in coordination with each other and with the medical staff to that end.

The administrator is responsible for the operating funds of the corporation, advises the board on matters of policy formation, proposes plans for organization of the facility, prepares plans for achieving hospital objectives, submits an annual budget for approval, recommends rates to be charged for services, and submits various periodic and special reports.

The administrator also may have duties imposed by state statute or regulation or by municipal ordinance, such as reporting vital statistics information to health authorities and furnishing communicable disease and gunshot wound treatment reports, unless state law imposes the duty on someone other than the hospital.

The most important skill needed to accomplish these varied responsibilites is the art of negotiation. Hospital administration is a series of negotiations in the interest of the institution and the community it serves accommodating the many groups with an interest in its activities. The following partial list of these groups demonstrates the complexity of the negotiations required: patients, their families, physicians, nurses, other hospital staff members, board members, community groups, insurers and other third party payers, bankers and other lenders, politicians, government officials, and reporters.

It is always possible for an adversary or any other party to find fault with the administrator's assessment of a situation, the strategy chosen to solve problems, or the decision made and the subsequent actions taken. The administrator's performance should be judged as a whole, however, since at any one time in the circle of diverse negotiations there is always somebody on the other side. The administrator has many persons to deal with and many interests to attempt to satisfy. Not every negotiation will be successful. Understanding of this broad context in which all decisions are made may help nurses when they seek administrative action.

To fulfill its responsibility for selecting an administrator, the board must select a competent individual who will set and maintain satisfactory standards of patient care. The board must evaluate the administrator's performance. Failure to remove an incompetent administrator or agent is as much a breach of the duty of due care and diligence as the failure to appoint a competent one.

LICENSING, ACCREDITATION, REGULATION

Health care facilities are among the most extensively regulated institutions in the United States. They are regulated by all levels of government and by numerous agencies within each level. As a result, they occasionally are confronted with conflicting mandates. Since this problem has been recognized, relief has been provided in some areas. However, problems remain because of the underlying conflicts in the goals of society. One example is the tension between the cooperation sought by the health planning laws and the competition sought by the antitrust laws. This section focuses primarily on hospitals but also includes nursing homes.

The terms licensure and accreditation are often confused. Licensure derives from the states' authority to regulate the operation of health care institutions in the public interest. The state legislature grants an administrative agency the authority to promulgate standards that health care institutions must meet, to grant licenses to institutions that meet the standards, and to enforce continuing compliance. Health care institutions that do not have a license are barred from operating in the state. A system is created to penalize institutions, or those who operate them, for violation of the standards when revocation is too severe a penalty. The important features of licensure that distinguish it from accreditation are that (1) it is a function of government and (2) it is mandatory for health care institutions.

In contrast, accreditation is granted by a private authority and is not mandated legally. Many hospitals are accredited by the Joint Commission on Accreditation of Hospitals (JCAH), an organization that includes representatives of the American College of Physicians, the American College of Surgeons, the American Dental Association, the American Hospital Association, and the American Medical Association. Hospitals wishing to be accredited apply to JCAH, pay a fee, and submit to an intensive survey to determine whether they satisfy the standards established by the JCAH and published in its *Accreditation Manual for Hospitals*.[11] Several states accept JCAH accreditation as a basis for either full or partial licensure without further state inspection. This is part of the effort to reduce duplicative inspections of hospitals. The American Osteopathic Association (AOA) accredits osteopathic hospitals and functions similarly to the JCAH.

Standards for hospitals and nursing homes also are established under the Medicare program. These standards are called "conditions of participation."[12] They are not licensing standards but health care institutions must comply with them or they cannot receive reimbursement from Medicare for most services to beneficiaries. The Medicare law and regulations provide that hospitals accredited by JCAH or AOA are deemed to meet most of the conditions of participation unless a special Medicare inspection determines they are not in compliance.

Some regulatory or accrediting agencies focus on the entire institution, others on individual services or activities such as the pharmacy or the elevators. For example, the agency granting certificates of need must give its permission before a new hospital, nursing home, or many services can be started. Numerous other regulations apply to other aspects of health care institutions such as financing, taxation, planning, waste disposal, communications, transportation, and labor relations. Other regulatory agencies that focus on licensing individuals are discussed in Chapter 2.)

Licensure of Institutions

Health care institutions are subject to regulation by the state through licensure. The major legal issues arising from this are the sources of authority for the licensing process, the scope and application of licensure regulations, and the sanctions that may be applied for violations.

The authority of state governments to regulate health care institutions is derived from the police power. All states have exercised this power by enacting hospital and nursing home licensing statutes. These statutes usually grant an agency the authority to promulgate standards, to grant licenses, and to enforce compliance with the standards through penalties or revocation of the license. The licensing statutes and regulations must be within the scope of the reasonable exercise of the police power and must not deny equal protection of the laws or due process.

For the agency's rules to be enforceable, they also must (1) be within the authority properly delegated to the agency in the statute and (2) be promulgated in accord with the procedure that the state specifies for administrative rulemaking. This usually includes public notice of the rule and an opportunity for the public to comment before it becomes final. Some states require additional steps such as an economic impact statement.

Licensing regulations usually address the organization of the hospital, requiring an organized governing body or some equivalent, an organized medical staff, an organized nursing department, and an administrator. The relationship among these elements is usually addressed. The regulations may require that general hospitals provide certain basic services, including laboratory, radiology, pharmacy, and some emergency services and that adequate nursing personnel be available. They also may establish standards for facilities, equipment, and personnel for specific services, such as obstetrics, pediatrics, and surgery. The standards may address safety, sanitation, infection control, record preparation and retention, and other matters. Nursing home licensing regulations are similar but frequently include more detail.

All standards do not have to be in objective numerical terms to satisfy due process requirements and thus be valid. However, courts are reluctant to uphold overly subjective rules. In 1978, a court found several of New York's nursing home rules to be invalid and unenforceable because they were too subjective and thus violated the due process requirement of adequate notice of the conduct required. The invalidated rules required sewage facilities, nursing staff, and laundering of linens to meet the "approval" and "satisfaction" of the Commissioner of the Department of Health but included no objective definitions of those standards. However, in the same decision, the court upheld another rule concerning the nursing staff that was based on the "needs of the patients." The court found this to be an objective standard because the needs would be "reasonably well identifiable by all competent observers."[13]

Courts recognize that in some areas objective standards are either impossible or would be too arbitrary so they have upheld enforcement of subjective standards if fairly applied. This is illustrated by a 1980 New York nursing home case in which somewhat vague standards were upheld because the actual violations clearly deviated from the objective of the rules and the agency had provided written explanations of the nature of the violations to the owners.[14]

Approval of the integrity of buildings is a major part of institutional licensure. Numerous special building and fire safety codes apply to health care institutions and frequently are enforced through the licensing mechanism. These codes usually provide for inspections of the institution.

The administrative agency often has the authority to permit exceptions to its rules by granting a waiver or variance. Undue hardship may result from unbending application of the rules, and the public's best interest may not be served by inflexibility. For example, one state required all hospital rooms to have a shower for the patient. When the rules were written, apparently no one thought of intensive care units where patients could not use showers, so it was necessary for hospitals in the state to obtain waivers until the rule could be changed. Waivers also may be necessary to implement innovative approaches.

For example, some hospitals are introducing systems that permit the ordering of medications or tests through a computer entry rather than a signed slip of paper. These systems may improve patient care while reducing its cost. Some licensing regulations require all such orders to be "signed" by a physician or other health professional so it is necessary to obtain a change in the rules or a waiver to convert to authentication through a computer code number. In general, waivers are granted only when (1) there is a substantial need for relief from the rule, (2) the public purpose will be better served by the exception, and (3) the exception will not create a hazard to the health and well-being of patients or others that is excessive in light of the public purpose being served.

Two of the fundamental elements of due process are notice and an opportunity to be heard. Unless the deficiencies of an institution immediately threaten life or health, the state can close it or impose other penalties for violations of the licensing law only after giving the facility adequate notice of the violations and an opportunity to be heard. Some states require that licensing agencies give the hospital an opportunity to correct deficiencies before they can apply sanctions.

Some statutes recognize that it may not be in the public interest to revoke a license for minor violations and thus provide a range of lesser penalties, reserving suspension or revocation for "substantial" violations. The states vary as to what they consider a substantial violation. However, at some point, if the violations become sufficiently serious, the institution's license will be revoked.[15]

Certificate of Need and Zoning Laws

A license no longer is sufficient authority to start a new health care institution in most states. Laws now require that the facility also obtain a permit titled a certificate of need before it can begin operations. Existing institutions must also obtain a certificate of need before they can begin some new services or make large capital expenditures. (These laws are discussed in detail later in this chapter.)

Zoning is another potential barrier to starting a new health care institution or substantially changing existing services. Zoning ordinances are laws adopted by local governmental subdivisions to provide for the safe and orderly development of the locality by specifying where certain types of land use are permitted or forbidden.

Licensure and Permits for Services

A facility that has an institutional license from one agency may also be required to obtain licenses or permits from the same or another agency for individual departments or services. For example, many state and local governments require that separate licenses or permits be obtained for hospital pharmacies, clinical laboratories, radiological equipment, renal dialysis facilities, substance abuse centers, food services, vending machines, elevators, hospital vehicles, waste disposal, and other services. Some states exempt some institutions from having to obtain a license or permit for some of these services but the exemption may be lost if the service is offered to persons other than the institution's patients and staff, so use of the service must be limited or a special license must be sought.

Regulation of Drugs and Medical Devices

One of the most heavily regulated aspects of health care is the use of drugs and medical devices. State laws regulate the operation of pharmacies, while federal laws cover most aspects of the production, distribution, and use of drugs and medical devices, especially those involved in interstate commerce. Federal law defines *medical device* broadly to include virtually all equipment and supplies used in patient care. In addition to such obvious devices as hip prostheses, pacemakers, and artificial hearts, the term includes common supplies such as catheters, endo-scopes, hospital beds, specimen containers, support stockings, scissors, adhesive tape, elastic bandages, tongue depressors, and sutures. Many states have laws that regulate intrastate commerce involving drugs not regulated by federal law. Operation of hospital pharmacies also is addressed in the standards of the JCAH and the Medicare conditions of participation.[16]

State Regulation

Some states require hospitals to obtain a separate license or permit for the pharmacy and to comply with the pharmacy licensing regulations. Other states regulate through the hospital licensing system, exempting hospital pharmacies from the system licensing other pharmacies.

Hospital Formularies

An area of controversy in the past has been the promotion of rational drug use through a hospital formulary system that selects the drugs that are to be available. A medical staff committee determines which drugs are equivalent and either selects one of them to stock or authorizes the hospital to accept bids from competing suppliers to determine which can be purchased at the least expense. When a physician prescribes a drug for which an equivalent is stocked, the equivalent is dispensed unless the physician specifies on the prescription form or order that no substitutions are permitted. Formulary systems have been adopted in a majority of hospitals. They have been successful in controlling the increase in the cost of drugs, especially when competition is promoted among multiple suppliers.

Periodically, drug manufacturers and others have challenged formulary systems, based primarily on state antisubstitution or generic substitution laws, federal or state drug laws, or trademark laws. These attacks have not been successful, mainly because there must be a substitution to establish violation of these laws. When the prescriber has an understanding or agreement that the dispenser may fill an order with an equivalent drug specified in a formulary, there is no substitution. The prescriber has agreed that the equivalent drug is what is actually being prescribed by the symbols on the form or order.

Controlled Substances Act

The Comprehensive Drug Abuse Prevention and Control Act of 1970, commonly known as the Controlled Substances Act, replaced virtually all preexisting federal laws dealing with narcotics, depressants, stimulants, and hallucinogens.[17] The act directly affects hospital distribution systems; it also deals with rehabilitation under community mental health programs, treatment of drug abuse and addiction, and importation and exportation of controlled substances.

The regulations implementing the Controlled Substances Act include hospitals as "institutional practitioners" that must register with the government. Each registrant must take a physical inventory every two years. A perpetual inventory is not required but a separate one is mandated for each registered location and for each independent activity registered. Each registrant also must maintain complete, accurate records of all controlled substances received and disposed of.

Controlled substances are classified into lists, called schedules, by the degree of control to which Congress ruled they should be subjected. Schedule I has the tightest controls. For all practical purposes, controlled substances in Schedules I through IV may be dispensed only upon the lawful order of a practitioner. For outpatients, the order must be in the form of a prescription that complies with the requirements of the law. For inpatients, a chart order satisfies the act's requirements for a lawful order so a separate prescription is not required. The practitioner who signs the order must be registered with the Drug Enforcement Administration of the Department of Justice. State law determines which professionals may be practitioners.

All institutional and individual registrants must provide effective controls and procedures to guard against theft and diversion of controlled substances. The central storage in a hospital should be under the direct control and supervision of the pharmacist. Only authorized personnel should have access to the area. When controlled substances are stored at nursing units, they should be kept securely locked and only authorized personnel should have access.

There are substantial federal criminal penalties, including fines and imprisonment, for violating the Controlled Substances Act, and violators can lose the authority to possess, prescribe, or dispense controlled substances.

Food and Drug Administration

The Food and Drug Administration (FDA) enforces a complex system of federal controls over the testing, manufacturing, labeling, and distribution of drugs, cosmetics, and devices.[18]

The definitions of drug and device are broad, so the applicable statutes, regulations, and court decisions should be consulted to determine whether a particular item is included. For example, human blood is considered to be a drug.

The law and regulations establish an elaborate procedure for determining that new drugs and devices are safe and effective before they can enter general use. The investigational new drug (IND) and investigational device exemption (IDE) requirements must be met to lawfully use investigational drugs and devices. With few exceptions, these drugs and devices can be used only in research projects approved by an institutional review board, conducted by a qualified investigator and sponsored by an appropriate company or institution.[19]

When the FDA is convinced that a new drug or device is safe and effective for certain uses, it approves it for general sale. The approval may permit sales either over the the counter or by order of a practitioner. Approval of devices may include additional restrictions on their use.

The approval specifies the approved uses of the drug or device that are to be included in the labeling. Frequently medical practice changes more rapidly than the FDA approval process so the actual use can be different from its labeled uses.

For example, drugs may be given for other conditions or in different dosages. It is not a violation of federal law for practitioners to order such unapproved uses or for pharmacists to dispense drugs pursuant to such orders. Unapproved uses that result in injuries to patients may result in liability.

However, courts generally have recognized that FDA approval lags behind medical practice so that deviation from FDA-approved uses alone does not conclusively prove negligence. Juries are permitted to consider the FDA's position along with other testimony concerning accepted practice in deciding whether the use was negligent. The must prudent practice is for the practitioner to explain the unapproved use to the patient, explain the reasons for it, and obtain the informed consent of the individual to the use.

Prescriptions must be properly documented. When prescription drugs are ordered in writing, either as a prescription or as an order on the patient's chart, the documentation requirement is clearly satisfied. In the case of oral orders, for drugs, the act states that such prescriptions must be ". . . reduced promptly to writing and filed by the pharmacist. . . ." Institutions should review these requirements as well as state requirements, such as hospital licensing regulations, to assure that telephone orders are accepted only by proper personnel. The most prudent practice is to require that a registered nurse or a pharmacist personally accept telephone orders.

Poison Prevention Packaging Act

The Poison Prevention Packaging Act is an example of the many other federal laws that regulate the pharmacy area.[20] This act requires that most drugs be dispensed in containers designed to be difficult for children to open. Exceptions are permitted when authorized by the prescribing practitioner.

ANTITRUST LAWS

Federal and state antitrust laws are designed to preserve the private competitive market system by prohibiting various anticompetitive activities. The primary federal laws are the Sherman Antitrust Act,[21] the Clayton Act,[22] the Federal Trade Commission Act,[23] and the Robinson-Patman Act.[24] These laws forbid many anticompetitive acitivities, including conspiracies to restrain trade, monopolization or attempts to monopolize, some exclusive dealing arrangements, acquisitions and mergers that have an anticompetitive effect, unfair or deceptive practices affecting competition, and discriminatory pricing that lessens competition.

Until the mid-1970s, many aspects of the federal antitrust laws were not thought to apply to health care because it was believed (1) health care providers were not engaged in interstate commerce, (2) activities by the learned professions were exempt, and (3) the federal health planning laws by implication created an exemption for health planning activities. In a series of decisions since then, however, the Supreme Court has made it clear that health care providers are treated in the same way as other industries for antitrust purposes.

In 1976, the Court ruled that a 49-bed proprietary hospital was involved in interstate commerce because it purchased $100,000 worth of medicines and supplies from out-of-state vendors and received considerable revenues from out-of-state insurance companies and federal payers. Thus, the hospital could sue the trustees of another hospital under the antitrust laws for an alleged conspiracy to restrain trade by blocking its expansion.[25] In 1975, the Court ruled that there was no learned professions exemption from the antitrust laws.[26]

In 1981, the Court ruled that implied exemptions to the antitrust laws are not favored and will be applied only to the limited extent necessary to fulfill the purposes of other laws. Blue Cross had refused to enter a reimbursement agreement with a hospital because the hospital had not obtained approval for its new building from the local health planning agency. However, state law did not require approval. The hospital claimed that the refusal by Blue Cross was a restraint of trade, and Blue Cross in turn claimed its refusal was protected by the national health planning law. The Court ruled that the Blue Cross refusal was not protected by the health planning law.[27] Other laws will provide implied protection from antitrust sanctions only when there is a clear repugnancy between the antitrust laws and the regulatory system under the other law. The protection will be recognized only to the minimum extent necessary to make the other law work.

The law has recognized some exemptions from antitrust liability for state actions, activities intended to induce governmental action, and the "business of insurance." In 1943, the Supreme Court ruled that state-compelled activities were immune from antitrust liability to preserve the state's authority to supervise economic activity within the state.[28] The state action doctrine was clarified in 1980 when the Court ruled that state authorization is not enough—the actions must be pursuant to a clearly articulated and affirmatively expressed state policy that is actively supervised by the state.[29] The Court also has ruled that the antitrust laws do not apply to most activities intended to induce governmental action, such as lobbying.[30] The Court based this doctrine on the right under the First Amendment to petition the government and on a judicial interpretation that lobbying activities were not restraint of trade. The petitioning must be for a legitimate purpose of influencing governmental policy. Sham efforts to bar the access of competitors to the government are not protected.

The McCarran-Ferguson Act created a statutory exemption for the "business of insurance" when the business is regulated by state law and does not constitute coercion, boycott, or intimidation.[31] The Supreme Court has taken a restrictive view of what constitutes the business of insurance entitled to this exemption. For example, in 1979, the Court defined the "business of insurance" as limited to the procedures and activities related to the spreading of risk among policyholders. It held that the special reimbursement arrangements between Blue Shield and participating pharmacies that were being challenged in the case were not within the business of *insurance,* but instead were merely the business of *insurers.*[32]

The courts have established that some practices are unlawful regardless of the rationale supporting them. These are called *per se* violations of the antitrust laws. Examples include price fixing, division of markets, group boycotts, and tying arrangements. In 1982, the Supreme Court ruled that a maximum fee schedule for physicians was price fixing and thus a *per se* violation.[33] The courts have concluded that the practices that are considered *per se* violations are unreasonable and usually will not examine their actual impact. When a practice is not considered a *per se* violation, it is analyzed under the "rule of reason" in which the court determines whether the practice actually imposes an unreasonable restraint on competition.

It should not be assumed that an activity violates the antitrust laws just because it is not exempt. In 1980, a United States Court of Appeals held that the different compensation formulas used by Blue Cross for participating and nonparticipating hospitals were not exempt under the McCarran-Ferguson Act "business of insurance" exemption but that the arrangement did not violate the antitrust laws because it was reasonable.[34]

The Robinson-Patman Act prohibits discriminatory pricing that lessens competition. There is a statutory exemption for purchases by nonprofit institutions "for their own use." Under this exemption, hospital pharmacies in nonprofit hospitals usually buy drugs from manufacturers at a discount not available to commercial pharmacies. These drugs can be used only "for their own use."

In 1976, the Supreme Court defined "for their own use" as limited to drugs for the following:

1. inpatients to be used in their treatment at the hospital
2. patients admitted to the hospital's emergency facility for use in treatment there
3. outpatients for personal use on the hospital premises
4. inpatients or emergency facility patients upon their discharge and for their personal use away from the premises
5. outpatients for personal use away from the premises
6. the hospital's employees or students (including nurses) for personal use or the use of their immediate dependents
7. physicians who are members of the hospital's staff, but who are not its employees, for personal use or the use of their immediate dependents.[35]

Thus, hospitals must limit sales of discount drugs to these groups to avoid possible civil liability, including treble damages, and the loss of the valuable discount. Purchasers who do not qualify include (1) former patients who wish to renew a prescription given when they were inpatients, emergency facility patients, or outpatients; (2) physicians who are members of the hospital's staff and who intend to dispense the drugs in the course of their private practice away from the hospital; and (3) walk-in customers who are not patients of the hospital. To avoid liability, hospitals either refuse to sell to these three categories of purchasers or set up a separate order system to fill their requests.

Health care institutions must consider the antitrust implications when entering group purchase or shared services agreements, mergers or agreements not to duplicate services, or exclusive contracts with a professional or group of professionals, as well as exchanging information with other institutions. Many of these actions can be permissible under the antitrust laws. However, those involved must understand what they are permitted to do and must be prepared to defend their action before engaging in these or other activities that might appear to have some anticompetitive effect.

HEALTH PLANNING

Health care planning in its broadest sense is a continuing process of assuring the community that its resources are being used properly to meet the people's health care needs. Effective planning has a combined focus on the individual health care institution, the health service area needs, and state and national health goals. This section focuses primarily on state and national governmental efforts to mandate and regulate health planning.

Health planning has been fostered through federal incentives and funding for local planning and federal mandates provided by a series of laws, including the Social Security Act Amendments of 1972,[36] the National Health Planning and Resources Development Act of 1974,[37] and the Social Security Amendments of 1983.[38]

The 1972 amendments promoted internal planning by mandating that all hospitals participating in Medicare develop a capital expenditures budget. They also promoted state planning by giving states the option under section 1122 of requiring state level review of certain capital expenditures of hospitals. The 1974 Act stated several national health planning priorities that are listed later in this chapter. It also created an elaborate structure to develop local health plans and to attempt to implement them through various steps, including the certificate-of-need laws (discussed later in this chapter). Federal health planning laws have become increasingly controversial because of their cost and the desire of some to return control of these issues to local areas.

Amendments to the 1974 act in 1979[39] and 1981,[40] among other changes, reduced the number of projects subject to review. Federal funding to reviewing agencies was cut drastically over the same period, reducing the scope of external planning activities. The Social Security Amendments of 1983 modified section 1122 to require states to implement review by October 1, 1986.[41] Other approaches to health planning are evolving, including community coalitions.

Social Security Act Amendments of 1972

The Social Security Act Amendments of 1972 require each Medicare provider, as a condition of participation in the program, to have a written overall plan, including an annual operating budget and a three-year capital expenditures budget.[42] Since the purpose of the requirements is to assure that providers conduct their own budgeting and planning, plans are not reviewed for substance by governmental authorities.

The 1972 amendments added section 1122,[43] which permits but does not require states to establish a program for review of capital expenditures of institutions participating in the Medicare reimbursement program. The Department of Health and Human Services (HHS) enforces the required review in the states that participate by refusing to pay Medicare's share of the capital costs of an unapproved or disapproved hospital project. Nearly every state implemented this provision through an agreement between the secretary of HHS and the governor. In return for funding and assistance, the governor designated an official state agency to administer the section.

Section 1122 originally provided for review of projects that change the bed capacity of the facility, substantially change its services, or cost more than $100,000. The Social Security Amendments of 1983 increased the $100,000 threshold to $600,000 and made section 1122 review mandatory by October 1, 1986.[44]

National Health Planning and Resources Development Act of 1974

The National Health Planning and Resources Development Act of 1974[45] added Titles XV and XVI to the Public Health Service Act. Title XV created a system of local planning agencies, called Health Systems Agencies (HSAs), that interfaced with state agencies called State Health Planning and Development Agencies (SHPDAs) and State Health Coordinating Councils (SHCCs). It was intended to restructure and expand the health planning process, leading to the development of state health plans under a national scheme and to efforts to implement those plans through certificate-of-need review and other mechanisms. Title XVI sought to integrate the federal health facility funding into the national health planning process of Title XV and at the same time redirect the flow of federal construction and modernization funds from inpatient to outpatient facilities. Title XVI had relatively little impact because Congress declined to appropriate sufficient funds.

The 1974 act has been amended several times, most extensively in 1979[46] and 1981.[47] The following discussion describes the Act as amended in 1981.

The national health planning framework created by Title XV has federal, state, and local elements. Congress also specified several national health priorities to be considered at all levels of planning. The original act had ten priorities, and seven more were added by amendment. The priorities include the promotion of:

1. primary care services
2. multi-institutional systems
3. health maintenance organizations and other alternate delivery systems
4. physician's assistants
5. shared services
6. quality care
7. geographic integration of care
8. disease prevention
9. accounting and reimbursement changes
10. health promotion
11. energy conservation
12. discontinuance of unneeded services
13. cost containment
14. institutional mental health care
15. outpatient mental health care
16. attention to the emotional and psychological components of health care
17. strengthening of competitive forces.[48]

Federal Level

The Secretary of the then Department of Health, Education, and Welfare (now HHS) was directed to develop national guidelines for health planning in consultation with various groups. In 1977 the department proposed numerical guidelines for hospital beds per 1,000 population and utilization of several types of services. The proposal stated that state and local plans could differ from the numerical guidelines only by setting lower maximums or higher minimums.[49] There was tremendous public reaction, particularly from rural states, that included more than 50,000 letters to the department. The House of Representatives unanimously adopted a resolution expressing the sense of Congress that there should be more flexibility for local characteristics. The final guidelines issued in 1978 were presented as benchmarks that could be adjusted to local conditions and needs.[50]

State Level

This level is composed of two entities. The first is a state government agency, frequently in the state health department and called the State Health Planning and

Development Agency (SHPDA). It performs health planning and fund allocation functions. The SHPDA is responsible for implementing state responsibilities under the comprehensive state health plan, serving as the designated planning agency (DPA) for "section 1122 review," administering the certificate-of-need program, and other functions. The second state-level entity is the Statewide Health Coordinating Council (SHCC). It is responsible for reviewing HSA budgets and applications for assistance, for reviewing the HSA and SHPDA health plans, and for approving the final state health plan. Members of the SHCC are named by the governor and include nominations by the HSAs.

Local Level

The act required the department to divide the nation into health service areas, so it designated more than 200. One HSA was established for each area with responsibility for collecting data on the health status of residents, taking inventory of health care resources and needs, and developing and implementing health plans.

The HSAs relied primarily on federal financing, although some were able to obtain some funding from other sources. Substantial reductions in federal funding caused many HSAs to curtail their operations. The 1981 amendments modified section 1536 of the Act to authorize HHS to approve an application of any governor to abolish the HSAs and have the SHPDA perform their functions. Several states have obtained this approval, so many HSAs have ceased operations. Some have reorganized to continue involvement in private health planning efforts (such as the community coalitions discussed later in this chapter).

Certificate-of-Need Programs

Section 1523(4) of the National Health Planning and Resources Development Act requires that each state have a certificate-of-need program or forego federal funding for health planning and several other health-related functions.

Such a law requires that a health care provider receive a certificate of need before making certain capital expenditures or program changes. The state agency establishes criteria to be used in analyzing the need for projects and evaluates whether they satisfy the criteria. The specific criteria, procedures, and scope of projects subject to review vary somewhat among the states. Note certificate of need review and section 1122 review are separate programs. Although they are coordinated in many states, they may have different thresholds for review. For example, the original federal laws provided for section 1122 review of capital expenditures in excess of $100,000, but did not require certificates of need until the project exceeded $150,000.

Some states began enacting certificate-of-need laws before federal incentives were enacted in 1975. New York pioneered the concept in 1964.

Scope of Projects Requiring Review

The federal regulations implementing the original law required review of: (1) all capital expenditures by health care institutions in excess of $150,000; (2) plans for the establishment of new institutions; (3) certain changes in bed capacity; and (4) proposals for new health services in institutions regardless of cost. Review of projects for physicians' offices was not required, although some states chose to cover some physicians' office projects, such as purchase of major equipment.

The 1979 amendments[51] specified in greater detail which projects must be reviewed and that any new service needed to be reviewed only if it involved a capital expenditure in excess of $150,000 or annual operating expenses of at least $75,000. The amendments also created several exceptions to the review requirement and permitted states to increase the $150,000 and $75,000 thresholds each year by an inflation factor approved by the department.

The 1981 amendments[52] increased the threshold for review of: (1) new services to $250,000 in annual operating expenses, (2) major medical equipment to $400,000 in capital expenditures, and (3) other capital expenditures to $600,000.

Review Criteria

Section 1532 requires that each HSA and SHPDA develop and publish criteria to be used in evaluating applications for certificates of need. The criteria must include consideration of the 14 listed in section 1532(c):

1. the relationship to applicable health plans
2. the relationship to the institution's long-range plan
3. the need of the service area's population
4. the availability of alternative methods
5. the relationship to the existing health care system
6. the availability of resources for proposed services, their impact on professional training programs, access of health professions schools, alternative uses of the resources, and accessibility to those to be served
7. the special needs and circumstances of institutions serving multiple health service areas
8. the special needs and circumstances of health maintenance organizations (HMOs)
9. the costs and methods of construction projects and their impact on the institution's costs and charges
10. the need for energy conservation
11. the effect on competition
12. the innovations in financing and delivery of services that promote competition, quality assurance, and cost effectiveness

13. the efficiency and appropriateness of the use of similar existing facilities
14. the quality of care provided in the past.

Additional criteria are required by the implementing regulations.[53]

The SHPDA must evaluate a proposed project based on properly defined standards. Courts have ordered the issuance of a certificate of need when a SHPDA's denial was not based on defined standards. For example, a Michigan court ordered a certificate for a new hospital because the SHPDA had used unpublished criteria that gave preference to existing facilities.[54]

Review Procedures

Section 1532(b) requires that certain procedures be followed in processing applications for certificates of need. State procedural requirements also must be followed. This principle is illustrated by a 1982 court decision involving section 1122 review that held that the state agency did not have authority to deny any applications because it had never published review rules as required by state law.[55] Compliance with federal procedures was not sufficient.

The Future of Health Planning

Congress has reduced the funding for health planning activities and pressure is on to further reduce the federal role in planning. Institutions will continue internal planning whether or not there are governmental mandates because it is necessary to cope with changing societal expectations, medical science and technology, and other aspects of the environment. It is likely that many states will continue some or all of their planning activities even if the federal government reduces its involvement. Local programs, both public and private, such as health care coalitions, are continuing to evolve.

In response to the declining federal support of health planning and the growing concern of some businesses over the cost of the health care benefits for their employees, there is increasing interest in voluntary community coalitions to address local health care issues, especially expenditures. In January 1982, the American Hospital Association, the American Medical Association, the Blue Cross and Blue Shield Association, the Health Insurance Association of America, the AFL-CIO, and the Business Roundtable endorsed the concept of voluntary coalitions and encouraged participation by their members.

Many coalitions have been formed since, focusing on a variety of issues, including data collection; utilization review; development and encouragement of HMOs and other alternate delivery systems; restructuring of insurance benefits; reduction of hospital capacity; other health planning, rate review, or regulation; ambulatory care; increasing access for the poor and unemployed; mitigating the impact of cuts in government support; and health promotion through wellness, exercise, and risk reduction programs.

FINANCING

One of the duties of the board of a health care institution is to maintain its financial integrity. Most actions necessary to accomplish this goal are the responsibility of the administrator, who must conceptualize and recommend actions to the board, then take steps to assure that the institution carries out the board's decisions.

The institution's financial requirements must be met or it cannot continue to operate. This is accomplished through establishing the scope of activities within available resources, developing a realistic budget allocating resources to carry out those activities, setting appropriate charges, obtaining third party reimbursement and collections from individuals, initiating cost containment measures, arranging for capital financing, protecting the institution's assets, and preserving tax exemptions.

Financial Requirements

The full financial requirements of a health care institution include its current operating needs plus an operating margin. In addition to caring for paying patients, many hospitals and other institutions provide charity care, education, and research, all of which contribute to their operating costs. An operating margin is necessary to provide working funds and meet other capital requirements. Proprietary institutions also seek a profit so they can pay dividends to their investors.

Working capital is needed to assure the institution's immediate stability and its ability to make timely payment of its current obligations without costly excessive short-term borrowing. Other capital requirements include renovations and major repairs, replacement of buildings and equipment, expansion, and acquisition of new technology. It is beyond the scope of this book to provide a full discussion of financial management, including budgeting, accounting, and auditing.

Setting Charges

The goal in setting charges is to meet the financial requirements of the institution. This is difficult because many payers, such as Medicare, Medicaid, and sometimes Blue Cross, pay less than the charges and some patients are unable to pay the charges in full. The complex process of calculating appropriate charges also is beyond the scope of this book; instead, this section focuses on some of the legal considerations involved.

Rate Regulation

Many states have an entity that prospectively monitors, reviews, or establishes charges or revenue limits for hospitals. The role of this entity varies greatly among the states—some programs are mandatory but others are voluntary, which means that a hospital can elect not to participate. Some programs are regulatory and require the hospital to comply with the decision of the entity, others are simply advisory. In the latter case, the hospital still may set the rates it chooses but it must be willing to accept the adverse publicity.

The programs vary in their scope. Some are limited to the rates of certain payers, others apply only to rates for inpatient services. They also vary on the type of data they use as a basis for their evaluations. Some programs establish peer groups of hospitals, then make comparisons among the facilities in each group; others focus on historical data from individual hospitals, comparing their current year with a base year.

The three basic approaches for evaluation of the data collected are: (1) formulas, (2) budget analysis, and (3) negotiation. Some states use a combination of these. Formula review involves comparing the submitted data to a standard that is calculated from a formula. Budget review involves analysis of the hospital's proposed budget to determine the appropriateness of particular expenditures. The hospital is permitted to set its own rates as long as the revenue generated does not exceed the approved budget. The negotiation approach establishes a process for reaching agreement between the hospital and the regulatory entity concerning the appropriate rates.

The Massachusetts Nurses Association challenged the state rate regulation system, claiming the reimbursement restrictions illegally interfered with collective bargaining efforts with hospitals. A United States Court of Appeals ruled in 1984 that the law did not violate the nurses' collective bargaining rights because it affected labor-management relations only indirectly.[56]

Bonding Covenants

When a health care institution borrows money through bonds or other mechanisms, it usually pledges certain property or revenues to guarantee repayment. One of these pledges usually is a promise to set rates sufficiently high to maintain the facility's operation until the loan is repaid. These pledges must be considered and complied with, to the extent permitted by law, in setting rates.

Reimbursement

Medicare

The 1965 Amendments to the Social Security Act[57] established a two-part program of health insurance for the aged known as Medicare. Persons are eligible to participate in Part A, the hospital insurance program, if:

1. They are 65 or older and are receiving retirement benefits under the Social Security Act or the Railroad Retirement Act.
2. They qualify under a special program for persons with endstage renal disease.
3. They qualify under the special transitional program that has complex requirements beyond the scope of this book.

Persons not qualifying otherwise and who are 65 or older still may participate in Part A by paying a premium. Anyone age 65 or older who is a United States citizen or has been a permanent resident alien for five years may elect to enroll in Part B, a program of supplementary medical insurance. Medicare applies to all qualified people without regard to financial need. It is administered federally and therefore is uniform throughout the country.

Part A is financed by a special tax on employers, employees, and the self-employed. The coverage includes a specified number of days of care in hospitals and extended care facilities for each benefit period, plus posthospital home care. Claims must be presented to trigger reimbursement. Until 1983, all reimbursement under Part A was based on the allowable costs of the facility providing the care but was subject to several reimbursement limits. This was changed by the Social Security Amendments of 1983.[58] Beginning in 1983-84, payment to hospitals for inpatient care is based on a prospectively determined amount per discharge according to the patient's diagnosis and the facility's location. During a transitional period of three years, the amount is modified based on the hospital's historical costs.

In addition to the payments by the Social Security System, beneficiaries have to pay certain deductible and coinsurance payments. A deductible is the amount of health care charges that the patient must incur and owe before Medicare pays for any of the remainder. Medicare will pay only a percentage of the remaining allowable costs for some services; the percentage not paid by Medicare is called a coinsurance payment and is owed by the patient.

Part B is a program of supplementary medical insurance covering a substantial part of physicians' and other practitioners' services, medical supplies, x-rays and laboratory tests incident to physicians' services, as well as other services not covered under Part A, such as ambulances and prosthetic devices. Enrollment is voluntary. The program is funded from contributions by beneficiaries and the federal government. Beneficiaries must pay a deductible and a 20 percent coinsurance amount. Reimbursement under Part B is based on reasonable charges for services.

The Department of Health and Human Services (HHS) has the overall responsibility for the program but it has delegated operation of the program to the Health Care Finance Administration (HCFA). Congress authorized the delegation of much of the day-to-day administrative burden to state agencies and public and private organizations operating under agreements with HHS. The processing of most claims for payment is done by agencies such as Blue Cross plans and commercial insurance companies on behalf of the government. Blue Cross and commercial insurers have entered into agreements to serve as "intermediaries" for Part A or "carriers" for Part B to make initial determinations whether services provided to beneficiaries are covered by the program and how much is due.

To be a participating provider of services and receive payment from the Medicare program, a hospital must sign an agreement with HHS and meet the "conditions of participation" specified in the Social Security Act and in the implementing regulations.[59] The only exception to these requirements is that Medicare will pay for some emergency services in hospitals that are not participating providers.

The participating provider agreement specifies that the hospital will not bill Medicare patients for services except for: (1) deductible and coinsurance payments required by law and (2) charges for services that Medicare does not cover. Charges can be made for noncovered services only if the patient has been given adequate notice that they are not covered. A hospital is deemed to meet the conditions of participation if it is accredited by the JCAH or the AOA unless a Medicare inspection indicates noncompliance.

The new Medicare hospital prospective payment system is based on diagnosis-related groups (DRGs). All Medicare inpatients now are divided into 470 DRGs based on their principal diagnosis. The principal diagnosis is the one chiefly responsible for the admission. Medicare will pay for 468 of the groups. Groups 469 and 470 involve unacceptable diagnoses and invalid data.

With a few exceptions, the hospital receives one payment for the entire admission based on the DRG and the facility's location. There is no extra payment for longer stays or more procedures unless the patient becomes an outlier. An outlier is a patient with an extraordinarily long length of stay or high total cost of care. Medicare makes an extra payment for part of the additional cost of outliers. Another exception is that capital costs, direct educational costs, and kidney acquisition costs are not included in the prospective payment; they are paid on a cost basis.

There is an adjustment for indirect educational costs that increases the payment to hospitals with medical residency programs. Children's hospitals, long-term hospitals, psychiatric hospitals and rehabilitation hospitals are exempt from the prospective payment system so they can continue to receive cost-based payment from Medicare. Psychiatric and rehabilitation units of general hospitals can be exempt if they apply for an exemption.

The new system of payment is prospective only in the sense that the amount paid is calculated based on circumstances at the time of admission. Prospective payment does not mean that the provider is paid before the services are provided. Payment is made after the services are provided.

This new payment system completely changes the implicit incentives. Under the previous cost-based system, there was an additional payment for additional days in the hospital and additional services. Thus, there was no disincentive to discourage giving patients all services that could possibly benefit them. In some situations, unnecessary services may have been provided, although if discovered, Medicare refused to pay for them.

Under the new system, there is an incentive to minimize services and shorten the length of stay to the greatest extent possible. Hospitals lose money if services to a patient exceed the prospective payment and they can keep the savings if the services cost less than the payment. Some hospitals will discontinue services that lose too much money. Most hospitals seek nurses' assistance in detecting ways to promote savings and to assure appropriate documentation of the diagnosis so that the patient is classified in the proper DRG.

Interhospital transfers constitute another important practice that is likely to be affected by the change to prospective payment. Those fashioning the system had wanted to make one payment to be shared by all hospitals that provided care to the patient but the Medicare revisions did not authorize this. The final rules provide for the hospital from which the patient is finally discharged to receive a full prospective payment based on the individual's DRG. A hospital that cares for a patient who is transferred to another hospital is to be paid at a per diem rate equal to the prospective payment for the DRG divided by the average length of stay. It is likely that there will be efforts to change the law to permit one payment that all of the hospitals would share. Regardless of the approach used, the payment policy can be expected to affect decisions as to whether to transfer a patient and the timing of the move.

The role of nurses in hospitals is being enhanced by the new reimbursement system.[60] Patient assessment, patient teaching, efficient and effective patient care, and discharge planning all have become of more critical importance. Patients must be discharged as soon as safely possible, thus requiring better preparation for self-care and home care and earlier arrangements for placement in other facilities. Nurses and others are endeavoring to find ways to safely reduce the length of stay while maintaining quality care.

Nurses are being challenged to reevaluate what they have believed to be essential for quality care. There will be difficult adjustments as they relinquish what eventually is recognized as unnecessary while defending retention of what is necessary. Because of their intimate knowledge of day-to-day patient care, nurses have a unique opportunity to influence the direction of developments. They also will be increasingly involved in analyzing costs, evaluating productivity, screening utilization by physicians, and managing supplies.

The new reimbursement system also will affect the roles of nurses involved in home and nursing home care. Patients in those settings will require increasingly sophisticated monitoring and treatment as they are discharged from hospitals sooner. The success of this transformation will depend on the patient and family education provided before and after discharge and on the supportive nursing services provided after discharge.

Medicaid

Medicaid is a joint federal-state program designed to provide medical assistance to individuals unable to afford health care. Medicaid is authorized by federal law[61] but states are not required to have a Medicaid program. Each state must pass its own law to participate (all have done so). Under Medicaid, the federal government makes grants to states to enable them to furnish: (1) medical assistance to families with dependent children and to aged, blind, or disabled individuals whose income and resources are insufficient to pay for necessary health services; and (2) rehabilitation and other services to help such families and individuals obtain or retain the capability for independence or self-care.

Any state adopting a Medicaid plan must provide certain minimum health benefits to the "categorically needy." These include individuals receiving financial assistance under the state's approved plan for Supplemental Security Income[62] or for Aid to Families with Dependent Children (AFDC).[63] Several other groups are included in the categorically needy if they would have qualified for financial assistance under the state plans except for certain characteristics that Medicaid requires to be ignored. The complex details concerning these characteristics and other aspects of Medicaid eligibility requirements are beyond the scope of this book.

States have the option of including other persons as "medically needy" if: (1) they would qualify for assistance under one of these programs if their incomes were lower and (2) their income would be low enough to qualify for assistance under such programs if they were permitted to subtract the health care expenses they have incurred already. This is sometimes called the "spend-down" option because the persons in effect must spend their income down to the threshold level for the other programs to be eligible for Medicaid.

State Medicaid plans must meet many conditions before they can be approved but states are permitted substantial flexibility in the administration of their programs. States may:

1. Decide, within federal guidelines, who in addition to the categorically needy will be eligible for medical assistance.
2. Reimburse directly physicians who provide covered services to the medically needy or pay the individual beneficiaries, thus leaving the individuals with the obligation to reimburse the physician.
3. Establish their own reimbursement methods for inpatient hospital services as long as the payments do not exceed Medicare's rates for the same services.

In determining the scope of benefits, states are required to provide only nine basic services to the categorically needy but are free to provide additional ones at their own option. The nine basic services are:

1. inpatient hospital services
2. outpatient hospital services
3. rural health clinic services
4. laboratory and x-ray services
5. skilled nursing facility services
6. early and periodic screening, diagnosis and treatment (EPSDT) for persons under age 21
7. family planning services
8. physicians' services
9. nurse midwives' services.

As a result of this flexibility, all states have developed Medicaid programs.

Medicaid is different from Medicare in that it provides medical assistance for categories of persons in financial need while Medicare provides medical assistance primarily to people 65 years of age or older without regard to need. Medicaid varies widely among the states while Medicare is uniform. Medicaid is financed by general federal and state revenues, while Medicare is financed by a special tax on employers and employees for hospital insurance and equal contributions by beneficiaries and the federal government for supplementary medical services. Medicaid is basically a welfare program while Medicare is a form of social insurance.

Eligible recipients must apply to the designated agency before Medicaid will pay for services they receive. Institutional service providers generally become Medicaid participants by applying to the state agency and contracting with it to provide services to Medicaid recipients for the payment permitted by the state. Payment cannot be collected from the patient except to the extent permitted by federal law. Noninstitutional providers of services generally are not required to enter into any contract with the state but participate merely by treating Medicaid recipients, then billing the state. However, payment for physician services can be made only if the physician agrees to accept charges determined by the state as full payment.

The 1981 Medicaid amendments increased the latitude of the states in determining services to be covered and payment amounts. As a result, many states began reducing services through such provisions as the 12-day limit on covered days of hospital care in South Carolina that was upheld by a federal court in 1982.[64] Other states placed new limits on the reimbursement of providers.

Medicare and Medicaid Fraud and Abuse

In 1977, Congress enacted the Medicare-Medicaid Anti-Fraud and Abuse Amendments[65] that strengthened the remedies for wrongful provider conduct. Many existing offenses were reclassified from misdemeanors to felonies and the possible fines and prison sentences for violators were increased.

Other Third Party Payers

A large part of health care is paid by third parties other than the government—the Blue Cross and Blue Shield plans, commercial insurance companies, self-funded health insurance plans of some industries, and various HMO and other alternate delivery systems (ADS).

Blue Cross and Blue Shield together are the largest private third party payers. They are different from most commercial insurers in that they usually contract with hospitals, physicians, and other providers who agree to offer services to their subscribers. The contracts specify the payment arrangements. Blue Cross covers hospital and related services. Blue Shield involves physician and related services.

Blue Cross and Blue Shield plans each cover a local region and have widely different practices concerning payment and other matters. Some Blue Cross plans contract with hospitals for payment based on costs, others pay all or part of billed charges, still others use other formulas to determine the amount. The hospital agrees to accept the amount determined by the contract as payment in full for all covered services. The subscriber can be responsible for paying a portion of the bill when the contract between the subscriber and Blue Cross requires certain out-of-pocket payments; the rest is paid by Blue Cross.

Because of the volume of services it pays for and the usual promptness of its reimbursement, saving hospitals some costs, Blue Cross contracts generally provide for a discount so that the company pays less than many other third party payers except Medicare and Medicaid, which generally pay much less than the actual cost of providing the services. These discounts for Blue Cross have been challenged in numerous court and regulatory cases and have been uniformly upheld.[66]

Most commercial insurance and self-funded plans are different from Blue Cross in that they usually do not contract directly with hospitals. Instead, commercial insurers generally reimburse their insureds for some or all of the expenses they have incurred. Most commercial insurers make their payments directly to the hospital if the patient so requests. If the insurer does not pay the entire bill, the insured still is responsible for the remainder of the charges.

HMOs and some ADSs differ from commercial insurance and Blue Cross plans by assuming responsibilities for providing care to their members in return for a prepaid premium. Some HMOs own their own hospitals but most HMOs and ADSs make arrangements with other facilities. These arrangements vary widely, with some providing for payment of full charges and others for a lower negotiated rate.

Collections

A difficult area for health care institution administrators is the control of the amount of money owed the hospital, called accounts receivable. Even though third party payers generally owe the majority of accounts receivable, collection from individual patients is a vital source of operating revenue. To ensure that collection of a bill can be pursued to the full extent permitted by law, the bill must be prepared and maintained accurately.

Adult patients are responsible for paying their bills. This principle is based on either an express or implied contract to pay for accepted services. Adults are responsible for the reasonable value of services furnished in good faith, even if they are unconscious, mentally incompetent, or incapacitated at the time. The major exceptions are when the competent, oriented adult has explicitly refused to accept the services or the law entitles the patient to free care.

Most states make a husband responsible for paying for necessary care for his wife; in most states, the wife has a reciprocal duty to pay for necessary care for her husband. Most states make the father responsible for paying for necessary care for minor children, and in many states the mother also is responsible. In some states, minors are not legally responsible for paying for care they receive unless they are emancipated but in other states are responsible for paying for necessary care received. When there is doubt under state law concerning the parents' responsibility, a parent's express promise to pay frequently is obtained.

Absent a statute or an express promise, other relatives or friends are not responsible for paying for care. Some state statutes make adult children responsible for the cost of their parents' care when their parents are unable to pay. By expressly promising to pay, a relative or friend may become responsible, especially if the promise is written. In most states, merely arranging for care or taking a person to the hospital does not make a relative or friend responsible for payment.

Some states make counties or other units of local government responsible for paying for some health care for their residents who are unable to pay although some provide that prior authorization must be obtained from appropriate government officials. Other statutes do not require prior approval to create an obligation, especially in emergencies.

When hospitals' internal collection procedures fail to produce payment, they frequently use collection agencies. Usually the hospital enters a written agreement with one or more such agencies specifying the terms and conditions for collection activities to assure compliance with laws and hospital policies. (Other collection matters are discussed in Chapter 5.)

Uncompensated Care

Many hospitals are required by law to provide uncompensated care to certain patients. State law requires many governmental hospitals to offer such care, especially to residents of the area that provides tax support to the facility. Federal law imposes this obligation on all hospitals that have received Hill-Burton grants or loans.

The federal Hill-Burton Act[67] provided public and nonprofit community hospitals with funding for construction and modernization. Hospitals that accepted this funding are required to provide a reasonable volume of services to persons unable to pay. For many years, this obligation was met by either: (1) certifying that free care provided was equal to 10 percent of all Hill-Burton assistance; (2) certifying that the amount was 3 percent of the hospital's operating costs, excluding expenses for Medicare and Medicaid patients; or (3) maintaining an open-door policy so that no person was turned away for lack of money. The obligation continued for 20 years after the construction was completed.

The open-door option was eliminated in 1979 and compliance became more difficult when HHS promulgated detailed regulations[68] specifying notice and recordkeeping requirements, qualifications patients must meet for their care to count toward satisfying the obligation, an inflation index so that the required amount under the 10 percent option increases each year, a requirement that any portion of the obligation not met in one year be added to the obligation for the next year, and numerous other changes.

Some patients have attempted to use a hospital's failure to comply with the Hill-Burton regulations on uncompensated care as a defense against collection suits. Courts have tended to reject this defense.[69]

Capital Financing

To meet the growing needs of consumers and to implement technological advances, hospitals and other health care institutions have increased the volume, variety, and complexity of services they offer. The combined effect of population growth and expanded services has produced increases both in operating costs and in capital outlays for modernization. Substantial capital also is required to renovate or replace obsolete facilities and equipment. The expansion of clinics, neighborhood health centers, intermediate care facilities, skilled nursing facilities, and home care programs also has increased capital requirements. These current needs and projections for future requirements have forced health care institutions to investigate a broad range of sources of capital financing, including internal financing, philanthropy, state grants, bonds and other borrowing, and leasing.

Asset Protection

Health care institutions must be concerned with protection against losses arising from injuries to patients or visitors and from damage to or destruction of physical facilities, equipment, and vehicles. Injuries to patients may result from acts of malpractice by professionals as well as from general negligence of nonprofessional employees. The institution is subject to the risk of legal action by such patients. The facility's physical property is subject to risk of fire, theft, and other hazards. Although it should attempt to minimize or eliminate these risks, a program of risk management includes proper insurance coverage against those risks.

TAXATION

Tax Exemption

Governmental and charitable institutions are granted exemption from many state and local taxes for property, sales, and income and from federal income taxes. Classification of a health care institution as exempt depends upon several factors that vary depending on the type of tax.

Property Tax Exemption

Each state has the power to tax the properties within its boundaries. A health care institution must prove it is qualified for an exemption or it is subject to property taxes. In some states, ownership by a nonprofit or governmental health care institution is not sufficient to establish exemption. It is necessary in those states to prove also that the property is used exclusively for hospital or health care purposes. In some states, simply providing health care on a nonprofit basis is sufficient to qualify; other states require that free care actually be provided to those unable to pay.[70]

Sales and Use Taxes

States that have sales and use taxes vary considerably in their coverage and exemptions. Health care institutions sometimes are exempted from paying taxes on some of their purchases. Some states exempt qualified charitable organizations for collecting sales taxes; others grant exemptions for specific products or services, rather than for entire institutions. There usually is an exemption for medicines and some medical products.

Federal and State Income Tax

Many nonprofit health care institutions are eligible for exemption from federal income tax under section 501(c)(3) of the Internal Revenue Code.[71] This section provides exemptions for organizations created and operated exclusively for certain purposes, including "charitable" purposes. The IRS accepts health care as "charitable." Prior to 1969, the IRS considered relief of the poor as one of the essential characteristics a hospital must meet to be "charitable." In 1969, it issued a ruling that recognized that promotion of health is one of the general purposes of the law of charity, so free or reduced-rate services are not required.[72]

A health care institution that has income tax exemption still must pay taxes on unrelated business income. In addition, if the unrelated business income is too large a portion of total revenues, the entire tax exemption can be lost.

Some governmental institutions obtain their federal income tax exemption under section 115 of the Internal Revenue Code[73] on the basis of being an instrumentality of the state, rather than under section 501(c)(3).

State income taxes (and city income taxes where they exist) apply to all profits or net proceeds accruing to an organization unless it has been approved for exemption under state law. The state qualifications for exemption may be different from the federal.

MEDICAL STAFF

Nurses in hospitals must interact with physicians every day and have an important role in assuring that the quality of care physicians provide is maintained. It thus is important for nurses to understand the relationship of the physician to the hospital. This relationship is different from that of most nurses: the nurse usually is an employee, while the physician is a private practitioner whose accountability is through the medical staff organization. (The efforts of nurses engaged in expanded or independent practice to obtain clinical privileges in hospitals are discussed in Chapter 5.)

Before being permitted to practice in a hospital, the physician must obtain an appointment to the medical staff and be granted clinical privileges by the governing board. Physicians may provide only the services for which they have clinical privileges. The board has the responsibility to exercise appropriate discretion in determining whether to grant an appointment and what the scope of privileges should be. The board also assures that there is periodic review of the physician and appropriate adjustments in privileges. It usually relies on the organized medical staff to conduct reviews and recommend board action. Each hospital is required to have an organized medical staff to comply with licensing regulations, accreditation standards, and third party payer requirements such as the Medicare conditions of participation.

This section discusses the responsibilities of the organized medical staff, appointment to that staff, clinical privileges, periodic review, modification and termination of such privileges, and the procedural due process rights of physicians.

The Organized Medical Staff

An important element of the governance of any hospital is the organized medical staff. In most hospitals, physicians are not employees or agents of the hospital but are accountable individually and collectively to the board for the quality of care they provide there. Their collective accountability is fulfilled through a medical staff organization. JCAH accreditation standards, Medicare conditions of participation, and most hospital licensure rules require that the medical staff be organized.

The board has the ultimate authority over the hospital and must exercise it consistent with satisfactory patient care. Through the bylaws, the board delegates to the medical staff the authority and duty to carry out the medical aspects of patient care. The board retains the authority and responsibility to approve appointments to the medical staff, to grant and decrease clinical privileges, and to assure that there is a mechanism for monitoring quality of care. It normally looks to the medical staff to conduct the monitoring and to provide expert advice on appointment and clinical privilege decisions.

The typical medical staff organization includes officers, such as a president; an executive committee to act in matters that do not require approval of the entire staff; and committees to address specific issues such as quality assurance, infection control, pharmaceutical utilization, credentials review, and other matters. In larger hospitals, the medical staff often is departmentalized along specialty lines so that there also is an organization at that level.

Functions of the organized medical staff include: (1) implementation of policies and procedures designed to provide patients with satisfactory care, (2) recommendation of appointments to the medical staff and of granting or changing clinical privileges, (3) development and implementation of a quality assurance mechanism, (4) provision of continuing medical education, and (5) other actions necessary to govern themselves and relate to the board.

The board cannot abdicate its responsibility by relying completely on the medical staff. Hospitals have been found liable for the actions of physicians when the institutions failed to properly evaluate them prior to appointment to the medical staff or failed to properly monitor their performance after appointment.[74] In 1981 the Wisconsin Supreme Court imposed liability on a hospital for injuries to a patient by a doctor because the hospital should never have appointed him to the medical staff.[75] The hospital had not checked his professional credentials and references. A check would have disclosed discrepancies and misrepresentations that would have led the hospital to deny him appointment to the medical staff.

Appointment to the Medical Staff

A physician does not have a right to practice in a particular hospital merely because of obtaining a medical license. Physicians must apply for appointment and prove that they satisfy the hospital's criteria for appointment or that the criteria are not permitted.

Since a modern hospital must fulfill its responsibility to screen applicants and a modern physician must have access to a hospital to practice, there have been many court cases involving appointment to the medical staff and other related issues. Courts have ruled that a hospital may require the physician to (1) complete an application form with a full, frank disclosure of requested information and an agreement to abide by hospital rules;[76] (2) provide references as long as the number of eligible referents is not limited inappropriately;[77] (3) provide evidence of the ability to work harmoniously with other physicians and hospital staff members;[78] (4) have a specified amount of malpractice insurance;[79] and (5) accept the responsibility for emergency room coverage on a rotational basis.[80] Hospitals cannot base their refusal to appoint a physician on (1) race, creed, color, sex, national origin, or handicap;[81] (2) failure to be a member of a medical association or society;[82] and (3) preappointment tests that are not uniformly applied to all applicants for certain clinical privileges.[83]

Delineation of Clinical Privileges

When a physician is appointed to the medical staff of a hospital, a determination must be made as to the scope of practice the individual will be permitted. A physician can act within the entire scope of medical practice without violating the medical license. However, because of the expansion of medical knowledge, no physician is actually competent to perform all medical procedures. The hospital protects the patient and the physician by examining the applicant's credentials and granting clinical privileges to engage in a certain scope of practice. A physician who acts outside the granted scope, except in an emergency, is subject to discipline, including termination of medical staff membership.

There are many ways to delineate clinical privileges. The key element is a written definition that the medical staff understands. Some hospitals grant privileges for individual procedures. Many hospitals use categories or levels of care. Broad categories of patient conditions and procedures are grouped into levels and physicians are granted privileges to perform everything in the appropriate group. Other hospitals grant privileges by specialty, defining what each is permitted to do. A hybrid of these approaches often is used.

Hospitals may place conditions on clinical privileges, such as a requirement that (1) a consultation be obtained before certain procedures are done, (2) assistants be used for certain procedures, or (3) certain procedures be supervised.

Review and Appointment

After physicians are appointed to the medical staff and receive clinical privileges, their performance is reviewed periodically as part of the process to determine whether to grant reappointment.[84] Failure to review performance and take appropriate action when necessary can result in hospital liability.[85]

The hospital and its medical staff can use a variety of methods to review performance. Traditionally, this has been accomplished through medical staff committees, such as the tissue committee, which reviews surgically removed tissues; the pharmacy committee, which reviews drug use; the medical records committee, which is concerned with timely, complete documentation; and similar committees for other functions. Although these committees continue to perform important functions, since the early 1970s there has been increasing focus on quality assurance programs that conduct patient care evaluations, problem-focused studies, and utilization review.

Patient care evaluations and problem-focused studies are directed toward evaluation of care provided for specific diseases or conditions or of clinical or administrative procedures. Criteria are established and a variety of data sources are used to measure performance. Variations are either justified or analyzed for appropriate corrective action, which often is an educational effort. A follow-up study then can be conducted to determine whether the action was successful. These techniques also are used to evaluate nursing care and procedures.

Utilization review focuses on the appropriateness of the physician's admitting individual patients to the hospital and of their length of stay. Utilization review can be conducted retrospectively by analyzing medical records or concurrently at the time the patient is in the hospital. Because of the pressure to reduce expenditures for hospital care by shortening length of stay, the focus now is on concurrent review.

In addition to this formalized review, day-to-day interaction with other physicians, with nurses, and with other hospital staff provides valuable information on problems. Nurses who become aware of potential problems should bring them to the attention of nursing supervisory personnel, who should notify medical staff officers or hospital administrators. Some courts will hold the hospital responsible for information known by a nurse even if the nurse does not communicate it, so it is important for problems to be identified and communicated quickly. When informed of problems, the hospital has a responsibility to determine what action is appropriate and to initiate that action. Usually educational efforts will be adequate but sometimes steps such as suspension or termination of all or some clinical privileges may be necessary.

In addition to the continuing review, a periodic systematic review is necessary to determine whether each medical staff member is still fulfilling the responsibilities of such membership and the clinical privileges granted. Thus, medical staff appointments are for a limited period, usually one or two years. Before the expiration of the appointment, each member is reviewed. The review includes clinical competence, compliance with hospital and medical staff policies, and fulfillment of other medical staff responsibilities, such as active involvement in assigned committees. Based on this review, a decision is made whether to reappoint the person to the medical staff and maintain the present clinical privileges or to modify them.

Difficult situations sometimes arise when physicians do not recognize their declining capabilities after long productive careers of service to the community. Fortunately, in most circumstances, they will recognize the change when approached tactfully and agree to adjust their scope of practice to fit their capabilities. However, if a physician will not agree to needed adjustments, the hospital and medical staff still have the difficult duty of protecting patients by taking action to reduce the physician's privileges to the appropriate scope.

Peer Review Organizations

The 1972 amendments to the Social Security Act required patient care evaluations and utilization review for all federally funded patients. The secretary of Health, Education, and Welfare (now HHS) was directed to divide the nation into areas, then designate a Professional Standards Review Organization (PSRO) for each area. The PSRO conducted utilization reviews to determine the medical necessity of the care and the appropriate level of treatment. The levels were care in hospitals, skilled nursing facilities, intermediate care facilities, and outpatient settings. The PSRO could delegate the patient care evaluation and utilization review functions to the hospital; if it did, it monitored the review activities of such facilities and could withdraw the delegated status if the reviews were not performed properly.

In 1982 the PSRO law was replaced by the Tax Equity and Fiscal Responsibility Act,[86] which required similar peer review by Utilization and Quality Control Peer Review Organizations (PROs). Transition provisions permitted existing PSROs to continue until a review organization had contracted under the new law to perform the function. Many PSROs were able to continue by contracting to be one of the new PROs. The Social Security Amendments of 1983 modified their role to focus their efforts on the potential problems created by prospective per-case payment based on diagnosis-related groups.[87]

The entire system of federally mandated review continues to be challenged politically by questions concerning whether its savings exceed its costs. Federal funding of the system has been curtailed, leading to changes in the review system so that it now focuses on potential problem areas rather than attempting to review all areas. Private health insurance companies and other third party payers are increasingly mandating that the care of patients for whom they pay be subject to the utilization review portion of the review system. Frequently, they contract with the same organizations that perform the federally mandated review, offsetting some of the diminished federal funding.

The new system focuses on utilization curtailment to reduce expenditures, so it cannot be relied on to fulfill the hospital's responsibility to review the quality of physicians' performance. Some elements of the federal program can be of assistance but hospitals must have their own system of review.

Modification or Termination of Privileges

The clinical privileges granted to physicians sometimes must be modified or terminated because of changes in their capabilities, violation of hospital or medical staff policies, changes in hospital standards, or other reasons. The primary legal issues in such cases concern the required due process procedures (discussed later in this chapter). The other major legal issue is the adequacy of the reason for the action.

The most frequent reason for temporary suspension of clinical privileges is failure to complete medical records within the time limits established by hospital policy. Most hospitals temporarily restrict admitting privileges of delinquent physicians until they complete all overdue records. The rationale is that physicians do not have enough time to accept responsibility for additional patients if they do not have enough time to complete records for past admissions. Courts accept the reasonableness of disciplinary actions for failure to complete records.[88]

Some physicians have challenged adverse actions on the basis that their due process rights were violated because the standards by which they were judged were too vague to inform them of what was expected. The courts generally have upheld actions taken on the basis of general subjective standards when they are applied in a reasonable way.

For example, in 1972, the Nevada Supreme Court upheld termination of clinical privileges based on the general standard of "unprofessional conduct."[89] The court recognized that it was not feasible to specify the variety of unprofessional conduct: The physician had touched a spinal needle without gloves before using it and had appeared for surgery in no condition to perform it, requiring cancellation. The court found that the standard was properly applied in this case.

Public Hospitals and Private Hospitals

Lawsuits arising out of governing body decisions concerning appointments and clinical privileges of physicians usually focus on the board's right to impose the rules applied or on the procedures followed in reaching the decision. Boards of public hospitals have less discretion in these matters than they do in private hospitals in most states. However, there is a trend toward reducing the discretion of private hospitals.

Public Hospitals

Public hospitals must satisfy the requirements of the Fourteenth Amendment to the Constitution which says that no state shall "deprive any person of life, liberty, or property, without due process of law. . . ." Actions of public hospitals are considered actions of the state. Courts have determined that the interest of physicians in practicing in a hospital is a liberty or property interest, so physicians are entitled to "due process of law" when a public hospital makes a decision concerning appointment to the medical staff or clinical privileges. However, physicians do not have a right to practice in any public hospital; they must demonstrate that they satisfy valid hospital rules before they may practice there.

To provide physicians with due process, the rules must be reasonable and must adequately express the intent of the hospital. Rules that are too arbitrary or vague may be unenforceable. In addition, physicians must be offered procedural protections or an adverse action may violate due process requirements. (Due process protections are discussed in detail later in this chapter.)

The Fourteenth Amendment also says that no state shall "deny to any person within its jurisdiction the equal protection of the laws." Equal protection means that like persons must be dealt with in like fashion. The equal protection clause is concerned with the justifiability of the classifications used to distinguish persons for various legal purposes. The determination of whether a particular difference between persons can justify a particular difference in rules or procedures can be difficult.

In general, the courts require that the government agency justify the difference with a "rational reason." The major exception is the strict scrutiny courts apply to distinctions based on "suspect classifications," such as race. Because of the comprehensive federal and state legislation prohibiting discrimination based on many characteristics, most challenges to alleged discriminatory actions are based on legislation rather than directly on this constitutional principle.

Private Hospitals

Most private hospitals are subject to fewer legal constraints than are public hospitals when taking actions concerning medical staff. The Fourteenth Amendment does not apply to private hospitals except in the unusual circumstance that their activities are found to be state action, such as when a majority of the hospital's board is appointed by state authorities. In most states, private hospitals are required only to follow their own rules in medical staff actions. However, in a growing number of states, legislatures and courts are requiring that medical staff members be provided some protections, although not always as formal as those for public hospitals.

State Action. It is rare for private hospitals today to be found to be engaged in state action and thus be subject to the Fourteenth Amendment. Prior to 1974, some courts ruled that private hospitals were engaging in state action when they had received Hill-Burton construction funds, were reimbursed by Medicare and Medicaid, and were heavily regulated by the state.

In 1974 the Supreme Court ruled that regulation or funding was not enough to establish state action.[90] The Court said that there must be a "sufficiently close nexus between the state and the challenged action of the regulated entity so that the action of the latter may be fairly treated as that of the state itself." The Court gave the following examples of such connection: (1) when the private entity exercises powers traditionally reserved to the state, (2) when the state directly benefits by sharing in the rewards and responsibilities of the private venture, and (3) when the state directs or encourages the particular act. All courts now agree that funding or regulation alone are not enough to convert private hospital actions to state action.

Hospital Rules. Most private hospitals have rules concerning the criteria and procedures to be followed in making decisions concerning medical staff membership and clinical privilege delineation. These rules usually appear in the medical staff bylaws and are required to obtain JCAH accreditation. After a private hospital has adopted such rules, most courts will require it to follow its own rules in making decisions.[91] However, courts are likely to overlook minor deviations as long as they do not significantly affect the fundamental interests of the physician.[92]

State Law Protections. There is a great range of state law protection for physicians in their relationship with private hospitals. Some states have not recognized any physicians' rights but others will enforce the rules of private hospitals. By statute or court decision, some states have limited the latitude of private hospitals. For example, New York law requires them to process all applications for membership or clinical privileges from physicians, podiatrists, and dentists.[93] It also specifies that membership or clinical privileges may be denied, curtailed, or terminated only after the reasons have been stated and that the only permissible reasons are "standards of patient care, patient welfare, the objectives of the institution, or the character or competency of the applicant."

A few state courts require private hospitals to provide some procedural protections for medical staff members, including notice of alleged shortcomings and an opportunity to be heard.[94] New Jersey has extended detailed additional procedural protections, including the right to be represented by a lawyer.[95]

Procedural Due Process

This section discusses the due process procedures required of public hospitals. The fair procedure required of private hospitals in some states may not include all of the elements discussed here.

Some courts recognize a distinction between the rights of applicants for appointments to the medical staff and the rights of those already on staff, especially in private hospitals. These courts find members to have a right to the procedures specified in the bylaws by virtue of their membership, but applicants do not have a right to make claims on the private organization until they actually are members. However, most hospitals follow the procedures specified in the bylaws for both applicants and members.

Situations involving potential immediate risk to patient well-being, such as a physician's incapacity due to alcohol or drugs, call for imposition of restrictions on a physician's practice before any due process procedures can be followed.[96] If the risk is not sufficiently immediate, such as when the incidents the action is based on did not occur recently, courts will enjoin immediate suspension.[97] In most circumstances it is possible to follow the required due process procedures before adverse action is taken.

The first step in providing due process is to give reasonable notice, in writing, of the reasons action is being considered and of the time and place where the physicians may present information on their behalf.[98] The second step is to provide an opportunity to present such information. In most situations, they will have had one or more opportunities to present information during the informal investigative steps that precede formal action. However, courts usually require another formal opportunity to do so after the formal recommendation of adverse action.

Courts have disagreed on whether there is a legal right to legal representation at the hearing.[99] The committee or individual conducting the hearing obviously must not be biased against the physician.[100] Courts have recognized that hospitals cannot compel witnesses to attend hearings because they do not have subpoena power. Thus, due process usually does not require an opportunity to cross-examine all those who may have complained about the physician's conduct.[101] However, a reasonable effort usually is made to have important witnesses present—among them, for example, nurses. Although the procedure is less formal than a court, it is important that all relevant information be provided so that both patients and physician can be protected.

Courts have permitted only the affected physician to seek judicial review of adverse decisions. For example, a New Hampshire court denied a petition by parents of a patient that the local hospital be required to grant temporary privileges to their physician so he could admit their child.[102] Courts generally require the physician to pursue all of the procedures available within the hospital before they will hear any appeal. If a physician refuses to participate in the hospital hearing, the court usually will not even consider the physician's contention that procedural due process was denied.[103]

When courts review actions of hospital medical staff concerning members, they usually show great deference to the judgment of the facility and its staff. They limit their review to a determination whether appropriate procedures were followed and whether the action appears to be arbitrary or capricious. If there is credible evidence supporting the action and proper procedures have been followed, the courts almost always will approve hospital actions. Thus, it is important to understand how to initiate and participate in hospital reviews.

NOTES

1. *Queen of Angels Hosp. v. Younger*, 66 Cal. App.3d 359, 136 Cal. Rptr. 36 (1977).
2. *E.g., Langrock v. Porter Hosp., Inc.*, 126 Vt. 223, 227 A.2d 291 (1967).
3. *E.g., In re Mt. Sinai Hosp.*, 250 N.Y. 103, 164 N.E. 871 (1928).
4. *E.g., Ray v. Homewood Hosp.*, 223 Minn. 440, 27 N.W.2d 409 (1947).
5. *Hulit v. St. Vincent's Hosp.*, 164 Mont. 168, 520 P.2d 99 (1974).
6. *Cobb County v. Prince*, 242 Ga. 139, 249 S.E.2d 581 (1978).
7. *Darling v. Charleston Community Memorial Hosp.*, 33 Ill.2d 326, 211 N.E.2d 253 (1965), *cert. denied* 383 U.S. 946 (1966).
8. *Johnson v. Misericordia Community Hosp.*, 99 Wis. 2d 708, 301 N.W.2d 156 (1981).
9. *E.g., Patient Care Services, S.C. v. Segal*, 32 Ill. App. 3d 1021, 337 N.E.2d 471 (1975).
10. *E.g., Fowle Memorial Hosp. v. Nicholson*, 189 N.C. 44, 126 S.E. 94 (1925).
11. Joint Commission on Accreditation of Hospitals, ACCREDITATION MANUAL FOR HOSPITALS, 1984 ed.
12. 42 C.F.R. § 405.1027 (1981).
13. *Koelbl v. Whalen*, 63 A.D.2d 408, 406 N.Y.S.2d 621 (1978).
14. *Eden Park Health Services, Inc. v. Whalen*, 73 A.D.2d 993, 424 N.Y.S.2d 33 (1980).
15. *E.g., Harrison Clinic Hosp. v. Texas State Bd. of Health*, 400 S.W.2d 840 (Tex. Civ. App. 1966), *aff'd*. 410 S.W.2d 181 (Tex. 1966).
16. 42 C.F.R. § 405.1027 (1981).
17. Pub. L. No. 90-513, 84 Stat. 1236 (codified as amended in scattered sections of 18, 21, 26, 42, 46, and 49 U.S.C.).
18. Federal Food, Drug and Cosmetic Act, which includes Medical Device Amendments of 1976, is codified in Title 21, U.S.C. FDA regulations fill Title 21, C.F.R.
19. 21 C.F.R. Pts. 50, 56, 312, 812, and 813.
20. Pub. L. No. 91-601, 84 Stat. 1670 (codified as amended in scattered sections of 7, 15, and 21 U.S.C.).
21. 15 U.S.C. §§ 1-7 (1976).
22. 15 U.S.C. §§ 12-27 and 44 (1976 & Supp. V 1981).
23. 15 U.S.C. §§ 41-58 (1976 & Supp. V 1981).

24. 15 U.S.C. § 13c (1976).

25. *Hospital Bldg. Co. v. Trustees of Rex Hosp.*, 425 U.S. 738 (1976).

26. *Goldfarb v. Virginia State Bar Ass'n*, 421 U.S. 773 (1975).

27. *National Gerimedical Hosp. and Gerontology Center v. Blue Cross of Kansas City*, 452 U.S. 378 (1981).

28. *Parker v. Brown*, 317 U.S. 341 (1943).

29. *California Retail Liquor Dealers Ass'n v. Midcal Aluminum, Inc.* 445 U.S. 97 (1980).

30. *Eastern R.R. Presidents Conf. v. Noerr Motor Freight, Inc.*, 365 U.S. 127 (1961); *United Mine Workers of Am. v. Pennington*, 381 U.S. 657 (1965).

31. 15 U.S.C. § 1012(b) (1976).

32. *Group Life and Health Ins. Co. v. Royal Drug*, 440 U.S. 205 (1979).

33. *Arizona v. Maricopa County Medical Soc'y*, 457 U.S. 332 (1982).

34. *St. Bernard Hosp. v. Hospital Services Ass'n of New Orleans, Inc.*, 618 F.2d 1140 (5th Cir. 1980).

35. *Abbott Labs. v. Portland Retail Druggists Ass'n, Inc.*, 425 U.S. 1 (1976).

36. Pub. L. No. 92-603, 86 Stat. 1329 (1972).

37. Pub. L. No. 93-641, 88 Stat. 2225 (1975).

38. Pub. L. No. 98-21, 97 Stat. 65 (1983).

39. Pub. L. No. 96-79, 93 Stat. 592 (1979).

40. Pub. L. No. 97-35, §§ 933-937, 95 Stat. 570-572 (1981).

41. Pub. L. No. 98-21, § 607, 97 Stat. 171 (1983).

42. 42 U.S.C. § 1395x(e)(8) and (z) (1976).

43. 42 U.S.C. § 1320a-1 (1976 & Supp. IV 1980), as amended by Pub. L. No. 97-35, § 2193(c)(3), 95 Stat. 827 (1981) and Pub. L. No. 98-21, § 607, 97 Stat. 171 (1983).

44. Pub. L. No. 98-21, § 607, 97 Stat. 171 (1983).

45. Pub. L. No. 93-641, 88 Stat. 2225 (1975).

46. Health Planning and Resources Development Amendments of 1979, Pub. L. No. 96-79, 93 Stat. 592.

47. Omnibus Budget Reconciliation Act of 1981, Pub. L. No. 97-35, §§ 933-937, 95 Stat. 570-572.

48. 42 U.S.C. § 300k-2 (1976 & Supp. IV 1980).

49. Fed. Reg. 48, 502-5 (September 23, 1977).

50. 42 C.F.R. §§ 121.201-121.211 (1982).

51. Pub. L. No. 96-79, §§ 117 and 126, 93 Stat. 614-620, 628, added 42 U.S.C. § 300m-6 (Supp. IV 1980) and amended 42 U.S.C. § 300n (Supp. IV 1980).

52. Pub. L. No. 97-35, § 936(a), 95 Stat. 572 (1981), amending 42 U.S.C. § 300n(5),(6), and (7) (Supp. IV 1980).

53. 42 C.F.R. § 123.412 (1982).

54. *Huron Valley Hosp., Inc., v. Michigan State Health Facilities Comm'n*, 312 N.W.2d 422 (Mich. Ct. App. 1981).

55. *First Fed. Sav. and Loan Ass'n of Lincoln v. Casari*, 667 F.2d 734 (8th Cir. 1982).

56. *Massachusetts Nurses Ass'n v. Dukakis*, 726 F.2d 41 (1st Cir. 1984).

57. Pub. L. No. 89-97, 79 Stat. 290 (1965).

58. Pub. L. No. 98-21, 97 Stat. 65 (1983); 49 Fed. Reg. 234-334 (Jan. 3, 1984).

59. 42 U.S.C. § 1395x(e) (1976 & Supp. IV 1980); 42 C.F.R. §§ 405.1011-405.1041 (1981).

60. "New Nursing Role Will be Vital to DRG Success, Says HCFA's Davis," 84 *Am. J. Nursing* (January 1984):112; "Nursing Leaders Sight Danger, Opportunity in Switch to DRGs," 83 *Am. J. Nursing* (December 1983):1707; "How DRGs Will Affect Your Hospital—and You," *RN* (May 1984):71.

61. 42 U.S.C. §§ 1396a-1396p (1976 & Supp. IV 1980), *as amended by* Pub. L. No. 97-35, 95 Stat. 785 (1981) and Pub. L. No. 97-248, 96 Stat. 367 (1982).

62. 42 U.S.C. §§ 1381-1383c (1976 & Supp. IV 1980), *as amended by* Pub. L. No. 97-248, 96 Stat. 404 (1982).

63. 42 U.S.C. §§ 601-613 (1976 & Supp. IV 1980), *as amended by* Pub. L. No. 97-248, 96 Stat. 395 (1982).

64. *Charleston Memorial Hosp. v. Conrad,* No. 81-2759-1 (D.S.C. April 16, 1982). *Medicare and Medicaid Guide* (CCH) ¶31,958.

65. Pub. L. No. 95-142, 91 Stat. 1175 (codified as amended in scattered sections of 42 U.S.C.).

66. *E.g., Travelers Ins. Co. v. Blue Cross of W. Pa.,* 361 F.Supp. 774 (W.D. Pa. 1972), *aff'd.* 481 F.2d 80 (3rd Cir. 1973), *cert.denied* 414 U.S. 1093 (1973).

67. 42 U.S.C. §§ 291a-291o-1 (1976 & Supp. IV 1980).

68. 42 C.F.R. pt. 124 (1983).

69. *E.g., Falmouth Hosp. v. Lopes,* 376 Mass. 580, 382 N.E.2d 1042 (1978); *but see Hospital Center at Orange v. Cook,* 177 N.J. Super 289, 426 A.2d 526 (N.J. Super. Ct. App. Div. 1981) [Failure to give required notice barred collection suit].

70. E.g., *Georgia Osteopathic Hosp. v. Alford,* 217 Ga. 663, 124 S.E.2d 402 (1962).

71. 26 U.S.C. § 501(c)(3) (1976).

72. Rev. Rul. 69-545, 1969-2 C.B.117; *modified by* Rev. Rul. 83-157, I.R.B. 1983-42, 9.

73. 26 U.S.C. § 115 (1976).

74. *E.g., Purcell v. Zimbelman,* 18 Ariz. App. 75, 500 P.2d 335 (1972).

75. *Johnson v. Misericordia Community Hosp.,* 99 Wis. 2d 708, 301 N.W.2d 156 (1981).

76. *E.g., Dunbar v. Hospital Auth. of Gwinnet County,* 227 Ga. 534, 182 S.E.2d 89 (1971); *Yeargin v. Hamilton Memorial Hosp.,* 225 Ga. 661, 171 S.E.2d 136 (1969), *cert.denied* 397 U.S. 963 (1970).

77. *E.g., Ascherman v. St. Francis Memorial Hosp.,* 45 Cal. App. 3d 507, 119 Cal. Rptr. 507 (1975).

78. *E.g., Sussman v. Overlook Hosp. Ass'n,* 95 N.J. Super. 418, 231 A.2d 389 (N.J. Super. Ct. App. Div. 1967); *but see McElhinney v. William Booth Memorial Hosp.,* 544 S.W.2d 216 (Ky. 1976).

79. *E.g., Pollock v. Methodist Hosp.,* 392 F.Supp. 393 (E.D.La. 1975).

80. *E.g., Yeargin v. Hamilton Memorial Hosp.,* 229 Ga. 870, 195 S.E.2d 8 (1972).

81. *E.g., Chowdhury v. Reading Hosp. and Medical Center,* 677 F.2d 317 (3rd Cir. 1982).

82. *E.g., Griesman v. Newcomb Hosp.,* 40 N.J. 389, 192 A.2d 817 (1963).

83. *E.g., Martino v. Concord Community Hosp. Dist.,* 233 Cal. App. 2d 51, 43 Cal. Rptr. 255 (1965).

84. Joint Commission on Accreditation of Hospitals, ACCREDITATION MANUAL FOR HOSPITALS, 1984 Ed., 101; 42 C.F.R. § 405.1023(d)(2) (1982).

85. *E.g., Elam v. College Park Hosp.,* 132 Cal. App. 3d 332, 183 Cal. Rptr. 156 (1982).

86. PEER REVIEW IMPROVEMENT ACT OF 1982, Pub. L. No. 97-248, §§ 141-150, 96 Stat. 382-395 (1982), codified as 42 U.S.C. §§ 1320c-1320c-12.

87. Pub. L. No. 98-21, § 602, 97 Stat. 167 (1983).

88. *E.g., Peterson v. Tucson Gen. Hosp.*, 114 Ariz. 66, 559 P.2d 186 (1976).

89. *Moore v. Board of Trustees of Carson-Tahoe Hosp.*, 495 P.2d 605 (Nev. 1976).

90. *Jackson v. Metropolitan Edison Co.*, 419 U.S. 345 (1974).

91. *E.g., Bricker v. Sceva Speare Memorial Hosp.*, 111 N.H. 276, 281 A.2d 589 (1971).

92. *E.g., Miller v. Indiana Hosp.*, 277 Pa. Super. 370, 419 A.2d 1191 (1980).

93. N.Y. PUBLIC HEALTH LAW § 2801-b (McKinney 1977).

94. *E.g., Silver v. Castle Memorial Hosp.*, 497 P.2d 564 (Hawaii 1972).

95. *Garrow v. Elizabeth Gen. Hosp. and Dispensary,* 79 N.J. 549, 401 A.2d 533 (1979).

96. *E.g., Storrs v. Lutheran Hosp. and Homes Soc'y of America, Inc.*, 609 P.2d 24 (Alaska 1980).

97. *E.g., Poe v. Charlotte Memorial Hosp.*, 374 F. Supp. 1302 (W.D.N.C. 1974).

98. *E.g., Woodbury v. McKinnon*, 447 F.2d 839 (5th Cir. 1971).

99. *E.g., Garrow v. Elizabeth Gen. Hosp. and Dispensary,* 79 N.J. 549, 401 A.2d 533 (1979) [Right to have attorney present]; *Anton v. San Antonio Community Hosp.*, 19 Cal. 3d 802, 567 P.2d 1162 (1977) [No right to have attorney present].

100. *E.g., Applebaum v. Board of Directors of Barton Memorial Hosp.*, 104 Cal. App. 3d 648, 163 Cal. Rptr. 831 (1980); *Laje v. R.E. Thomason Gen. Hosp.*, 564 F.2d 1159 (5th Cir. 1977).

101. *E.g., Woodbury v. McKinnon*, 447 F.2d 839 (5th Cir. 1971).

102. *Bradley v. Lakes Region Hosp. Ass'n,* No. E-80-0060 (N.H. Super. Ct., Belknap Co., July 2, 1980).

103. *E.g., Suckle v. Madison Gen. Hosp.*, 499 F.2d 1364 (7th Cir. 1974).

BIBLIOGRAPHY

Creighton, Helen. "Value of Careful Personnel Records." *Nursing Management* 14, no. 6 (June 1983):38.

Grimaldi, Paul, and Micheletti, Julie. "DRG Reimbursement: RIMs and the Cost of Nursing Care." *Nursing Management* 13, no. 12 (December 1982):12.

Haddad, Amy. "The Nurse's Role and Responsibility in Corporate-Level Planning." *Nursing Administration Quarterly* 5, no. 2 (Winter 1981):1.

Trandel-Korenchuk, Keith, and Trandel-Korenchuk, Darlene. "Legal Forum: Conflicting Loyalties of the Nurse." *Nursing Administration Quarterly* 6, no. 2 (Winter 1982):63.

Trandel-Korenchuk, Keith, and Trandel-Korenchuk, Darlene. "Legal Forum: Restrictions on Male Nurse Employment in Obstetric Care." *Nursing Administration Quarterly* 6, no. 1 (Fall 1981):87.

Chapter 4

The Nurse as Employee

Most nurses work as employees of health care institutions, public or private agencies, private practitioners, or businesses. A significant determinant of whether good quality, compassionate care is provided to patients or clients is the quality and performance of the nurse and the relationship between the nurse and the employer.

Employers must be careful in selecting, training, supervising, and disciplining nurses and other employees. Nurses need to know the rights and the responsibilities of employees and employers to understand and respond to actions concerning their employment. Detailed state and federal regulations control many aspects of employee relations, including equal employment opportunities, compensation and benefits, occupational safety, labor-management relations, and other matters. The trend has been toward more federal regulation and reduced state control.

GENERAL EMPLOYEE RELATIONS ISSUES

Selection

Employers must exercise care in selecting their employees. Employers should verify any required licenses and check references and other information provided to confirm that it is reasonable to believe the applicant is qualified for the position. Nurses should expect this verification to occur. It is not because a prospective employer has doubts concerning the individual applicant or nurses in general; it is a prudent step that helps protect patients from unqualified nurses and helps protect qualified nurses from being assigned to work with unqualified ones. Selection also must be in compliance with applicable equal employment opportunity laws (discussed later in this chapter).

Health Screening

Health care employers should screen nurses and other employees to identify conditions, such as contagious diseases, that may constitute a risk to patients and take appropriate steps to assure that persons who constitute a risk do not have contact with patients or objects that could transmit their condition. Employers that choose to perform health screening of applicants before hiring must require it for all applicants for covered positions. Selective screening of individual applicants violates section 504 of the Rehabilitation Act of 1973.[1]

Training and Supervision

As discussed in Chapter 6, employers are liable for injuries caused by the negligence of their employees. To optimize patient care and minimize liability exposure, health care employers must assure that employees receive necessary training and supervision. It is important for nurses to participate in continuing education to maintain and improve their skills. While employers should facilitate continuing education, in most states there is no obligation to provide it without cost to the employee or during compensated time.

Discipline and Dismissal

Health care employers have a responsibility to take steps to enforce institutional policies to maintain patient care and the integrity of the institution or agency. It is important that proper procedures be followed and that the action be based on legally permissible grounds. Generally, employees are considered employees at will. That means employers may terminate employees at will at any time without cause unless there is a contract that specifies a specific period of employment or a statute that lists criteria or procedures for termination.[2] Some nurses have attempted to convince courts that their state's nursing licensing law created procedural rights, but courts have rejected this contention.[3]

Most courts will require health care employers to follow their own procedures when pursuing disciplinary measures or dismissal.[4] However, courts have disagreed on what constitutes an enforceable policy or procedure. The Delaware Supreme Court ruled that statements in employee handbooks do not change an employee's at-will status unless they specify a definite term of employment.[5] A Florida appellate court ruled that hospital personnel policies might be enforceable and ordered a trial court to reconsider the matter.[6] Some public employees are covered by civil service laws that require certain procedures.

When employees are covered by individual employment contracts or collective bargaining agreements, the procedures they specify should be followed. Such contracts do not have to be in writing to be enforceable. A Louisiana court found a hospital liable for breaching an oral promise to five certified registered nurse anesthetists that they would be given a six-month notice of termination. The court awarded payment of salary for the six months, less the amount they actually earned during the six months.[7] This illustrates the principle that courts generally will not order employees reinstated unless a statute authorizes it; instead, they will order that employees be paid for their lost wages and other damages when they are wrongfully discharged.

One issue that is receiving increasing attention is whether employees should be protected from retaliatory discharge for certain conduct. Some statutes specifically forbid retaliatory discharge of employees who make certain reports to governmental agencies[8] and some courts have extended such protection to employees who make other reports, such as Workers' Compensation claims.[9] There may be some protection for employees or other staff members of public institutions who are discharged for exercising their rights of free speech,[10] but this does not extend to employees of private employers. For example, an Illinois court ruled that, even if a nurse had been terminated solely in retaliation for reporting incidents to a newspaper, she would not be entitled to any more protection than other at-will employees of private employers.[11]

Some provisions of the National Labor Relations Act also apply when employees are not represented by a union. The equal employment opportunity laws described later in this chapter apply to all aspects of employment, including discipline and dismissal, so they may offer recourse for nurses in actions with a discriminatory basis.

Certain grounds for dismissal are not considered "just cause" by state unemployment compensation agencies, so employers are required to pay unemployment compensation to the dismissed nurse. (Unemployment compensation issues are discussed later in this chapter.)

Communications About Former Staff

Many types of employers, including hospitals, have been sued for libel or slander by former staff members based on statements in unfavorable evaluations, termination notices, and responses to inquiries from prospective employers. Some supervisory personnel have been reluctant to communicate deficiencies accurately because of limited understanding of what they may legally say. It is essential that supervisors understand what they can communicate so that present and prospective employees can obtain accurate evaluations with minimum legal risk.

In general, there can be no liability based on libel or slander for communicating the truth. However, since it often is difficult to prove the absolute truth of a statement, the law extends a "qualified privilege" to certain communications. This means that there is no liability as long as the communication was not made with malice. The qualified privilege applies to communications to certain persons who have a legitimate interest in the information given, as long as the information is limited in scope commensurate with the legitimate interest and is provided in a proper manner so that others do not learn of it inappropriately. Courts generally have recognized that an employer or prospective employer has a legitimate interest in employment-related information.[12] The best way to avoid exceeding the qualified privilege is to limit the communication to factual statements and avoid comments concerning personality or personal spite. Neutral factual statements can communicate the deficiencies that need to be expressed without creating the appearance of malice.

EQUAL EMPLOYMENT OPPORTUNITY LAWS

Congress has enacted laws to expand equal employment opportunities by prohibiting discrimination on various grounds. The measures include Title VII of the Civil Rights Act of 1964, the Equal Pay Act of 1963, the Age Discrimination in Employment Act (1967), and sections 503 and 504 of the Rehabilitation Act of 1973. Numerous state laws also address equal employment opportunities.

Title VII of the Civil Rights Act of 1964

Title VII of the Civil Rights Act of 1964[13] prohibits disparate employment treatment based on race, color, religion, sex, national origin, or pregnancy. It applies to hiring, dismissal, promotion, discipline, terms and conditions of employment, and job advertising. It applies to nearly all employers; governmental agencies were included by the 1972 amendments. One of the few exemptions permits religious institutions to consider religion as a criterion in their employment practices.

The primary enforcement agency is the Equal Employment Opportunity Commission (EEOC). In some situations, the EEOC can defer to enforcement by local or state agencies or through individual suits. Three legal theories are used as the basis for finding employment discrimination:

1. Violations can be found on the basis of disparate treatment when work rules or employment practices are not applied in a consistent fashion because of a discriminatory motive.
2. Violations can be found on the basis of disparate impact when an employment practice, such as a written test, has an adverse impact on minorities and cannot be justified as job-related.
3. Violations can be found based on carryover of past discrimination when minorities are in a disadvantageous position because of prior discriminatory practices.

Employers are prohibited from retaliating against employees who oppose discrimination by engaging in reasonable activities. In 1984, a federal court of appeals found that a hospital had violated this provision when it fired a black registered nurse who had complained about black patient care.[14]

In some circumstances, sex or features related to religion or national origin are bona fide occupational qualifications reasonably necessary to the normal operation of a particular business. When hospitals can demonstrate this, the use of the qualification is not a violation of the law.

In 1981, a federal court ruled that it was not illegal sex discrimination for a hospital to employ only female nurses in its obstetrics-gynecology department.[15] The court noted that the policy was based on the patients' privacy rights, not just their preference. In the same year, another federal court ruled that it was not illegal discrimination based on national origin for the hospital to require all employees to have some facility in communication in the English language.[16] The court recognized that ability to communicate in English was a bona fide occupational qualification for virtually every position in a sophisticated medical center.

In 1978, Title VII was amended to prohibit discriminatory treatment of pregnant women for all employment-related purposes. No special considerations are required. However, for example, if leaves are offered for disabilities, similar leaves must be offered for maternity. Mandatory maternity leaves that are not based on inability to work violate Title VII. Pregnancy itself is not considered a disability, but if a pregnant worker becomes unable to work, then disability benefits offered for other disabilities must be offered to such a woman. Some states require employers to offer a leave of absence for pregnancy.

The EEOC has published guidelines on sexual harassment[17] that indicate the employer can be liable for such activities by coworkers and nonemployees as well as by supervisory and managerial staff.

Some groups have sought to convince the courts that Title VII requires the adoption of a comparable worth doctrine. This doctrine would require employers to revise wage scales so that pay is based on the comparable worth of the work done by persons in different job classifications when work categories that are predominantly filled with females have been assigned lower wage scales. This comparable worth doctrine goes beyond the Equal Pay Act (discussed in the following section) that requires equal pay for essentially identical work.

Nursing groups have been in the forefront of the effort to establish the comparable worth doctrine. However, courts generally have ruled that Title VII does not require wage scales based on comparable worth.[18] One exception is a federal court decision in 1983 involving a broad range of public jobs in the state of Washington. The court applied comparative worth principles to find the state's wage scales in violation of Title VII. The decision was appealed.[19]

Title VII does not preempt the entire field of equal employment opportunity. While state law cannot permit something prohibited by Title VII, it can assure more opportunities. Thus, many state laws that limit the types of work women may perform are superseded by federal law but those requiring employers to offer pregnancy leaves are not.

Equal Pay Act of 1963

The Equal Pay Act[20] is designed to prohibit discriminatory compensation policies based on sex. It requires equal pay for equal work, which it defines as work requiring equal skill, equal effort, and equal responsibility that is performed under similar working conditions. The payment of higher wages to male orderlies than to female aides has been challenged in several cases. In general, the courts have required equal pay for male orderlies and female aides except when the hospital has been able to prove actual differences in the work performed during a substantial portion of work time. The courts have adopted a case-by-case approach to the determination of whether work is equal.

Age Discrimination in Employment Act

The Age Discrimination in Employment Act[21] prohibits discriminatory treatment of persons from 40 to 69 years of age for all employment-related purposes. Mandatory retirement is prohibited for persons under 70, except for certain exempted executives. The law applies to governmental and private employers of 20 or more persons. There are exceptions for bona fide occupational qualifications, bona fide seniority systems, and reasonable factors other than age, such as physical fitness.

Rehabilitation Act of 1973

The Rehabilitation Act of 1973 prohibits discrimination on the basis of handicap.[22] Section 503 prohibits discrimination by government contractors and section 504 by entities that receive federal financial assistance. In 1984, the Supreme Court ruled that any entity receiving federal financial assistance may not discriminate in either services or employment.[23] Medicare and Medicaid reimbursement have been interpreted to be federal financial assistance.

When the Rehabilitation Act applies, the institution is prohibited from discriminating against any qualified handicapped person who, with reasonable accommodation, can perform the essential functions of the job in question. Inquiries about handicaps prior to employment are prohibited, except that applicants can be asked if they are able to perform the job. Preemployment physical examinations may be required only if all applicants for similar positions must undergo the same examination. A hospital may refuse to hire a person on the basis of behavioral manifestations of the handicap, such as excessive absenteeism by an alcoholic.

COMPENSATION AND BENEFIT LAWS

Several federal laws regulate employee compensation and benefits, including the Fair Labor Standards Act, the Federal Wage Garnishment Law, and the Employee Retirement Income Security Act. In addition, numerous state laws address these issues.

Fair Labor Standards Act

The Fair Labor Standards Act[24] establishes minimum wages and maximum hours of employment. Employees of all nonprofit and proprietary hospitals are covered by this act and hospitals must conform. However, bona fide executive, administrative, and professional employees are exempted from the wage and hour provisions when salaried. While it is clear that these categories would include physicians and administrators, Department of Labor regulations must be consulted to determine the status of other classifications of employees.

The 1974 amendments to the act extended its minimum wage and overtime provisions to almost all employees of state and local governments. However, the Supreme Court in 1976 declared the application of these provisions to state employees violated the Tenth Amendment to the Constitution, which reserves to the states powers not granted to the federal government.[25] This decision did not affect other federal labor legislation, including the Equal Pay Act and the Age Discrimination in Employment Act.

Most employers are required to pay overtime rates for work that exceeds 40 hours in seven days. However, the law permits hospitals to enter into agreements with employees establishing an alternative work period of 14 consecutive days, rather than the usual seven-day week. If the alternative period is chosen, the hospital need pay the overtime rate only for time worked in excess of 80 hours during the 14-day period. It should be noted that, if the alternate 14-day work period is established, the hospital is not relieved from paying overtime rates for hours worked in excess of eight in any one day, even if no more than 80 are worked during such a period.

The Fair Labor Standards Act also regulates the hours and conditions of employment of children. However, it does not preempt more protective state or local laws that establish a higher minimum wage, a shorter minimum work week, or more protection for children.

Federal Wage Garnishment Law

One way to enforce a court judgment against another person is to impose garnishment of the debtor's wages. Garnishment is a court order to an employer to pay a portion of the debtor's paycheck to the creditor until the debt is paid. The Federal Wage Garnishment Law[26] and various state laws restrict how much of a paycheck may be garnisheed. State law may limit garnishment to an amount smaller than under federal law. Federal law prohibits employers from discharging employees because of garnishment for one indebtedness. The limits on garnishment do not apply to certain bankruptcy court orders or debts due for state or federal taxes.

Employee Retirement Income Security Act of 1974

The Employee Retirement Income Security Act of 1974 (ERISA)[27] regulates nearly all pension and benefit plans for employees, including pension, profit-sharing, bonus, medical or hospital benefit, disability, death benefits, unemployment and other plans. The law applies to all employers (including health care institutions) except for government agencies and some plans of churches. It regulates many features of the plans, including nondiscrimination, benefit accrual, vesting of benefits, coverage, responsibilities of plan managers, termination of plans, descriptions of plans, and required reports.

OCCUPATIONAL SAFETY AND HEALTH

Congress enacted the Occupational Safety and Health Act (OSHA) of 1970[28] to establish standards and to provide for their enforcement. Standards developed for various industries are mandatory for all covered employers. The statute provides that when no federal standard has been established, state safety rules remain in effect. OSHA applies to health care institutions.

The federal act mandates that each state enact legislation to implement the standards and procedures promulgated by the Department of Labor. Litigation has arisen over inspections by federal and state officials to enforce the OSHA standards. The courts have held consistently that an employer may refuse an inspection unless the inspector obtains the consent of a duly authorized agent of the employer or has a valid search warrant issued in accordance with state law. The Supreme Court ruled unconstitutional an OSHA provision that permitted ''spot checks'' by OSHA inspectors without a warrant.[29]

Under the law of some states, employers are charged by statute with the duty of furnishing employees with a safe place to work. Of course, even in the absence of such statutes, employers are liable for most injuries workers suffer as a result of employment unless the doctrine of governmental immunity is applicable. In most situations, the employee must pursue compensastion through Workers' Compensation rather than through the courts.

In addition to provisions relating to unsafe conditions in the workplace, other state statutes require the presence of certain facilities there. These facilities, such as lavatories, are to be provided for the convenience and safety of employees. Ordinances and laws of the city and county in which an employer is located also may include requirements, such as sanitary and health codes, to promote and safeguard the safety and health of employees and others. In most instances, these laws do not exempt institutions because of their charitable status. However, in most states, state institutions are exempt from local regulation unless state law grants local government the authority to encompass such institutions.

LABOR-MANAGEMENT RELATIONS

Unions have become a significant factor in relations between health care institutions and their employees in many parts of the country. A number of different types of labor organizations now are recognized as collective bargaining representatives for groups of hospital employees: craft unions, whose primary organizing efforts are devoted to skilled employees such as carpenters and electricians; industrial unions and governmental employees' unions that seek to represent large groups of relatively unskilled or semiskilled employees; and professional and occupational associations and societies, such as state nurses' associations, that represent their members. The professional organizations are labor unions to the extent that they seek goals directly concerned with wages, hours, and other employment conditions and engage in bargaining activities on behalf of employees.

Labor-Management Relations Act

The Labor-Management Relations Act,[30] which defines certain conduct of employers and employees as unfair labor practices and provides for hearings upon complaints alleging that such practices have occurred, explicitly exempts governmental employees from its coverage. This act consists of the National Labor Relations Act of 1935,[31] the Taft-Hartley amendments of 1947,[32] and numerous other amendments, including the Labor-Management Reporting and Disclosure Act of 1959.[33] The Act is administered by the National Labor Relations Board (NLRB). The NLRB (1) investigates and adjudicates complaints of unfair labor practices and (2) conducts secret-ballot elections among employees to determine whether they wish to be represented by a labor organization and, if so, which one.

The exemption for governmental hospitals has been interpreted by the NLRB to apply only to hospitals that are owned and operated by governmental agencies. For example, a municipal hospital operated under contract may be considered a private entity subject to the NLRB if overall daily control is by a private contractor. Exempt governmental hospitals usually are subject to state laws concerning governmental employees.

For-profit hospitals were never exempt from the NLRB. Nonprofit hospitals were exempted until the amendments of 1974 eliminated the exemption.[34] The 1974 amendments attempted to deal with some of the unique aspects of health care by providing legislative direction on collective bargaining, mediation, conciliation, and strikes.

Exempt Staff

Several groups are excluded from the NLRB's jurisdiction, including independent contractors, supervisors, managerial employees, confidential employees, and some students. Each of these groups has been defined by numerous NLRB and court decisions, but the details are beyond the scope of this book.

Unfair Labor Practices

Section 7 of the National Labor Relations Act established four fundamental rights of employees: (1) the right to self-organize; (2) the right to engage in concerted activities for the purpose of collective bargaining or other mutual aid or protection; (3) the right to engage in collective bargaining; and (4) the right to refrain from union activities.

Employer Unfair Labor Practices. An employer commits an unfair labor practice through: (1) interference with any of the four rights recognized in section 7; (2) domination of a labor organization; (3) discouragement or encouragement of union activity; (4) discrimination against employees who file charges or testify in an NLRB proceeding; or (5) violation of the other obligations, including good faith bargaining, specified in section 8(a) of the NLRA.

The NLRA applies to employers that do not have employees represented by a labor organization. Employees' rights to engage in concerted activities for the purpose of mutual aid or protection can apply to isolated incidents. For example, the NLRB ruled that a small group of unorganized staff were protected when they left their work station to complain to hospital officials concerning work conditions.[35]

Labor Organization Unfair Labor Practices. A labor organization commits an unfair labor practice through: (1) restraint or coercion interfering with exercise of the four rights recognized in section 7 or interference in management's selection of its representatives; (2) attempts to cause the employer to discriminate to encourage or discourage membership in a labor organization; (3) failure to bargain in good faith; (4) prohibited secondary boycotts; (5) excessive union initiation fees; (6) causing employers to pay for services not performed; or (7) picketing solely to compel an employer to recognize a union (recognitional picketing) or to persuade employees to join the union (organizational picketing) without filing a petition for an election within the appropriate time limit.

Employee Representation

A labor organization seeking representation rights for employees may petition the NLRB for a secret-ballot election. The petition must make a ''showing of interest'' supporting the petition—that is, at least 30 percent of the workers who ultimately will make up the bargaining unit must support it and show their interest by signing union authorization cards.

Bargaining Unit Designation. The employer may take the position that certain persons (supervisors, confidential employees, temporary employees) should be excluded from the unit or argue that the unit would be inappropriate because of the employer's organization. The NLRB then will conduct a representation hearing to determine the appropriate bargaining unit, examining whether the proposed unit is characterized by a "community of interest" and whether it will be likely to promote collective bargaining within the institution.

The board must respect the congressional intent in the 1974 amendments to avoid proliferation of bargaining units in the health care industry. The board has recognized only five basic units in health care institutions: (1) clerical; (2) service and maintenance; (3) technical, including licensed practical nurses; (4) professionals; and (5) registered nurses. Section 9 of the NLRA forbids including professional employees in bargaining units with nonprofessionals unless a majority of the included professions vote in favor of inclusion.

The designation of a unit solely for registered nurses still is controversial because hospitals view it as constituting the proliferation Congress sought to avoid. Several United States Circuit Courts of Appeals have refused to enforce board orders designating units solely for registered nurses when the board has relied entirely on a finding of community of interest without addressing the congressional mandate to avoid proliferation of units.[36] However, the courts have indicated it is possible for an order establishing a registered nurse unit to be upheld if the board finds it appropriate after considering all required factors, including avoidance of proliferation.[37]

Solicitation and Distribution. Most hospitals have rules concerning solicitation of employees and distribution of materials in the hospital to avoid interference with patient care. The NLRB examines each policy on a case-by-case basis. Some general guidelines can be derived from past decisions. Nonemployees generally may be prohibited access to the facility for solicitation or distribution. Employees can be prohibited from solicitation or distribution during work time. Solicitation or distribution can be limited to nonpatient care areas at all times.[38] In general, a genuine likelihood of patient disturbance is necessary, so areas where visitors have general access such as cafeterias and lounges usually cannot be prohibited.

Election. A labor organization can become the exclusive bargaining agent for a bargaining unit by winning the secret ballot election conducted by the NLRB. After an election, the employer or the labor organization can challenge the outcome by filing an objection alleging misconduct during the process. If the NLRB finds misconduct, it can set aside the results and order a new election.

Recognition without an Election. An employer can voluntarily recognize a labor organization as the exclusive bargaining agent without an election. If the employer participates in certain actions, such as checking the union authorization cards or polling the employees, those actions sometimes can constitute recognition. However, recognition without an election can constitute an unfair labor practice in some circumstances, especially when other labor organizations also are seeking to represent the employees. Thus, most employers avoid all actions that could be interpreted as a voluntary recognition of a labor organization.

A second way that a labor organization can be recognized without an election is by order of the NLRB. When the NLRB finds serious unfair labor practices, it has the authority to order the extraordinary remedy of recognition of the union. A third way is accretion. If a labor organization has negotiated a contract for a bargaining unit with an employer that subsequently acquires a new facility, under some circumstances the new facility is considered to be accreted to the existing one, and new unit employees are covered automatically by the preexisting contract.

Collective Bargaining and Mediation

After a labor organization has been recognized as the exclusive bargaining agent, the employer and union both have a duty to negotiate in good faith. They must bargain concerning mandatory subjects, including wages, hours, and other terms and conditions of employment, and they may bargain on other permissive subjects but are not legally obligated to do so. It is unlawful to bring negotiations to an impasse, to strike, or to lock out employees over permissive subjects.

Several special notice, mediation, and conciliation safeguards were built into the law for the health care industry to avoid strikes when possible. For example, 90 days' notice is required if a party intends to terminate or modify a bargaining agreement, and the Federal Mediation and Conciliation Service (FMCS) must be given 60 days' notice. When notified, the FMCS is required to attempt to bring about an agreement, and all parties must participate fully and promptly in meetings called by the agency to aid in a settlement. In the event of a threatened strike, the FMCS, under certain conditions, can establish an impartial board of inquiry to investigate the issues and provide a cooling-off period of up to 30 days.

Strikes

Another special provision for health care institutions is a 10-day advance notice of intention to engage in concerted economic activities, including strikes, picketing, or any other joint refusal to work. This provision is designed to allow a hospital to make plans for continuity of patient care in the face of a work stoppage. Some courts have ruled that individual unorganized employees do not have to give a 10-day notice. One federal court ruled in 1980 that two physicians who walked out of the hospital and joined the picket line of a lawful strike by other employees did not have to give the notice.[39] The court noted that the action was inconsiderate and ethically suspect, but protected.

In some circumstances, the "ally doctrine" allows a union to strike against a secondary employer not involved in the original dispute. The strike is permitted when the secondary employer loses its neutrality by performing work during the course of the labor dispute that would have been done by the striking employees of the primary employer. The legislative history of the 1974 amendments modifies the "ally doctrine" by permitting a hospital to accept the critically ill patients of a struck hospital without losing its status as a neutral employer. In an advice memorandum issued by the NLRB in September 1977, a union was said to violate the act when it threatened to picket two neutral hospitals because they received critically ill patients and 46 pregnant women transferred from the struck hospital.[40]

Administering the Contract

After negotiating a labor agreement, the hospitals and labor organizations should spend no less care on its administration. Rights that have been established at the bargaining table, sometimes at a high price, can be eroded or entirely lost through inattention. Employees should be knowledgeable concerning their rights and responsibilities. The entire managerial team, especially first-line and second-line supervisors, should know the aspects of the contract applicable to their responsibilities. Of particular importance is the problem of discipline. They must be trained to ensure that discipline is administered for the right reasons and by the appropriate procedures under the contract.

Reporting and Disclosure

The Labor-Management Reporting and Disclosure Act of 1959[41] places controls on labor unions and their relationships with their members. It also requires employers to report payments and loans to officials or other representatives of labor organizations. Payments to employees to persuade them or cause them to persuade other employees to exercise or not exercise their rights to organize and bargain collectively also must be reported. Many of these payments are illegal, and the reporting requirement does not make them legal.

Expenditures with the object of interfering with employees' rights to organize and bargain collectively, as well as agreements with labor relations consultants under which such persons undertake to interfere with employees' rights, must also be reported. Reports required under this law must be filed with the Secretary of Labor and are made public. Both charitable and proprietary hospitals making such payments or entering into such agreements must file the reports. Governmental hospitals are not subject to these provisions. There are substantial penalties for failure to make required reports or for making false reports.

Hospitals are intended to receive special considerations from the NLRB because of their sensitive mission, but the board will continue to make individual rulings on each of these areas on the basis of many factors in addition to the uniqueness of the industry.

STATE LAWS

State labor legislation is being increasingly preempted by federal programs; however, state laws still apply in at least two situations: (1) If the federal law does not cover an area or activity, the state may regulate it. (2) If the courts have ruled that the state law does not conflict with the federal law on the same matter, the state law will be declared to be enforceable.

Despite the broad sweep of the doctrine of federal preemption, states continue to possess the power to regulate labor relations activity that also falls within the jurisdiction of the NLRB where the regulated conduct touches interests deeply rooted in local feeling and responsibility. Thus, violence, threats of violence, mass picketing, and obstructing streets may be regulated by the states.

Many states do not have labor relations statutes, but in others there are two types that directly affect the rights of employees to organize and bargain collectively: (1) anti-injunction acts and (2) laws regulating union security agreements. Other state labor legislation deals with equal employment opportunity, child labor, safety, Workers' Compensation, and unemployment compensation. Many states have laws concerning the relationship between public employees and governmental employers that apply to governmental hospitals.

Anti-Injunction Acts

The federal government and many states have enacted anti-injunction acts, reducing the power of the courts to issue injunctions in labor disputes by setting strictly defined standards as to when injunctions can be granted concerning strikes, picketing, and related activities. The federal courts are bound by the Norris-La Guardia Act,[42] which severely limits their authority to grant injunctions in "labor disputes." A number of states have similar statutes that restrict the authority of state courts.

Union Security and Right-to-Work Laws

Labor organizations frequently seek to enter into one of two types of union security contracts with employers: (1) the "closed shop," which provides that only members of a particular union may be hired, and (2) the "union shop," which makes continued employment dependent upon membership in the union although the employee need not be a union member at the time of hiring.

By statute or constitution, many states have made such contracts unlawful. Statutes forbidding such agreements generally are called "right-to-work" laws on the theory that they protect employees' "right to work" even if they refuse to join the union. Other states have statutes or decisions that restrict union security contracts or provide for procedures to be completed before such agreements may be made. Some states permit forms of union security contracts if authorized by an employee election. Some states permit a union shop agreement but not a closed shop. State "right-to-work" laws are not preempted by the NLRA because section 14(b) of the NLRA explicitly authorizes them.

If such agreements are illegal in the state, a health care facility must refuse any request for such a contract and can obtain an injunction to stop a strike or picketing designed to induce the employer to enter into such a contract. In states that permit a union security contract, there is no legal obligation to enter into such a contract. It is one of the matters on which there may be bargaining.

Workers' Compensation

Every state has some form of workers' compensation legislation that is designed to assure that employees will be compensated for losses resulting from accidental on-the-job injuries. These acts replace the common-law remedy that required the employee to sue the employer for negligence, which usually was unsuccessful. Most employers are subject to the act, although some states provide exceptions. In cases not routinely paid by the insurance carrier, the matter will go to hearings before a state commission to determine questions of liability.

State statutes define employee, injury, and other terms and have comprehensive schedules stating payment amounts for types of injuries. Where the workers' compensation law applies, the employee is barred from suing the employer for the injury. The only way courts become involved is if there is an appeal concerning the decisions of the state official or agency administering the law.

Considerable litigation takes place in each state to settle the questions arising in the many situations in which employees are injured. One sensitive area involves whether the injury occurred "out of and in the course of employment," a key phrase in qualifying for compensation. A related issue is whether the injury was truly caused by an "accident" or was instead the "natural and probable result of that particular job." Numerous exclusions are stated for preexisting or congenital physical conditions, as well as injuries caused by horseplay and other causes not incidental to employment.

Initially, an employee must give written notice of the injury to the employer. This and the report of the medical treatment provided ordinarily constitute the basis for compensation. Usually employees cannot receive compensation under workers' compensation laws: (1) if the injury was caused by the intoxication of the injured worker(s); (2) if the injury was caused by their willful intent to injure themselves or another; or (3) if (in some states) the injury was caused by the willful act of another directed against the employee for personal reasons.

Unemployment Compensation

State law generally provides for payment of unemployment compensation to many unemployed individuals. Generally persons who have been discharged for misconduct forfeit all or part of the compensation they would have received otherwise. Thus, there is considerable litigation concerning what constitutes misconduct.

For example, the Pennsylvania Supreme Court found a nursing assistant guilty of misconduct for smoking in a patient's room contrary to hospital rules. Therefore, she was denied unemployment compensation after her discharge.[43] However, the Vermont Supreme Court ruled that a nurse who had been discharged for giving a patient medications by intravenous (IV) push instead of IV drip was entitled to unemployment compensation because her error had been in good faith.[44]

Public Employees

Since the NLRA does not apply to employees of state and local agencies, the relations between these public employees and their governmental employers are controlled by state law, which often varies from the federal act. There is significant variation among the states. Some prohibit collective bargaining by public employees, so that workers' rights are determined by state civil service laws and individual agency policies. Many states authorize representation by a labor organization and collective bargaining. A state agency similar to the NLRB usually is established to administer the authorizing law. State laws frequently limit the subjects that may be determined by collective bargaining. Many states prohibit strikes by all or some public employees and require that an arbitration procedure be used to resolve impasses.

NOTES

1. 29 U.S.C. § 794 (Supp. V 1981).

2. *E.g.*, *Lampe v. Presbyterian Medical Center*, 590 P.2d 513 (Colo. Ct. App. 1978) [Head nurse terminated for inability to follow staffing procedures and stay within budget].

3. *E.g.*, *Lampe; Kurle v. Evangelical Hosp. Ass'n*, 88 Ill. App. 3d 45, 44 Ill. Dec. 357, 411 N.E.2d 326 (1980).

4. E.g., *People ex rel. Miselis v. Health and Hosps. Governing Comm'n*, 44 Ill. App. 3d 958, 3 Ill. Dec. 536, 358 N.E.2d 1221 (1976).

5. *Heideck v. Kent Gen. Hosp.*, 446 A.2d 1095 (Del. 1982) [Dismissal for failure to heed patient's plea for privacy on bedside commode].

6. *Falls v. Lawnwood Medical Center*, 427 So.2d 361 (Fla. Ct. App. 1983) [Alleged abuse of patient].

7. *Hebert v. Woman's Hosp. Found.*, 377 So.2d 1340 (La. Ct. App. 1979).

8. *E.g.*, Iowa Code § 135C.46 (1984) [Reports by employers of health care facilities to the facility licensing agency].

9. *Kelsay v. Motorola, Inc.*, 74 Ill. 2d 172, 23 Ill. Dec. 599, 384 N.E.2d 353 (1979).

10. *Hitt v. North Broward Hosp. Dist.*, 387 So.2d 482 (Fla. Ct. App. 1980) [Private duty nurse put flyers concerning nursing group on public hospital bulletin board].

11. *Rozier v. St. Mary's Hosp.*, 88 Ill. App. 3d 994, 44 Ill. Dec. 144, 411 N.E.2d 50 (1980); *see also Maus v. National Living Centers, Inc.*, 633 S.W.2d 674 (Tex. Civ. App. 1982) [Discharge of nurse's aid by nursing home for complaints to superiors concerning patient care].

12. *E.g.*, *Gengler v. Phelps*, 589 P.2d 1056 (N.M. Ct. App. 1978), *cert. denied* 92 N.M. 353, 588 P.2d 554 (1979) [Communication concerning nurse anesthetist].

13. 42 U.S.C. §§ 200e-2000e-17 (1976 & Supp. IV 1980).

14. *Wrighten v. Metropolitan Hosp., Inc.*, 726 F.2d 1346 (9th Cir. 1984).

15. *Backus v. Baptist Medical Center*, 510 F.Supp. 1191 (E.D. Ark. 1981), *vacated as moot* 671 F.2d 1100 (8th Cir. 1982).

16. *Garcia v. Rush-Presbyterian Medical Center*, 660 F.2d 1217 (7th Cir. 1981).

17. 29 C.F.R. § 1604.11 (1982).

18. *E.g.*, *Lemons v. City of Denver*, 620 F.2d 228 (10th Cir. 1980); *Briggs v. City of Madison*, 536 F.Supp. 435 (W.D. Wis. 1982).

19. *A.F.S.C.M.E. v. Washington*, 578 F.Supp. 846 (W.D. Wash. 1983).

20. 29 U.S.C. § 206(d) (1976).

21. 29 U.S.C. §§ 621-634 and 663(a) (1976 & Supp. V 1981), as amended by Pub. L. No. 97-248, § 116(a), 96 Stat. 353 (1982).

22. 29 U.S.C. §§ 701-794 (1976 & Supp. V 1981).

23. *Consolidated Rail Corp. v. Darrone*, 52 U.S.L.W. 4301 (U.S. 1984).

24. 29 U.S.C. §§ 201-219 (1976 & Supp. V 1981).

25. *National League of Cities v. Usery*, 426 U.S. 833 (1976).

26. 29 U.S.C. § 1671-1677 (1976).

27. Pub. L. No. 93-406, 88 Stat. 829 (1974) (codified as amended in scattered sections of 5, 18, 26, 29, 31, and 42 U.S.C.).

28. Pub. L. No. 91-596, 84 Stat. 1590 (1970) (codified as amended in 29 U.S.C. §§ 651-678 and scattered sections of 5, 15, 18, 29, 42, and 49 U.S.C.).

29. *Marshall v. Barlow's, Inc.*, 436 U.S. 307 (1978).

30. 29 U.S.C. §§ 141-187 (1976 & Supp. V 1981).

31. Act of July 5, 1935, ch. 372, 49 Stat. 449.

32. Act of June 23, 1947, ch. 120, 61 Stat. 136.

33. Pub. L. No. 86-257, 73 Stat. 519.

34. 29 U.S.C. §§ 152(2), 158, and 169 (1976).

35. *E.g.*, *Mercy Hosp. Ass'n, Inc.*, 235 N.L.R.B. 681 (1978).

36. *E.g.*, *Presbyterian/St. Luke's Medical Center v. NLRB*, 653 F.2d 450 (10th Cir. 1981).

37. *E.g.*, *NLRB v. Federick Memorial Hosp., Inc.*, No. 81-1672 (4th Cir. October 13, 1982).

38. *NLRB v. Baptist Hosp.*, 442 U.S. 773 (1979).

39. *Montefiore Hosp. and Medical Center v. NLRB*, 621 F.2d 510 (2d Cir. 1980).
40. Memorandum from Dietz, Associate General Counsel, NLRB, to Siegel, Director, Region 31, September 2, 1977, concerning cases No. 31–CC–820, 821 and 31–CG–7,8.
41. 29 U.S.C. §§ 401–531 (1976 and Supp. V 1981).
42. 29 U.S.C. §§ 101–111 (1976).
43. *Selan v. Unemployment Comp. Bd. of Review*, 433 A.2d 1337 (Pa. 1981).
44. *Porter v. Department of Employment Sec.*, 139 Vt. 405, 430 A.2d 450 (1981).

BIBLIOGRAPHY

Beletz, Elaine. "Nurses Participation in Bargaining Units." *Nursing Management* 13, no. 10 (October 1982):48.

Ginzberg, Eli. "The Economics of Health Care and the Future of Nursing." *The Journal of Nursing Administration* 9, no. 3 (March 1981):28.

Greenlaw, Jane. "Legally Speaking." *RN* 45, no. 8 (August 1982):71.

Regan, William. "Legally Speaking: Does Freedom of Speech Cover Staff Disputes?" *RN* 45, no. 3 (March 1982):85.

Sheridan, Donna. "The Health Care Industry in the Marketplace: Implications for Nursing." *The Journal of Nursing Administration* 8, no. 9 (September 1983):36.

Chapter 5

The Nurse as Independent Contractor

With the emergence of nursing specialties and certification for advanced practice, many nurses have begun the independent practice of a specialty. Nurse practitioners, nurse anesthetists, and clinical nursing specialists are examples of those who practice independently or contract with an agency, such as a clinic or hospital, to provide services. Others, including nurse anesthetists, pediatric and family nurse practitioners, and mental health practitioners, practice under the supervision of an agency or an employing physician.

Generally, nurse practitioners and nurse anesthetists are registered nurses who have completed a practitioner program of specialized clinical and academic preparation, not necessarily leading to a master's degree, while clinical nursing specialists are registered nurses who have received a master's degree. Increasingly, states are requiring that specific criteria be met before nurses can represent themselves as qualified to practice in an expanded role. Many states have developed separate licensing for advanced practice.

The opportunities for nurses to practice in expanded roles have grown as a result of increased nursing knowledge and specialization, shortages of physicians in some areas, and consumers' demands for primary caregivers. Nurses have assumed a greater role in providing patients with services such as health maintenance and promotion, education, information about diseases and treatment, and anticipatory guidance, often in nontraditional health care settings such as schools, factories, and clinics as well as in hospitals and doctors' offices.

The expanded role refers to the enlargement of the individual's functions in utilizing all aspects of problem-solving processes: delineation of the field of the problem, assessing and implementing care, and evaluating outcomes. The result is a qualitative change in the nurse's delivery of patient care services.

Role expansion is based on theory, utilizing natural and behavioral sciences that give direction to nursing action. Knowledge and skill are applied to decision making as well as to performance. The nurse assumes or shares the responsibility for the health care services delivered to the patient and establishes plans and goals alone or in consultation with other professionals.[1]

A nurse functioning in an expanded role acts on knowledge that reflects theory, for example, determining the need for a pap smear and dealing constructively with the behavioral factors that inhibit the patient from taking the recommended action.

This chapter addresses some of the legal issues associated with nurses engaged in expanded or independent practice, covering three basic patterns of practice: (1) nurses who maintain their own practice, (2) nurses who engage in expanded practice and contract to provide services to an agency, and (3) nurses who function in an expanded role under the supervision of another health professional. Some of the legal issues covered include the types of practice arrangements, scope of practice, payment and collections, clinical privileges, and liability.

PRACTICE ARRANGEMENTS

Nurses engage in expanded practice in a number of types of settings, with wide variation in their job functions and responsibilities. Typical responsibilities of the nurse practitioner or expanded practitioner include history taking, physical examination, identification of problems, counseling, and referral. Some states allow nurse practitioners to prescribe treatments and drugs and many permit them to prescribe within standing orders or protocols. Most nurse practitioners work in a clinic or office, but they also are found in hospitals, in industrial settings, and as consultants. Some work independent of an agency or supervisor, on a fee-for-service basis. The most common ways in which an independent practice can be structured are described next.

Sole Proprietorship

In a sole proprietorship an individual has sole responsibility for all aspects of the enterprise, including hiring employees, collection of fees, liability, and policy determination and decision making. The sole proprietor may hire employees on salary. The income from the business will be taxed by the federal government at the same rate as income from any other job. The owner is personally liable for all aspects of the business, including the actions of the employees (as discussed in Chapter 6). If the owner dies or leaves the business it does not automatically continue.

General Partnership

When two or more individuals enter into a business enterprise, sharing both the responsibilities and the profits or losses, a general partnership exists unless the business is incorporated. Each partner is responsible for the management and liabilities. If the partnership does not have sufficient assets to meet its obligations, the partners may be required to use their personal assets. If one partner is found liable for negligence arising out of the partnership, all the partners will be responsible for the damages. One partner can bind the other partners to an agreement. Income from a partnership is taxed as personal income, and a partnership usually ends when one of the partners dies or leaves the partnership.

Limited Partnership

A limited partnership consists of two types of partners: general partners whose rights and obligations are the same as those in a general partnership, and limited partners who have made an investment in the business and whose liabilities extend only to the extent of that investment. Limited partners do not participate in the management or operations of the business.

Business Corporation

The business corporation is a legal entity, organized under the laws of the state, with the same power as a natural person to engage in acts consistent with its stated purpose. The corporation is organized under a board of directors, which manages the corporation, and is owned by shareholders. There are several advantages to the corporate form of business. Since the law recognizes the corporation as a separate entity, it can own property, make binding agreements, and exist indefinitely, independent of the individuals who own or operate it. The shareholders also have limited liability if the corporation is found liable for negligence.

The income of a corporation generally is taxed at a lower rate than personal income but the profits are taxed again at personal income rates whenever they are distributed to stockholders. The corporation can offer some tax-free fringe benefits to its employees but these are being increasingly restricted. The corporation must comply with the laws and regulations governing corporations in the state, limiting management flexibility of the practice to some extent.

Professional Corporation

An increasingly popular type of business organization in the health care field is the professional corporation. It has many of the features of a business corporation. In many states, all of the members must be licensed in the same profession but some states permit multiple professions to form one corporation. In some states all members are jointly liable for malpractice committed within the practice of the professional corporation but in other states, unlike partners, individual members are not liable for malpractice of others in the corporation. Liability for matters not related to the professional practice generally is limited to the investment.

Independent Practice

A nurse entering independent practice should be familiar with the advantages and disadvantages of each type of business organization and should review the state laws pertaining to each. It is important to consult an attorney when making any practice agreements. There are several disadvantages to independent practice arrangements, including the necessity of hiring employees, bookkeeping, interaction with government agencies, arranging third party payment, and financial risks.

Many nurse practitioners engage in a modified independent practice in which they contract with a physician or agency to provide services. The services usually are in the nature of expanded practice and the nurses have a significant measure of independence. They are liable for their own acts of negligence and may be liable for those of others acting under their direction even if not their employees. An agreement between a nurse and an agency should indicate clearly what provisions exist for liability coverage, payment of fees, and referral.

In the most common practice arrangement, the nurse practitioner is employed by an agency or a physician to provide expanded services to a group of patients. Typically there is indirect supervision over the nurse, who practices within a list of protocols developed jointly with the agency. Protocols attempt to standardize the diagnosis and management of specified patient complaints.

SCOPE OF PRACTICE

One major legal issue is the legally permissible scope of practice for nurses in an independent role. Traditionally, the nurse's responsibilities were ministerial and administrative in nature, and the physician had sole responsibility for diagnosis, treatment, and prescription. In recent years, however, developments in nursing and in legislation have expanded the scope of practice and blurred the distinction between the activities of nurses and physicians in some areas.

There is no dispute that nursing practice still includes the traditional elements of ministerial care of patients, including meeting their needs for safety, comfort, and carrying out prescribed treatments and other orders. The scope of the nurses' role in defining, prescribing, and monitoring treatment has expanded, however, and can be expected to continue to grow.

This has taken two forms: (1) the expansion of the definition of basic nursing practice through nurse practice acts, regulations, and judicial decisions; and (2) the trend toward advanced practice licensure.

A review of state statutes shows that only three jurisdictions have not amended their laws in recent years to authorize nurses to diagnose and treat patients and to recognize nurse practitioners.[2] The scope of practice also may be defined through the state medical practice act, judicial decisions, and attorney general's opinions.

Nurses should be familiar with each of these sources in the state in which they practice.

An example of the relationship of all of these sources to the scope of practice is the prescription of medications by nurses, which was prohibited by early acts. When states began to authorize expanded practice, they frequently left it to the boards of medicine and nursing to work out the details of the changes. Many assumed that if the statute allowed nurses to diagnose and treat patients, it inferentially authorized nurses to prescribe. Idaho, the first state (in 1971) to authorize expanded practice, took this approach.[3] In some states, the statute specifically authorizes nurses to prescribe medications, some grant prescriptive authority by rule, some specify that it be authorized by contract with an agency or health department. Several states' attorney generals have issued opinions that describe circumstances under which nurse practitioners can prescribe medications.[4]

A judicial definition of the appropriate scope of nursing practice is found in *Sermchief v. Gonzales*.[5] The case involved two certified family nurse practitioners who were providing services in a family planning clinic. The services included breast and pelvic examinations, pap smears, gonorrhea cultures, blood serology, birth control methods, pregnancy testing, and information and education. The services were provided according to standing orders and protocols agreed upon jointly by the nurse practitioners and the five physicians with whom they worked.

A written complaint was filed with the Missouri Board of Registration for the Healing Arts alleging that the nurse practitioners were practicing medicine without a license. After an investigation, the board recommended criminal prosecution of the two. The Circuit Court of St. Louis County ruled that the two nurses were not practicing nursing but were practicing medicine without a medical license. The court stated that determining the existence or nonexistence of contraindications to the use of contraceptives required an individual to draw upon education, judgment, and skill based upon knowledge and application of principles in addition to and beyond biological, physical, social, and nursing sciences. The court also found that by authorizing the use of protocols the physicians were abetting the unlawful practice of medicine.

On appeal, however, the Missouri Supreme Court overturned the ruling, holding that the Missouri legislature, in passing the Nursing Practice Act in 1976, indicated its intent to avoid statutory constraints on the evaluation of new functions for nurses delivering health services and that those performed by the practitioners were clearly within their scope of practice as defined by the act. The court stated, "We believe the acts of the nurses are precisely the types of acts the legislature contemplated when it granted nurses the right to make assessments and nursing diagnoses."[6] On the question of the distinction between a nursing diagnosis and a medical diagnosis, the court said:

There can be no question that a nurse undertakes only a nursing diagnosis, as opposed to a medical diagnosis, when she or he finds or fails to find symptoms described by physicians in standing orders and protocols for the purpose of administering courses of treatment prescribed by the physician in such orders and protocols.[7]

The court also stated:

The broadening of the field of practice of the nursing profession authorized by the legislature and here recognized by the court carries with it the profession's responsibility for continuing high educational standards and the individual nurse's responsibility to conduct herself or himself in a professional manner. The hallmark of a profession is knowing the limits of one's professional knowledge. The nurse, either upon reaching the limit of her or his knowledge or upon reaching the limits prescribed for the nurse by the physician's standing orders and protocols, should refer the patient to the physician."[8]

The Missouri court thus determined that professional nurses in Missouri had a right to practice within the limits of their education and experience. It also said nurses had a professional duty to make a timely referral of patients whose needs exceed the scope of the practitioners' expertise. The case was not appealed.

PAYMENT

Payment to nurses in private or expanded practice is important both in terms of professional status and in assuring the viability of a business enterprise. For those reasons the issue of reimbursement of third party payers for nursing services has become important. Traditionally, payments for nursing services provided in an institution or in the home have been made to the employing agency. Nurses now are seeking to receive reimbursement for services directly from Medicare, Medicaid, and private insurers rather than through a physician or agency.

The 1965 Amendments to the Social Security Act[9] created the Medicare and Medicaid programs (described in detail in the section on Reimbursement in Chapter 3). As noted there, Medicare Part B provides for direct reimbursement of nurse practitioners and nurse midwives practicing in rural areas.[10] The authority for Medicaid, the joint federal-state program, is Title XIX of the Social Security Act[11] and individual state statutes. Federal Medicaid regulations authorize payment to licensed practitioners within the scope of their practice as defined by the law of the state, which undoubtedly includes nurses in expanded roles.

A large part of health care is paid for by third party payers other than the government, including Blue Cross and Blue Shield, commercial insurance companies, self-funded health insurance plans of some industries, health maintenance organizations, and other alternative delivery systems. Blue Cross covers hospital and related services, and Blue Shield covers physician and related services. Blue Cross and Blue Shield plans cover local regions and have widely different practices concerning payment and other matters. Consequently, there is wide variation among regions as to the reimbursement of nurses and nurse practitioners.

Some restrictive reimbursement policies of private third party payers have been successfully challenged in the courts. For example, a group of psychologists challenged the practice of the Blue Shield plan of Virginia to reimburse for such services only if they were billed through a physician. A federal court held that this was a violation of the antitrust laws and ordered Blue Cross and Blue Shield to reimburse psychologists directly.[12] The same reasoning could be used to challenge some restrictions on private insurers' payment to nurses. Most commercial insurance policies do not provide for direct reimbursement to nurse practitioners but will cover their services if billed through a hospital or agency.

COLLECTIONS

A difficult area for any health care provider is the collection payments for services. Although third party payments may constitute a portion of nurses' accounts receivable, collection from individual patients is an important source of revenue. To ensure that a bill can be pressed to its legal limits for collection, it must be accurately prepared and maintained. The correct name and address of the patient and the name of the person responsible for payment must be obtained, services provided and dates clearly described, and the recording of any payments or other credits promptly reflected on the account.

An unpaid bill for professional services frequently is turned over to a collection agency. Practitioners usually enter into a written agreement with one or more collection agencies specifying the terms and conditions for their activities to assure compliance with the law.

A bill for services is evidence of a contract to pay for care provided and is enforceable by legal action. Although small bills usually are not worth the cost of judicial proceedings, legal collection actions sometimes serve to educate patients about their obligation to pay medical bills just as they pay other bills. A court judgment can be obtained against a debtor and enforced through several mechanisms such as garnishment of wages.

Several state and federal laws regulate collection practices, including the Consumer Credit Protection Act,[13] the Federal Debt Collection Practices Act,[14] and federal bankruptcy laws. Nurse practitioners engaged in collection of bills should consult with an attorney to make sure that the legal requirements are met.

CLINICAL PRIVILEGES

Some nurses in expanded or independent practice seek to obtain hospital privileges. Before they may practice in a hospital, they must be granted clinical privileges by its governing board. Some boards delegate the responsibility for granting privileges to an administrative official or committee. Practitioners may provide only the services for which they have clinical privileges, and the board has the responsibility to exercise its discretion in determining whether to grant an appointment and the scope of privileges. Some institutions grant nurse practitioners hospital privileges, some give limited privileges to function under a sponsoring physician, and some have decided not to admit them. When a hospital does decide to accept such nurses, it must consider the criteria and procedures for determining whether any specific practitioner will be granted privileges.

Public hospitals must satisfy the requirements of the Fourteenth Amendment to the Constitution—that no state shall "deprive any person of life, liberty, or property, without due process of law." Actions of public hospitals are considered actions of the state. Courts have determined that the interest of a practitioner in obtaining hospital privileges is a liberty or property interest so that "due process of law" is required.[15]

To provide due process, hospital rules must be reasonable and adequately express the facility's intent. They must provide adequate procedural protections or an adverse action may violate due process requirements. Rules that are too arbitrary or vague may be unenforceable.

The primary procedural protections that must be offered are notice and an opportunity to appear in person to present information on behalf of the applicant and the shortcomings that are the basis for any proposed rejection.

The Fourteenth Amendment also says that no state shall "deny to any person within its jurisdiction the equal protection of the laws." This means that persons who are similarly situated must be dealt with in similar fashion. The equal protection clause is concerned with the justifiability of the classifications used to distinguish persons for various legal purposes. In general, the courts require that any distinction must be justified with a "rational reason."[16]

Most private hospitals are subject to fewer legal constraints than public facilities when taking action concerning privileges. However, statutes and court decisions in some states require private hospitals to provide some procedure for challenging adverse decisions.[17]

When a hospital decides not to permit any independent practice by nurses, different legal principles apply because the decision does not reflect on the qualifications of individual nurses. In nearly all states, hospitals probably can refuse legally to permit independent practice by nurses since the governing body has broad latitude in deciding what services will be provided and by whom.

One possible basis for challenge are state and federal antitrust laws. Courts have been increasingly willing to permit antitrust suits in the health care field challenging efforts by competitors to improperly restrict competition.[18] Most of the suits against hospitals have been by physicians, but few have been successful. It may be more difficult for nurse practitioners to win because most of their services can be provided outside the hospital. This makes it difficult to prove that foreclosing such practice by nurses tends to create a monopoly of the services by the hospital.

Some restrictive hospital policies may be challenged successfully if they are the result of a conspiracy between the institution and competing physicians. However, conspiracies usually are difficult to prove. If the board has properly made an independent decision that it does not believe independent practice by nurses is best for the hospital, it will be difficult to mount a successful challenge.

LIABILITY

The expansion of nursing practice into some areas traditionally defined as medical in nature has led to an increased risk of liability. In addition to the standard liability principles (discussed in Chapters 6 and 7) applicable to nurses generally, those practicing in an expanded role may be at increased risk of criminal liability for practicing medicine without a license and of civil liability for failing to refer a patient in a timely manner.

Changes in the scope of practice make it difficult to say with certainty when a practitioner has a duty to refer a patient to a specialist. Physicians and other health care providers have long been recognized to have a duty to refer. Generally, providers have a duty to disclose to the patient the advisability of seeking other treatment if they know or should know that the ailment is beyond their ability to treat. In other words, a general practitioner has a duty to refer a patient to a specialist when the condition demands it.[19] It is likely that this duty will be applied to nurse practitioners.

NOTES

1. Nursing: A Social Policy Statement, pt. 3, Specialization in Nursing Practice, *American Nurses' Association.*

2. E.g., Delaware, Rhode Island.

3. Idaho Code, § 54-1413, as amended 1971; Idaho Board of Nursing and Board of Medicine, *Guidelines for Nursing Practitioners Writing Prescriptions;* Minimum Standards, Rules, and Regulations for the Expanding Role of the Registered Professional Nurse, June 1972.

4. E.g., Michigan, New York.

5. *Sermchief v. Gonzales,* 600 S.W.2d 683 (Mo. *en banc* 1983).

6. Id. at 689.

7. Id. at 689–90.

8. Id. at 690.

9. Pub. L. No. 89-97, 79 Stat. 290 (1965).

10. 42 C.F.R. part 405.2401–405.2430 (1983).

11. 42 U.S.C. § 1396a-1936p (1976 & Supp. IV 1980) as amended by Pub. L. No. 97-35, 95 Stat. 785 (1981) and Pub. L. No. 97-248, 96 Stat. 367 (1982).

12. *Virginia Academy of Clinical Psychologists v. Blue Shield of Va.*, 624 F.2d 476 (4th Cir. 1980). *See also* related case, *Blue Shield of Va. v. McCready*, 454 U.S. 962 (1982).

13. 15 U.S.C. §§ 1671-1677 (1976).

14. 15 U.S.C. §§ 1692-1692o (Supp. V 1981).

15. *Klinge v. Lutheran Charities Association of St. Louis*, 523 F.2d 56 (8th Cir. 1975); *Poe v. Charlotte Memorial Hosp., Inc.*, 374 F. Supp 1302 (W.D.N.C. 1974).

16. *Sosa v. Board of Managers of Val Verde Memorial Hospital*, 437 F.2d 173 (5th Cir. 1971).

17. *Woodward v. Porter Hosp., Inc.*, 125 Vt. 419, 217 A.2d. 37 (1966).

18. *Malini v. Singleton and Associates*, 516 F. Supp. 440 (S.D. Tex. 1981).

19. *E.g., Manion v. Tweedy*, 257 Minn. 59, 100 N.W.2d 124 (1960).

BIBLIOGRAPHY

Braitman, Arthur. "Pennsylvania Senate Bill 361: Direct Third-Party Reimbursement to Nurse-Midwives." *Health Matrix* 1, no. 2 (Summer 1983):55.

Cohn, Sarah. "A Survey of Legislation on Third Party Reimbursement for Nurses." *Law, Medicine, and Health Care* 11, no. 6 (December 1983):260.

Creighton, Helen. "Nurse Practitioner." *Nursing Management* 13, no. 1 (January 1982):14.

Cushing, Maureen. "When Medical Standards Apply to Nurse Practitioners." *American Journal of Nursing* 82, no. 8 (August 1982):1274.

Greenlaw, Jane. "*Sermchief v. Gonzales* and the Debate over Advanced Nursing Practice Legislation." *Law, Medicine, and Health Care* 12, no. 1 (February 1984):30.

Wille, Rosanne, and Fredrickson, Keville C. "Establishing A Group Private Practice in Nursing." *Nursing Outlook* 29, no. 5 (September 1981):522.

Wolff, Michael. "Court Upholds Expanded Practice Roles for Nurses." *Law, Medicine, and Health Care* 12, no. 1 (February 1984):26.

Chapter 6

General Principles of Civil Liability

Everyone involved in the delivery of health care is acutely aware of the potential for patients or their families to make legal claims seeking money because of injuries they believed were caused by malpractice or other wrongful conduct. Much of this concern on the part of nurses is caused by the mystery and uncertainty surrounding the legal process and principles of liability. This chapter is designed to take away some of that mystery. By developing a basic understanding of liability principles, nurses can help to minimize claims and to facilitate proper handling of claims that are made.

Civil liability is the liability, or legal responsibility, imposed through mechanisms other than criminal law. Civil liability can be divided into liability that is based on contract and liability that is based on tort. A tort is a private or civil wrong committed by a person or persons against the person or property of another. It generally is based on a violation of a duty owed to the injured party. The review of tort law includes: (1) the three basic types of tort liability: strict liability, liability for intentional torts, and liability for negligent torts; (2) the basis for personal and institutional liability; and (3) recent attempts to reform tort law. (Specific cases illustrating the tort liability of nurses are surveyed in Chapter 7.)

CONTRACTS

A contract is a legally enforceable agreement. Nurses may work under a contract of employment and in all likelihood will provide care to patients who are being cared for under a contract between a hospital or agency and a governmental agency or third party provider. Nurses also work under numerous agreements between the hospital and business or labor organizations, including contracts for rental of equipment and labor contracts specifying terms of employment.

The primary purpose of a written contract is to describe clearly the elements of the agreement. It is important that the agreement be clear among all parties to facilitate compliance, not to prepare for litigation. It is essential that all elements of contracts be carefully thought through and clearly articulated. This section outlines just some of the problems associated with contracts, for the law of contracts is complex.

Enforcement and Nonenforcement

To be enforceable, every contract must specify certain things, including the participants in the agreement, the terms (what each participant agrees to do or not do), and dates within which it is effective. Generally, a person's signature on a contract binds only that person to the terms of the agreement, but some persons, known as agents, are authorized to act for others, and the agents' signature is binding on the people or organizations they represent.

Some agreements are not enforceable, including those to agree in the future. In most situations, the courts require all participants in the agreement, called parties, to promise to do something or not to do something in order for there to be a contract. This is called consideration for the contract. In some situations, when one party has not promised or provided any consideration, the courts will not enforce the contract.

There are many other contracts that the courts will not enforce: illegal contracts, those viewed by the courts as being against public policy, oral contracts of the type the law requires to be written, and unconscionable contracts. Unconscionable contracts are those that shock the conscience of the court, usually because they are extortionate. Generally, courts apply the unconscionability doctrine only to consumer contracts. Some hospital contracts with patients, such as exculpatory contracts purporting to limit the patient's right to sue, could be found to be unconscionable and thus unenforceable.

Courts tend to limit their review of contracts to what is stated in the written document by applying the "parol evidence rule" under which prior oral agreements are assumed to be incorporated into the written contract. Under this rule, an oral promise made during negotiations that is not included in the final written agreement is assumed to have been negotiated away. The court will not hear evidence on an oral promise that is not reflected in the final document. If oral statements are important to the understanding, they should be in the written contract.

Litigation and Damage Awards

The purpose of a contract is to document careful planning for completion of an agreement and for dealing with contingencies that preclude completion. As a last resort, litigation can be required to deal with breach of contract. In a few situations, the court will compel performance of a contract that has been breached by one of the parties. Courts sometimes will issue an injunction prohibiting another party from violating a restrictive covenant, such as an agreement not to disclose a trade secret.

In most situations, however, the only remedy the court will award is money, called damages. When it will be difficult to calculate the damages resulting from a breach of contract, the parties sometimes agree in advance what the amount will be; this agreed amount is called liquidated damages. Although courts usually will not enforce contract provisions that are considered penalties, they frequently do enforce liquidated damages provisions as long as the amounts are reasonable.

Contracts can address other issues concerning dispute resolution. They can specify which state's law will govern the contract and where litigation can be brought. Some specify that disputes will be resolved by arbitration rather than court litigation.

There are several defenses to contract suits, including waiver and default. Sometimes courts interpret conduct of the parties, such as regular acceptance of late delivery without complaint, to imply a modification to the agreement and thus a waiver of rights. Under default defense, the law recognizes that some promises are dependent on others and that a sequence of events is either express or implied. If one party fails to perform an earlier step in the sequence, it can be found to be in default, excusing the other parties from carrying out subsequent steps.

Promise to Cure or to Use a Certain Procedure

Most malpractice suits against nurses and hospitals are based on tort law, not on contract law. However, a few suits against health care professionals and hospitals are based on contract principles. One type is the allegation that the physician promised a certain outcome that was not achieved. Absent a specific promise to cure, the law does not consider the physician to be an insurer of a particular outcome. However, if the physician is incautious enough to make a promise, the law will enforce it.

One of the most publicized cases was a 1971 Michigan court decision (*Guilmet v. Campbell*) upholding a jury's finding that the physician had promised to cure a bleeding ulcer and was liable for the unsuccessful outcome even though the physician was not negligent in providing the care.[1] In 1974, the Michigan legislature adopted a statute[2] making promises to cure unenforceable in Michigan unless they are in writing, in effect overruling *Guilmet*.

Another type of breach of contract suit involves the physician's failure to use a specific procedure. For example, in a 1957 Michigan case, the patient had been promised that her child would be delivered by a Caesarean operation. The physician failed to arrange for a Caesarean operation and the baby was stillborn. The court upheld the jury's finding that the physician had breached his promise to arrange for a Caesarean operation.[3]

These cases based on oral promises are unusual but they demonstrate that nurses, physicians, and others should be careful what they say to patients so they do not go beyond reassurance to promising an outcome that may not be possible.

GENERAL PRINCIPLES OF TORT LIABILITY

A tort is a civil wrong that is not based on a violation of contract. Tort liability almost always is based on fault; that is, something was done incorrectly, or something that should have been done was omitted. This act or omission can be intentional or can result from negligence. There are some exceptions to the requirement of fault where there is strict liability for all consequences of certain activities regardless of fault.

The Negligence Factor

Most cases involving nurses are based on negligence, and it is interesting to note the development of causes of action over the years. The earliest malpractice litigation involving nurses generally was based on patient injury sustained as a result of the nurse's improperly carrying out a physician's order. Most of these early cases involve patients being burned by hot water bottles. Another common action was based on postoperative patients who were discovered to have had a sponge or surgical instrument left in the incisional site.

The legal issues in these cases usually involved the extent of the physician's liability for the actions of the nurse. A third common case resulted from an improperly administered injection that led to the patient's sustaining nerve damage. Recent cases have focused on the duties of nurses to observe the patient, report to the physician, and make independent judgments.[4]

INTENTIONAL TORTS

Although most incidents involving the issue of a nurse's liability for harm to a patient result from negligence, a nurse also may be liable for intentional wrongs. An intentional tort always involves a willful act that violates the patient's rights. Intentional torts include assault and battery, defamation, false imprisonment, invasion of privacy, and the intentional infliction of emotional distress.

Assault and Battery

An assault is an action that puts another person in apprehension of being touched in a manner that is offensive, insulting, provoking, or physically injurious without lawful authority or consent. No actual touching is required; the assault is simply the credible threat of being touched in this manner. If actual touching occurs, then it is called battery. Liability for these wrongs is based on individuals' right to be free from unconsented invasions of their persons.

Assault or battery can occur (1) when medical treatment is attempted or performed without lawful authority or consent and (2) in other circumstances, such as in attempts to restrain patients who are competent and oriented without lawful authority.

When an assault and/or a battery has occurred, the law provides the injured person with the right to recover payment, called damages, for the interference. Thus, the injured person can sue the wrongdoer for the injury suffered. Even if no actual harm occurs, the law presumes a compensable injury to the person from the assault and/or battery.

In the health care context, the legal principles related to assault and battery are closely related to the requirement for consent to medical and surgical procedures. Procedures performed on the patient without consent can give rise to a suit for assault and/or battery. Even if a procedure has improved the patient's health, an individual who did not consent to the touching may be entitled to damages.

For example, in an early Minnesota case, the patient had consented to surgery on her right ear. When the patient was anesthetized and the physician could examine her ears, he discovered that the left ear was more seriously involved than the right ear. The physician operated on the left ear, although the patient had consented to surgery on her right ear. The court concluded that there was a battery since surgery was performed on the left ear, without consent.[5] While the legal principle established by this case is still sound—that a procedure performed without the patient's consent can give rise to civil liability—it is unlikely that this will be a basis for a cause of action against a nurse.

Assault and battery cases also have been brought on behalf of nurses who were injured by patients. For example, a private duty nurse in Hawaii was hit on the head by a patient who was having delirium tremens. The court held that, in accepting employment with the patient, the nurse did not "assume the risk" of injury unless she could have, in the exercise of due care, prevented the injury. Thus, she could sue the patient.[6]

Defamation

Defamation is the wrongful injury to another person's reputation. Written defamation is called libel and spoken defamation is called slander. The defamatory statement must be communicated to a third person; defamatory statements made only to the injured party are not grounds for an action. A claim of defamation can arise from the inappropriate or inaccurate release of medical information or from untruthful statements about other members of the hospital or medical staff.

Essentially, there are two defenses to a defamation action: truth and privilege. A statement that is damaging to another person's reputation will not be the basis for liability if it can be shown that the statement is true. A privileged communication is a disclosure that might be defamatory under different circumstances but is not because of a legally recognized higher duty that the person making the communication must honor.

Courts have recognized the importance of communications concerning a staff member's performance to supervisory staff and on up through the organizational structure. Such communications are protected by a "qualified privilege" when they are made in good faith to the persons who need to know. This means that liability will not be imposed for defamation even if the communication is false as long as it was made without malice. For example, one federal court held that a report submitted to a nursing supervisor concerning a disagreement over a doctor's order could not be the basis for a libel suit.[7] For a communication to be privileged, it must be made within appropriate channels to a person who has a legitimate reason to receive the information. Discussions with others will not be protected by the qualified privilege.

Many courts have recognized a qualified privilege for assessments provided by a former employer to a prospective employer. This is illustrated by a Michigan case in which the director of a department of health that had employed a nurse was found not liable for providing a prospective employer with information concerning the nurse's abilities. The court ruled that the qualified privilege applied, and no malice had been shown.[8] Many employers do not release information regarding former employees unless a written request is received, so they do not need to rely on the court to decide that the qualified privilege applies. Of course, liability still could be imposed for untruthful information released with malice.

False Imprisonment

False imprisonment is the unlawful restriction of a person's freedom, including physical restraint or unlawful detention. Holding a person against the individual's will by physical restraint, barriers, or even threats of harm can constitute false imprisonment if not legally justified. Claims of false imprisonment can arise from patients' being detained inappropriately in hospitals or from patients challenging their commitments for being mentally ill. Hospitals do have the common-law authority to detain patients who are disoriented. All states also have a legal procedure to obtain authorization to detain some categories of persons who are mentally ill, are substance abusers, or have contagious diseases. When a patient is oriented, competent, and not legally committed, nurses should avoid detaining the person unless authorized by an explicit hospital policy or by a hospital administrator.

Mentally ill patients may be detained in the hospital if there is a danger that they will take their own life or jeopardize the lives and property of others. Patients who are mentally ill or insane can be restrained only if they present a danger to themselves or others. Only as much force as is reasonably necessary under the circumstances may be used. The use of excessive force in restraining a patient may produce liability for battery for the hospital and the nurse. If a mentally ill patient is detained in the hospital, commitment procedures should be begun expeditiously.

Invasion of Privacy

The legal right of privacy is the right to be free from unwarranted publicity and exposure to public scrutiny, as well as the right to avoid having one's name, likeness, or private affairs made public against one's will. Hospitals, physicians, and nurses may become liable for invasion of privacy if they divulge information from a medical record to improper sources or if they commit unwarranted intrusions into a patient's personal affairs. Examples of unwarranted intrusion include some uses of a patient's photograph without permission.

Information concerning a patient is confidential and should not be disclosed without authorization. Claims for invasion of privacy can arise from the unauthorized release of information concerning a patient. However, not all releases of information violate the right to privacy. For example, the Minnesota Supreme Court found that, even though a patient had explicitly requested that the information not be released, it was not an invasion of privacy to disclose orally the fact that she had been discharged from the hospital and that she had given birth, as long as the information was given in response to a direct inquiry concerning the patient and at a time reasonably near the time of her stay in the hospital.[9] The case involved an inquiry by the patient's sister as to whether the patient had been discharged. The sister was told that the patient had gone home but the baby was still hospitalized. The court stated that the oral disclosure of the information did not involve "medical records" and was not covered by the state statute governing confidentiality of medical records. However, state law and regulations in some states may not permit this disclosure. Most hospitals also prohibit such disclosure by policy. The better practice would be to avoid the release of discharge and birth information when the patient requests nondisclosure.

Obviously, institutional policies concerning confidentiality must be followed because some courts will impose liability for failure to do so. Occasionally, a nurse may be required to disclose certain information. The reporting of communicable diseases, wounds of violence, child abuse, and other matters are required by law in most states, and the disclosure of such information to the appropriate officials (but not necessarily to the general public or the press) is justified by public policy.

Intentional Infliction of Emotional Distress

Intentional infliction of emotional distress is another intentional tort. It includes several types of outrageous conduct that cause emotional trauma. It should be easy to avoid this tort by remembering to treat patients and their families in a civilized fashion. This apparently was forgotten in the following two examples involving actions after the deaths of patients.

In a Tennessee case, a mother sought the body of her baby who had died in the hospital. A hospital staff member gave the body to her preserved in a jar of formaldehyde.[10] Another example, in Ohio, dealt with communications after death. A woman died and a month later her family physician's office sent a notice for her to come in for a periodic checkup. The court said that this first notice was an excusable error. Her husband sent the doctor a letter explaining that the patient had died. The husband later sued the doctor for malpractice in her death. After the suit was filed, the doctor's office sent two more reminders for the dead woman to come in for a checkup, one of which was addressed to the youngest daughter of the deceased. The court said that the second and third reminders could be the basis for liability.[11]

Malicious Prosecution and Abuse of Process

Suits for malicious prosecution and abuse of process provide some recourse when there is unjustifiable or harassing litigation. The person alleging malicious prosecution and suing for damages must prove the defendant used the legal process for improper ends. This proof includes showing that (1) the defendant brought an action against the plaintiff, (2) the proceeding was terminated in favor of the party sued, (3) probable cause for the proceeding was absent, and (4) the defendant brought the action because of malice.

Some physicians who have been sued for malpractice and who have been successful in defending themselves have in turn sued the patient and the patient's attorney for malicious prosecution. Generally, public policy favors giving persons an opportunity to present their case to the courts for redress of wrongs, so the law protects them when they act in good faith upon reasonable grounds in commencing either a civil or criminal proceeding. Thus, few countersuits have been successful.[12]

NEGLIGENT TORTS

The most frequent basis for liability of nurses, physicians, and hospitals is the negligent tort. Fortunately, negligence by itself is not enough to establish liability; there must also be an injury caused by the negligence. Four elements must be proved to establish liability for negligence: (1) duty (what should have been done), (2) breach of duty (deviation from what should have been done), (3) injury, and (4) causation (the injury was the direct and legal cause of the deviation from what should have been done). These elements are discussed in more detail next.

There is a "fifth element" that courts do not discuss but that nurses should remember: there must be someone willing to make a claim. Health care providers who maintain good relationships with their patients before and after incidents are less likely to be sued. If a hospital staff member suspects that an incident has occurred, the persons responsible for risk management in the institution should be notified promptly so steps can be taken to minimize the chance of a claim. In addition, after an incident has occurred, nurses and other staff members, whether in institutional or independent practice, should try to maintain a good relationship with the patient and the family.

Duty

The first element that must be proved in any action for negligence is the duty. Duty has two aspects: (1) it must be proved that a duty was owed to the person harmed; (2) the scope of that duty, sometimes called the standard of care, must be proved.

In general, common law does not impose a duty on individuals to come to the rescue of persons for whom they have no other responsibility, although some states recently have attempted to impose such a duty by statute. Under the common-law rule, an individual walking down the street has no legal obligation to come to the aid of a heart attack victim, unless: (1) the victim is the individual's dependent; (2) the individual contributed to the cause of the heart attack; (3) the individual owns or operates the premises where the heart attack occurred; or (4) the individual has a contractual obligation to come to the person's aid, for example, by being on duty as a member of a public emergency care team. In most situations involving potential liability for incidents in hospitals or other institutions, it is not difficult to establish a duty based on the admission of the patient.

After the existence of a duty is established, the second aspect, the scope of the duty, must be established. This sometimes is called the obligation to conform to the standard of care. The standard of care for nurses is the degree of care that would be exercised by a "reasonably prudent nurse" acting under similar circumstances. A judge or jury will make this determination based on one or more of the following: (1) expert testimony, (2) common sense, or (3) published standards.

Expert Testimony

The technical aspects of care must be proved through expert testimony, usually by other health professionals engaged in similar practice. Several court decisions have addressed the issue of who is the appropriate expert in nursing practice cases.

In early malpractice actions, physicians frequently testified as to the standard of care for nurses. In more recent cases, nurses have been used increasingly as experts. For example, in a 1983 Louisiana case the court held that a nurse's testimony could be used to prove that a nurse should diligently monitor a heparinized patient in an intensive care unit.[13]

Common Sense

Nontechnical aspects of care can be proved by nonexperts. Some courts will permit juries to use their own knowledge and common sense when the duty is considered common knowledge. For example, many courts consider one of the nontechnical aspects to be how a disoriented patient should be protected from falling out of bed. Another issue many courts consider nontechnical is how to protect patients from burns.

Published Standards

Some courts will look to published standards, such as licensure regulations, institutional rules, standards promulgated by professional and specialty organizations, and accreditation standards. Courts have permitted published standards to be used in two ways: (1) In many cases, published standards are used in place of expert testimony; the jury may consider them along with all other evidence to determine the standard of care. (2) In other cases, published standards are presumed to establish the standard of care unless the defendant can prove otherwise. In most cases, published standards are used in addition to expert testimony and do not create a presumption of the standard of care.

Violations of statutes or government regulations can be used to establish the standard of care when the plaintiff is a member of the class of people that the rule is designed to protect and the injury suffered is of the general type that it is designed to prevent. For example, a Maryland court found a hospital liable for injuries because of failure to comply with a licensing regulation requiring segregation of sterile and nonsterile needles.[14] The patient had a liver biopsy with a needle that was suspected of being nonsterile, requiring postponement of other therapy and requiring immediate treatment with a series of painful gamma globulin injections to prevent infection from the needle. This clearly was the type of patient that the regulation was designed to protect and the kind of harm it was intended to prevent.

Hospital policies and procedures also can be used to establish the standard of care. For example, the highest court of New York ruled that a hospital could be liable for injuries because of failure to raise the patient's bedrails when the institution had a rule requiring bedrails to be raised for all patients over the age of 50.[15]

It is important for nurses to be familiar with and act in compliance with the rules and policies of their institution applicable to nursing practice. If the rules are impossible to follow, steps should be taken to modify them instead of ignoring them. Eliminating all rules, however, is not a solution, as the failure to adopt necessary regulations can be a violation of the standard of care for hospitals. In Michigan a hospital was found liable for the transmission of infection by a transplanted cornea because it did not have a procedure to assure that the relevant medical records of the proposed donor were reviewed prior to the transplant.[16]

The violation of a hospital policy also can be the basis for a finding of nursing liability for negligence. In a West Virginia case a patient who was being treated for a broken wrist developed signs of severe infection. The nurse reported the patient's symptoms to his physician, who took no action, nor did the nurse. Later, the patient's arm was amputated. The court ruled that liability could be based on the nurse's failure to comply with a hospital policy that required any nurse who had reason to doubt or question the care of a patient to report it first to the attending physician, then to the department head if the problem was not resolved.[17]

Respected Minority Rule

The proof of duty can become confused when there are two or more accepted approaches to a situation. This is particularly true in nursing practice where there may be several different, equally safe and effective ways to perform a procedure. The courts have attempted to resolve this through the "respected minority" rule. If a health professional follows the approach used by a respected minority of the profession, then the duty is to follow that approach properly. The courts will not permit liability to be based simply on the decision not to follow the majority approach.

Locality Rule

In the past, some courts limited the standards of hospitals and health care professionals to the practice in the same or similar communities. This meant that experts testifying on the standard of care had to be from the same community or, in states that allowed the standards of similar communities to be considered, from a similar setting.

This rule was designed to avoid finding rural hospitals and physicians liable for not following the practices of urban medical centers. In practice the rule made it very difficult to obtain expert testimony. The rule has been abandoned in nearly every state for hospitals and physicians, so that experts from anywhere generally can testify if they are familiar with the relevant standard of care. However, the applicability of the locality rule to nursing practice still is an open issue in many states.

Legally Imposed Standards

Courts occasionally will impose a new duty not previously recognized by the profession. A court may find that the whole profession is lagging in its standards so it imposes a more stringent legal standard. In a 1974 case, the Washington Supreme Court determined that an ophthalmologist was negligent in failing to administer a simple glaucoma test to a patient, although there was uncontradicted expert testimony that it was the universal practice for ophthalmologists not to administer glaucoma tests to patients under age 40. The court said the reasonable precaution of giving the test to the patient was so important that the fact that it was not the standard of the ophthalmology profession was no excuse.[18] In another case, the California Supreme Court found liability for a psychiatrist's failure to warn a woman that his patient had threatened to kill her, even though other psychiatrists would have acted in the same manner.[19]

Breach of Duty

After the duty is proved, the second element that must be proved is the breach of this duty; that is, that there was a deviation in some manner from this standard. Something was done that should not have been done or something was not done that should have been done. The proof of breach of duty hinges on a showing that the care of the patient was substandard. This can be shown through the nursing record or the testimony of witnesses.

Injury

The third element that must be shown in order to prove negligence is injury. The person making the claim must demonstrate physical, financial, or emotional injury. In many malpractice cases the existence of the injury is very clear by the time the suit is brought, although there still may be disagreement concerning the dollar value of the injuries.

With few exceptions, most courts will not allow suits based solely on negligently inflicted emotional injuries; generally, the emotional injuries are compensated only when they accompany physical injuries. Intentional infliction of emotional injury is compensated without proof of physical injury. In some states, negligently inflicted emotional injuries are compensable without accompanying physical injuries in a few circumstances.

The most widely accepted circumstance is when the plaintiff was in the "zone of danger" created by the defendant's negligence, that is, when the plaintiff has been exposed to risk of injury. A few states have extended this to when the plaintiff is not in the zone of danger but witnesses injury of a close relative. A California court permitted a father to sue for his emotional injuries when he was present in the delivery room when his wife died, and he placed his hands on her body after her death and felt the unborn child die.[20] There is a trend toward compensating more negligently inflicted emotional injuries without requiring physical harm.

Causation

The fourth element is causation: the breach of duty must be proved to have legally caused the injury. For example, a treatment may be negligently administered (which is a breach of duty) and the patient may die (which is an injury), but the person suing still must prove that there was a substantial likelihood that the person would have lived if the treatment had been administered appropriately. Thus, causation can be the most difficult element to prove.

There have been several cases involving the negligence of nurses in which causation of the injury was a key issue. An Illinois case addressed a child in an incubator who became overheated, had febrile seizures, and eventually was found to be brain damaged. There was no thermometer in the incubator and the practice was to check the infants' temperatures once daily. There was conflicting expert testimony on the cause of the baby's brain damage. The court was critical of the nursing care given to the baby but said that causation was not proved.[21]

Another example is a Texas case concerning a nurse who gave a patient solid food immediately after colon surgery (which is a breach of duty), and eight days later the ends of the sutured colon came apart (which is an injury). Because of the time lag, the patient was not able to prove causation.[22] Causation can be proved in many cases, however, as illustrated in a Colorado case in which a nurse had put a 3-year-old patient in an adult-sized bed. The child slipped through the siderail and strangled. The court held that the nurse violated her duty to furnish adequate attention to the patient and that her acts were the direct cause of the child's death.[23]

Res Ipsa Loquitur

There is a major exception to the requirement that the four elements be proved. This is the doctrine of *res ipsa loquitur,* "the thing speaks for itself." In England, in the nineteenth century, the courts were confronted with a case arising from a barrel flying out of an upper story window and hitting a pedestrian. The pedestrian tried to sue the owner of the building, who claimed that the four elements of negligence had to be proved. Of course, the person suing could not find out the specifics of what went wrong in the upper story room, so the case would have been lost. However, the court said the owner could not take advantage of the rules to escape liability in cases like this when someone clearly had done something wrong. Therefore, the court developed the doctrine of *res ipsa loquitur.*

The courts have said that all that needs to be proved is: (1) the accident is of a kind that does not happen without negligence, (2) the apparent cause is in the exclusive control of the defendants, (3) the person suing could not have contributed to the difficulties, (4) evidence of the true cause of the injury is inaccessible to the person suing, and (5) the fact of the injury is evident.

Courts frequently have applied this rule to two types of malpractice cases: (1) sponges and other foreign objects left unintentionally in the body and (2) injuries to parts of the body distant from the site of treatment, such as a leg laceration during eye surgery. Some courts have extended the applicability of the rule to other types of malpractice cases. An example is a California case in which a patient had a cardiac arrest and subsequently died as a result of the nurses' failure to observe, monitor, exercise appropriate care in performing procedures, and institute emergency resuscitation. The court applied the doctrine of *res ipsa loquitur*.[24]

Liability is not automatic in *res ipsa loquitur* cases. The persons being sued may attempt to explain why the injury was not the result of negligence. This can be done successfully in some circumstances. For example, a physician could establish the absence of negligence by proving the sponge was left in the body because the patient had to be closed quickly on an emergency basis to save the person's life and there was no time for a sponge count, as in cases of sudden life-threatening deterioration of the patient. The evidence necessary to avoid liability varies among states because there is variation to the degree to which the burden of proof shifts to the defendant in *res ipsa loquitur* cases.

Defenses

Several defenses are available in a negligence action, including time limits within which suits must be started, releases, contributory or comparative negligence, and immunity statutes.

Statute of Limitations

The statute of limitations specifies the time limit within which a lawsuit must be filed, with suits barred after the period has expired. The time varies depending on the nature of the suit; in many states, for malpractice suits it is one or two years. In most states, the time for a malpractice suit begins when the patient discovers that the injury may have been caused by negligence. Actual knowledge is not required. If the patient through reasonable diligence should have known the injury was due to negligence, discovery is legally considered to have occurred, starting the time period.

For example, in a Utah case a patient who was a nurse began to have pain and numbness in her jaw immediately after receiving two injections from a dentist. She did not determine that the cause of her pain was the negligence of the dentist until more than two years after the injection—and two years was the time limit for malpractice suits in the state. She claimed that she had not discovered that her injury was due to negligence until she actually had determined the cause. The court ruled she should have known the cause sooner, so her suit was barred.[25]

Some states have enacted absolute time limits for most malpractice suits. For example, in Iowa, a malpractice suit must be commenced within two years of discovery of the potential suit, but no longer than four years after the occurrence of the injury, unless a special exception applies.[26]

Many states have special exceptions for cases involving minors, foreign objects unintentionally left in the body, and other situations. In many states, a suit involving a minor patient may be commenced at any time before the minor's 19th birthday if the time period would otherwise expire before that date.[27] A few states have adopted shorter time limits for malpractice suits involving minors.[28]

In some states that have enacted absolute time limits for most malpractice suits, a special exception is retained for cases involving foreign objects unintentionally left in the body, so that these have no absolute time limit. However, these suits still are subject to a time limit that begins with the discovery of the foreign object.[29] When there is no statutory exception for foreign object suits, some courts have created similar exceptions by judicial interpretation. For example, an Ohio court ruled that leaving a surgical needle in an incision was not "malpractice" for purposes of the statute of limitations, so that the longer time period for "personal injuries" applied. Thus, the suit against the responsible nurse and her hospital employer was not barred.[30]

Some lawsuits, especially those involving care of newborns, can be started many years after the care is provided. Since few people have memories that long, it is important to thoroughly document the care given to patients. The records will be the only way to prove what was done. Most courts assume that if it was not written down, it was not done. (Charting is discussed further in Chapter 11.)

The Release

Another defense is a release. As part of the process of settling a claim, the claimant is usually asked to sign a release of all future claims arising from the same incident. In most cases, if such a release has been signed, it will bar a future suit based on the same incident. An exculpatory contract is different from a release because it is signed before the care is provided and generally will not be a successful defense. For example, some providers have asked patients to sign an exculpatory contract agreeing not to sue or agreeing to limit the amount of any suit but courts have refused to enforce such contracts on the ground that they are against public policy.[31]

Contributory and Comparative Negligence

Contributory negligence is a defense to a claim of a negligent tort. Contributory negligence occurs when the patient does something wrong that contributes so much to the injury that the health care provider is not responsible for the damage.

In other words, the patient is unable to prove the fourth element, causation of the injury by the provider's error.

Contributory negligence can occur when (1) the patient fails to follow clear orders and does not return for follow-up,[32] (2) the patient walks on a broken leg,[33] (3) the patient gets out of bed and falls,[34] (4) the patient lights a cigarette in bed when unattended,[35] or (5) the patient deliberately gives false information that leads to the wrong antidote's being given for a drug overdose.[36]

The success of this defense depends on the intelligence and degree of orientation of the patient. Obviously, a patient who does not appear to be able to follow orders cannot be relied on to follow orders, so contributory negligence would not be a successful defense against a claim by such a person.

A majority of the states have abandoned the all-or-nothing contributory negligence rule; instead, they apply comparative negligence, which means the award is decreased by the percentage of the patient's responsibility for the injury.[37] Some states that have adopted this rule provide that a patient responsible for 50 percent or more of the cause cannot collect anything.[38]

State Immunity Statutes

Some states have statutes that extend some degree of immunity from some types of suits. These statutes are another source of defense. A suit still may be filed but an attorney can win dismissal if the statute applies. The most widely adopted type of immunity statute is the Good Samaritan Law that applies to care provided gratuitously in an emergency situation. In most states, persons who provide care in emergencies are protected if their actions are in good faith and not reckless, but it is helpful to be familiar with the details of the applicable statute because there are variations in the protection. For example, in Florida, the Good Samaritan Law does not apply if the patient objects to the care provided.[39] As a practical matter, negligence actions against persons who attempt to provide aid at the scene of an accident are rare.

Breach of Implied Warranties and Strict Liability

The major exception to the requirement that liability be based on fault involves breach of implied warranties and strict liability in tort. This is an area of the law where liability based on contract and liability based on tort overlap. The implied warranties of merchantability and fitness for a particular use are based on contract. These warranties form the basis for finding liability without fault for many of the injuries caused by use of goods and products. Normally, the seller is liable for the breach of the warranties, but in some situations persons who lease products to others have been found liable.

Strict liability applies to injuries caused by the use of a product that is unreasonably dangerous to a consumer or user and that reaches the user without substantial change from the condition in which it was sold. Usually it is the manufacturer or seller of the product who is liable. Strict liability in tort does not require a contractual relationship between the seller and the person injured to establish the seller's liability. Some courts have extended strict liability to persons who furnish goods or products without a sale.

Hospitals almost always are considered to be providing services, not selling or furnishing products, so they seldom have been found liable for breach of warranties or strict liability. However, plaintiffs and their attorneys have made numerous efforts to convince courts to apply these principles to make it easier to establish liability. These efforts have been based on services involving blood transfusions, drugs, radiation, and hospital equipment.

Blood Transfusions

One of the known risks of blood transfusions is the transmission of diseases such as serum hepatitis. In 1954, the New York courts ruled that blood transfusions were a service, not a sale, so that hospital liability could not be based on breach of warranty or strict liability.[40] However, in the late 1960s and early 1970s, courts in several other states began applying these product liability principles to blood transfusions. For example, in Illinois, the court ruled that strict liability in tort could be used against hospitals for hepatitis transmitted by blood transfusions.[41] Legislatures in nearly all states enacted statutes intended to reverse these court decisions.[42] Some of the statutes state that providing blood is a service, not a sale. Other statutes expressly forbid liability based on implied warranty or strict liability. These immunity statutes have been found to be constitutional.[43] Of course, the hospital or nurse administering a blood transfusion or blood product still can be liable for negligent administration of the blood or monitoring of the patient.

Drugs

Efforts to use implied warranties or strict liability to impose liability on hospitals for the administration of drugs generally have been unsuccessful. For example, a Texas court refused to apply these product liability principles to the administration of a contaminated drug.[44]

Radiation

In Illinois, the Supreme Court reversed a lower court's application of strict liability principles to x-ray treatment. The court ruled that the issue in the case was the decision to use a certain dosage.[45] The x-rays themselves were not a defective product, so strict liability in tort was not applicable.

Hospital Equipment

Courts also have declined to apply implied warranties or strict liability in tort to hospital equipment. For example, a California court ruled that the hospital was the user, not the supplier, of a surgical needle that broke during an operation.[46] Of course, the hospital still may be liable based on negligence and the manufacturer may be liable based on implied warranties or strict liability in tort.

WHO IS LIABLE?

Liability can be divided into personal liability, liability for employees and agents, and institutional liability.

Individual Liability

Individual staff members are liable for the consequences of their own acts. Individual liability almost always is based on the principle of fault. To be liable, the person must have done something wrong or failed to do something that should have been done.

Employer Liability

Employers can be liable for the consequences of the job-related acts of their employees or agents even if the employer is not at fault personally. Institutions can be liable for the consequences of breaches of duties owed directly to patients and others, such as the maintenance of buildings, grounds, and equipment, and selection and supervision of employees and medical staff.

Respondeat Superior

As noted, employers can be liable for the consequences of their employees' job-related acts whether or not the employer is at fault. This legal doctrine is called *respondeat superior,* which means "let the master answer." Under this doctrine, the employer can be liable for any consequence of an employee's activities within the course of employment for which the worker could be liable. The employer need not have done anything wrong. Thus, for example, if a nurse employed by a hospital injures a patient by giving the wrong medication, the hospital can be liable even if the nurse was properly selected, properly trained, and properly assigned the responsibility.

The supervisor is not the employer. Since the supervisor also is an employee, *respondeat superior* does not impose liability on the supervisor for acts or omissions of persons being supervised. Supervisors are liable only for the consequences of their own acts or omissions. Of course, the employer also can be liable for the acts and omissions of both the supervisor and the person being supervised.

The liability of the employer under *respondeat superior* is for the benefit of the person who is injured, not the employee. The employer's liability does not mean that the employee must be provided with liability protection. It means that the person who is injured can sue the employer, the employee, or both. If the employee is individually sued and found liable, the employee must pay. If, as usually occurs, the employee is not individually sued, then the employer must pay. Technically, the employer can sue the employee to get the money back. The repayment is called indemnification. However, indemnification is almost never sought because of the negative effects on future recruiting efforts. In addition, many employers provide individual liability protection for their employees (as is discussed in the insurance section at the end of this chapter).

Borrowed Servant and Dual Servant

In some situations hospitals may not be liable for the consequences of negligent acts of nurses and other employees because of the "borrowed servant" doctrine. In some states, when the hospital delegates its right to direct and control the activities of its employees to an independent staff physician who assumes the responsibility, the employee becomes a borrowed servant. The physician, rather than the hospital, is then liable under *respondeat superior* for the acts of the employee.

Courts in many states do not apply the doctrine when the nurse continues to receive substantial direction from the hospital through its policies and rules. Thus, the trend appears to be toward abandoning the "borrowed servant" doctrine or replacing it with a dual servant doctrine under which both the physician and the hospital are liable under *respondeat superior* for the acts of the employee. For example, a Kentucky court held that both the surgeon and the hospital could be liable for a negligent instrument count by the operating room nurse assisting the surgeon.[47]

Many court decisions have addressed the extent of liability for sponges and surgical instruments left inside patients. In the first cases brought for injuries sustained in this manner, the surgeon generally was held liable under the so-called "captain of the ship" doctrine: the surgeon was considered to be in control of everything that went on in the operating room, so that nurses acting under the surgeon's direction were temporarily not hospital employees. Now, some cases find that both the surgeon and hospital are liable, but most recent cases hold that the nurses and their hospital employers are responsible for errors in sponge and instrument counts unless there are extenuating circumstances.

Other cases have addressed the nurse acting on behalf of or as the "agent" of the physician. Some hospitals have attempted to convince courts the nurse is acting as the agent of the doctor when the nurse is carrying out orders and thus the hospital is not liable for errors or omissions. Courts have rejected this argument unless the nurse actually is employed by the doctor and not the hospital.

Institutional Liability

Institutions can be liable for the consequences of breaches of duties owed directly to the patient. These duties, as noted, include the maintenance of buildings and grounds, the selection and maintenance of equipment, and the proper selection and supervision of employees. Failing to exercise reasonable care in the discharge of any of these duties can impose liability on the institution for resulting injuries.

In a 1978 Washington case, another form of institutional liability was imposed. The court found the hospital liable for the treatment provided in an emergency room by an independent professional corporation because it considered the emergency services to be an inherent function of the hospital's overall enterprise for which it bears some responsibility.[48] Other courts have not adopted this position.

Liability of Contracting Agency

Since the late 1970s there has been a proliferation of agencies that employ nurses and contract with hospitals or other health care centers to provide services. Under these circumstances, the nurse's employer is the personnel agency, and the allocation of liability for a nurse's negligent acts can be complex. Generally, the employing personnel agency will be liable for the negligent acts of the nurse under *respondeat superior*. The hospital, however, could be liable in whole or in part for a nurse's negligence if it did not exercise due care in the selection of the agency or in the assignment and supervision of the nurse.

The agreement between a personnel agency and a health care facility should allocate liability and the responsibility for maintaining insurance. A nurse who is employed by such an agency should understand its scope of liability coverage. This is particularly essential if the nurse works in more than one setting, since there are likely to be differences in institutional liability coverage among various settings and institutions.

TORT REFORM

In the mid-1970s, the cumulative effect of the increasing number of medical malpractice cases and the growing cost of individual cases led to a surge in the cost of malpractice insurance and, in some areas of the country, a reduction in its availability for some medical specialists. The malpractice insurance crisis led nearly every state to review and revise its laws concerning tort suits. These tort reforms can ge grouped into (1) changes in dispute resolution mechanisms, (2) changes in the amount of the award and how it is paid, (3) changes in the time in which the suit must be brought, and (4) various other changes. These tort reforms have received a mixed reception in the courts, which have disagreed on whether they violate various state and federal constitutional provisions.

Dispute Resolution Mechanisms

The two primary changes in mechanisms for dispute resolution have been the introduction of screening panels and the authorization of binding agreements to arbitrate disputes.

Screening Panels

Several states have enacted laws that require all malpractice claims to be screened by a panel before a suit can be filed. These screening panels are designed to promote settlement of meritorious claims and abandonment of frivolous claims.

A few courts have held screening panels to be an unconstitutional infringement of rights under state constitutions to access to the courts.[49] The Florida Supreme Court declared the state's medical mediation requirement unconstitutional on the ground that it violated due process by being arbitrary and capricious in operation because of its arbitrary ten-month limitation on the mediation process.[50] The process was not completed in more than half of the cases because there was no procedure to extend the time, so the court ruled the law unconstitutional in its entirety.

Most courts have upheld the required use of screening panels since the plaintiffs still have the right to sue after the screening process is completed.[51] The federal courts require plaintiffs to complete the screening process, if required by applicable state law, before pursuing a malpractice claim in federal court based on the court's diversity jurisdiction, that is, jurisdiction based on the fact that the parties to the suit are from different states.[52]

Arbitration

Several states have authorized binding agreements to arbitrate future malpractice disputes. In many states agreements to arbitrate were not valid unless signed after the dispute arose, so changes in the law were necessary to make agreements signed before the dispute enforceable. When there is a valid agreement to arbitrate, the dispute is submitted to an arbitrator who decides whether there should be any payment and, if so, how much. Many agreements provide for an arbitration panel rather than a single arbitrator. Several states specify that certain elements must be included in agreements to arbitrate, such as a right to withdraw from the agreement within 30 days after signing, or 60 days after discharge.[53] The laws vary on which health care providers are eligible to enter arbitration agreements.

Arbitration is favored by some health care providers and patients because it is faster and less costly than litigation. It is a less formal process, avoiding adverse publicity and the complex rules of litigation that promote adversarial positions. Others are opposed to arbitration because they prefer having their disputes decided by a jury using procedures with which attorneys are more familiar. Some providers believe they have a better chance of avoiding any payment in a jury case, while some patients believe that if they win they will be awarded a larger payment.

Amount and Payment of Award

The amount of the award has been limited in a few states by imposition of a ceiling. Some have abolished the "collateral source" rule, reducing the amount paid. State payment mechanisms that pay part of any malpractice award have been created. Award of periodic payments has been authorized.

Ceilings

Limitations on the amount that can be awarded in a malpractice suit have been one of the most controversial approaches to tort reform. Few states have enacted limits. Courts have disagreed on their constitutionality. For example, the Illinois Supreme Court declared ceilings to be an unconstitutional violation of equal protection because it could find no rational justification for treating those injured by medical malpractice different from those injured by other means.[54] The Indiana Supreme Court declared ceilings to be unconstitutional because it found the need for a risk-spreading mechanism for malpractice liability at a reasonable cost to assure the continued availability of health services to be a rational justification.[55]

Collateral Source Rule

In most states, the defendant must pay for the entire cost of the injuries even if the plaintiff already has been compensated in part by some other source such as insurance or Workers' Compensation. This is called the collateral source rule. Several states have abolished the collateral source rule, so the amount of compensation the plaintiff receives from other sources is deducted from the amount the defendant owes. This has been declared constitutional by several courts.[56]

State Payment Mechanisms

Some states have created insurance mechanisms that pay part of any malpractice award. These laws generally have been upheld, including the requirement that all health care providers contribute to the fund.[57]

Periodic Payments

Under common law, court judgments must be paid in a single lump sum. One of the advantages of settling cases involving large liabilities is that the parties can agree to periodic payments that are more reasonable for the defendant to pay. Some states have passed laws that authorize courts to direct that large judgments be paid by means of periodic payments. The courts have not agreed on whether these laws are constitutional.

Statute of Limitations

The statute of limitations specifies the time period in which suits must be filed or forever barred. One form of tort reform has been to shorten the time period. Prior to the malpractice crisis amendments, nearly all statutes of limitations permitted minors to wait to file suits until after they became adults. One type of amendment limits minors to a specific number of years after the right to sue accrues. In 1982, the Ohio Supreme Court upheld a one-year limit on the time minors have to sue.[58]

Other Tort Reforms

Other tort reform amendments: (1) limit the grounds for suits based on lack of informed consent,[59] (2) restrict contingency fees for lawyers or give courts the authority to modify them,[60] (3) prohibit asking for a certain amount of money in the suit,[61] and (4) restrict who can give expert testimony.

RISK MANAGEMENT

Beginning in 1980, the Joint Commission on Accreditation of Hospitals standards mandated a quality assurance program that includes the correction of identified patient care problems.[62] One mechanism used to implement this standard is risk management. The concept of risk management, originated by the insurance industry in the 1950s, focuses on loss prevention by advising clients how to evaluate potential risks and prevent injuries from them. In hospitals, risk management includes evaluating and controlling environmental hazards that affect the condition of patients or staff members. An effective risk management program focuses on prevention but also identifies existing risks and documents actions taken to minimize damage and avoid future injuries from the same cause.

Two factors are critical in the evaluation of risks to patients: accurate data collection and appropriate data analysis. Data collection requires a system that will record all incidents of patient injury or system breakdown in an accurate, complete, and objective manner. Analysis of incidents includes detection of trends or patterns, identification of potentially compensable incidents, and timely action.

In all risk management systems there is a tension between the desire to collect and analyze needed information and the desire to avoid creating documentation that will increase the liability exposure of the hospitals, nurses, and other staff members. These factors are balanced differently in each institution, depending on state law, risk exposure, insurance policies, and institutional philosophy.

A significant consideration in the design of all systems is a desire to minimize the possibility that the most sensitive documentation can be seen or used by the patient or the patient's lawyer. State law varies concerning the extent of protection of risk management documents and what must be done to qualify for the protection. It is important for nurses to respect and follow institutional policies because their defense will be based on the assumption that the policies are being followed. If there are apparent deficiencies in the policies, formal change should be sought rather than making ad hoc, unilateral changes that could jeopardize the nurse and institution.

Hospitals differ in their approaches to the evaluation and minimization of patient injuries. Several of these programs are described next. Frequently a combination of approaches is used.

Incident Reports

Some type of reporting of incidents is an essential element of any risk management program. Incidents cannot be recorded, analyzed, or responded to unless someone identifies their occurrence and reports them. Nurses have a central role in reporting because they usually are the first to discover incidents and frequently are responsible for follow-up.

All types of unusual occurrences should be reported unless institutional policy expressly provides some other procedure for addressing particular types of events. When there is any doubt, an incident should be reported. Most institutions have adopted broad definitions of "incidents" to encourage reporting. Thus, any unusual occurrence not consistent with the routine operation of the institution or the routine care of a particular patient should be reported, whether it is a potential danger or results in an actual injury and whether it involves a patient, visitor, or staff member. Incidents include patient falls, medication errors, and blood mishaps. It is important to document system breakdowns (such as the wrong patient being sent to the operating room) as well as physical hazards and injuries.

Traditionally, incident reports have included a narrative description of what happened and a list of witnesses. The reports sometimes include a place to document follow-up or consequences. The reports are routed through channels specified in institutional policy and are evaluated to determine whether immediate action is required. If not, they are used for statistical analysis of emerging trends or common factors.

Some institutions have adopted notification forms in place of the traditional incident report form. The notification form is designed to quickly notify appropriate officials of an unusual occurrence and of its type but not the details or the follow-up. If the officials believe the event warrants special investigation, it is conducted by a member of the risk management staff or an attorney. This approach has been adopted: (1) to avoid delays in initial reporting by making the form easier to complete quickly; (2) to reduce the time of nursing and other patient care staff devoted to the forms; (3) to assure consistency in how occurrences are investigated and reported; and, (4) in some states, to reduce access of patients and their representatives to detailed reports. The forms also may be designed so that the information can be put into a computer easily for faster and more comprehensive statistical analysis.

A frequent question associated with incident reports is whether they are subject to discovery, that is, whether they can be obtained for use in a lawsuit. The answer depends on the institution's procedure and use of the report. Generally, if a report is prepared for the hospital's attorney for the purpose of obtaining advice on how to handle the incident, the report is protected by the attorney-client privilege. Since discovery applies to nonprivileged information, it does not extend to materials that are privileged. Information obtained by the attorney in anticipation of or in preparation for litigation also is protected. Incident reports prepared primarily for nursing or hospital administration are not protected, however.

Some nurses are reluctant to report incidents, especially ones for which they may share responsibility. Prompt reporting is in the best interest of the involved nurse. It helps to protect the nurse, patient, other staff members, and the institution by facilitating (1) prompt action to minimize injuries from the incident, (2) proper interaction with the patient to decrease the likelihood of a claim, and (3) appropriate action to reduce the likelihood of similar incidents in the future. Incident reporting should lead not to punishment but to positive action. If there is a perception in an institution that incident reporting leads to inappropriate punishment, nursing and institutional officials should be told so they can foster a better climate for reporting. Nurses should not fear liability for defamation for making reports as long as they are made through official channels and without malice. There is a risk of liability for defamation if reports are made outside of official channels.[63]

Each institution should have a policy specifying how unusual occurrences should be reported and investigated. Some states mandate certain reporting procedures.[64] Nurses should be familiar with the policies of all institutions in which they practice.

Closed Claims Studies

One method of risk management consists of using information obtained from insurance companies regarding claims against hospitals and health professionals. These data then are analyzed to identify areas of high risk to patients or employees.

Review of Medical Records

Review of medical records addresses only unusual incidents that are documented in the patient's medical record. It can be a useful adjunct to other approaches if it is remembered that other methods must be used to address incidents not reflected in the medical record. This method allows complete data analysis because of the availability of the information on the patient's subsequent hospital course.

The Nurse's Role in Risk Management

To establish a basis for analysis, prevention, and follow-up of actual or potential patient injuries, the first important step is the documentation of incidents. This will require the cooperation of all levels of nursing personnel likely to discover incidents. Reports should be completed as soon as possible after the incident is discovered, and should be clear, complete, and legible.

When nursing unit administrators are charged with immediate investigation of potentially compensable injuries, they need to focus on three areas: (1) checking the report for clarity and accuracy, (2) interviewing the person reporting and witnesses for additional details, and (3) ensuring that the medical record is complete and accurate, unless these responsibilities are assigned to someone else by hospital policy. Steps must be taken, at all times, to ensure confidentiality. There should be immediate notification of nursing department or hospital administrators when any major event occurs. A serious accident or problem of potential liability should go first to a supervisor or administrator for timely intervention, with retrospective analysis of the report assuming a secondary role.

SAFEKEEPING OF PATIENTS' PROPERTY

At the time of admission, most hospitals direct that patients send home the belongings they will not need. Patients also are encouraged to place valuables such as money and jewelry in the hospital safe to minimize the chances of loss or theft. Nevertheless, many patients keep some money and a variety of items of personal property. Some hospitals have patients sign a release of responsibility for loss or breakage of items. This serves to notify them that there will be no reimbursement for loss or damage to property kept against hospital advice. A release form may not excuse the hospital if staff members assume responsibility for patient property or are directly responsible for its loss or damage.

There are some circumstances in which the hospital may accept responsibility for patient property, such as when the person is transferred or goes to the operating room. The nurse who accepts responsibility for patient property but fails to take appropriate steps to safeguard it may incur personal liability for lost articles or cause liability for the hospital.

The basis for this liability is the law of bailments. A bailment is the delivery of property by one party to another party to be held by the latter. When property is held by a hospital or nurse for a patient, a contract of bailment arises and the hospital or nurse has a duty to exercise reasonable care in keeping the property and delivering it to the patient on demand. The law imposes liability on hospitals and staff members for the loss of or damage to property for which they have assumed responsibility or that they have lost or damaged.

. Many common incidents of damage to property involve patients' dentures. In a New York case involving a private duty nurse's liability for the loss of a patient's false teeth, the court found that the evidence was insufficient to establish that the nurse had assumed responsibility for the dentures. However, it assumed that the nurse would have been liable for the loss if responsibility had been accepted.[65]

When a nurse becomes aware that a patient has property of substantial value in a hospital room, institutional officials should be notified promptly so that steps can be taken to (1) remove the property from the hospital, or (2) provide security, or (3) identify and evaluate the property and obtain a release from liability.

INSURANCE

All practitioners should know the extent of insurance coverage for their activities. Many employing agencies provide some level of liability protection for their employees. For example, governmental employers in Iowa are required to provide employees with liability protection for acts committed in the scope of employment and are prohibited from suing employees to recover money paid out in a judgment against them.[66]

This does not mean that the employer must buy commercial insurance. Many employers choose to provide individual liability protection through self-insurance. Most who do so cover only job-related activities, so some nurses in such cases elect to purchase coverage for their outside activities, such as volunteer services not covered by the insurance of the organization for which they are providing the volunteer services. Personal malpractice insurance may not cover nurses for some activities outside the scope of nursing practice. Each nurse should be aware of the scope of the state nurse practice act and the institutional policies that define nursing practice for employees. The nurse who is not aware of what protection is provided by the employer should request a statement of clarification in order to evaluate the need for additional personal liability coverage.

Professional liability policies include the following: the insurance agreement, the amounts payable under the policy, the defense and settling of claims, the period of time during which the policy covers the practitioner, and conditions that must be met to assure that coverage will be provided. Typically, the nurse must notify the insurance company of claims within a certain period. The company then will select and pay attorneys to defend the nurse for claims made while the policy was in effect. Some policies require the nurse's approval for any settlement.

Most policies limit coverage in some way such as excluding criminal acts or actions outside the scope of nursing practice. Some policies limit coverage to assigned job responsibilities and exclude actions outside the hospital.

Several suits between practitioners and their insurers have arisen out of situations in which the company refuses to pay a claim. In some cases, this is because the nurse did not meet the requirements of the policy, such as notification to the company. For example, when a doctor failed to notify the company of the claim pending against him, the Tennessee Court of Appeals upheld the denial of benefits.[67]

Other suits have involved questions of whether the alleged negligent acts occurred during the period covered by the insurance. Traditional insurance policies, called "occurrence" policies, cover all claims arising out of acts or commissions during the period they cover, regardless of when the claim is made. However, some insurance policies, called "claim made" policies, cover only claims made during the time they are in effect so professionals must continue renewing them in order to maintain coverage for past incidents, unless they purchase a relatively expensive special policy that covers future claims. Generally, the special policy is not purchased until the professional wishes to end active practice or to change insurance companies. The nurse should find out whether an institutional or personal liability policy covers future claims so that if it does not, arrangements can be made for desired coverage.

In the decision whether to acquire a personal professional policy, nurses should consider several factors, including that fact that if they lose a judgment and they are not covered by insurance, personal assets may be used to satisfy the award. In most states, judgments remain open until satisfied or dropped. Carrying a personal professional liability insurance policy can mean duplication in circumstances where the employer also has malpractice coverage. However, duplication usually is preferable to having a portion of liability not covered.

NOTES

1. *Guilmet v. Campbell*, 385 Mich. 57, 188 N.W.2d 601 (1971).
2. Mich. Comp. Laws 566.132 (1979).
3. *Stewart v. Rudner and Bunyan*, 349 Mich. 459, 84 N.W. 2d 816 (1957).
4. E.g., *Howard v. Piver*, 279 S.E.2d 876 (N.C. 1981); *Baur v. Mesta Machine Co.*, 176 A.2d 684 (Pa. 1962).
5. *Mohr v. Williams*, 95 Minn. 261, 104 N.W. 12 (1905).

6. *Burrows v. Hawaiian Trust Co.*, 417 P.2d 816 (Hawaii 1966).

7. *Malone v. Longo*, 463 F. Supp. 139 (E.D.N.Y. 1979).

8. *Wynn v. Cole*, 91 Mich. App. 517, 204 N.W.2d 144 (1979).

9. *Koudski v. Hennepin County Medical Center*, 317 N.W.2d 705 (Minn. 1982).

10. *Johnson v. Women's Hosp.*, 527 S.W.2d 133 (Tenn. Ct. App. 1975).

11. *McCormick v. Haley*, 37 Ohio App. 2d 73, 307 N.E.2d 34 (1973).

12. *Spencer v. Burglass*, 288 So. 2d 68 (La. App. 1974); *but see Bull v. McCuskey*, 615 P.2d 957 (Nev. 1980) and Taub, Malpractice Countersuits: Succeeding at Last? 9 LAW, MEDICINE, AND HEALTH CARE 17 (December 1981).

13. *Belmont v. St. Francis Cabrini Hosp.*, 427 So. 2d 541 (La. 1983).

14. *Suburban Hosp. Ass'n v. Hadary*, 22 Md. App. 186, 322 A.2d 258 (1974).

15. *Haber v. Cross County Hosp.*, 37 N.Y. 2d 888, 340 N.E.2d 734 (1975).

16. *Ravenis v. Detroit Gen. Hosp.*, 63 Mich. App. 79, 234 N.W.2d 411 (1975).

17. *Utter v. Hospital Center, Inc.*, 236 S.E.2d 213 (W. Va. 1977).

18. *Helling v. Carey*, 83 Wash. 2d 514, 519 P.2d 981 (1974).

19. *Tarasoff v. Board of Regents*, 17 Cal. 3d 425, 551 P.2d 334 (Cal. 1976).

20. *Austin v. Regents of Univ. of Cal.*, 89 Cal. App. 3d 354, 152 Cal. Rptr. 142 (1979).

21. *Horowitz v. Michael Reese Hosp.*, 5 Ill. App. 3d 508, 284 N.E.2d 4 (1972).

22. *Lenger v. Physician's Gen. Hosp.*, 455 S.W.2d 703 (Tex. 1970).

23. *St. Luke's Hosp. Ass'n v. Long*, 125 Colo. 25, 240 P.2d 917 (1952).

24. *Sanchez v. Bay Gen. Hosp.*, 116 Cal. 3d 678, 172 Cal. Rptr. 342 (1981).

25. *Hove v. McMaster*, 621 P.2d 694 (Utah 1980).

26. IOWA CODE, § 614.1(9) (1983).

27. *E.g.*, IOWA CODE, § 614.8 (1983).

28. *E.g.*, FLA. STAT. ANN., § 95.11(4)(b) (West 1982).

29. *E.g.*, IOWA CODE § 614.1(9) (1983).

30. *Neilson v. Barberton Citizens Hosp.*, 446 N.E.2d 209 (Ohio App. 1982).

31. *E.g.*, *Tatham v. Hoke*, 469 F.Supp. 914 (W.D.N.C. 1979).

32. *E.g.*, *Roberts v. Wood*, 206 F.Supp. 579 (D.Ala. 1962).

33. *E.g.*, *Shirley v. Schlemmer*, 223 N.E.2d 759 (Ind. App. 1967).

34. *E.g.*, *Jenkins v. Bogalusa Community Medical Center*, 340 So. 2d 1065 (La. App. 1976).

35. *Seymour v. Victory Memorial Hosp.*, 60 Ill. App. 3d 366, 376 N.E.2d 754 (1978).

36. *E.g.*, *Rochester v. Katalan*, 320 A.2d 704 (Del. 1974).

37. *E.g.*, *Goetzman v. Wichern*, 327 N.W.2d 742 (Iowa 1982).

38. *E.g.*, *Bradley v. Appalachian Power Co.*, 256 S.E.2d 879 (W. Va. 1979).

39. *E.g.*, *Botte v. Pomeroy*, 438 So. 2d 544 (Fla. Dist. Ct. App. 1983).

40. *Perlmutter v. Beth David Hosp.*, 308 N.Y. 100, 123 N.E.2d 792 (1954).

41. *Cunningham v. MacNeal Memorial Hosp.*, 47 Ill. 2d 443, 266 N.W.2d 897 (1970).

42. *E.g.*, IOWA CODE, § 142A.8 (1983).

43. *McDaniel v. Baptist Memorial Hosp.*, 469 F.2d 230 (6th Cir. 1972).

44. *Shivers v. Good Shepherd Hosp.*, 427 S.W.2d 104 (Tex. Civ. App. 1968).

45. *Dubin v. Michael Reese Hosp.*, 83 Ill. 2d 277, 415 N.E.2d 350 (1980).

46. *Silverhart v. Mount Zion Hosp.*, 20 Cal. App. 3d 1022, 98 Cal. Rptr. 187 (1971).

47. *Somerset v. Hart*, 549 S.W.2d 814 (Ky. 1977).

48. *Adamski v. Tacoma Gen. Hosp.*, 20 Wash. App. 98, 579 P.2d 970 (1978).

49. *E.g., State ex. rel. Cardinal Glennon Memorial Hosp. v. Gaertner*, 583 S.W.2d 107 (Mo. 1979).

50. *Aldana v. Holub*, 381 So. 2d 231 (Fla. 1980).

51. *E.g., Paro v. Longwood Hosp.*, 373 Mass. 645, 369 N.E.2d 985 (1977); *Johnson v. St. Vincent Hosp., Inc.*, 404 N.E.2d 585 (Ind. 1980).

52. *E.g., Feinstein v. Massachusetts Gen. Hosp.*, 643 F.2d 880, (1st Cir. 1981).

53. *E.g.,* CAL. CODE OF CIV. PROC., § 1295 (1982).

54. *Wright v. Central DuPage Hosp. Ass'n*, 63 Ill. 2d 313, 347 N.E.2d 736 (1976).

55. *Johnson v. St. Vincent Hosp., Inc.*, 404 N.E.2d 585 (Ind. 1980).

56. *E.g., Rudolph v. Iowa Methodist Medical Center*, 293 N.W.2d 550 (Iowa 1980).

57. *E.g., Johnson v. St. Vincent Hosp., Inc.*, 404 N.E.2d 585 (Ind. 1980).

58. *Baird v. Loeffler*, 434 N.E.2d 194 (Ohio 1982).

59. *E.g.,* FLA. STAT. ANN. § 768.46 (1983 Supp.).

60. *E.g.,* IOWA CODE, § 147.138 (1983).

61. *E.g.,* IOWA CODE, § 619.18 (1983).

62. Joint Commission on Accreditation of Hospitals, ACCREDITATION MANUAL FOR HOSPITALS, (1980 ed.):151–54; (1984 ed.):147–49.

63. *E.g., Malone v. Longo*, 463 F.Supp. 139 (E.D.N.Y. 1979).

64. *E.g.,* FLA. STAT. ANN. § 768.41; FLA. ADMIN. CODE CHAP. 100–75.

65. *Fischer v. Sydenham Hosp.*, 176 Misc. 7, 26 N.Y.S.2d 389 (1941).

66. IOWA CODE, §§ 25A, 613A (1983).

67. *Osborne v. Hartford Accident and Indem. Co.*, 476 S.W.2d 265 (Tenn. 1971).

BIBLIOGRAPHY

Acton, W.G. MALPRACTICE. Boston: Little, Brown & Co., 1977.

Bernstein, Arthur. "Why Another Hospital Malpractice Insurance Crisis?" *Hospitals* (November 1, 1980).

———. "*Darling* is Alive and Well in California." *Hospitals* (October 1, 1982):114.

Bianco, R.C. "What Turns a Patient Into a Plaintiff?" *International Ophthalmology Clinics* 20, no. 4 (April 1980):43.

Creighton, Helen. "Malpractice Insurance." *Nursing Management* 12, no. 12 (December 1981):15.

———. "Incident Reports Subject to Discovery?" *Nursing Management* 14, no. 2 (February 1983):55.

Guarriello, Donna Lee. "Legally Speaking," *RN* 47, no. 2 (February 1984):19.

Chapter 7

Tort Liability and Nurses

The previous chapter reviewed the general principles of civil liability. This chapter discusses the application of these principles in a variety of specific situations involving nurses, illustrating many of the duties of nurses to patients, clients, and others.

A professional nurse is held to the standard of care generally observed by other competent nurses under similar circumstances. The standard may vary depending on the circumstances. For example, a Texas court ruled that a nurse specialist is held to the standard of care observed by those in the same specialty under similar circumstances.[1] A Louisiana court held that when a person assisting a physician performs a task deemed medical in nature, such as removal of a cast with a Stryker saw, the person is held to the standard of care applicable to physicians.[2] The standard of care applicable to nursing students is the same as that for professional nurses. The standard of care is an essential element that must be proved to establish liability. As discussed in Chapter 6, to establish liability, it must be shown that a patient's injury was caused by the failure to meet the applicable standard of care.

The first half of this chapter reviews areas of potential liability in each step of the nursing process: (1) assessment, (2) plan, (3) intervention, and (4) evaluation. The second half analyzes special problems involving supervisors, students, nursing specialists, and nurses in various nonhospital settings.

ASSESSMENT

The nurse has a responsibility to assess the health status and needs of the patient or client and to communicate that assessment properly. Assessment is a process of gathering information and analyzing it to reach a working decision concerning status and needs. The decision is subject to revision at any time because of subsequent assessments. The steps required will vary, depending on the setting

141

and the degree of involvement of other health professionals in the care of the patient.

Assessment errors can arise from (1) failure to take appropriate steps to gather information, (2) failure to recognize the significance of information gathered, and (3) failure to communicate steps taken or information gathered.

Monitoring and Other Steps to Gather Information

Steps to gather information include asking questions, taking vital signs, and making other observations, and taking further actions, such as probing wounds. For example, a Mississippi hospital was found liable when an emergency room nurse failed to obtain necessary information from the ambulance personnel who had brought a profusely bleeding patient to the hospital. The nurse transferred the patient, a veteran, to a Veterans Administration hospital without making any effort to assess the extent of the bleeding or to stop it. The patient died because the bleeding was not stopped.[3] In a California industrial accident case, a worker who had received a puncture wound on his forehead went to see the nurse in his employer's first aid room. She swabbed the wound with mercurochrome and bandaged it. The nurse and her employer were found liable for subsequent injuries to the worker because she did not probe the wound before bandaging it.[4]

Generally nurses do not have to reexamine areas checked by other nurses or physicians if the earlier exam is reliable, properly communicated, and not outdated. If a nurse has reason to suspect that the earlier exam is incomplete, inaccurate, or outdated because of the patient's changing condition, then reexamination by the nurse or a physician is warranted. If no physician is involved or available, the nurse may be expected to examine areas that normally would be the physician's responsibility. The probing of the wound in the California case is an example.

When a nurse has the responsibility to monitor a patient over a period of time, information gathering is a continuing responsibility that requires repeated observation. When a patient reaches a condition that could have been avoided by earlier intervention, a question is raised whether the responsible nurse should have detected it earlier. This usually becomes a question of whether the nurse observed the patient frequently enough. Most courts recognize that few patients can be observed continuously so the appropriate frequency for observations is determined by reference to institutional policy, physician orders, and the patient's needs.

In 1982 a District of Columbia court found a hospital liable when an elderly disoriented patient fell out of bed after having not been checked during the hour prior to the fall.[5] There was a question whether the patient had been restrained prior to the fall. The court concluded that whether or not she had been restrained, she should have been checked more frequently. Expert testimony was not required to establish that duty. A hospital policy requiring restrained patients to be checked at least every half-hour helped establish the standard. In 1973 a California hospital was found liable for the death of a patient because of a nurse's failure to follow the physician's orders concerning observations. The nurse had been ordered to check the patient's vital signs every 30 minutes but did not do so.[6]

Physicians' orders will not protect nurses from liability when reasonable nursing judgment would require more frequent observations. A Massachusetts trial court dismissed a suit against a nurse because of the suicide of a psychiatric patient for whom she was responsible. The court based its decision in part on its belief the nurse should not be responsible because three days before the death a psychiatrist had determined that suicide precautions were not necessary. The appellate court overruled the dismissal and ordered a trial.[7] The court ruled that a jury could find the nurse liable because deterioration in the patient's condition during the three days should have led either to closer supervision or at least to a request for permission to do so. The nurse had not observed the patient for the 40 minutes prior to the discovery that the patient had drowned in a bathtub. A nurse expert testified that the patient's condition required observations every 15 minutes.

Some patients, especially young children and persons recovering from anesthesia, require virtually continuous observation. A Tennessee court found a nurse and her physician employer liable for the death of a 22-month-old child the nurse had left unattended on a treatment table. The patient vomited while lying on his back on the table. The court concluded there was sufficient evidence that the nurse could have saved the child if she had been present.[8]

The condition of patients recovering from anesthesia is sufficiently unstable to require virtually minute-by-minute observation. In 1982 a Hawaii court upheld a $400,000 judgment against the state of Hawaii for the death of an 8-year-old boy from cardiac and respiratory arrest during the postoperative period after a tonsillectomy and adenoidectomy. The arrest occurred sometime between the 8:35 a.m. and 8:45 a.m. checks on the patient's condition. Resuscitation restored circulation and respiration but the patient did not regain consciousness before dying two weeks later. The one registered nurse in the recovery room had been busy with another patient between 8:35 and 8:45. She attempted to convince the court she had detected the arrest at 8:40 and had initiated intervention then, but all of the records indicated discovery at 8:45, and the court did not believe her testimony because of her evasive and inconsistent answers during the trial.[9]

The negligence must be the legal cause of the injury before there can be liability. This is illustrated by a Minnesota case that arose from a cyanotic episode with a newborn who later had severe mental retardation and other injuries.[10] There were no recorded observations of the patient for the half-hour prior to the discovery of the cyanotic condition. There was testimony that observations every 15 minutes were required, so there was evidence of negligence. However, since there were several other likely causes of the patient's condition, the court ruled that causation of the injury had not been demonstrated, so there was no liability.

The actions of patients can create a duty to observe or assist them more frequently. The Vermont Supreme Court found a hospital liable for the failure to respond to a call light.[11] The sedated patient used the call light to attempt to obtain a bedpan. When there was no response, she attempted to go to the lavatory and fell, causing back injuries. The court concluded that responding to a call light was an element of routine care, so no expert testimony was needed to establish the duty to respond.

Juries often will recognize that nurses cannot be in two places at the same time. In a 1975 Utah case the jury was asked to decide whether the nurse was negligent for not making a vaginal examination of a pregnant patient (in labor) when the nurse was busy with another complicated emergency delivery.[12] The woman who was not examined had a stillborn baby. The jury found the defendants not liable. This case illustrates the importance of exercising appropriate judgment when confronted with multiple responsibilities. When time and available staffing permit, assistance should be sought to avoid postponing necessary care.

Recognition of Significance of Information

Nurses have a responsibility to understand the significance of the information they gather within the limits of ordinary prudent nursing knowledge. They are not expected to have full medical knowledge. In some situations, the nurse's only responsibility is to understand that the information should be communicated to a physician. In other situations, the nurse should understand the significance and be able to plan and initiate appropriate intervention.

A 1981 California case illustrates a combination of failure to make timely observations, failure to understand the significance of the observations made, and failure to respond to the observations.[13] The case dealt with a patient who had undergone an elective laminectomy. She received appropriate care until transferred to a postoperative unit. No vital signs, neurological examinations, or tests for responsiveness were taken upon transfer. Her chart was not examined, so the nurses on the unit (1) did not know she had been vomiting, so no suctioning equipment was ordered, and (2) did not know she had an atrial catheter, so they believed it to be a peripheral intravenous line. Ten minutes after transfer to the unit her blood pressure, pulse, and respiration were measured and reflected a substantial decrease, but the nurses were not aware of this because they did not compare the results to earlier measurements. Since they did not understand the significance of the measurements, no one was informed of the patient's deteriorating condition. She vomited, which was reported to the nursing team leader, who merely rechecked the vital signs. When the patient's heart arrested 25 minutes after the transfer, the nurse panicked and did nothing to assist her. When an emergency room physician arrived, he was not told that the line was an atrial catheter so he mistook it for a peripheral intravenous line and had all medications administered through it. The patient entered a vegetative state that lasted until death two months later. The court applied the doctrine of *res ipsa loquitur* and found the hospital liable. This case also illustrates that it is often necessary to compare measurements to previous data to detect changes and understand the significance of the newer ones.

A 1983 Louisiana case arose from the failure of a nurse to recognize and respond properly to the signs of hemorrhage.[14] A heparinized patient in an intensive care unit complained to the nurse concerning pain at 7:30 a.m. At 9:30, the nurse charted the complaint of pain and her observation of swelling. She did not call the physician until the patient complained of pain again at 11:50 a.m. because she did not see evidence of a hematoma. When the physician arrived at noon, he discovered a large hematoma. The patient experienced extended hospitalization and permanent disability to her hand and arm because the physician was not called when the swelling was first observed. The hospital was found liable as the employer of the nurse because she did not understand that she should report the swelling.

Communication

Part of the assessment process is communication of observations and knowledge gained. This communication includes timely oral notification, when necessary, and proper documentation.

Oral communications may include information that (1) was gained during the initial contact with a new patient, (2) results from monitoring a patient, (3) should be shared with others who are working with the patient at the same time, and (4) should be shared with those who are assuming responsibility for care of the patient.

In emergency rooms nurses frequently are given information concerning new patients that they have a responsibility to convey accurately to the responsible physician. Liability can arise when patients are injured by failure to fulfill this duty. In 1977, a Maryland case concerned misdiagnosis of two children taken to an emergency room with rashes.[15] The mother told the nurse she had removed two ticks from one child several days earlier. The nurse did not tell the physician this. A routine tick search ordered by the physician was fruitless so he diagnosed measles and prescribed appropriate treatment for that. One child died of Rocky Mountain spotted fever before it was diagnosed accurately. The other child then was treated and cured. The hospital was found liable for the nurse's failure to report the ticks, delaying the proper diagnosis.

Telephone communications tend to lead to more problems. A 1982 Alaska court decision addressed an early morning emergency room visit by a person who had taken a drug overdose.[16] The court did not criticize the practice in the remote community of having the nurse telephone the on-call physician concerning emergency patients and having the physician decide whether he needed to come to the hospital to see the patient. The content of the telephone conversation was the issue. The patient had told his wife before going to the hospital that he had taken 30 Darvon pills but told the nurse he had taken ten pills. She observed the patient and found him coherent and with vital signs within the normal range. She called the physician to report this information. While she was on the phone, the wife told her he actually had taken half a bottle of pills. The nurse reported this to the physician by saying that maybe the patient had taken a few more than ten pills. The doctor concluded it was not an emergency and did not see the patient, so the man was sent home and died that night of a large overdose of Darvon and alcohol. The jury ruled in favor of the doctor and hospital. This decision may have been due to the jury's determination the nurse's communication was sufficiently accurate or the jury's suspicion that the fatal dose was taken after the patient left the emergency room. Even though the defendants won, this illustrates the potential injury to patients and the potential liability from such communications.

In some areas of the country, particularly urban areas, telephone communications never are considered sufficient. A federal court in Pennsylvania found that the standard in Philadelphia was for a licensed physician to personally examine the patient or the patient's chart before anyone was discharged from an emergency room.[17] The judge found the United States liable for the death of a woman whose subarachnoid hemorrhage was not diagnosed in a Navy hospital emergency room because she was seen by only a nurse and a physician's assistant.

Nurses have a duty to monitor the patient. They are expected to distinguish abnormalities in the patient's condition and determine whether nursing care is a sufficient response or whether assistance from a physician or others may be required. The nurse also has a responsibility to inform the physician promptly of abnormalities that may require the physician's attention. A Kansas nurse and hospital were sued because of injuries to a woman during delivery of a baby without the attendance of a physician.[18] The nurse had refused to call the physician despite the clear signs of imminent delivery. The nurse and hospital were found liable for the nurse's failure to give timely notification to the physician of the impending delivery. A Massachusetts hospital was found liable when a nurse attended seven hours of labor of a patient before calling a physician, despite the woman's vomiting and despite fluctuating fetal heartbeats.[19] The nurse called the physician when she no longer could detect a fetal heartbeat. An emergency Caesarean section was performed, but there was a stillbirth. A West Virginia court ruled that the hospital could be found liable for the death of a patient when the nurse failed to notify the physician of the patient's symptoms of heart failure for six hours.[20]

A 1979 Minnesota decision illustrates both liability for failure to notify the physician and an application of the comparative negligence rule described in Chapter 6.[21] A patient with a wrist fracture had a cast applied and was admitted to the hospital. Two days later, the nurses observed that his hands and fingers were swollen and bluish. Although they were concerned, they did not call the physician until five days after admission. The physician immediately removed the cast. The patient left the hospital against medical advice 17 days later and engaged in activities he was told to avoid. Two months later his arm had to be amputated below the elbow.

The $350,000 in damages were allocated as follows: (1) 10 percent from the patient for not following advice; (2) 30 percent from the physicians for making the cast too tight and other errors; and (3) 60 percent from the hospital for the nurses' delay in reporting the swollen and bluish hand and fingers.

Nurses do not have to report every patient complaint orally to the physician. For example, a hospital and nurse were found not liable for injuries resulting from grande mal seizures of a patient with a history of epilepsy.[22] The physician had withdrawn all medications upon admission to reestablish appropriate levels. The nurse called the physician at 5 a.m. to report that the patient was restless, coughing, and complaining of pain. The physician ordered a medication. At 5:25 a.m. the patient said she felt she was going to have an unconscious spell. The nurse gave the ordered medication and did not call the physician again. The next morning the patient had six seizures, causing significant damage. The court concluded there was no duty to report the 5:25 a.m. complaint and no evidence that the lack of a report caused the harm. It was within the range of appropriate nursing judgment to decide whether another report was immediately necessary.

When a nurse has information that should be reported to the physician, failure to report is not excused by the nurse's belief the physician is not likely to respond. If the physician does not respond, the nurse has a duty to notify her supervisors or follow other institutional procedures to bring the nonresponse to the attention of those who can provide necessary care for the patient. A California court ruled that two nurses and a hospital could be sued for the death of a woman from severe bleeding from an incision made to assist her to give birth to a child.[23] Although the nurses believed the patient was bleeding heavily, they did not notify the physician until nearly three hours later, when the patient went into shock. One nurse explained that she did not call the physician because she did not believe he would respond. The court concluded that she should have notified the attending physician and taken other steps to safeguard the life of the patient by notifying her superiors in the event the physician did not or could not respond rapidly enough.

A Kansas hospital was exposed to liability by the failure of several nurses to make sufficient efforts to obtain a physician's presence.[24] A patient asked the nurses to call a physician because of pain. A nurse tried to call the physician at 11:01 a.m. When she could not reach him, she talked to his partner, who ordered Demerol. The nurse documented 12 more efforts by the patient to convince them to find a physician but made no further efforts to do so. When the physician finally arrived at 9:30 p.m., he found the patient suffering from acute gastric dilation.

In the famous case of *Darling v. Charleston Community Memorial Hospital*, one of the reasons for the hospital's liability for the amputation of the patient's leg was the failure of the nurses to inform administration of the progressive gangrenous condition of the leg and the inappropriate efforts of the attending physician to address the condition.[25] No effective alternative channel had been established for direct nursing notification of the medical staff and for appropriate medical intervention. The court held that hospital administration should have been notified so it could provide appropriate medical staff intervention.

Most hospitals today have established direct communication channels between nursing administration and the medical staff leadership so direct hospital administration involvement is less frequent. These channels must be used when necessary. A West Virginia hospital was found liable for the failure of the nurses to comply with its nursing manual and report the patient's deteriorating condition to the department chairman when the attending physician failed to respond adequately to the worsening status.[26]

Nurses have a responsibility to communicate orally information that is needed by those working with the patient at the same time. The United States was found liable when a nurse-anesthetist did not inform a nurse who was inserting a catheter that the patient was under light anesthesia.[27] The catheter broke when the patient moved his arm.

When a patient is transferred to another unit or facility, it is necessary to assure that appropriate information is communicated to those assuming responsibility for the patient. In some circumstances, this communication is the nurse's responsibility. A Florida nursing home transferred a patient to a hospital without reporting his senility and need for special supervision.[28] The nursing home was found liable for the patient's death when he wandered away from the hospital.

In addition to the responsibility to communicate certain information orally, there is a responsibility to document the assessment of the patient. A California nurse, acting pursuant to a telephone order from a physician, gave an injection of Phenergan in the buttock of a woman in labor.[29] The patient reported immediate pain radiating downward from her buttock and later made repeated complaints of a similar nature. The nurse did not record any of the complaints and did not contact the physician. Even though the patient did not include the failure to contact the physician as one of the grounds for her suit, the court ruled that the failure to document the complaints could be the basis for liability of the nurse's employer.

Sometimes nurses claim to have observed the patient more frequently than is indicated in their documentation. The jury or judge has to decide whether the error was a failure to make the observation or a failure to document it. Courts tend to conclude that if an observation is not documented, it did not occur. An Illinois hospital was sued for the loss of a patient's leg.[30] The patient had been admitted for treatment for a broken leg. The admitting physician entered an order to "watch condition of toes" and testified at the trial that routine nursing care required frequent monitoring of a seriously injured patient's circulation, even in the absence of a physician's orders. The patient developed irreversible ischemia in his leg, requiring its amputation. The nursing notes for the seven-hour period prior to the discovery of the irreversibility of the ischemia did not reflect any observations of the patient's circulation. The court ruled that the jury could conclude that absence of entries indicated the absence of observations. Thus, the nurse and hospital could be liable even if the nurse actually had made the observations. In these circumstances, it is as important to document no change as it is to document changes, so that the time when changes occur can be identified.

Deficiencies in charting must contribute to the patient's injuries before they can lead to liability. In a 1983 Louisiana case a woman experienced severe hemorrhaging after childbirth.[31] Her physicians performed a series of operations resulting in removal of her uterus and cervix. The court found that the records concerning her vital signs were incomplete and poorly kept but concluded that these deficiencies played no part in causing her problems.

PLAN

A nurse must plan appropriate nursing care for each patient based on the information gathered and assessed. A nurse also must plan how to carry out physicians' orders. Few court decisions focus on this step because planning almost always must result in an act or omission of intervention before liability is likely. The decision then focuses on the act or omission.

One example of poor planning was the decision by a licensed practical nurse in a Veterans Administration hospital to send a patient unaccompanied to a laboratory for a test when the licensed practical nurse was aware the patient had been administered several drugs and had suffered chest pains.[32] The United States was found liable for the amputation of the patient's finger from injuries received when the individual fainted while standing in line.

Another example of poor planning arose when a woman with a Dalkon Shield, an intrauterine contraceptive device, sought help from a health plan in Massachusetts.[33] The woman was experiencing a foul odor and a nurse practitioner told her to douche with yogurt. When the woman called again reporting pain, the nurse told her to wait until she had a fever before calling back. When she finally was examined by a physician, multiple abscesses were found, requiring a total hysterectomy.

The court noted that the douche was a substandard lay remedy and that the failure to recommend a prompt examination by a physician was substandard. The nurse practitioner also had a duty to inform the patient of the risks associated with the Dalkon Shield or arrange for a physician to do so. She had a duty to keep herself informed of well-publicized current developments in areas about which she was advising patients. The problems with Dalkon Shields had been well publicized prior to the first call from the patient. Thus, the court ruled the health plan that employed the nurse practitioner could be liable for her advice to the patient.

Planning decisions of supervisory nurses concerning allocation of staff time have resulted in liability. Examples are discussed in the Supervisors section of this chapter.

INTERVENTION

Intervention is the carrying out of the plan derived from the assessment. Intervention can involve carrying out nursing care that does not require physician orders as well as implementing physicians' orders. Obtaining physician attention, as necessary, can be viewed as an intervention but it also can be one of the communication responsibilities that are part of assessment, which is the way it is addressed in this chapter.

Duty to Interpret and Carry Out Orders

Nurses have a duty to interpret and carry out orders properly. They are expected to know basic information concerning the proper use of drugs and procedures they are likely to be ordered to use. When an order is ambiguous or apparently erroneous, the nurse has a responsibility to seek clarification from the ordering physician. This almost always will result in correction or explanation of the order. In the unusual situations when that does not occur, the nurse has a responsibility to inform nursing, hospital, or medical staff officials designated by the institution's policy who can initiate review of the order and, if necessary, other appropriate action. Pending review, if the drug or procedure appears dangerous to the patient, the nurse should decline to carry out the order, but should immediately notify the ordering physician.

Hospitals should have established procedures for nurses to follow when they are not satisfied with the appropriateness of an order. Frequently, this procedure will involve notification of a nursing supervisor, who then will contact appropriate medical staff officials. Hospital administration occasionally may need to become involved to resolve individual issues.

A Louisiana court focused attention upon the responsibility of a nurse to obtain clarification of an apparently erroneous order from a patient's physician.[34] The order, as entered in the chart, was incomplete and subject to misinterpretation. Believing the medication order to be incorrect because of the dosage, the nurse asked two physicians whether it should be given as ordered by the patient's physician. They did not interpret the order as the nurse did and therefore did not share the nurse's concern, commenting that the attending physician's instructions did not appear out of line. The nurse did not contact the attending physician and administered the misinterpreted dosage of the medication, leading to the patient's death.

The appellate court upheld the jury's finding that the nurse had been negligent in failing to contact the attending physician before giving the medication, and the nurse and her employer were held liable, as was the physician who wrote the ambiguous order that led to the fatal dose. This case illustrates the way in which a nurse's conduct is measured against the practice of competent and prudent nurses. There had been testimony at the trial that a prudent nurse, when confronted with an ambiguous or confusing medication order, will obtain clarification from the prescribing physician. However, the nurse who administered the medication did not seek such clarification and the departure from the standard of competent nursing practice provided the basis for holding the nurse liable for negligence.

Sometimes an order that is correct when originally given becomes apparently erroneous because of changes in the patient's condition or because the therapy ordered usually should not be continued for such a long period without reevaluation. An Indiana hospital was found liable because a nurse did not question an excessively long, continuous intubation of a patient.[35] After the endotracheal tube had been in place for five days, the physician ordered the nurse to remove it, but she could not do so. The physician immediately removed it, and injuries to the throat and vocal cords were discovered. Experts testified that the tube should not have been left in continuously for more than four days. The nurse should have brought the problem to the physician's attention and, if he did not respond, to her supervisor's attention.

Of course, in some situations, nurses are given authority to adjust the amount of some drugs or other substances being given to patients within guidelines established by the physician. In such situations, the nurse has the added responsibility to exercise the appropriate judgment in making those adjustments. In many states, there are legal limits on the discretion that can be delegated concerning some drugs and substances, so familiarity with local law is important. In addition, as with all delegations, the physician should provide guidance and delegate this responsibility only to nurses who are able to make the required judgments.

In 1979 a California court recognized the appropriateness of delegating to a nurse the decision concerning when a prescribed pain medication was needed.[36] The patient suffered cardiopulmonary arrest and died soon after she was given the pain medication. The court ruled that it was appropriate for the trial court to give the jury two special instructions usually used only for physicians because the case involved a nurse who was exercising independent judgment delegated by the physician. One instruction emphasized that perfection was not required, so liability could not be based on a mere error in judgment by a nurse who possessed the necessary learning and skill and exercised the care ordinarily exercised by reputable nurses under similar circumstances. (It should be noted that the standard applied was the conduct of nurses, not physicians.) The other instruction emphasized that when there is more than one recognized method of treatment, it is not negligent to select one of the approved methods that later turns out to be wrong or to be not favored by certain other practitioners. The appellate court upheld the jury verdict in favor of the nurse and hospital.

Unless an order is ambiguous or apparently erroneous, the nurse has a responsibility to carry it out:

- A New York nurse and hospital were held liable for the scalding of a young tonsillectomy patient by water that was served as part of his meal by a nurse, contrary to the dietary instructions ordered by the attending physician.[37]
- A Texas hospital was sued because a nurse gave a patient solid food after a colon resection, contrary to orders.[38] The hospital avoided liability because the patient could not prove that the solid food was the cause of the separation of the sutured ends of the colon several days later.
- A Georgia hospital was held liable when a patient fell after a nurse instructed the patient to use the bathroom without supervision, contrary to the physician's order requiring an attendant.[39]
- A New York hospital was sued for the blindness of an infant caused by too much oxygen when a nurse gave six liters per minute instead of the four liters per minute ordered by the physician.[40] The hospital presented evidence that six liters per minute was within the range of permissible dosages. The court found this irrelevant because the nurse had not been given authority to deviate from the physician's order and, thus, had breached her duty to the patient.

Nurses cannot assume that orders have remained unchanged from previous shifts. They have a duty to check for changes in orders. A Delaware physician wrote an order on the patient's order sheet changing the mode of administration of a drug from injection to oral.[41] When a nurse, who had been off duty for several days, was preparing to give the medication by injection, the patient objected and referred the nurse to the physician's new order. The nurse, however, told the patient she was mistaken and gave the medication by injection. Either the nurse had not reviewed the order sheet after being told by the patient that the medication was to be given orally or did so in a negligent manner and did not note the physician's entry. In either case, the nurse's conduct was held to be negligent. The court stated that the jury could find the nurse negligent by applying ordinary common sense, so expert testimony was not necessary to prove the applicable standard of care.

When a nurse carries out an order that is neither ambiguous nor apparently erroneous, the order provides significant protection from liability. A Nebraska hospital was unsuccessfully sued when a schizophrenic patient fractured her arm.[42] The physician had ordered the patient restrained the first four days of the admission, then had directed that the restraints be removed. The requests of the patient's daughter that the restraints be restored had been conveyed to the physician but he declined to do so. The court ruled there was no liability for the nurse because there was no duty to restrain when the physician did not order restraints, and there was no reason to believe the order was so erroneous as to require intervention.

A Montana court ruled that a hospital could not be liable for failing to lock the door of a security room while an irrational patient had an attendant present when the physician had ordered the door locked only when the patient was unattended.[43] The patient had forced himself past the attendant, run to a window outside the security room, and jumped to the ground 20 feet below. The court ruled that the nurses had to follow the physician's orders unless there was an emergency.

Orders do not excuse the nurse from the duty to use proper care for the safety of the patient and to carry out the orders nonnegligently. A Kentucky physician ordered a patient to be exercised after her surgery.[44] The patient became violently ill at the first attempt. The physician ordered a second attempt but the patient protested when two nurses tried to carry out the order. The patient collapsed, hitting the floor and suffering permanent pain. The court ruled that the jury could find the nurses did not use proper care for the safety of the patient. Many of the other ways orders have been carried out negligently are discussed in the next section.

Errors in Carrying Out Interventions

Many types of negligent errors in carrying out interventions have led to lawsuits. Some of these interventions were initiated by nurses and some were ordered by physicians. This section gives examples of errors involving: (1) patient identity, (2) patient positioning, (3) changing sheets, (4) medications, (5) injections, (6) sterile techniques, (7) catheterization, (8) foreign objects left in the body, (9) incubators, (10) restraints and falls, and (11) patient instructions. This is not a complete list of the areas leading to liability, but it illustrates the range.

Patient Identity

The identity of the patient should be checked before initiating major interventions. A patient scheduled for conization of the cervix was taken to the operating room by a surgical technician at the time a thyroidectomy was scheduled for another patient.[45] The mistake was discovered after the incisions of the thyroidectomy were made but before excision of the thyroid. No one checked the patient's identification bracelet. They erroneously relied on the patient who had answered to the wrong name. The court found the hospital liable for the nurse's failure to check the bracelet. The patient's erroneous answer was not accepted as a defense.

In a Louisiana case, a nurse's aide was sent to the laboratory to obtain two extra units of blood before an operation.[46] The lab gave her blood intended for a different patient on a different floor. The circulating nurse checked the number on the blood with the number on the slip accompanying the blood, which matched, but she never checked the name. The O positive patient received 600ccs of A positive blood. The hospital was found liable.

Patient Positioning

Improper positioning of a patient for some procedures can result in injuries and liability. A Missouri hospital was held liable when a nursing assistant improperly adjusted a proctoscopic table and improperly positioned the patient, resulting in neck injuries.[47] An employee of a Michigan hospital failed to properly pad an elbow when restraining the patient for an appendectomy.[48] The hospital was found liable for the resulting impairment of the conduction of nerve impulses in the left ulnar nerve that caused numbness in two fingers. One of the grounds of a suit against a Minnesota hospital was that a nurse incorrectly positioned an infant for a lumbar puncture shortly before the infant had a cardiac arrest resulting in a semicomatose condition.[49] However, there was no liability because the family did not prove the positioning could have caused the cardiac arrest.

Changing Sheets

Even changing sheets can lead to suits and potential liability. A minor patient in a Florida hospital had his leg in traction to avoid any movement that might lead to a fracture because he had a degenerative bone disease that made fractures likely.[50] A nurse pulled the sheets from under the patient without assistance, causing his body to twist. He immediately felt his leg had broken, which was confirmed later. The court ruled that a jury should decide whether the nurse's actions caused the fracture.

Medication Errors

Medication errors can arise from giving the wrong substance or wrong dose, using the wrong route of administration, or giving the substance at the wrong time.

Wrong Substance. Liability resulted when a patient was injured because a scrub nurse filled a syringe with a solution different from the one ordered by the physician.[51] In another case, a Maryland hospital and nurse settled a claim arising out of mismatched blood.[52] A physician ordered the nurse to get another unit of Rh negative blood for a 15-year-old female victim of an auto accident. The nurse mistakenly picked up a unit of Rh positive blood and gave the patient 0.5cc before detecting the error and stopping. The patient had an itching rash for half an hour and was permanently sensitized so any pregnancy would be more complicated.

Wrong Dose. A North Carolina patient attempted to prove that damage to his hand and skin was caused by an excessive dose of potassium chloride through an intravenous line into his hand.[53] The trial judge refused to allow a nurse trained in

IV therapy to testify concerning the cause of damage, so the patient did not have expert testimony concerning causation, and the hospital won. The appellate court ruled that the nurse should have been permitted to testify and ordered a new trial.

An Alaska case involving an overdose illustrates the defense of the statute of limitations.[54] A nurse mistakenly administered an overdose of lidocaine, causing a cardiac arrest. Upon directions of a physician, hospital records were altered to delete references to the overdose. Despite this cover-up attempt, another physician told the patient's family about the overdose two days later. The physician who attempted to cover up was suspended from the hospital staff. This was reported in detail in the newspaper, including the reasons and the patient's last name. Normally statutes of limitation do not apply during periods of cover-ups. The court ruled that the statute of limitations began to apply when the newspaper reports appeared. Since the suit was not filed for more than two years after that, and the time limit for malpractice suits in Alaska is two years, the suit was barred. Since newspaper reports such as these are rare, it is never advisable to attempt a cover-up; cover-ups only extend the exposure to liability.

Wrong Route. Medications can be given orally; by injection into a vein, the skin, or a muscle; or by application to the surface of the skin, as well as by other means. When drugs are given by the wrong route, injuries and liability can result.

A Kansas hospital was held liable when a nurse used a needle that was too short to inject dramamine into the hip of a large patient.[55] Since the needle was too short, the drug was injected subcutaneously rather than the intended intramuscular route. The injection caused a painful odoriferous wound and recurring back pain. A New York hospital was held liable when a licensed practical nurse who was attempting to inject penicillin intramuscularly accidently pierced a vein, injecting the drug into the blood stream.[56] The patient died from anaphylactic shock.

Wrong Time. Another type of error is a delay in administering a prescribed medication. Most minor delays will not have serious consequences but sometimes the results can be substantial. A 1979 Utah case resulted when a nurse did not administer a psychiatric medication until 10 p.m. although it had been ordered to be given immediately at 8 p.m. At 2:40 a.m. the patient broke a window of his room on the sixth floor and jumped to a roof five stories below. He was permanently paralyzed. The trial court granted summary judgment for the defendants. The Utah Supreme Court ruled that the jury should have been permitted to decide whether the delay contributed to the jump.[57]

An Illinois hospital was sued for the death of a 14-month-old child from measles.[58] The nurse's two-hour delay in administering prescribed medications was one of the grounds of the suit. There was conflicting testimony whether this contributed to the death and whether it was a deviation from the standard of care, since other medications were given just before the two hours began. The jury ruled in favor of the defendants.

Injections

Injections can lead to liability for all of the reasons discussed in the medication errors and sterile technique sections plus other reasons unique to injections.

A frequent source of liability is damage to the sciatic nerve during injections in the buttocks. For example, an Oregon hospital was held liable in 1980 for a Nembutal injection by a nurse that injured the sciatic nerve.[59]

A California court ruled that the jury could apply *res ipsa loquitur* to a case involving wrist drop that resulted from an injection in the arm by a nurse in a physician's office.[60]

In 1982 a federal appeals court was presented with an unusual case involving an outpatient hemodialysis facility and its nursing supervisor.[61] A patient had used abusive, disruptive, and threatening language with the staff and used an extension phone to eavesdrop on the nursing supervisor's telephone calls. When his dialysis was completed, the nursing supervisor had disconnected him from the machine, called him a "black son of a bitch," and left the dialysis needles in his arm. He refused all offers of assistance from other staff personnel, left the facility and later removed the needles himself with substantial loss of blood. Staff members at the facility testified that it was not unusual for the needles not to be removed immediately and for other staff members to do so later. The court discounted this testimony because the nursing supervisor's actions were associated with name-calling, indicating unprofessional conduct. The court held the facility liable despite the extreme provocation by the patient, but allocated 40 percent of the fault to the patient because he had refused other assistance, so the patient received payment for only 60 percent of his damages.

Sterile Technique

In the past, courts found hospitals liable for infections when the patient proved they had unsanitary conditions. With improvements in infection control and in determining types and sources of infections, courts increasingly have recognized that nurses, physicians, and hospitals cannot guarantee the absence of infections and that infections do occur for many reasons other than negligence. Thus, most courts require proof of a causal relationship between the infection and a deviation from proper practices.

A hospital in Washington State was held liable for a staphylococcus infection because the patient proved that nurses failed to take the necessary precautions, such as handwashing, to avoid cross-infection from the other patient in the semi-private room who was infected with the same organism.[62] The patient who suffered the cross-infection recently had undergone hip surgery and the infection entered his hip, requiring its fusing into a nearly immovable position.

A jury found a New York hospital liable for the loss of a patient's eye from an infection after a nurse put over the eye a patch that had fallen on the floor.[63]

However, the judge overruled the jury because there was no evidence that that particular type of infection could be transmitted by the patch.

In the past, there frequently were suits when nurses failed to sterilize needles and other equipment.[64] The use of presterilized supplies has reduced both the risk to the patient and the liability exposure. If a patient is infected by a presterilized item, the manufacturer usually will bear the liability unless the item was contaminated by negligent conduct of the nurse or other health professionals or there was a pattern of infection that should have led to discontinuance of use of the supply of the item.

For example, a Georgia physician was found not liable for an infection because an office nurse had properly used a prepackaged, presterilized needle and syringe.[65] However, an Iowa surgeon was held liable for a patient's infection from contaminated sutures because he knew they were contaminated when he used them since an earlier patient had become infected through use of sutures from the same supply.[66]

Catheterization

Improper insertion or removal of catheters and failure to catheterize a patient have led to negligence suits. A Utah patient had a series of catheterizations after a hysterectomy.[67] When a nurse performed the 12th catheterization, the patient experienced pain and later the urine bag filled with blood. There was conflicting testimony concerning the cause of the injury, with one expert saying it could be from a hematoma from the surgery. The jury decided that causation was not proved and ruled in favor of the defendants.

A Florida hospital was held liable when a nurse removed a Foley catheter without first deflating the cup, resulting in bladder damage.[68] An Oklahoma court ruled that a hospital could be liable for the refusal of nurses to catheterize a patient for 22 hours, despite repeated requests from the person.[69] Stitches from a prior operation tore and the bladder fell.

Foreign Objects

When foreign objects such as sponges or surgical instruments are left in patients during surgery, there usually is liability. As discussed in Chapter 6, most courts apply the doctrine of *res ipsa loquitur* to such cases. Thus, liability is avoided only when the defendants can show that the injury was not caused by negligence. For example, if the patient has to be quickly closed in an emergency, the failure to make an instrument or sponge count can be justified.

Most foreign object cases center on whether the hospital or surgeon is liable. It is generally recognized that a nurse is responsible for the count of the sponges and instruments. A California court held that a hospital could be liable for a clamp left in a patient even though it was not local practice at that time (1956) to take a count.[70] The court ruled that hospitals should require counts by their nurses.

The hospital, as employer of the nurse, is generally liable in foreign object cases. In the past, the surgeon often was liable as captain of the ship but today generally is liable only when exercising specific control or personally making errors. For example, a Missouri doctor was held not liable, while the hospital was held liable, for a laparotomy sponge left after a gall bladder operation.[71] The court ruled that the injury resulted from the failure of the circulating nurse to announce the sponge count correctly. The surgeon had not exercised specific control and could not do so without violating proper sterile technique. (The interrelationship of the liability of the nurse, hospital, and surgeon in the operating room is discussed further in the nurse-anesthetist section of this chapter.)

Incubators

Infants have burned and overheated in incubators. A Georgia court ruled that a hospital could be sued when an infant was burned in an incubator.[72] The nurse placed the infant so that a foot was in contact with a preheating electric light bulb. Severe burns required amputation of most of the foot. The court noted that liability could be based on failure to turn off the preheating bulb and on the incorrect positioning of the infant.

In another case, an infant became extremely overheated in an incubator, was dehydrated, and experienced convulsions and twitching.[73] A few days after discharge, the infant developed central nervous system disorders, cerebral palsy, and mental retardation. When the suit was decided more than 20 years later, the jury decided in favor of the defendants, probably because there was testimony that the patient's condition was caused by prenatal injuries, not the overheated incubator.

Although incubator design has changed, nurses still need to be aware of potential risks to infants and to take appropriate steps to reduce those risks.

Restraints and Falls

Nurses have a responsibility to provide proper attention for disoriented, disabled, and mentally ill patients. This frequently includes a duty to restrain or provide proper attendance. Although some emergency restraints may be applied temporarily, based on nursing judgment, most restraints—especially for extended periods—require a physician's order. Such orders provide substantial protection for the nurse, as discussed earlier, if the order is carried out nonnegligently.

Liability generally arises after patients fall or escape and injure themselves or others. Courts frequently take the position that juries do not need expert testimony to establish what the nurse should have done; juries are allowed to apply common sense.

Leaving a patient in a risky situation without an attendant or proper restraint has led to suits and liability. A Louisiana hospital was held liable when a patient fell, lacerating his penis, after a nurse left him unattended in a bathroom.[74] The court held he should have been attended because he was drugged and had previously had an arm amputated. A North Carolina court ruled that a hospital and nurse's aide could be liable for leaving a patient unattended on a bed pan in an armchair, even though the absence was for only four minutes for the purpose of patient privacy.[75] The armchair was not in reach of a call buzzer. The patient fell, breaking a hip. The court ruled that expert testimony concerning the standard of care was necessary, and that expert testimony from a nurse was sufficient.

Courts are especially critical when they believe the nurse has left the patient unattended to do something considered less important. An Ohio hospital was held liable when a patient fell from a bed in the labor room.[76] The patient was under sedation, restless, and repeatedly attempting to climb out of bed. The nurse left the room briefly to do some charting, then agreed to accompany a physician to see another patient since hospital rules prohibited physicians from attending a woman in labor unless a nurse was present.

A Texas hospital was held liable when a patient fell from an emergency room table.[77] The nurse was busy having the father of the patient sign papers and refused to respond when the patient started to turn white and vomit. The patient fainted and fell to the floor, breaking two teeth, fracturing a thumb, suffering a concussion, and bruising a shoulder. The court criticized the nurse for being more attentive to forms than to the patient.

When nurses remove ordered restraints they need to be particularly careful to assure attendance. A Wisconsin court ruled that a hospital could be liable when a patient fell, breaking his hip, after a nurse removed his restraint and left him unattended.[78] The nurse had removed the restraint to permit the patient to feed himself. The court ruled that expert testimony was not necessary to establish the need for restraints since the patient was confused and irrational.

The nurse does not have to be present continuously when the patient does not need an attendant. In cases when the need is marginal, the request of the patient to be left alone may excuse the nurse from liability. An elderly patient refused assistance from a nurse while disrobing in a Connecticut physician's office.[79] While the nurse was waiting a few feet away in an adjacent room, the patient fell. The jury found the defendant physician not liable because the patient had refused assistance, there was no physician order requiring an attendant, and the patient demanded to be left alone.

Failure to provide a patient with a signaling device and failure to respond to a signal can lead to liability. A Florida court ruled that a hospital and nurse could be liable for a fall in an emergency room.[80] The patient presented with chest pains, was given medications, and was left lying for nearly two hours on a stretcher in an empty room without a signaling device. When nurses did not respond to his oral calls, he attempted to go to the bathroom unassisted and fell, injuring himself. A Louisiana hospital was found liable when nurses failed to respond to a call light for

15 minutes.[81] A drugged patient attempted to go to a bathroom unassisted and fell, suffering a compression fracture of the vertebra.

There can be liability when restraints are not applied properly. An example concerning a patient restrained during surgery is discussed in the earlier section on patient positioning.[82] Another example is an Arizona case in which a hospital was found liable when a patient struck another patient with a chair.[83] The assailant extricated himself from restraints five times, and the incident occurred after the fifth escape. The court ruled that no expert testimony was needed to prove that properly applied restraints should have precluded multiple escapes.

Patient Instructions

Some interventions require cooperation of or special care by the patient, for which nurses need to give appropriate instructions. However, if proper instructions are given to a competent patient who does not follow them, liability is unlikely unless proper nursing care calls for additional precautions that are omitted.

An Indiana physician ordered a 24-hour urine collection that required all the urine to be transferred into a jug with hydrochloric acid.[84] There was conflicting evidence whether the nurse advised the patient how to safely collect the urine and pour it into the jug through a funnel. The patient voided directly into the jug and the acid reacted, burning his penis. The jury believed the nurse had provided appropriate instructions so it found no liability.

EVALUATION

Evaluation is the review and documentation of the effect of the intervention step to assure it is completed properly. If further action may be warranted, the nurse returns to the assessment step. Although important, the evaluation step itself seldom leads to liability; liability arises from failure to perform a proper assessment or failure to carry out proper intervention.

For example, a California nurse detected problems when evaluating the effects of an intravenous infection.[85] Her assessment included observation of increased swelling and redness in the area of the intravenous tube. She notified the physician several times of the swelling but he ordered continuation of the procedure. There was conflicting testimony at the trial concerning (a) whether the nurse had communicated the seriousness of the swelling when it became markedly worse and (b) whether the nurse had the authority to discontinue the intravenous infusion without a physician's order. The court overturned the trial court's decision in favor of the hospital and physician and ordered a new trial so a jury could determine these issues. In this case, the potential liability arose from the assessment and intervention phases, not the evaluation. Today a nurse confronted with this situation would either (1) discontinue the procedure if authorized to do so by institutional policy or (2) follow the institutional procedure for reporting apparently erroneous orders.

SUPERVISORS

Because the nursing supervisor is not the employer of the nurses supervised, *respondeat superior* does not impose liability on the supervisor for the negligent acts of those people supervised. Supervisors will be held liable for their own negligent acts or omissions and the employer will be held liable for the supervisor's negligence under *respondeat superior*.

Generally, a nursing supervisor will be held liable for negligent acts of supervision. Liability also can be imposed on a supervisor who is negligent in providing care while assisting in patient treatment on a unit she supervises. For example, in one case, the superintendent of the hospital was acting as a circulating nurse in the operating room when she applied straps to the patient's feet so tightly that circulation was cut off and the patient developed gangrenous sores.[86] The patient successfully sued the hospital and the nurse as an individual for negligence. In another case a nursing supervisor whose duties included covering the emergency room as a staff nurse was held by the court to be acting as a hospital employee when she administered an injection to a patient in the emergency room.[87]

The liability of a supervising nurse was involved in another case in which a needle was left in a patient's abdomen during surgery and discovered after the operation had been completed.[88] The patient brought suit against the surgeons, the hospital, a nurse, and the nursing supervisor of the operating room.

The court dismissed the suit against the nursing supervisor saying, ''It appears that she, as supervisor of the operating rooms, assigned two competent nurses to attend the operation, that she was not present at the operation or any other place with the plaintiff, and she had no control or custody of plaintiff. Furthermore, she was acting as a supervisory employee of the hospital in assigning the nurses and she . . . would not be liable by reason of the assignment.'' The court ruled that the doctrine of *respondeat superior* is not applicable to the relationship between a supervisor and subordinate employees.

Another case that illustrates the potential liability of a nursing supervisor was decided by a Canadian court in British Columbia.[89] The court found both the supervising nurse and her employer, the hospital, liable for injuries to a woman who was not observed often enough in a postoperative recovery room. The patient had a cholecystectomy without complications and was transferred to the recovery room. The hospital had provided two staff nurses for the area, which the court accepted as adequate staffing, but the supervising nurse permitted one nurse to leave for a coffee break just before three patients were admitted. One of the patients suffered a respiratory obstruction that was not observed until the lack of oxygen caused permanent brain damage.

The court ruled that the supervising nurse was liable for permitting the other nurse to leave the area at a time when she knew that the operating schedule would result in several admissions to the unit. The court said that even if she had not known the operating schedule she still would be liable for not knowing the aspects of the schedule that applied to the staffing needs of the area she supervised. Since the supervising nurse also provided direct care to the patients in the area, she also was liable for failing to personally observe the patient more frequently.

The court also ruled that the nurse who left the area would have been liable had she been included in the suit because she should have known the aspects of the operating schedule that applied to the staffing needs of the area in which she worked. The hospital also was liable for the acts of both nurses under the doctrine of *respondeat superior*.

Two years later, a similar case was decided in the same province in Canada.[90] A 10-year-old boy who had undergone plastic surgery for overprominent ears suffered a cardiac arrest resulting in a permanent coma for over four years until his death. The cardiac arrest occurred in the postanesthesia area while three of the five nurses assigned to the area were on a coffee break. The hospital was found liable for negligence for the same reasons described in the earlier case.

In a New York case a patient who had been disoriented was found on a balcony outside a second-story window.[91] After the patient was returned to the hospital room, a physician told the staff to arrange to have the person watched. The charge nurse called the patient's family to tell them to arrange to have someone do so. The family said someone would be at the hospital in 10 or 15 minutes. By the time the family member arrived, the patient had fallen out the window and was seriously injured.

The hospital was found liable for failing to remove the patient to a secure room, apply additional restraints, or find someone to watch the patient for the 15 minutes. There was one charge nurse, one new registered nurse in orientation, one practical nurse, and one aide on a unit with 19 patients. The court found that all except the aide had been engaged in routine duties that could have been delayed for 15 minutes, and that the aide had been permitted to leave for supper during the period. The court said this was evidence that there was sufficient staffing to provide continuous supervision for a patient in known danger for 15 minutes. The failure of the supervising nurse to properly allocate the time of the available staff was one of the grounds for the hospital's being held liable.

In a 1942 California case, the hospital was held liable for the death of a patient from tetanus following a successful hernia operation.[92] Evidence showed that the patient had demonstrated symptoms of tetanus for some time, the supervisory nurse and other nursing staff knew of the symptoms, and none of them had reported the symptoms. The court said that for a supervisory nurse to knowingly permit a patient recovering from a major operation to suffer symptoms indicating a growing pathology for three days merely because the attending physicians were not available amounted to negligence.

In summary, a supervisor can be held liable if:

1. The supervisor assigns a subordinate to do something the supervisor knows or should know the person is unable to do.
2. The supervisor does not provide the subordinate the degree of supervision the supervisor knows or should know is needed.
3. The supervisor is present and fails to take action when possible to avoid an injury.
4. The supervisor does not properly allocate the time of available staff, for example by permitting breaks from areas where there are critical needs at times when the supervisor knows or should know that the staff will be needed.

STUDENT NURSES

Student nurses will be held liable for their own acts of negligence committed in the course of clinical experiences. If they are performing duties that are within the scope of professional nursing, they will be held to the same standard of skill and competence as registered professional nurses. A lower standard of care will not be applied to the actions of nursing students. To fulfill their responsibilities to their patients and to minimize exposure to liability, nursing students should make sure that they are properly prepared to care for assigned patients and should ask for additional help or supervision if they feel inadequately prepared for an assignment.

A nursing instructor is responsible for assigning students to the care of patients and for exercising reasonable supervision over the students. The instructor could be held liable for injuries that resulted from the assignment to a patient of a student who is not competent and prepared for the assignment or from the instructor's failure to supervise the student's performance adequately.

Traditionally, cases arising from the negligent acts of student nurses resulted in their being treated as employees of the hospital, which was held liable under *respondeat superior*. In a 1921 case, two student nurses volunteered to work in the pediatric ward to care for a 2½-year-old child.[93] No trained nurses were available to provide special nursing services for the child because of an influenza epidemic. The child was having difficulty breathing and a lighted vaporizer containing alcohol and eucalyptus oil was placed in the bed. One of the students left the child unattended for a few minutes and when she returned the bed was in flames. The child died a few hours later. The court held that, even though the student was acting voluntarily, the hospital's authorization of her actions amounted to an assignment and she was acting within the scope of employment. The hospital was found liable for damages resulting from the child's death.

Several other cases imposed liability for the actions of students. In a 1954 case, parents were awarded damages for their infant's death when a student nurse placed an unshielded light bulb two inches from the blankets in the crib.[94] Later, when the student checked the baby, the crib was in flames. In a 1962 case, a student failed to heed a warning on a medication vial to the effect that the drug was for intravenous use only and injected the medication into a baby's buttock, resulting in serious injury.[95] The parents sued the child's physician and received an out-of-court settlement.

Failure to provide a student with reasonable supervision also can be the basis for liability. In a 1957 case the court ordered an osteopathic hospital to pay damages to a patient who had been injured by a student.[96] The patient had gone to a clinic for evaluation and treatment of back problems. A student, attempting to treat the patient without supervision, struck him in the back, precipitating a ruptured disk. The court said that a student in a clinical situation must be given reasonable guidance and supervision.

Today, most nursing students would not be considered employees of the agencies in which they receive clinical experience since associate and baccalaureate degree programs generally contract with agencies to provide student experiences. However, nursing students probably will continue to be viewed as agents of hospitals and other agencies (such as public health agencies) when participating in patient care at the hospital. Thus, future cases involving the liability of students probably will hold both the hospital or agency and the educational institution potentially liable for students' actions.

Students should expect to satisfy requirements of both the college and the agency during clinical experiences and to comply with the policies of each agency in which clinical experiences are obtained. When a nurse employed by the hospital or other agency accepts responsibility to supervise a nursing student, even for a short time, the nurse becomes a supervisor and has the liability exposure described in the earlier section on supervisors. If no one else is supervising a student and a nurse permits a student to aid in the care of a patient, that nurse usually will be considered to have accepted the responsibility of supervising. It is advisable that the nursing staff on any unit where students are in training clarify the roles of the student, instructor, and staff nurse in the care of each patient to assure that appropriate supervision actually is provided.

NURSING SPECIALTIES

Nurses who claim to be specialists in a particular area generally are expected to meet the higher standard of care of specialists when providing such services. The most common types of nursing specialists in practice are nurse anesthetists, nurse practitioners, and nurse midwives.

Nurse Anesthetists

It is not surprising that there has been more litigation involving nurse anesthetists than any other subspecialty because of the high risks associated with anesthesia and their longer recognition as specialists. A nurse anesthetist is a registered nurse who has completed a program of clinical training in planning anesthesia, administering anesthetic agents, and monitoring the anesthetized patient. Nurse anesthetists have several practice arrangements, including employment by a hospital or by an anesthesiologist, or a practice made up exclusively of nurse anesthetists.

The earliest reported cases involving nurse anesthetists focused on whether the administration of anesthetics by a specially trained nurse constituted the practice of medicine. A 1917 Kentucky case held that a nurse anesthetist who was employed by a physician and administered anesthetics under the doctor's direction was not practicing medicine within the meaning of the state medical practice statute.[97] A 1936 California case reached a similar result.[98] The court held that a nurse anesthetist was not practicing medicine without a license since she was not diagnosing or prescribing and her actions were under the control of the surgeon. In a 1938 case involving interpretation of an Arizona law that allowed a nurse anesthetist to administer anesthesia under the direction of a surgeon, the court included dental surgeons in the meaning of the statute.[99]

The Question of Liability

There has been considerable litigation on allocating liability for negligent acts of nurse anesthetists. They clearly are liable for the results of their own negligence but the legal question has been: Who also is liable? There have been four general results: (1) the nurse anesthetist's employer has been liable under the principle of *respondeat superior*; (2) the surgeon has been liable under the "captain of the ship" doctrine or for the surgeon's personal negligence; (3) both the employer and the surgeon have been liable under the dual servant doctrine; or (4) only the nurse anesthetist has been liable.

When nurse anesthetists are employees, the employer generally will be liable for the results of their negligence under *respondeat superior*. For example, several anesthesiologists were ordered to pay $500,000 for the death of a patient when a nurse anesthetist they employed failed to call for assistance when she had problems ventilating a patient.[100] Similarly, a California hospital was found liable for the death of a child because of errors by a nurse anesthetist it employed who gave the child too much ether during a tonsillectomy.[101]

In the past, when charitable hospitals were exempt from liability, several courts imposed liability on the surgeon for injuries caused by nurse anesthetists employed by the hospital. The courts reasoned that the surgeon was like the "captain of the ship" during the operation and was legally accountable for all actions of the operating crew, including the nurse anesthetist. The courts said that the hospital had loaned the nurse to the surgeon and as a loaned servant or borrowed servant was in effect an employee of the surgeon, not the hospital, for purposes of liability.[102]

Today courts seldom use the captain of the ship doctrine. The surgeon generally is liable only under the general principles applicable to supervisors unless the surgeon actually employs the anesthetist. The surgeon is liable only for personally doing something wrong. For example, an Illinois court ruled that a jury could find a surgeon liable for his personal decisions concerning draping the patient and not remaining in the room until the patient resumed breathing.[103] The court ruled that the surgeon was not automatically liable for the actions of the nurse anesthetist who was a hospital employee.

Similarly, the Ohio Supreme Court ruled that a surgeon could be liable for the actions of a nurse anesthetist when the surgeon "does control or realistically possesses the right to control events and procedures."[104] The court held that there could have been sufficient control in the case because the surgeon had instructed, assisted, and watched the anesthetist intubate the patient prior to a laminectomy.

When sufficient actual control is not possessed or exercised, courts that apply this approach rule in favor of the surgeon. A New Jersey court overturned a judgment against a surgeon, ruling that it was valid only against the employing hospital because the surgeon did not exercise sufficient control to be responsible for injuries to the mother's teeth and mouth due to intubation during childbirth.[105]

A few courts rule that both the surgeon and the employer can be liable under the dual servant doctrine. They reason that both have sufficient control over the activities of the nurse through either direct supervision or through policies and procedures so that each should be legally accountable.[106]

Sole Liability

There are three situations in which nurse anesthetists may not have anyone with whom to share liability: (1) when they are self-employed and the court determines the surgeon has not exercised sufficient control to have assumed responsibility, (2) when their employer is immune from liability, or (3) when the patient decides to sue only the nurse anesthetists.

In a 1981 Louisiana case a nurse anesthetist had attempted a nasal intubation that failed, resulting in the death of the patient. The family settled with the nurse anesthetist's insurer for $264,728. The family then sued the surgeon, but the court ruled in his favor because it found he had not exercised sufficient control.[107]

In a 1976 North Carolina case a newborn was burned by a hot water bottle that was under the control of a nurse anesthetist.[108] The court held that the surgeon was not liable because he had not been in control of the heating and was not aware of the problem. The court also ruled that the hospital was immune because it was a charitable institution. This left the nurse as the only defendant. Charitable immunity has since been eliminated in North Carolina and nearly all other states but it still is possible for governmental hospitals in some states to be protected by sovereign immunity.

When both the nurse anesthetist and someone else are sued for the negligence of the former, if the court holds that the nurse is not liable then it cannot find the other defendants liable for the nurse's actions. Of course, the other defendants still could be found liable for their own acts of negligence. In a 1969 Virginia case a patient had died of a stomach rupture because of insufflation of gas.[109] The jury found that the nurse anesthetist had not been negligent and thus not liable. The court ruled that since the jury had exonerated the nurse, the hospital employer could not be liable for the acts of the nurse. There was no evidence of another basis for hospital liability, so the plaintiff lost the case.

In some cases, the patient chooses to sue only the employer. In a 1982 Missouri case, the patient dropped the claim against the nurse and sued only the hospital. The jury decided that the hospital owed $4 million but the judgment was reversed on a technicality concerning the trial procedure.[110]

Some plaintiffs have attempted to convince courts that it is negligent for a hospital to permit nurse anesthetists to provide anesthesia services. Their position has been that all anesthesia should be provided by anesthesiologists. Courts have uniformly rejected this position.[111] It is proper to permit properly trained nurse anesthetists to administer anesthesia to most patients under appropriate supervision.

Nurse Anesthetist and Physician Roles

Some cases have made a clear distinction between the roles of nurse anesthetists and physicians and analyzed the duties separately for purposes of liability. In one case the court said it is customary for the physician to rely on the anesthetist for the selection and administration of drugs and that the statute that authorized nurse anesthetist practice did not require constant direct supervision by a physician.[112] In another case, the court distinguished between matters of judgment that were exclusively the concern of the physician and those within the duties of the nurse anesthetist.[113]

When the physician turns the care of the patient over to the nurse anesthetist, the latter will be liable for any injuries that result from acts that occur while the patient is under the nurse's control. In one case a nurse anesthetist was found liable for negligently monitoring anesthesia of a patient undergoing a tonsillectomy when the doctor was called out of the room.[114]

The nurse anesthetist also will be held liable for negligence in basic nursing care functions such as reporting, monitoring, and maintaining patient safety. For example, the employer of a nurse anesthetist was held liable for damages when she failed to inform a nurse who was inserting a catheter in the patient's arm that the patient was under "light" anesthesia.[115] The patient moved his arm when the catheter was inserted, the catheter broke in the arm, and he developed carpal tunnel syndrome. In another case, a nurse anesthetist was held liable for burns sustained by a newborn patient when she failed to monitor the temperature of water being used to warm the patient.[116]

The standard of care for nurse anesthetists was described in a 1980 Michigan case.[117] The court said that nurse anesthetists are professionals who have expertise in an area akin to the practice of medicine. Because their responsibilities are greater than those of general duty nurses, and because those responsibilities lie in an area of "medical" expertise, the standard of care is based on the skill and care normally expected of those with the same education and training.

The standard of care for nurse anesthetists was held to be a national standard in a 1982 Alabama case[118] in which the nurse had trouble ventilating a patient but did not call for assistance. Expert testimony attempted to show the nurse complied with the standard of care for the city—Mobile. The court said that the local and national standards were the same and that the failure of the nurse anesthetist to call for assistance when she first realized there was a problem was a departure from the accepted standard of care in the national medical community.

A critical element for nurse anesthetists is the duty to seek assistance from a supervising physician when the situation demands it. Other areas in which they must exercise reasonable care are the selection of anesthetic agents, administration of anesthesia, monitoring the patient, maintaining safety precautions on behalf of the patient, communicating with the surgeon about the anesthetic agent being used, and performing procedures.

Nurse Practitioners

Several cases involving nurse practitioners have addressed both negligence and scope of practice issues. In a 1980 case a patient brought suit against a physician and a nurse practitioner.[119] The patient had a Dalkon Shield intrauterine contraceptive device implanted in 1972. In June of 1974 she read an article concerning the shield and subsequently consulted her doctor about the risks of pregnancy and infection that the article had described. The doctor advised her that he knew of no risks associated with the device. Several months later, in mid-April, 1975, the patient began to experience a foul vaginal odor. She called the Harvard Health Plan for an appointment and was told by a nurse practitioner to douche with yogurt. A little over a week later the patient called again complaining of intense abdominal pain. The nurse practitioner told the patient that she probably had the flu and to call back if she developed a fever. On April 30, when the patient kept a scheduled appointment with the plan she could hardly walk. She was given antibiotics and her Dalkon Shield was removed. When she returned on May 2, multiple abscesses were diagnosed and she underwent a total hysterectomy three days later.

The patient offered testimony by an expert as evidence of negligence. The expert had considerable experience working with a supervising nurse practioner. The expert stated that the doctor and nurse practitioner were under a continuing obligation to inform the patient of the risks known to be associated with the Dalkon Shield. Failure of the physician to inform the patient in June of 1974 probably determined the patient's retention of the device and contributed to the development of the infection.

The expert said that the nurse's management of the patient in April clearly was in error, her recommendations being substandard and inappropriate. The delay in scheduling diagnosis and treatment constituted substandard care, and the delay was the factor that caused the need for a total hysterectomy. The patient's expert said articles published in both professional journals and the lay press had analyzed problems with the Dalkon Shield. The court found that the expert testimony created sufficient question about the adequacy of care to warrant a trial. The case was remanded for trial.

An interesting feature of this case was the expert's testimony that it was difficult to evaluate the situation because the records were ''sketchy.'' The court said it was difficult to determine how sketchy the records were because many of them were totally illegible. Nurse practitioners, like other health care providers, should keep complete, legible records of patient visits and telephone counseling.

A 1981 California case addressed the standard of care for nurse practitioners.[120] A 34-year-old man noticed chest pains several times in a four-day period. He made an appointment at the Kaiser Health Plan and was examined by a nurse practitioner. After taking a history and examining the patient, the nurse gave him a prescription for valium and told him he was suffering from muscle spasms. The following morning the patient awoke with severe chest pains and went to the emergency room, where he was given pain medication and again told that he was having muscle spasms. Later that day he returned to the emergency room where an electrocardiograph showed that he had suffered a heart attack. The patient sued the health care provider, alleging that his condition should have been diagnosed earlier and that earlier diagnosis would have reduced the residual effect of the heart attack, which included a reduced life expectancy.

The trial court instructed the jury that the standard of care required of a nurse practitioner is the same as that of a physician. On appeal, the nurse practitioner claimed that this instruction was erroneous and the Court of Appeals agreed that the standard of care required of a nurse practitioner is not the same as for a physician. However, the court said this was a ''harmless error'' because the patient had sued the employer, not the nurse individually. The employer was responsible for satisfying the standard of care of a physician when a patient was treated in the clinic even though the care actually was provided by a nurse practitioner.

Another case alleging negligence of a nurse practitioner involved telephone consulting of an injured patient.[121] A woman who had stepped on a thumb tack causing a puncture wound in the ball of her foot was treated in an emergency room. Three days later her daughter phoned a clinic and told the nurse practitioner on duty that the toes on her mother's foot were turning purple, there was redness around the purple areas, the flesh around the toes was very white, and her mother was very cold. The nurse practitioner allegedly told the daughter "not to worry, that purple was a good color." Four days after this conversation, the mother underwent amputation of two toes.

The mother sued, alleging that the nurse practitioner was negligent in undertaking to provide a medical diagnosis and recommendation, failing to recognize obvious symptoms of infection and gangrene, failing to refer her to a physician, and giving inappropriate instructions concerning her condition. She also sued the clinic, claiming that it was negligent in: (1) failing to maintain adequate supervision and control over its employees, (2) failing to establish appropriate standard operating procedures to correct misinformation, and (3) failing to ensure that its personnel were trained to recognize ailments or trained to be aware of their inability to recognize such elements.

While the court dismissed the case on procedural grounds, the facts raise significant issues of negligence by nurse practitioners. It is clear that they should be very careful in their responses during telephone consultations and should keep accurate records documenting the occurrence of calls and the advice given. Agencies that employ nurse practitioners also should have guidelines to direct them in their handling of such calls.

There is one reported case of a nurse practitioner's license being suspended for treating patients without a physician's supervision.[122] The court upheld the suspension for treating two patients by providing medication to one and therapy for the other. Nurse practitioners should be familiar with their permitted scope of practice to avoid liability to their patients and to retain their licenses.

Nurse Midwives

Midwifery became a regulated, legally recognized profession in some states in the early 1900s. Prior to that time it was practiced by women who learned about birth from other women and their own experiences and often practiced without compensation in areas where there were no other health care providers. The first nurse midwifery education program was opened by the Maternity Association in New York City in 1952; currently, 25 university-affiliated programs are accredited by the American College of Nurse Midwifery.

The practice of nurse midwifery is not clearly illegal anywhere, although in at least one jurisdiction (North Dakota) there is an apparent conflict in the laws. In North Dakota the state's medical practice act defines the practice of medicine as "the practice of medicine, surgery, and obstetrics," and is open to restrictive interpretation. The state's nurse practice act is permissive, as the section which prohibited diagnosis and treatment was deleted. Authorization for the practice of nurse midwifery may be found in nurse practice acts, medical practice acts, rules and regulations pertaining to nursing or midwives, public health laws, allied health laws or separate nurse midwife practice acts. Depending on the jurisdiction, various state agencies may have regulatory authority over nurse midwives.

Midwifery practice includes the independent management of essentially normal newborns and women for prenatal, intrapartum, postpartum, and gynecological care in a system that provides for medical consultation and collaborative management or referral.[123] Generally, state regulations permit the full range of practice, although there have been legislative attempts to limit or restrict nurse midwifery practice in several states. For example, in 1981, restrictive regulations that would limit nurse midwives' practice were proposed, but not adopted, in Kentucky and Maryland. The New Jersey Board of Medical Examiners tried unsuccessfully to limit nurse midwives' scope of practice. These initiatives are the result of several factors, including limited supply and public awareness of the role of the nurse midwife. It is likely that other attempts to restrict the practice of nurse midwives will occur, through attempts to limit the scope of practice, denial of hospital privilege, or denial of reimbursement.

The earliest cases addressed the question of whether midwifery constituted the practice of medicine. An 1894 Illinois case sought to penalize a midwife for practicing medicine without a license.[124] The court ruled that the midwife was practicing in violation of the medical practice act. It said that midwifery was an important part of medicine and was recognized as such in the medical practice act, and that people who engaged in the practice of midwifery should possess special knowledge and skill. Subsequently, midwives worked to establish a clear legal status for their practice, including the licensure of lay midwives who are not registered nurses.[125]

Liability of nurse midwives is based on patient injuries resulting from their negligent actions. In a 1925 case, a midwife was attending a patient after delivery.[126] The patient suffered a seizure and a physician was called. The doctor ordered that hot water bottles and flatirons be placed on the patient, and the midwife carried out the orders. The patient was burned and sued the physician.

The court, affirming a judgment that the doctor was not negligent, said: "Mrs. Frost was a woman of 12 years' experience as a midwife who had been employed by plaintiff's husband to attend her at this time. Wrapping the irons so they would not burn and so the wrappings would remain in place required no professional skill. Mrs. Frost or any person of common intelligence and experience was competent to do it. It cannot be said that the doctor was guilty of negligence in trusting Mrs. Frost to perform this service and in relying on her to perform it properly." In effect, the court said that a physician would not be liable for the actions of a midwife that should have been governed by common sense.

There have been several recent criminal indictments of unlicensed midwives for manslaughter following the deaths of newborns whose births they attended. In addition, there have also been actions brought against unlicensed midwives for the unauthorized practice of medicine.

To protect themselves from liability, nurse midwives should first be sure that they are properly licensed and practicing as legally defined by statute or rule. They must familiarize themselves with the regulations that govern midwife practice in their jurisdiction. In a negligence action, they will be held to the standard of care of other reasonable, competent nurse midwives. As a practical matter, physicians probably will provide the expert testimony on the standard of care.

A significant element in the duty of a nurse midwife is to refer a patient who requires medical care or to seek assistance when complications arise. The failure to do so in a timely manner may be the basis for a negligence action, as well as put the nurse midwife in the position of having to act beyond the permissible scope of practice in the course of providing care. Criminal and civil liability may be imposed on a nurse midwife who is found guilty of the unauthorized practice of medicine.

SCHOOL NURSES

Most school nurses are employed by a state department of education or a local school board. Their general duties include health screening, recordkeeping, planning and implementing health education programs, first aid, and prevention of injuries. The duties also may be described in rules or regulations promulgated by the local or county board of education. These should be examined regularly to ensure that they are consistent with the state's nurse practice act.

School nurses should have approved procedures for situations that occur frequently. They generally will be held liable for acts of negligence but their employer also will be liable for damages under the doctrine of *respondeat superior* unless the school nurse-employee was acting outside the scope of the prescribed duties.

School nurses cannot make a medical diagnosis and cannot prescribe medications. The importance of this rule, while it may seem overly restrictive, is clear when the consequences of incorrect diagnosis or medications are considered. School nurses should seek a statement from their employer detailing the extent, scope, and limitations on their practice as well as the extent of liability insurance coverage extended by the employer.

Several areas have legal consequences and are of particular concern to school nurses, such as child abuse, drug abuse, venereal disease, and parental consent. (Authorization for treatment of these conditions and parental consent issues are discussed in Chapter 9.) Parental consent usually is not required for basic health screening. If anything more than measurement or observation is contemplated, parental permission must be obtained unless state law authorizes the minor to consent. If psychological testing or referral is planned, parents must be involved because such tests have the potential for invading the privacy of the family.

Another area of concern to school nurses is access to records (discussed in Chapter 11). School records generally are not open to the public, so some degree of confidentiality can be maintained. Nurses have a professional and ethical obligation to maintain confidentiality of information received from a patient until legally compelled to disclose the information. However, the records can be subpoenaed and a nurse or teacher can be compelled to testify about them since in most states no privilege applies to school nurses.

PUBLIC HEALTH NURSES

The duties of public health nurses include health screening, teaching, assessment, referral, and planning and implementing programs of health education for individuals and the community. In addition, the public health nurse may, in the course of a home visit, perform procedures related to patient care. The employer of a public health nurse may be held liable for the acts of the employee under *respondeat superior*. If the employer is a government agency, it might not be liable for damages in the absence of a statutory provision authorizing such liability. If government immunity does apply, the public health nurse may be the only party from whom damages may be obtained.

Avoiding liability when working as a public health nurse involves: (1) good judgment, (2) careful performance of procedures and screening, (3) appropriate referrals, and (4) clear policies that define the role and appropriate actions. Such policies should specifically address documentation, phone counseling, verbal orders, referrals, reporting of patient conditions, and access to records. There should be procedures for basic nursing care tasks performed (such as assessment or injections), as well as responses in emergencies (such as anaphylactic reactions). There also should be guidelines for how many visits may be made without medical supervision or reporting to the patient's physician.

Written orders should be obtained for treatments and procedures performed when they do not involve exclusively nursing judgments. Verbal and telephone orders should be recorded, copied, and the original sent to the physician for signature. The nurses' notes should reflect each consultation and order. Written consent must be obtained for treatment, use of photographs, or release of information outside of the agency or treating physician.

Public health nurses should know the extent of liability insurance coverage provided for them by the employing agency. Specifically, they should clarify their protection while traveling to home visits, while using their own or an agency car, for transporting patients and equipment, and for their own injuries or those sustained by others.

Public health nurses must keep records that are as accurate and complete as possible. There have been cases where a public health nurse's records have been used as evidence in a legal action.[127] Records also may serve as the basis for reports submitted to court on issues such as parental fitness and termination of parental rights.[128]

A 1983 case involved a public health nurse's liability in a suit in which a couple alleged trespass, conversion of property, and deprivation of civil rights arising out of the destruction of their mobile home.[129] The Iowa Supreme Court affirmed a damage award against a public health nurse because, at the request of the sheriff, she had written a letter declaring the couple's home a health hazard. The home then was demolished without notifying the owners, who were vacationing out of state. In this case, the nurse was found liable for violating the rights of the couple even though they were not her patients.

OCCUPATIONAL HEALTH NURSES

The nurse employed by a company to administer nursing and emergency services to its employees generally is viewed as an employee of the company, which will be liable for the nurse's negligent actions under *respondeat superior*. As a result, in some states the only recourse is through the workers' compensation law, since in many states an employer can be sued only under that law.

For example, the Pennsylvania Supreme Court found an employer responsible under the Workers' Compensation Act when a company nurse failed to call a doctor although an employee had severe chest pains, vomiting, chills, and perspiring—and died a few hours later.[130] In other states, occupational health nurses are considered independent contractors even though salaried by the company, so the nurse, but not the employer, can be sued outside the workers' compensation process. For example, an Indiana court ruled that an occupational nurse could be sued for administering a hypodermic injection that damaged the patient's left ulnar nerve.[131]

Several potential legal problems are associated with nurses practicing in the occupational health setting. First, they must be sure they are within the acceptable limits of nursing practice as defined by statute and rule in the jurisdiction. Second, they must recognize situations in which referral is appropriate. Finally, nurses performing procedures such as dressing or cleansing wounds will be held to the same standard of care as those in the hospital.

In one case, an employee brought a malpractice action against an occupational health nurse and the company that employed her.[132] The employee had sustained a puncture wound in his forehead. The nurse bandaged the wound but did not probe it for foreign objects. After several months, the wound healed, but a small red area remained and eventually became puffy. During this time the patient visited the nurse several times to point out that the wound did not seem to be healing.

Ten months after the injury the patient requested that he be referred to a doctor. After the doctor's examination, the patient had a basal-cell carcinoma removed from his forehead. The court found the company and the nurse liable for damages. The court noted two bases for its finding of liability against the nurse: (1) her failure to examine the wound for foreign bodies, and (2) her failure to refer the patient to a doctor when the wound did not heal.

Similar factors were issues in another case.[133] An employee coughed, then felt an intense pain down her leg. A few hours later she reported to the company nurse, who told her the pain was caused by a sciatic nerve spasm that could be relieved by soaking in a tub of hot water. The nurse also gave the woman two green pills. Several days later it was determined that the patient had a ruptured disk.

The court affirmed a decision against the patient because the claim already had been litigated and denied under the Workers' Compensation Act. The facts of the case, however, disclose two areas of concern: (1) the nurse did not keep records of nonwork-related complaints, and (2) the company had a policy of dispensing mild analgesic preparations to employees who complained of discomfort. To avoid liability, a company nurse should keep records of all visits and should not dispense medications independently unless specifically authorized to do so by state law.

OFFICE NURSES

A nurse who works for a physician or dentist usually will be considered an employee. The employing physician generally directs and controls the work of the office nurse to an extent that will support the application of *respondeat superior*. Thus, the employer can be held liable for the negligent acts of the nurse. Most lawsuits based on the actions of office nurses are filed against both the nurse and the physician.

The duties of an office nurse generally include assisting with procedures, carrying out orders, charting, recording measurements, and health counseling. They may include history taking, physical assessments, screening examinations, and other procedures. The office nurse must comply with the accepted standard of care for nurses generally when attending to patients or performing treatments and procedures. The office nurse should be especially careful to record and report symptoms and other observations, telephone inquiries, and what information is given to a patient.

Office nurse liability arises from four general areas: (1) failure to assist patients, (2) failure to maintain confidentiality, (3) failure to perform procedures according to the accepted standard of care, and (4) failure to monitor or refer the patient.

In one case, a patient fell down while disrobing at the doctor's office.[134] The family sued the physician for the negligence of his office nurse, claiming that they were negligent in failing to assist the patient and in leaving her unattended. The doctor knew that the elderly patient had a tendency to fall backward. The nurse offered to help but the patient refused. The court said that the physician who employs a nurse is liable for any wrongful conduct on the nurse's part in following the physician's instructions and in any breach of nursing duty but upheld a finding of no liability since the patient had accepted the risk by refusing assistance while competent to do so.

The failure to maintain confidentiality of patient information can subject the office nurse to liability based on defamation or invasion of privacy. In a California case an office nurse was found liable for saying that a patient had syphilis when the person actually was being treated for a false positive test for syphilis.[135] A nurse employed in a physician's office has a duty not to disclose confidential patient information.

Most cases involving the liability of office nurses occur when they perform a procedure incorrectly, leading to patient injury. In one case, a judgment against a nurse and her employer was upheld when the nurse, acting on the orders of the doctor, used a Stryker saw to remove a cast from a patient's arm.[136] While the nurse was cutting the cast, the patient complained but the nurse told the patient she was only feeling the heat from the blade. In fact, the saw made a cut in the patient's arm the length of the cast. The nurse testified that she continued to use the same amount of pressure even after the patient complained. The court found that the nurse's failure to respond to the patient's complaints did not conform to the standard of care.

In another case a patient suffering from neck pain underwent a diathermic treatment prescribed by her doctor.[137] The physician's assistant placed the electrodes on the patient and turned on the current. The patient immediately complained of a burning sensation but the assistant took no action and left the room. After repeated complaints, the electricity was turned off but the patient suffered severe burns. The court found that both the physician and his assistant were liable for negligence.

A nurse was held to be negligent in a case where a woman brought her son in for examination by a doctor and the office nurse requested that the woman help her hold another child for an x-ray.[138] In the process of assisting, the woman was burned by an electric current and injured in a fall. She recovered damages for the nurse's negligence. In another case, the California Court of Appeals reversed a judgment in favor of an office nurse and her employing physician.[139] A patient suffered injuries to his right arm following an injection given by the nurse. The appellate court held that the jury could have properly been instructed to apply *res ipsa loquitur,* saying that it is common knowledge among laymen that injections in the muscles of the arm do not cause trouble unless they are unskillfully done or there is something wrong with the medication.

A patient who suffered punctured ear drums when an office nurse washed wax from his ears was not allowed to recover damages in a 1968 case.[140] The doctor was not in the office and the patient insisted that the nurse wash out his ears. The nurse protested but eventually performed the procedure, stopping when the patient complained of pain. The court found that the patient was contributorily negligent and not entitled to recover. Nurses should not accede to patients' demands for inappropriate therapy. As discussed in the previous chapter, under the comparative negligence rule that is replacing the contributory negligence rule in most states, the nurse could be found liable today for a substantial portion of the damages in cases such as this.

In another case, a surgeon asked a nurse to provide him with a 1% procaine solution and the nurse negligently prepared a solution of formaldehyde.[141] Even though the nurse was under the direction and control of the surgeon, the court held that the surgeon was entitled to rely on the skill of the nurse and was not liable for the nurse's negligence. This case illustrates the proposition that a physician generally will not be liable for the negligence of a nurse when the physician has no reason to believe that the nurse is not competent.

A nurse and her physician employer were found liable for negligence in the death of a 22-month-old child who died from aspiration after the nurse left him lying on his back unattended.[142] The child had been seen by the physician earlier in the day and his mother brought him back to the office as she thought he was much worse. The nurse told the doctor, who was out of the office, that the child was about the same condition as earlier so the doctor had lunch before returning to the office. The nurse went to lunch before the doctor returned, leaving a receptionist in charge of the office. The child vomited while positioned on his back and died a few minutes later. The court found both the nurse and the physician liable for negligence. The court noted that if the nurse had been with the child or available to help, she could have done several things to save the boy's life.

NURSES IN NURSING HOMES

The general standard of care required of staff members dealing with patients in a nursing home is the degree of care, skill, and diligence characteristic of such facilities. While some of the rules applicable to hospitals apply also to nursing homes, distinctions must be made between the two because a hospital generally has more extensive facilities, greater control over and access to physicians, and a larger number of staff members. The duties of a nursing home to its patients sometimes are treated as contractual in nature and also are affected by statutes, regulations, and agreements with reimbursement entities. The elements of the contract or the regulations for nursing homes represent the minimum standard of care that must be met.

The general rule in nursing homes is that nurses must exercise the degree of care and skill required by the patients' condition and capabilities and must take into account their ability or inability to care for and protect themselves. Litigation involving nursing staff members of such homes is based primarily on an alleged breach of the duty to maintain patient safety. The cases fall into three general categories: (1) falls, (2) burns and other injuries, and (3) patients wandering away.

The most common cause of action involves patient injuries in falling. The significant facts include whether or not the patient was attended, whether the patient was appropriately restrained, and the person's general condition. Most often, the outcome of the case turns on two questions: (1) Would a reasonably competent nurse, in the same circumstances, have taken additional precautions to protect the patient? (2) Would these precautions have prevented the injuries? Expert testimony often is used to provide the basis for a judge or jury answering those questions. However, some courts do not require expert testimony for fall cases.

Cases that find liability for negligence on the part of the home are those in which the nursing staff: (1) failed to follow a physician's orders to restrain a patient, (2) left a patient who had a known tendency to fall unattended in a chair, or (3) failed to provide help for a patient who was unsteady.

When safety precautions can be documented, through the patient's record or through standard institutional procedures, liability generally is not imposed. A patient who falls should be evaluated and observed closely for any injuries. The nursing home was held liable for injuries in a case in which a patient's leg was broken in a fall but it was not noted until nine hours later.[143] The court noted that the patient should have been watched closely after the fall, and that the client's complaints of pain should have alerted the staff that something was wrong.

Several cases involve burned or scalded patients. Circumstances in which the nursing home staff exercised exclusive control over the cause of the injury—such as heat lamps, radiators, or hot water bottles—generally result in a finding of liability against the home. For example, the Alabama Supreme Court affirmed a $500,000 judgment against a nursing home and subsequently treating hospital after a patient died as a result of a scalding in a bathtub in the nursing home.[144] A nursing aide had left the 26-year-old severely retarded patient unattended in an empty bathtub and another retarded patient had turned on the hot water, scalding the first patient. Some circumstances, such as when competent patients smoke in bed in violation of instructions, will lead to a finding of no liability for the institution.[145]

Suits against nursing homes also involve patients who wander away and are injured. In one case, the nursing home was found liable for negligence when it sent an elderly, senile patient to the hospital without giving the hospital instruction about his special need for supervision.[146] The patient wandered away from the hospital and was found dead several days later. In many cases the nursing home is held not to be liable, since it is not possible to provide constant supervision of all patients. The responsibility of the nursing home extends to a reasonable standard of care, taking into account the patients' mental and physical condition.

NOTES

1. *Webb v. Jorns*, 473 S.W.2d 328 (Tex. Civ. App. 1971), *rev'd on other grounds*, 488 S.W.2d 407 (Tex. 1972).

2. *Thompson v. Brent*, 245 So. 2d 751 (La. Ct. App. 1971).

3. *New Biloxi Hosp. v. Frazier*, 245 Miss. 185, 145 So. 2d 882 (1962).

4. *Cooper v. National Motor Bearing Co.*, 136 Cal. App. 299, 288 P.2d 581 (1955).

5. *Washington Hosp. Center v. Martin*, 454 A.2d 306 (D.C. Ct. App. 1982).

6. *Cline v. Lund*, 31 Cal. App. 3d 755, 107 Cal. Rptr. 629 (1973).

7. *Delicata v. Bourlesses*, 80 Mass. App. 963, 404 N.E.2d 667 (1980).

8. *Crowe v. Provost*, 52 Tenn. App. 397, 374 S.W.2d 645 (1963).

9. *Yorita v. Okumoto*, 643 P.2d 820 (Haw. Ct. App. 1982); *see also Goldfoot v. Lofgren*, 135 Or. 533, 296 P. 843 (1931) [adult with lung abscess due to aspirated material during recovery]; *Thomas v. Seaside Memorial Hosp. of Long Beach*, 80 Cal. App. 2d 841, 183 P.2d 288 (1947) [8-month-old died during recovery].

10. *Lhotka v. Larson*, 238 N.W.2d 870 (Minn. 1976).

11. *Newhall v. Central Vermont Hosp.*, 349 A.2d 890 (Vt. 1975).

12. *Nelson v. Peterson*, 542 P.2d 1075 (Utah 1975).

13. *Sanchez v. Bay Gen. Hosp.*, 116 Cal. App. 3d 776, 172 Cal. Rptr. 342 (1981).

14. *Belmon v. St. Francis Cabrini Hosp.*, 427 So. 2d 541 (La. Ct. App. 1983).

15. *Ramsey v. Physicians Memorial Hosp., Inc.*, 36 Md. App. 42, 373 A.2d 26 (1977).

16. *Baker v. Warner*, 654 P.2d 263 (Alaska 1982).

17. *Polischeck v. United States*, 535 F.Supp. 1261 (E.D. Pa. 1982).

18. *Hiatt v. Groce*, 215 Kan. 14, 523 P.2d 320 (1974).

19. *Samii v. Baystate Medical Center, Inc.*, 8 Mass. App. 911, 395 N.E.2d 455 (1979).

20. *Duling v. Bluefield Sanitarium, Inc.*, 149 W. Va. 567, 142 S.E.2d 754 (1965).

21. *Sandhofer v. Abbott-Northwestern Hosp.*, 283 N.W.2d 362 (Minn. 1979).

22. *Howard v. Piver*, 279 S.E.2d 876 (N.C. Ct. App. 1981).

23. *Goff v. Doctors General Hosp. of San Jose*, 166 Cal. App. 2d 314, 333 P.2d 29 (1958).

24. *Karrigan v. Nazareth Convent & Academy, Inc.*, 212 Kan. 44, 510 P.2d 190 (1973).

25. *Darling v. Charleston Community Memorial Hosp.*, 33 Ill. 2d 326, 211 N.E.2d 253 (1966), *cert. denied* 383 U.S. 496 (1966).

26. *Utter v. United Hosp. Center, Inc.*, 236 S.E.2d 213 (W. Va. 1977).

27. *Corson v. United States*, 304 F.Supp. 155 (E.D. Pa. 1969).

28. *Krestview Nursing Home, Inc., v. Synowiec*, 317 So. 2d 94 (Fla. Dist. Ct. App. 1975).

29. *Frantz v. San Luis Medical Clinic*, 81 Cal. App. 3d 34, 146 Cal. Rptr. 146 (1978).

30. *Collins v. Westlake Community Hosp.*, 57 Ill. 2d 388, 312 N.E.2d 614 (1974).

31. *Trichel v. Caire*, 427 So. 2d 1227 (La. Ct. App. 1983).

32. *Thompson v. United States*, 368 F.Supp. 466 (W.D. La. 1973).

33. *Gugino v. Harvard Community Health Plan*, 403 N.E.2d 1166 (Mass. 1980).

34. *Norton v. Argonaut Ins. Co.*, 144 So. 2d 249 (La. Ct. App. 1962).

35. *Poor Sisters of St. Francis v. Catron*, 435 N.E.2d 305 (Ind. Ct. App. 1982).

36. *Fraijo v. Hartland Hosp.*, 99 Cal. App. 3d 331, 160 Cal. Rptr. 246 (1979).

37. *Striano v. Deepdale Gen. Hosp.*, 54 A.D.2d 730, 387 N.Y.S.2d 678 (1976).

38. *Lenger v. Physician's Gen. Hosp., Inc.*, 455 S.W.2d 703 (Tex. 1970).

39. *Doctor's Hospital of Augusta, Inc., v. Poole*, 144 Ga. App. 184, 241 S.E. 2d 2 (1977).

40. *Toth v. Community Hosp. at Glen Cove*, 22 N.Y.2d 255, 239 N.E.2d 368 (1968).

41. *Larrimore v. Homeopathic Hosp. Ass'n of Del.*, 54 Del. 449, 181 A.2d 573 (1962).

42. *Wees v. Creighton Memorial St. Joseph's Hosp.*, 194 Neb. 295, 231 N.W.2d 570 (1975).

43. *Hunsaker v. Bozeman Deaconess Found.*, 588 P.2d 493 (Mont. 1978).

44. *Arnold v. James B. Haggin Memorial Hosp.*, 415 S.W.2d 844 (Ky. Ct. App. 1967).

45. *Southeastern Ky. Baptist Hosp., Inc., v. Bruce*, 539 S.W.2d 286 (Ky. 1976).

46. *Parker v. St. Paul Fire & Marine Ins. Co.*, 335 So. 2d 725 (La. Ct. App. 1976).

47. *Goodenough v. Deaconess Hosp.*, 637 S.W.2d 123 (Mo. App. 1982).

48. *Koepel v. St. Joseph Hosp. & Medical Center*, 381 Mich. 440, 163 N.W.2d 222 (1968), *rev'g* 8 Mich. App. 609, 155 N.W.2d 199 (1967).

49. *Plutshack v. University of Minn. Hosps.*, 316 N.W.2d 1 (Minn. 1982).

50. *Truluck v. Municipal Hosp. Bd. of Lakeland*, 162 So. 2d 549 (Fla. Dist. Ct. App. 1964).

51. *Hudmon v. Martin*, 315 So. 2d 516 (Fla. Dist. Ct. App. 1975).

52. *Kyte v. McMillion*, 256 Md. 85, 259 A.2d 532 (Md. Ct. App. 1969).

53. *Maloney v. Wake Hosp. Sys., Inc.*, 262 S.E.2d 680 (N.C. Ct. App. 1980).

54. *Sharrow v. Archer*, 658 P.2d 1331 (Alaska 1983).

55. *Barnes v. St. Francis Hosp. & School of Nursing, Inc.*, 211 Kan. 315, 507 P.2d 288 (1973); see also *Su v. Perkins*, 133 Ga. App. 474, 211 S.E.2d 421 (1974) [prescribing physician not liable when nurse selects wrong needle size].

56. *Rodriguez v. Columbus Hosp.*, 38 A.D.2d 517, 326 N.Y.S.2d 438 (1971); *see also* note 41 *supra* for another case involving wrong route of administration.

57. *Farrow v. Health Servs. Corp.*, 604 P.2d 474 (Utah 1979).

58. *Gasbarra v. St. James Hosp.*, 85 Ill. App. 3d 32, 40 Ill. Dec. 538, 406 N.E.2d 544 (1980).

59. *Macy v. Presbyterian Intercommunity Hosp., Inc.*, 46 Or. App. 791, 612 P.2d 769 (1980).

60. *Bauer v. Otis*, 133 Cal. App. 2d 439, 284 P.2d 133 (1955).

61. *Hall v. Bio-Medical Applications, Inc.*, 671 F.2d 300 (8th Cir. 1982).

62. *Helman v. Sacred Heart Hosp.*, 62 Wash. 2d 69, 381 P.2d 605 (1963).

63. *DeFalco v. Long Island College Hosp.*, 393 N.Y.S.2d 859 (N.Y. Sup. Ct. 1977).

64. *E.g. Kalmus v. Cedars of Lebanon Hosp.*, 132 Cal. 2d 243, 281 P.2d 872 (1955).

65. *Cochran v. Harper*, 115 Ga. App. 277, 159 S.E.2d 461 (1967).
66. *Shepard v. McGinnis*, 251 Iowa 35, 131 N.W.2d 475 (1964).
67. *Schmidt v. Intermountain Health Care, Inc.*, 635 P.2d 99 (Utah 1981).
68. *Zack v. Centro Español Hosp.*, 319 So. 2d 34 (Fla. Dist. Ct. App. 1975).
69. *Skidmore v. Oklahoma Hosp.*, 137 Okla. 133, 278 P. 334 (1929).
70. *Leonard v. Watsonville Community Hosp.*, 47 Cal. 2d 509, 305 P.2d 36 (1956).
71. *Robinson v. St. John's Medical Center, Joplin*, 508 S.W.2d 7 (Mo. Ct. App. 1975).
72. *Porter v. Patterson*, 107 Ga. App. 64, 129 S.E.2d 70 (1962).
73. *Horwitz v. Michael Reese Hosp.*, 5 Ill. App. 3d 508, 284 N.E.2d 4 (1972).
74. *Daniel v. St. Francis Cabrini Hosp.*, 415 So. 2d 586 (La. Ct. App. 1982).
75. *Page v. Wilson Memorial Hosp.*, 49 N.C. App. 533, 272 S.E.2d 8 (1980).
76. *Jones v. Hawkes Hosp. of Mt. Carmel*, 175 Ohio St. 503, 196 N.E.2d 592 (1964).
77. *McEachern v. Glenview Hosp., Inc.*, 505 S.W.2d 386 (Tex. Civ. App. 1974).
78. *Cramer v. Theda Clark Memorial Hosp.*, 45 Wis. 2d 147, 172 N.W.2d 427 (1969).
79. *Levett v. Etkind*, 158 Conn. 567, 265 A.2d 70 (1969).
80. *Cavenaugh v. South Broward Hosp. Dist.*, 247 So. 2d 769 (Fla. Dist. Ct. App. 1971).
81. *Leavitt v. St. Tammany Parish Hosp.*, 396 So. 2d 406 (La. Ct. App. 1981).
82. *See* n. 48 *supra*.
83. *Doctors Hosp., Inc. v. Kovats*, 16 Ariz. App. 489, 494 P.2d 389 (1972).
84. *Chamberlain v. Deaconess Hosp., Inc.*, 324 N.W.2d 172 (Ind. Ct. App. 1975).
85. *Mundt v. Alta Bates Hosp.*, 223 Cal. App. 2d 413, 35 Cal. Rptr. 848 (1963).
86. *Palmer v. Clarksdale Hosp.*, 57 So. 2d 476 (Miss. 1952).
87. *Lewis v. Davis*, 410 N.E.2d 1363 (Ind. Ct. App. 1980).
88. *Bowers v. Olch*, 120 Cal. App. 2d 108, 260 P.2d 997 (1953).
89. *Laidlaw v. Lions Gate Hosp.*, 8 D.L.R.3d 730 (B.C. Sup. Ct. 1969).
90. *Krujelis v. Esdale* [1972] 2 W.W.R. 495 (B.C. Sup. Ct. 1971).
91. *Horton v. Niagara Falls Memorial Medical Center*, 51 A.D.2d 152, 380 N.Y.S.2d 116 (1976).
92. *Valentin v. La Société Française de Bienfaisance*, 76 Cal. App. 2d 1, 172 P.2d 359 (1946).
93. *Longuy v. Société Française de Bienfaisance Mutuelle*, 52 Cal. App. 370, 198 P. 1011 (1921).
94. *Cadicamo v. Long Island College Hosp.*, 308 N.Y. 196, 124 N.E.2d 279 (1954).
95. *O'Neil v. Glens Falls Indemnity Co.*, 310 F.2d 165 (8th Cir. 1962).
96. *Christiansen v. Des Moines Still College of Osteopathy*, 248 Iowa 810, 82 N.W.2d 741 (1957).
97. *Frank v. South*, 175 Ky. 416, 194 S.W. 375 (1917).
98. *Chalmers-Francis v. Nelson*, 6 Cal. 2d 402, 57 P.2d 1312 (1936).
99. *State v. Borah*, 51 Ariz. 318, 76 P.2d 757 (1938).
100. *Lane v. Otis*, 412 So. 2d 254 (Ala. 1982).
101. *Cavero v. Franklin General Benevolent Soc'y*, 36 Cal. 2d 301, 223 P.2d 471 (1950).
102. *Jackson v. Joyner*, 236 N.C. 259, 72 S.E.2d 589 (1952).
103. *Foster v. Englewood Hosp. Assoc.*, 19 Ill. App. 3d 1055, 313 N.E.2d 255 (1974).
104. *Baird v. Sickler*, 69 Ohio St. 2d 652, 433 N.E.2d 593 (1982).
105. *Sesselman v. Muhlenberg Hosp.*, 124 N.J. Super. 285, 306 A.2d 474 (N.J. Super. Ct. App. Div. 1973).

106. *Tonsic v. Wagner*, 458 Pa. 246, 329 A.2d 497 (1974) [nursing case not involving a nurse anesthetist].

107. *Hughes v. St. Paul Fire & Marine Ins. Co.*, 401 So. 2d 448 (La. Ct. App. 1981).

108. *Starnes v. Charlotte-Mecklenberg Hosp. Auth.*, 28 N.C. App. 418, 221 S.E.2d 733 (1976).

109. *Whitfield v. Whittaker Memorial Hosp.*, 210 Va. 176, 169 S.E.2d 563 (1969).

110. *Yoos v. Jewish Hosp. of St. Louis*, 645 S.W.2d 177 (Mo. Ct. App. 1982).

111. *Whitney v. Day*, 100 Mich. App. 707, 300 N.W.2d 380 (1980); *Starnes v. Charlotte-Mecklenberg Hosp. Auth.*, 28 N.C. App. 418, 221 S.E.2d 733 (1976).

112. *Brown v. Allen Sanitorium, Inc.*, 364 So.2d 661 (La. Ct. App. 1978) *cert. denied* 367 So. 2d 392 (La. 1979).

113. *Weinstein v. Prostkoff*, 13 A.D.2d 539, 213 N.Y.S.2d 571 (1961).

114. *Willinger v. Mercy Catholic Medical Center*, 362 A.2d 280 (Pa. Super. Ct. 1976).

115. *Corson v. United States*, 304 F.Supp. 155 (E.D. Pa. 1969).

116. *Starnes v. Charlotte-Mecklenburg Hosp. Auth.*, 28 N.C. App. 418, 221 S.E.2d 733 (1976).

117. *Whitney v. Day*, 100 Mich. App. 707, 300 N.W.2d 380 (1980).

118. *Lane v. Otis*, 412 So.2d 254 (Ala. 1982).

119. *Gugino v. Harvard Community Health Plan*, 403 N.E.2d 1166 (Mass. 1983).

120. *Fein v. Permanente Medical Group*, 121 Cal. App. 3d 135, 175 Cal. Rptr. 177 (1981).

121. *Flickinger v. United States*, 523 F.Supp. 1372 (E.D. Pa. 1981).

122. *Hernicz v. Florida*, 390 So. 2d 194 (Fla. Dist. Ct. App. 1980).

123. American College of Nurse Midwives, OFFICIAL DEFINITIONS (1978).

124. *People v. Arendt*, 60 Ill. App. 89 (1894).

125. *Bowland v. Santa Cruz Court*, 18 Cal. 3d 479, 556 P.2d 1081, 134 Cal. Rptr. 630 (1976).

126. *Olson v. Bolstad*, 161 Minn. 419, 201 N.W. 918 (1925).

127. *E.g., McCarthy v. Maxon*, 134 Conn. 170, 55 A.2d 912 (1947).

128. *E.g., In re Hoppe*, 289 N.W.2d 613 (Iowa 1980).

129. *Dickerson v. Young*, 332 N.W.2d 93 (Iowa 1983).

130. *Baur v. Mesta Mach. Co.*, 405 Pa. 617, 176 A.2d 684 (1962).

131. *McDaniel v. Sage*, 419 N.E.2d 1322 (Ind. Ct. App. 1981).

132. *Cooper v. National Motor Bearing Co.*, 136 Cal. App. 2d 299, 288 P.2d 581 (1955).

133. *Akins v. Hudson Pulp & Paper Co.*, 330 So. 2d 757 (Fla. Dist. Ct. App. 1976).

134. *Levett v. Etkind*, 158 Conn. 567, 265 A.2d 70 (1969).

135. *Schessler v. Keck*, 125 Cal. App. 2d 827, 271 P.2d 588 (1954).

136. *Thompson v. Brent*, 245 So. 2d 751 (La. Ct. App. 1971).

137. *Wood v. Miller*, 158 Or. 444, 76 P.2d 963 (1938).

138. *Kelly v. Yount*, 338 Pa. 190, 12 A.2d 579 (1940).

139. *Bauer v. Otis*, 133 Cal. App. 2d 439, 284 P.2d 133 (1955).

140. *Brockman v. Harpole*, 444 P.2d 25 (Or. 1968).

141. *Hallinan v. Prindle*, 11 P.2d 426 (1932); *rev'd*, 220 Cal. 46, 29 P.2d 202 (1934); *aff'd in part, rev'd in part*, 17 Cal. App. 2d 656, 62 P.2d 1075 (1936).

142. *Crowe v. Provost*, 52 Tenn. App. 397, 374 S.W.2d 645 (1963).

143. *Powell v. Parkview Estate Nursing Home, Inc.*, 240 So. 2d 53 (La. Ct. App. 1970).

144. *Estes Health Care Center, Inc., v. Bannerman*, 411 So. 2d 109 (Ala. 1982).
145. *LeBlanc v. Midland Nat. Ins. Co.*, 219 So. 2d 251 (La. Ct. App. 1969).
146. *Krestview Nursing Home, Inc., v. Synowiec*, 317 So. 2d 94 (Fla. Dist. Ct. App. 1975), *cert. denied* 333 So. 2d 463 (Fla. 1976).

BIBLIOGRAPHY

Creighton, Helen. "Refusal to Treat Patient." *Supervisor Nurse* 12, no. 4 (April 1981):67.

———. "Nursing Assessment." *Nursing Management* 12, no. 11 (November 1981):

———. "Negligence in Releasing Psychiatric Patient." *Nursing Management* 14, no. 11 (November 1983):53.

Cushing, Maureen. "An Occupational Nurse's Liability." *American Journal of Nursing* 81, no. 12 (December 1981):2206.

———. "A Matter of Judgment." *American Journal of Nursing* 82, no. 7 (July 1982):990.

———. "Failure to Communicate." *American Journal of Nursing* 82, no. 10 (October 1982):1597.

———. "Expanding the Meaning of Accountability." *American Journal of Nursing* 83, no. 8 (August 1983):1202.

Fortin, J. et al. "Legal Implications of Nursing Diagnosis." *Nursing Clinics of North America* (September 1979), p. 553.

Greenlaw, Jane. "Liability for Nursing Negligence in the Operating Room." *Law, Medicine, and Health Care* 10, no. 5 (October 1982):262.

Regan, William. "Legally Speaking." *RN* 46, no. 5 (May 1983):87.

———. "Legally Speaking." *RN* 47, no. 1 (January 1984):23.

Chapter 8

Beginning and Ending the Patient Relationship

The legal relationship between a nurse and an institutional patient is unique because of the continuous personal responsibility during the period the nurse is on duty coupled with the ending of that responsibility when a replacement takes over at the end of the duty period. The legal relationship between nurses in independent practice and their patients is similar to the physician-patient relationship. There have not been many court decisions discussing the beginning and ending of the nurse-patient relationship; instead, nearly all of the decisions have focused on physicians and hospitals.

This chapter discusses the ways the nurse-patient relationship begins and ends. It also explores the physician-patient and hospital-patient relationships because it is important for nurses to understand the responsibilities of physicians and hospitals.

NURSE-PATIENT RELATIONSHIP

The nurse-patient relationship shares characteristics of both the physician-patient and the hospital-patient relationships.

Most nurses in institutional or other employment relationships assume responsibility for a designated group of patients during a specified time period, a shift. Unlike the physician who is expected to be physically present only episodically, the nurse has continuous responsibility for monitoring and caring for those patients during the shift. However, unlike the physician who continues to be individually responsible for the patient around the clock, the nurse is expected to transfer the care of the client to another nurse at the end of the assigned period. Of course, the nurse cannot abandon the patient at the end of that period if the replacement does not arrive on time but must continue to provide care until other coverage can be arranged. After the appropriate transfer of responsibility, the nurse is not legally responsible to return to care for the patient while off duty unless the contract with

184

the employer requires it. The physician is legally responsible to return whenever personal attendance is required.

Nurses are expected to allocate their time properly while on duty and to be knowledgeable concerning the anticipated workload involving both existing patients and expected additional admissions. Nurses can be legally liable for taking a break or leaving a unit at a time when they should know that the demand for care on the unit will require their presence, if a patient is harmed because of their absence.[1]

Nurses are expected to exercise professional judgment concerning the needs of the patients to whom they are assigned and not to abandon any who need their services. In a 1983 California case, a circulating nurse left the operating room to assist with another surgery before the first patient was transferred to the recovery room. One of the circulating nurse's responsibilities was to monitor the patient and assist the anesthesiologist. After the nurse left, the patient went into cardiac arrest and suffered a severe loss of oxygen, resulting in permanent, total paralysis and a semicomatose state. The nurse's only defense was that she was being yelled at. The court ruled that nurses' abandonment of a patient at a life-endangered time is so obviously negligent that no expert testimony was required to establish liability. The nurse's employer, the hospital, under the doctrine of *respondeat superior,* was ordered to pay $982,000.[2]

Failure to be present for a scheduled shift without adequate excuse has not generally been viewed as nursing malpractice. This is another indication that the law has not viewed the legal nurse-patient relationship as extending beyond each assigned shift. Of course, a nurse who is absent without adequate excuse may be subject to employment sanctions and, in some states, discipline by licensing agencies.

If the institution assigns a nurse to care for a different group of patients on subsequent shifts, it does not violate the legal nurse-patient relationship with those the nurse cared for on previous shifts unless there is a special contract promising that a particular nurse will continue to care for a particular patient. Although many nurses establish meaningful relationships with individual patients that extend over an entire period of hospitalization, the legal relationship does not; instead, it ends when the patient is transferred to another unit or to the care of another nurse after the end of the shift. The legal relationship is recreated each time the nurse reports for a shift and is assigned to the patient. Employed nurses generally are not authorized to make promises to patients concerning being present during future shifts, so they must avoid such promises unless the officials responsible for scheduling give them special authorization and the nurses are willing to accept the responsibility for fulfilling the promise.

The contracts of institutional nurses and most other employed nurses include an express or implied agreement to provide care to all patients to whom they are assigned. This is similar to the contract most employed physicians enter. Thus, employed nurses generally do not have the right to refuse to care for patients to whom they are assigned. Many employers attempt when feasible to accommodate severe personality incompatibilities but, as every experienced nurse knows, some patients are difficult for anyone to care for so the only accommodation possible may be a rotation of responsibility.

Nurses in private practice may create a relationship similar to the physician-patient relationship described in the following section unless the contract with the patient or client limits their responsibility. A nurse in private practice has the same latitude as other independent professionals to decide whether or not to accept a particular patient or client, unless the nurse has entered a contract to care for a certain population. The nurse may assume a 24-hour a day responsibility to personally provide necessary services. When such a relationship has been established, the nurse has the same options for ending it as does the physician.

PHYSICIAN-PATIENT RELATIONSHIP

Beginning the Relationship

Generally a physician has the right to accept or decline establishing a professional relationship with any person. A physician does not have a legal responsibility to diagnose or treat anyone unless there is an express or implied agreement to do so. Likewise, an individual does not have an obligation to accept diagnosis or treatment from any particular physician unless the situation is one in which the law authorizes that the person be cared for involuntarily.

There are three ways a physician can establish a patient relationship: (1) by contracting to care for a certain population and to have one of that population seek care, (2) by entering an express contract with the patient or the patient's legal representative by mutual agreement, or (3) by engaging in conduct from which a contract can be implied.

Contracts to Care for a Certain Population

A physician who enters a contract to care for members of a certain population must provide care for them to the extent required by the contract. For example, physicians enter contracts with hospitals to care for emergency patients or to provide certain services such as radiology or pathology. Usually these contracts include restrictions on the freedom of the physician to refuse to care for individual hospital patients requiring those services. Physicians frequently enter contracts with other institutions and organizations, such as athletic teams, schools, companies, prisons, jails, nursing homes, and health maintenance organizations, that include an agreement to provide certain kinds of care to all members of certain populations.

Express Contract

The most frequent way that the physician-patient relationship is begun is by mutual agreement of the physician and the patient or the person's representative, such as the parent or guardian of a minor or the guardian or next-of-kin of an incompetent adult. The physician may limit the scope of the contract and not assume responsibility for all the patient's medical needs.

For example, the services can be limited to a particular specialty, so that an internist can refuse to perform surgery.[3] An obstetrician can refuse to participate in home deliveries.[4] Physicians may limit the geographic area in which they practice—they are not obligated to travel to another town to see a patient who becomes ill while visiting out of town.[5] A consulting physician who examines a patient at the request of the primary physician can limit the involvement to the consultation and not accept continuing responsibility as long as this limitation is made clear to the patient and the primary physician.

Some limitations on the scope of the contract are not permissible. For example, an admitting physician assumes the responsibility to examine the patient and offer appropriate treatment until the physician-patient relationship is terminated. In a 1975 Florida case, a physician who was at home recovering from an illness had agreed to admit a patient to the hospital as a favor to a friend but attempted to limit his contract solely to the act of admission by making it clear he could not treat the patient. The patient died of an undiagnosed brain abscess within a few days. The physician never saw her. The court ruled that there was a physician-patient relationship that included a duty to see the patient, so the father of the patient could sue the physician for malpractice.[6]

Implied Contract

Sometimes a relationship with all of its attendant responsibilities is inferred from the physician's conduct. If the physician commences treatment of a person, the courts generally will find a physician-patient relationship. However, some courts have found a relationship from lesser contact. The Iowa Supreme Court ruled that a physician-patient relationship was established when a physician told a patient he would perform surgery.[7] A New York court based an implied contract on the fact the physician had listened to a recital of the patient's symptoms over the telephone.[8] Thus, physicians who do not wish to assume the responsibility of a relationship should limit telephone calls to advising the caller to seek medical assistance elsewhere.

In some situations, very limited conversations may not be interpreted as creating a relationship. For example, a Georgia hospital employee sued the hospital medical director for giving her erroneous medical advice when he responded with a few suggestions to her questions while stopped in the hospital hallway. The court found that this was not enough to conclude that the physician had agreed to treat her or advise her as a physician.[9]

Although some specialists, such as pathologists and diagnostic radiologists, seldom see their patients, a physician-patient relationship is still established. This does not usually include the responsibility for continuing care that is one of the elements of most relationships but it does include responsibility for consequences of intentional or negligence errors in providing pathology or radiology services.

Ending the Relationship

A physician has a duty to continue to provide medical care until the relationship is terminated legally. A physician who discontinues care before that occurs can be liable for abandonment.

The relationship can be ended if: (1) medical care no longer is needed, (2) the patient withdraws from the relationship, (3) the care of the patient is transferred to another physician, (4) the physician gives the patient ample notice of withdrawal, or (5) the physician is unable to provide care.

If the patient withdraws from the relationship, the physician has a duty to attempt to warn the person if further care is needed and upon request should advise the successor physician, if any, of information necessary to continue treatment. If care still is needed, the physician usually should request the patient to provide written confirmation of the withdrawal, realizing that in many situations the patient will decline to do so.

The care of a patient can be transferred to another physician. It is recognized that physicians attend meetings, take vacations, and have other valid reasons they cannot be available. A physician can fulfill the duties of the relationship by providing a qualified substitute. A physician can withdraw without providing a substitute by giving reasonable notice in writing with sufficient time to locate another physician willing to accept the person if continuing care is required. Some of the reasons for withdrawal are noncooperation or failure to pay bills when able to do so.

Finally, a physician can be excused from the responsibilities of the relationship when unable to provide care. A physician who is ill should not accept additional responsibilities and should attempt to arrange for a substitute. However, it is recognized that sometimes physicians become too ill to be able to arrange a substitute. It also is recognized that a physician cannot be with two patients simultaneously. Thus, the necessity of attending another patient may provide a valid excuse as long as the physician has exercised prudence in determining the priority. The physician cannot entirely give up one patient to attend another. The frequency of attendance of each patient will be an important factor in assessing whether one patient has been abandoned.

A physician who fails to see a patient with whom there is a relationship without an acceptable reason may face liability for breach of contract or, if the patient is injured as a result, malpractice.

Physicians do not have to be with the patient continuously to satisfy their responsibility. They can leave orders for others to administer medications or other care, as long as they return at intervals appropriate to the patient's condition. When admission to a hospital is not indicated, the patient usually can be sent home with instructions to call if further care is needed. The patient then has the responsibility to call.

The major exception to this is when the patient and those responsible for the individual are unable to provide the needed care in the home. The physician should then have arrangements made for other assistance or placement. Finally, the patient or patient's representative can be told to follow certain instructions or to return at a certain time. It is not abandonment if the patient fails to return or follow instructions; however, if the individual has a known debility, it may be necessary to follow up if the patient does not return.

HOSPITAL-PATIENT RELATIONSHIP

This section addresses the hospital's responsibilities to persons who are not in need of emergency care; responsibilities to persons who need emergency care; and issues concerning discharge.

Nonemergency Patients

Under common law, a person who does not need emergency care usually does not have a right to be admitted to a hospital. The hospital can legally refuse to admit any person unless one of three broad categories of exceptions applies: (1) the common law, (2) contractual exceptions, and (3) statutory exceptions. Several statutes forbid discriminatory admission policies but do not grant a right to be admitted. All of these rights to be admitted are contingent on the necessity for hospitalization, appropriateness of the hospital for the patient's needs, and availability of space.

Common-Law Rights to Admission

A person generally has a right to be admitted when the hospital is responsible for the original injury that caused the need for hospitalization. In some circumstances, a person who becomes ill or injured in the hospital buildings or on the grounds may have a right to be admitted even if the facility is not otherwise responsible for the problem. If a hospital begins to exercise control of a person by examining or beginning to provide care, that may start a hospital-patient relationship, entitling the patient to be admitted.

Contractual Rights to Admission

If a hospital has made a contractual promise to accept members of a certain population, then they have a right to be admitted when they need care that institution is able to provide. Some hospitals have entered contracts with employers to provide services to their employees or with health care insurers, such as Blue Cross or health maintenance organizations, agreeing to accept patients covered by the insurer.[10]

Hospitals that accepted Hill-Burton construction grants or loans agreed to a "community service" obligation. The regulations defining this obligation specify that no person residing in the area served by the hospital will be denied admission to the portion of the facility financed by Hill-Burton funds on any grounds other than the individual's lack of need for services, the availability of the needed services in the hospital, or the individual's ability to pay.[11]

Inability to pay cannot be a basis for denial when the person needs emergency services or the facility still has a Hill-Burton uncompensated care obligation. Emergency patients who are unable to pay and for whom services are not available under the uncompensated care obligation may be discharged or transferred to another facility that is able to provide necessary services. However, there must be a medical determination that the discharge or transfer does not substantially risk deterioration in the patient's medical condition. Advance deposits can be required if the hospital permits alternative arrangements when patients who are able to pay do not have the necessary cash.

Hospitals may require admission by a physician with clinical privileges only if enough physicians on the staff are willing to admit the patients who must be admitted under the community service obligation. If not enough physicians on the medical staff will admit certain types of individuals, such as Medicaid patients, the hospital must either hire physicians who will admit them, condition appointment to the medical staff on an agreement to admit some of them, or grant temporary admitting privileges to their personal physicians. Any hospital that received construction funds after the 1974 amendments must provide this access to persons who work in the area served by the facility, in addition to those who reside in the area.

Statutory Rights to Admission

Some hospitals, especially governmental ones, are obligated by statute to accept all patients from a certain population that may be defined in terms of geographic area of residence, inability to pay for care, or a combination of both. For example, county hospitals in Iowa are required to provide care and treatment to any resident of the county who is sick or injured and observes the rules of conduct adopted by the governing body.[12]

Nondiscrimination Statutes

Several statutes forbid discrimination in admission but do not grant a right to be admitted. Title VI of the Civil Rights Act forbids discrimination on the basis of race, color, or national origin in any institution that receives federal financial assistance.[13] A hospital must comply with this statute and its implementing regulations[14] if it receives Medicare or Medicaid reimbursement. The Rehabilitation Act of 1973 forbids discrimination on the basis of handicap in any institution that receives federal financial assistance.[15] A hospital that receives Medicare and Medicaid reimbursement must comply with the provisions of that statute and its implementing regulations.[16] Most substance abusers are considered handicapped under this law, so hospitals cannot discriminate against alcoholics and drug abusers.

Reasons for Nonadmission

Even when a person otherwise has a right to be admitted to a hospital, several reasons are generally recognized as justifying nonadmission. First, if hospitalization is not medically necessary, there is no right to admission. A hospital is not a hotel; it is an institution for the provision of necessary medical services. Second, if the hospital does not provide the services the patient needs, it does not have to admit the patient. If the patient needs emergency care to prepare for transfer to an appropriate facility, the hospital usually will be expected to provide such care.

Generally, when space is not available, the hospital may refuse to admit a patient. This rule usually applies even when a court orders admission.[17] However, not all courts adopt this realistic position[18] so court orders should not be violated except upon advice of legal counsel knowledgeable concerning local law.

Emergency Patients

In the past, the general rule was that persons did not even have a right to emergency care in a hospital except in the circumstances discussed earlier in which they would be entitled to any necessary hospital services. In many states, the rule now is that there is a special right to hospital care in actual emergencies. In states that have not yet formally adopted the rule, hospitals that maintain an emergency room should provide necessary emergency care because it is unlikely that many courts will rule today that such care may be denied.

In some states, some or all hospitals are required by statute or regulation to provide necessary emergency services to anyone who arrives at their door. For example, in Texas it is a crime for any officer or employee of a general hospital supported with public funds to deny a person emergency services available in the facility on the basis of inability to pay if a physician has diagnosed that the patient is seriously ill or injured.[19]

Many courts have recognized a common-law right to emergency services in states that do not have statutes. In a Delaware case, a hospital had refused to accept a baby as a patient because the family's personal physician was not available. The emergency room staff asked the parents to return the next day with the baby but the infant died at home that afternoon. The court ruled that in an unmistakeable emergency, patients have a right to care in a hospital that maintains an emergency room, so the hospital was liable for the child's death.[20] Courts in several other states have reached the same conclusion.[21] Often they base the right on an implied invitation to the public by operating an emergency room. However, even when the hospital clearly is operated only for a limited population, some courts still impose an obligation to offer emergency care.[22]

When care is provided under the emergency obligation to patients the hospital would not otherwise accept, the facility generally does not have a duty to provide continuing treatment if arrangements can be made to transfer the individual to an appropriate hospital without substantial danger to the person. This is recognized by the Hill-Burton community service regulations discussed earlier.

For example, the Alabama Supreme Court ruled that the hospital had no obligation to admit a patient after providing proper emergency care.[23] It held that the patient had no right to stay in the hospital and that the institution had fulfilled its responsibility by arranging for transfer to a charitable facility. However, if the emergency care had created a dangerous condition requiring further treatment, the hospital would have had a duty to admit the patient under the general common-law responsibility that everyone has to assist persons they have put in peril.

If the hospital cannot provide the care the patient needs, it has a duty to attempt to arrange a transfer. A California court found a hospital and treating physician liable for the negligent care of a severely burned patient in part because the hospital did not have the facilities to care for severe burns.[24]

If a transfer is required, the hospital has a duty to properly prepare the patient for the move and to make arrangements for it. Preparation of the patient includes an appropriate examination and stabilization. In a Mississippi case, a veteran who went to a community hospital emergency room bleeding profusely had been transferred to a Veterans Administration hospital by an emergency nurse who made no effort to stop the bleeding.[25] The community hospital was found liable for the death because the nurse did not obtain information concerning his condition from the people who presented him, did not tell the physician on call of the extent of the bleeding, and did not do anything to stop the bleeding.

Appropriate transfer arrangements include appropriate attendants and appropriate speed. When ambulances and helicopters staffed with emergency medical technicians, emergency nurses, or physicians are available, it will be difficult to convince a court of the appropriateness of an interhospital transfer of a critically ill patient in an unequipped vehicle that is not staffed with specially trained personnel.

However, emergency room staff members can take actions based on the reasonably available information. They do not have to be able to foresee the future in the absence of information. For example, a Florida hospital was sued by the wife of a man who had been stabbed by a person who had been seen briefly in the emergency room. A grandmother had taken her grandson to the emergency room because she suspected he had taken LSD, but the hospital did not have the testing facilities to determine the presence of the substance. While the grandmother was driving the grandson to another hospital, he jumped out of the car, ran into a building, and fatally stabbed the plaintiff's husband. The court found that the hospital was not liable because the patient had exhibited no behavior there that would have led the personnel to suspect a risk of this outcome.[26] If there had been reason to suspect this, other arrangements would have had to be made for transport.

Other Health Care Institutions

Similar rules apply to relationships between patients and other health care institutions, such as skilled nursing and intermediate care facilities. Although it is unlikely that medical circumstances will arise compelling emergency admissions to such facilities, there are circumstances after admission that may require transfer to a hospital. Questions then arise concerning the scope of the right to be readmitted when hospitalization no longer is required. The scope of the right will vary depending on state licensing rules, transfer agreements between the health care institution and the hospital, contracts between the patient and the health care institution, and applicable rules of the agency paying for the patient's care.

DISCHARGE FROM AN INSTITUTION

There is a fundamental tension between the liability that can result from holding a patient too long and the liability that can result from releasing a patient too soon. This section discusses the liability for false imprisonment, for discharge of patients in need of additional care, refusal to leave, temporary releases, and escapes.

False Imprisonment

False imprisonment is holding persons against their will without lawful authority. Physical restraint or a physical barrier is not necessary. Threats leading to a reasonable apprehension of harm can provide enough restraint to establish false imprisonment.

In the past, a few cases of false imprisonment arose when hospitals attempted to hold patients until their bills were paid.[27] There have been no reported court decisions concerning this situation in more than 20 years, which indicates that hospitals now understand this practice is unacceptable. The only vestige of this problem arises when unsophisticated parents offer their children as collateral. Hospital staff members must explain that this is inappropriate and unnecessary.

In some cases, hospitals inappropriately restrain patients as part of treatment, leading to liability. An unreported 1970 Michigan Circuit Court decision is an example.[28] A patient who had been transferred from the coronary care unit to a semiprivate room decided to leave the hospital because he did not like the room. When he tried to leave, several staff members returned him to the hospital room and restrained him in the bed. He escaped from the restraints and fled through the window, receiving injuries in his fall to the ground. Since there was no evidence that the patient was disoriented or mentally unsound, the court found the hospital liable.

In many situations, it not only is appropriate but also is a duty of the hospital to detain or restrain a patient. All states have laws providing procedures for the commitment of persons who are seriously mentally ill, are substance abusers, or are a danger to the public health because of contagious disease. They also have laws that provide procedures for obtaining custody of minors who are neglected or abused. Generally, a hospital can hold these persons while reporting them to authorities and obtaining commitment or custody orders. When these laws do not apply, the hospital still has a common-law duty to protect temporarily disoriented patients.

Physicians and hospitals have authority under the common law to temporarily detain and even restrain disoriented medical patients without court involvement. This responsibility generally can be delegated to nurses to the extent necessary to deal with emergencies in which there is insufficient time to contact the physician before restraints are initiated.

The authority of physicians and hospitals to detain and restrain is inferred from the cases in which institutions have been found liable for injuries to patients because they were not restrained during temporary disorientation. This common-law authority does not apply when the patient is being detained for treatment for mental illness or substance abuse. The applicable statutory procedures should be followed in those cases. This common-law authority also does not apply when the patient is fully oriented, but the hospital usually can maintain custody long enough for the person's status to be determined if there is reasonable doubt.

If parents try to take children out of the hospital when removal presents an imminent danger to their life or health, most states either authorize the health care provider to retain custody or provide an expeditious procedure for obtaining court authorization to retain custody. Some states give only physicians or hospital administrators authority to retain custody, so nurses must get an appropriate order before doing so. Most parents will agree to an acceptable treatment or at least postpone precipitous withdrawal when advised that these procedures will have to be invoked.

An adult patient who is neither disoriented nor commitable generally has a right to leave unless it is one of the other unusual situations when courts will order treatment (see Chapter 9). Interfering with this right can lead to liability. Honoring the patient's wishes to leave can cause nurses and other staff members great distress. For example, nearly all physicians or nurses are distressed when an oriented patient with a spinal fracture insists on leaving the hospital, risking paralysis or even death that probably could be prevented by appropriate care in the hospital. This distress does not change the patient's right to leave. It will affect the efforts to convince the patient to stay and to explain the risks of leaving.

Patients who decide to leave against medical advice should be advised of the risks, if possible, and should be urged to reconsider if further care is needed. The explanation should be provided by the physician, if possible, and should be documented. Patients should be asked to sign a release form that they are leaving against medical advice and that the risks have been explained to them. However, they cannot be forced to sign. If they do refuse, the explanation and refusal should be documented in the medical record by the staff persons involved.

Discharge of Patients Needing Additional Care

A patient should be discharged only with a written order of a physician familiar with the person's condition or decision to leave against medical advice. This helps to protect the patient from injury and the hospital from liability for premature discharge.

Most premature discharge cases arise from misdiagnosis but sometimes they result from releasing patients who are ready to leave but for whom adequate arrangements have not been made. It is essential for children, the infirm aged, and others unable to care for themselves to be discharged only to the custody of someone who can take care of them. A California physician was found liable for discharging an abused 11-month-old child to the abusing parents without first giving the state an opportunity to intervene.[29]

Patients do not have to be kept in the hospital until cured. When they no longer need the level of care provided in a hospital, they can be transferred to a nursing home or discharged to home care. When they no longer need the level of hospital care in a referral center or begin to need more specialized care, interhospital transfer is appropriate and sometimes necessary.

If a patient becomes sufficiently difficult or disruptive, it is permissible in some situations for the hospital to discontinue providing care. In 1982, a California court refused to order a physician and several hospitals to continue to provide chronic hemodialysis to a noncooperative, disruptive female patient who had even refused to comply with the conditions of a court order that provided for continued treatment during the litigation.[30] The physician had given her due notice of his withdrawal from the physician-patient relationship with ample time for her to make other arrangements. The court clearly was troubled by the possibility that the patient would not be able to receive necessary care but concluded that several alternatives were available.

Courts are more comfortable with discharges when the patient's condition is not so severe. For example, an Arizona court ruled that the physician and hospital were not liable for discharging a difficult patient who had been admitted for treatment of lesions on his lips.[31] The court observed that the patient was uncomfortable but not helpless, and the hospital staff had done nothing to actively retard his treatment or worsen his condition.

Any discharge of a patient in need of continued care could become controversial so most hospitals usually limited these releases to situations that interfere with the care of other patients or threaten the safety of staff members. Hospital administration usually reviews each case to minimize legal liability and other adverse effects on the institution. When the attending physician desires an inappropriate discharge, the hospital may have to arrange for the transfer of the care of the patient to another physician or to discuss with the physician the compatibility of the proposed discharge with the hospital's standards for continued membership on the medical staff.

Refusal to Leave

Patients and their representatives do not have the right to insist on unnecessary hospitalization. If patients refuse to leave, or their representatives refuse to remove them after the physician's discharge order, the patients are trespassers and the hospital can take appropriate steps to effect their removal. If the situation is simply a delay in discharge because of difficulties in arranging placement, hospitals usually make reasonable efforts to assist in making arrangements. However, if patients and their representatives will not cooperate, it may be necessary to use reasonable force to remove them or to get a court order.[32] As with the discharge of noncooperative and disruptive patients, hospital administration should make decisions concerning forceable removal after appropriate review.

Temporary Releases

Sometimes children, incompetent adults, cooperative committed patients, or competent adults who need continuing supervision or care ask to leave the hospital for a short time. This is permissible in many situations and may assist the care of the patient. Since there is a possibility of liability, certain precautions should be taken. Hospital policies should be followed, which usually include the following precautions:

- There should be a written physician's authorization indicating that the temporary release is not medically contraindicated.
- There should be written authorization from competent adult patients or from the parent or guardian of other patients acknowledging that the hospital is not responsible for the care of the patient while the person is out of the custody of the hospital.
- There should be release (of patients who are not able to take care of themselves and are not a danger to others) only to an appropriate adult who has been instructed concerning the needs of the patient, such as medications and wheelchair use, and how to contact the hospital for information or assistance if needed. If arrangements are made for such patient needs, the risks associated with temporary releases are minimized.

If patients who are a danger to themselves or others are temporarily released and are harmed or harm others, the hospital could be liable. For example, a Florida court ruled that the hospital could be sued by a person who was injured in an automobile accident caused by a patient on a temporary release because the hospital should have known she would attempt to operate an automobile and could not do so safely.[33] This illustrates the significance of careful review by the physician before authorizing the release.

Escape

Hospitals frequently are sued when patients who have escaped either commit suicide, are injured or killed in accidents, or injure or kill others. The courts usually focus on: (1) how much those involved in the care of the patient knew or should have known about the dangerousness of the patient to self or others and (2) the appropriateness of the precautions taken to prevent escape in the light of that knowledge.

Generally, if the injury was not foreseeable, there is little likelihood of liability for failure to take additional precautions. If the injury was foreseeable, courts will examine the reasonableness of the precautions, and liability will be more likely. However, many courts have recognized the therapeutic benefits of more open patient care units and found them to be reasonable even for some patients at risk. In other cases, the precautions have been found to be inadequate, and liability has been imposed.

THE EFFECT OF PROSPECTIVE PAYMENT

As discussed in the Medicare section of Chapter 3, changes in approaches to payment for health care services are focusing attention on prompt discharge of patients to the lowest level of care possible. This has resulted in increased emphasis on discharge planning. Through patient education, nurses now are preparing patients and their families to assume more responsibility for the care. There is increased pressure for communities to develop adequate resources to provide support for home care and for increased availability of more sophisticated services in skilled nursing and intermediate care facilities. Nurses increasingly are called upon to assure that arrangements are made for the prompt, safe discharge of patients to these facilities.

Knowledge as to the care in the available settings, as well as to the patient's needs and capabilities, is essential to assure that a planned discharge is appropriate. Nurses are involved in explaining to physicians, patients, families and others why certain discharges are appropriate while others are not. This can involve explaining how surprisingly sophisticated care can be given in another facility or the home and why certain needed care cannot be delivered in a proposed setting.

This actually is just another manifestation of the nurse's traditional role of patient advocate, which always has included pushing the patient and the family to make efforts they think they would prefer to postpone.

NOTES

1. *E.g., Laidlaw v. Lions Gate Hosp.*, 8 D.L.R.3d 730 (B.C. Sup. Ct. 1969).

2. *Czubinsky v. Doctor Hosp.*, 139 Cal. App. 3d 361, 188 Cal. Rptr. 685 (1983).

3. *Skodje v. Hardy*, 47 Wash. 2d 557, 288 P.2d 471 (1955).

4. *Vidrine v. Mayes*, 127 So. 2d 809 (La. Ct. App. 1961).

5. *McNamara v. Emmons*, 36 Cal. App. 2d 199, 97 P.2d 503 (1939).

6. *Giallanza v. Sands*, 316 So. 2d 77 (Fla. Dist. Ct. App. 1975).

7. *McGulpin v. Bessmer*, 241 Iowa 1119, 43 N.W.2d 121 (1950).

8. *O'Neil v. Montefiore Hosp.*, 202 N.Y.S.2d 436 (N.Y. App. Div. 1960).

9. *Buttersworth v. Swint*, 53 Ga. App. 602, 186 S.E. 770 (1936).

10. *E.g., Norwood Hosp. v. Howton*, 32 Ala. App. 375, 26 So. 2d 427 (1946).

11. 42 C.F.R. §§ 124.601–124.607.

12. IOWA CODE, § 347.16 (1983).

13. 42 U.S.C. §§ 2000d–2000d–6 (1976 & Supp. IV 1980).

14. 45 C.F.R. pt. 80 (1981).

15. 29 U.S.C. § 794 (Supp. V. 1981).

16. 45 C.F.R. pt. 84 (1981).

17. *E.g., People ex rel. M.B.*, 312 N.W.2d 714 (S.D. 1981).

18. *E.g., Pierce County Office of Involuntary Commitment v. Western State Hosp.*, 644 P.2d 131 (Wash. 1982).

19. TEX. REV. CIV. STAT. ANN. art. 4438a (Vernon 1976).

20. *Wilmington Gen. Hosp. v. Manlove*, 54 Del. 15, 174 A.2d 135 (1962).

21. *E.g., Stanturf v. Sipes*, 447 S.W.2d 558 (Mo. 1969).

22. *E.g., Guerrero v. Copper Queen Hosp.*, 537 P.2d 1329 (Ariz. 1975).

23. *Harper v. Baptist Medical Center-Princeton*, 341 So. 2d 133 (Ala. 1976).

24. *Carrasco v. Bankoff*, 220 Cal. App. 2d 230, 33 Cal. Rptr. 673 (1963).

25. *New Biloxi Hosp. v. Frazier*, 245 Miss. 185, 146 So. 2d 882 (1962).

26. *Nance v. James Archer Smith Hosp.*, 329 So. 2d 377 (Fla. Dist. Ct. App. 1976).

27. *E.g., Gadsden Gen. Hosp. v. Hamilton*, 212 Ala. 531, 103 So. 553 (1925).

28. *Smith v. Henry Ford Hosp.* (Wayne County, Mich. Cir. Ct., 1970).

29. *Landeros v. Flood.* 17 Cal. 3d 399, 551 P.2d 389 (1976).

30. *Payton v. Weaver*, 131 Cal. App. 3d 38, 182 Cal. Rptr. 225 (1982).

31. *Modla v. Parker*, 17 Ariz. App. 54, 495 P.2d 494 (1972), *cert.denied* 409 U.S. 1038 (1972).

32. *E.g., Jersey City Medical Center v. Halstead*, 169 N.J. Super. 22, 404 A.2d 44 (N.J. Super. Ct. Ch. Div. 1979); *Lucy Webb Hayes Nat. Training School v. Geoghegan*, 281 F.Supp. 116 (D.D.C. 1967).

33. *Burroughs v. Board of Trustees of Alachua Gen. Hosp.*, 328 So. 2d 538 (Fla. Dist. Ct. App. 1976).

BIBLIOGRAPHY

Aroskar, M. "Ethics of Nurse-Patient Relationships." *Nurse Educator* (March-April 1980):18.

Smith, S. et al. "Ethical Dilemmas: Conflicts Among Rights, Duties, and Obligations." *American Journal of Nursing* 80, no. 8 (August 1980):1463.

Trandel-Karenchuk, Darlene. "Legal Forum: Patients' Rights and the Preservation of Human Dignity." *Nursing Administration Quarterly* 6, no. 4 (Summer 1982):83.

Chapter 9

Authorization for Treatment

Health care providers must obtain appropriate authorization before examining a patient or performing diagnostic or therapeutic procedures. In most circumstances the express or implied consent of the patient or the patient's representative constitutes the authorization. The law requires that the patient (or representative) be given sufficient information concerning the available choices so that the consent is an informed consent. If the decision is not to consent, the examination or procedure usually cannot be performed. However, in several circumstances the law overrides the decision and provides authorization for involuntary treatment, such as for some mental illness and for substance abuse. In a few situations, consent is not sufficient authorization because some procedures are illegal under some circumstances.

Physicians and other independent practitioners have the primary responsibility for obtaining informed consent or other authorization for treatment. Nurses are not responsible for obtaining consent unless they are in independent practice or are assigned responsibilities associated with obtaining consent by their employer. If nurses happen to become aware of a lack of informed consent or other authorization, they generally have a responsibility to inform the responsible physician or other independent practitioners and, in some circumstances, inform institutional officials.

Hospitals and other health care institutions generally are not liable for the physician's failure to obtain authorization, unless (1) the physician is an employee or agent of the hospital or (2) the hospital happens to be aware of the lack of consent and fails to take appropriate action. Thus, nurses need to be familiar with the principles discussed in this chapter.

The requirements of consent and informed consent, the decision-making roles of patients and their representatives, and the exceptions to the consent requirement are discussed in this chapter. Decisions concerning reproductive issues are discussed in Chapter 12. Withholding and withdrawing treatment from dying patients are discussed in Chapter 10.

THE DISTINCTION BETWEEN CONSENT AND INFORMED CONSENT

The common law has long recognized the right of persons to be free from harmful or offensive touching. The intentional harmful or offensive touching of another person without authorization is called battery (as discussed in Chapter 6). When there is no consent or other authorization, the physician or other practitioner doing a medical procedure can be liable for battery, even if the procedure is properly performed, beneficial, and has no negative effects. The touching alone leads to liability.

The physician or other practitioner responsible for the procedure has a separate legal duty to disclose sufficient information so that the consent is based on an informed decision. Failure to disclose the necessary information does not invalidate the consent, so the procedure is not a battery. However, failure to disclose is a separate wrong for which there can be liability based on principles applicable to negligent torts (as discussed in Chapter 6). Thus, uninformed consent protects from liability for battery but informed consent is necessary to protect the health care provider from liability for negligence.

In California, the courts have extended the informed consent doctrine to require informed refusal. In 1980 the California Supreme Court ruled that a physician could be liable for a patient's death from cancer of the cervix based on failure to inform the woman of the risks of not consenting to a recommended Pap smear.[1] The Pap smear probably would have discovered her cancer in time to begin treatment that would have extended her life.

CONSENT

Consent may be either express or implied. Express consent is consent that is given by direct words, either oral or written. There are a few procedures, especially those involving reproduction, for which some states require written consent. With those exceptions, either oral or written consent can be legally sufficient authorization. However, it often is difficult to prove oral consent so most providers seek to get consent in writing.

Implied consent can be divided into consent that is inferred from the patient's conduct and consent that is presumed in certain emergencies. When a patient voluntarily submits to a procedure with apparent knowledge of its nature, the courts usually will find implied consent. For example, the Massachusetts Supreme Judicial Court ruled that a woman had given her implied consent to being vaccinated by extending her arm and accepting the vaccination without objection.[2] This implied consent is the reason explicit consent is usually not sought for physical examinations or minor procedures on competent patients.

Consent is presumed to exist in medical emergencies unless the provider has reason to believe that it would be refused. This presumption clearly applies when there is an immediate threat to life or health. The Iowa Supreme Court found implied consent to the removal of a mangled limb that had been run over in an accident with a train.[3] The court accepted the physician's determination that the amputation was necessary to save the patient's life.

Courts have disagreed on whether pain is enough justification to find implied consent.[4] In addition, some courts have found implied consent to extensions or modifications of surgical procedures beyond the scope specifically authorized when unexpected conditions arise, especially when the additional action is necessary to preserve the patient's life.[5] Many surgical consent forms include explicit authorization of extensions or modifications to preserve the patient's life or health. This minimizes disagreements over the scope of the authorization by providing an opportunity for patients to specify extensions or modifications that they forbid.

Express consent or consent implied from the patient's conduct must be voluntary. While there are no reported cases dealing with this issue outside of a research context, in an unusual situation a consent might be challenged on the basis that it allegedly was obtained through coercion or undue inducement.

Exceptions to the requirement of consent in which the law authorizes treatment despite the refusal of the patient (or representative) are discussed later in this chapter.

INFORMED CONSENT

The courts have developed two standards for determining the adequacy of the disclosure—the professional or reasonable physician standard and the reasonable patient standard. Courts in many states use the professional standard of accepted medical practice. In those states, the physician or other independent practitioner has a duty to make the disclosures that a reasonable medical practitioner would make under the same or similar circumstances.[6] Expert testimony is required to prove the required disclosure.

The reasonable patient standard has been adopted by an increasing number of states. This provides that the duty to disclose is determined by the information needs of the patient, not by professional practice. Information that is "material" to the decision must be disclosed. One court defined a risk to be material "when a reasonable person, in what the physician knows or should know to be the patient's position, would be likely to attach significance to the risk or cluster of risks in deciding whether or not to forego the proposed therapy."[7] No expert testimony is required on the scope of disclosure, although expert testimony may be necessary to establish what the risks and alternatives are.

A few states have adopted hybrid standards. For example, in Iowa the reasonable patient standard applies if the procedure is elective, but the reasonable physician standard applies if the procedure is necessary.[8]

The usual elements of the explanation are the patient's medical condition, the nature and purpose of the proposed procedure, its consequences and risks, and the feasible accepted alternatives, including the consequences of no treatment. Only risks that are known or should be known by the physician to occur without negligence are required to be disclosed. Nearly all courts recognize that not all risks can be disclosed. One useful guideline is to disclose the risks of the most severe consequences and the risks that have a large probability of occurring.

Some nurses have suggested that the elements be expanded to include an explanation of the postoperative treatments that they and therapists will provide. While it is beneficial for patients to have this information to avoid surprises, courts have not required proof that this information was provided unless the patient can prove it was requested. Courts have attempted to focus on disclosure of the more permanent effects of procedures, rather than the accompanying transitory experiences, in recognition of the practical limits on what may be disclosed and understood in a reasonable period of time.

When the patient indicates the need for additional information, there can be a duty to provide it. For example, a patient had told the physician that his ability to work was crucial, so an Arizona court ruled that the physician should have informed the patient of the risks that could affect that ability to work.[9]

The most difficult element for the patient to prove in an informed consent case is causation. Since informed consent suits are based on the principles of liability for negligent torts, the plaintiff must prove that the deviation from the standard caused the injury. Thus, the plaintiff must prove that consent would not have been given if the risk involved had been disclosed or a possible alternative had been disclosed.

The courts have developed two standards. Some jurisdictions apply an "objective" standard of what a prudent person in the patient's position would have decided if informed of the risk or alternative.[10] Other courts apply a "subjective" standard so that the plaintiff must prove that the patient would have refused consent if informed of the risk or alternative.[11] Either of these standards provides substantial protection for the conscientious health care professional who discloses the major risks and then has a more remote risk occur. A patient who consents to a procedure knowing of the risk of death and paralysis will find it difficult to convince a court that knowledge of a minor risk would have led to refusal. However, courts may be more easily convinced when there are undisclosed alternatives.

Exceptions to the Disclosure Requirement

The courts have recognized four exceptions to the disclosure requirement in circumstances where consent still must be obtained—emergencies, the therapeutic privilege, patient waiver, and prior patient knowledge.

In emergencies when consent is implied to exist, there is a corollary modification of the disclosure requirement. When there is no time to obtain consent, there clearly is no time to make disclosures. Courts have recognized that even when there is time, emergency situations still may make possible only abbreviated disclosure.[12]

Most courts recognize a therapeutic privilege when disclosure poses a significant threat of detriment to the patient. Courts have tried to carefully limit the privilege so it is not applicable when the health care professional solely fears that the information might lead the patient to forego needed therapy. Thus, the privilege should be relied on only when a patient's anxiety is documented to be significantly above the norm. Some courts have ruled that when the therapeutic privilege is applied to keep information from the patient, the information must be disclosed to a relative. Before the procedure can be performed, the informed relative must concur with the patient's consent.[13] However, at least one court has ruled that no disclosure needed to be made to relatives.[14]

A patient can waive the right to be informed.[15] However, it is doubtful that courts will accept a waiver initiated by a health care professional so a prudent practitioner should not suggest a waiver but instead should encourage reluctant patients to be informed. There is no liability for nondisclosure of risks that are common knowledge or that the patient has experienced previously.

One state by statute eliminated the requirement of disclosure of risks. The Georgia Code states that health care professionals need only disclose "in general terms the treatment or course of treatment" to obtain an informed consent.[16] The Georgia courts have interpreted this to eliminate the requirement that risks be disclosed, so they no longer base liability on failure to disclose risks.[17]

RESPONSIBILITY FOR OBTAINING CONSENT

It is the physician's responsibility, not the hospital's, to provide the necessary information and to obtain informed consent. Other independent practitioners, including nurses in independent practice, who order procedures have the same responsibility concerning the procedures they order. A hospital or other health care institution generally is not liable for the failure of the physician or other independent practitioner to get informed consent unless the professional is an employee or agent of the institution. This principle has been applied in several court decisions, and some states have enacted it in their statutes.[18] There have been increasing efforts to convince courts to require hospitals to intercede in the professional relationship with the patient by imposing liability on the institution for inadequate disclosures by independent physicians. These efforts have not been successful with few exceptions such as one Illinois appellate court decision.[19]

One of the earliest court decisions addressing professional liability for operating without consent observed that while a hospital generally is not liable for nonconsensual operations by physicians who are independent contractors, it may be liable for failing to intervene when it has actual knowledge that the procedure is being performed without authorization.[20] Some attorneys believe this could be extended to situations in which the hospital should have known there was no authorization.

It is generally recognized that it is not feasible for the hospital to be responsible for the content of the professional disclosure underlying the consent because the necessary monitoring could destroy the professional relationship with the patient. However, the hospital could be liable if it failed to intervene when it knew the disclosure was not proper.

Nurses can potentially be involved in obtaining patient consent to four types of procedures: (1) procedures offered by nurses in independent practice roles; (2) nursing procedures not directly related to medical procedures; (3) nursing aspects of medical procedures where the primary procedure is being provided by another practitioner; and (4) medical procedures being provided by another practitioner.

Nurses have the same responsibility as physicians to obtain informed consent for the first type—the procedures they authorize or perform in independent practice roles.

Nurses, regardless of their position, clearly should provide information to patients concerning the second type of procedures. This does not mean that formal informed consent must be obtained. Only in the most unusual circumstances would a signed consent form be appropriate. However, it does mean that nurses should continue to explain what to expect from nursing procedures the patient will be experiencing. The patient's acquiescence is implied consent. If the patient withdraws consent by objecting, the procedure should be discontinued as expeditiously as possible without endangering the individual. When the patient is unable to understand, implied consent is derived from the person's admission to the institution by the family or guardian or from the emergency doctrine in cases where such others are not involved.

There is disagreement over the appropriate role of nurses within the third type of procedure. Good patient education includes explaining many postoperative procedures before they are begun. The disagreement concerns whether they should be disclosed before consent is obtained for the operation and, if so, by whom—the nurse or the physician. There is no general legal duty to explain postoperative nursing procedures as part of the disclosure before consent to operative procedures. Some nurses advocate that nurses actively explain postoperative procedures before consent to the operation is obtained. The other position is to place the disclosure responsibility on the physician and give additional nursing explanations only with the physician's authorization or after consent to the operation is obtained. The latter probably is the better approach because it avoids conflicting explanations that could confuse the patient and because it minimizes the nurse's exposure to liability. Nurses should encourage physicians to orient patients to postoperative procedures or to authorize the nurse to do so. One approach is for nurses to contribute to the development of booklets and other educational aids, such as audio and visual recordings, that orient the patient to the full course of the procedure.

There is disagreement concerning the extent of the nurse's involvement in obtaining consent for the fourth type of procedures that are primarily the responsibility of other health care professionals, especially physicians.[21] Some hospitals permit nurses to obtain the signature of the patient or the patient's representative on the consent form. Some hospitals permit nurses to provide some or all of the information necessary for an informed consent. Both of these practices may impair the physician-patient relationship by reducing the opportunity for adequate communication and negotiation. These practices could shift the liability for disclosure inadequacies to the nurse and to the hospital as the employer of the nurse. One attempt to shift responsibility was a 1979 Missouri case that arose when a nurse gave a patient a consent form authorizing a vaginal hysterectomy. The nurse did not know the physician had failed to explain the procedure to the patient. The patient asked questions about what the form authorized. The nurse replied that the physician knew what the patient wanted. The patient later experienced complications from the surgery (a vesicovaginal fistula) and sued the physician and the hospital employer of the nurse alleging lack of informed consent. After the physician settled, the court ruled that the nurse and hospital were not liable because they were not responsible for obtaining the informed consent.[22] Some states might have imposed liability because the nurse failed to notify the physician of the patient's questions.

To avoid these adverse consequences, some hospitals do not permit nurses to obtain signatures on consent forms. In hospitals where this rule is not practical, nurses who get the forms signed should not attempt to answer patient questions concerning the procedure unless authorized to do so by the hospital and physician. The physician may legally delegate the obtaining of an informed consent to a nurse or other appropriate person but will be liable if such consent is not obtained. The nurse and the nurse's employer also will be potentially liable, so a nurse should not accept this delegation unless authorized to do so by the employer. Absent authorization from the employer and physician, if the patient seeks additional information or expresses reluctance the nurse should contact the physician instead of attempting to convince the patient to sign the form.

To help protect the hospital or health care facility from the risk of liability for lack of consent, most institutions require the use of a standard form before major procedures. The battery consent form described in the next section will fulfill this purpose. The role of nurses and other staff members usually should be limited to (1) screening for completion of the form or alternative authorization and (2) conveying information to the physician.

For procedures for which the hospital requires consent, nurses and other staff members should be assigned the responsibility of ascertaining whether the consent is appropriately documented or that there is another type of authorization before permitting the procedure to be performed. A staff member who becomes aware of a patient's confusion or change of opinion regarding a procedure should notify the responsible physician. If the physician does not respond, appropriate supervisors, medical staff, or institutional officials should be notified so they can determine whether intervention is necessary.

DOCUMENTATION

Most attorneys who represent health care professionals and hospitals agree that the best way to document consent is to obtain the signature of the patient (or representative) on an appropriate form. Usually, if there is a proper form signed by the appropriate person, the courts accept it as proof of consent unless the plaintiff can prove there were special circumstances so that the form should be ignored.

A few attorneys disagree with that position and recommend that a note be written in the medical record concerning the discussion with the patient or representative. These attorneys are concerned that courts will consider a consent form to contain all information given to the patient and not believe testimony that additional information was provided. The attorneys who recommend the use of forms write them to make clear that they do not contain all information provided by the professional.

Joint Commission on Accreditation of Hospitals (JCAH) standards concerning medical records require "evidence of appropriate informed consent" for procedures or treatments for which it is required by hospital policy.[23] The hospital should have a policy that is consistent with legal standards. The JCAH does not specify the procedures or treatments and does not require the consent to be documented by the signature of the patient or representative. Several hospitals that do not require the use of signed consent forms are accredited.

Whenever developing or applying a policy involving consent forms, it is essential to remember that the actual process of providing information to the person giving consent and of determining that individual's decision is more important than the form itself. The form is evidence of the consent process, not a substitute for it. There should be someone who has the authority to determine that there is actual consent even when the form has been lost or inadvertently not signed prior to sedation of the patient or when other circumstances make it difficult to obtain the signature. In those circumstances, a note in the medical record describing the circumstances and the consent can be substituted for the missing form.

Consent Forms

There are three basic types of consent forms: (1) the blanket consent, (2) the battery consent, and (3) the detailed consent.

Blanket Consent Forms

In the past, many hospitals provided consent forms that authorized any procedure the physician wished to perform. Courts have ruled that these blanket consent forms are not evidence of consent to major procedures because they do not specify the procedure.[24] Some attorneys recommend the continued use of a blanket admission consent form to cover procedures for which individual special consent is not sought. There is disagreement whether these admission forms provide more protection than the implied consent that is inferred from admission and submission to minor procedures. Institutional policy concerning admission consent forms should be followed.

Battery Consent Forms

For major procedures, most hospitals now provide consent forms that include space for the name and a description of the specific procedure. In addition, the form states (1) the person signing has been told about the medical condition, consequences, risks, and alternatives; and (2) all questions have been answered to that person's satisfaction. This type of form almost always will preclude a successful claim of battery as long as the proper person signs it and the procedure described is performed. This form also provides strong support for the reasonableness of the hospital's lack of suspicion that the person who signed was uninformed while providing some support for the professional's assertion that the patient was in fact informed. However, the person who signed still could convince a court that the information concerning consequences, risks, and alternatives was not actually given.

Detailed Consent Forms

Some physicians and other independent professionals use forms that detail the medical condition, procedure, consequences, risks, and alternatives. Such forms have been mandated for federally funded sterilizations and research. It is much more difficult for the patient to prove that the information included in the form was not disclosed. The primary difficulty with detailed consent forms is that it is costly and time consuming to prepare them for each individual procedure. Thus, some professionals who use detailed forms do so only for procedures, such as cosmetic surgery, where there is a higher risk of misunderstanding and unsatisfactory results.

Challenges to Consent Forms

Although the forms are strong evidence of informed consent, they usually are not conclusive. A person challenging the adequacy of the consent process usually will be permitted an opportunity to convince the court that informed consent was not actually obtained. This can be done by proving that the person who signed the form was not competent, for example, because of transient impairment by medication. Thus, it is important that the explanation be given and the signature be obtained at a time when the person is able to understand.

Another basis for challenging a consent form is that the wording was too technical or in a language the person did not understand. In general, persons are presumed to have read and understood documents they have signed. However, courts sometimes will not apply this rule when the document is too technical or in a language foreign to the patient. Thus, it is important that forms be written so that the person signing can understand.

There has been increasing criticism that many forms require too high a level of reading ability. Several journal articles have been published that describe how to simplify the wording of forms.[25] If the person has difficulty understanding English, then someone should translate the form. It usually is not necessary to have forms in other languages, although it is advisable to have them in the primary languages used by a substantial portion of the patients served by the hospital. It usually is sufficient to have the form translated orally and have the translator certify that the form and discussion of the procedure have been translated orally for the person signing.

Another basis for challenge is that the signature was not voluntary. The person signing would have to demonstrate that there had been some threat or undue inducement to demonstrate that the signature was not voluntary, so it is unlikely this will apply in hospital situations or most other situations in which nurses might become involved.

Exculpatory Clauses

Some providers include in their forms a paragraph that states that the person signing waives the right to sue for injuries or agrees to limit any claims to not more than a specified amount. These are called exculpatory clauses. Courts will not enforce them in suits on behalf of patients against health care providers. For example, in 1979 a federal court refused to enforce a $15,000 limit on liability in an agreement that the patient had signed before surgery.[26]

Period of Validity of Consent Forms

There is no absolute limit on the period of validity of a consent or the documentation of that consent by a signature on a form. If the patient's condition or the available treatments change significantly, the earlier consent no longer is informed and a new consent should be obtained. Otherwise, the consent is legally valid until withdrawn unless institutional policy limits the period of validity. A claim that consent was withdrawn becomes more credible as time passes, so the guideline some hospitals follow is to recommend a new consent each time the patient is admitted. The consent may be obtained in the physician's office before the admission, if appropriate documentation is inserted in the hospital's records, unless hospital policy precludes preadmission consents.

Some hospitals use a guideline that forms should be signed no more than 30 days before the procedure. Hospitals are not legally required to have guidelines but generally are required to follow their own rules. Thus, most hospitals that adopt guidelines (1) state that they are not a requirement, or (2) identify who has authority to make exceptions to the requirement to deal with repetitive treatments for chronic disease, situations when the person who gave consent is no longer competent or available, and other unusual circumstances.

Impact of Statutes

Some states have adopted statutes concerning consent forms. Several of these provide that, if the form contains certain information and is signed by the appropriate person, it is conclusive evidence of, or creates a presumption of, informed consent.[27] Such statutes address how the courts shall consider forms that contain certain information. They do not address forms that do not contain the information. Thus, it is not a violation of these statutes to use a form that contains different information or to forego the use of a form. However, especially in states that make certain forms conclusive evidence, health care professionals should give serious consideration to using forms that qualify.

Supplements to Documentation

Some health care professionals supplement their explanations to patients with other educational materials, such as booklets and movies. Some are making audio and visual recordings of the consent process to supplement or even substitute for written consent. Some are giving their patients tests of knowledge or are having their patients write their own forms to determine and document the level of understanding. None of these steps are legally required today, but they should be given serious consideration whenever controversial procedures are being used.

THE DECISIONMAKER

The person who makes the decision concerning the treatment or procedure must be legally and actually competent to do so and must be informed, unless one of the exceptions applies. Competent adults and some mature minors make decisions regarding their own care; someone else must make the decisions for incompetent adults and other minors.

Competent Adults

The age of majority is established by the legislature of each state. In most states, it now is 18, but there still is some variation. In some states, a person can become adult before the established age by certain actions, such as marriage.

Adults are competent if: (1) a court has not declared them incompetent; and (2) they generally are capable of understanding the consequences of alternatives, weighing them by the degree they promote their desires, and choosing and acting accordingly. There is a strong legal presumption of continued competence.

For example, a Pennsylvania court found a woman to be competent to refuse a breast biopsy even though she was committed to a mental institution with a diagnosis of chronic schizophrenia and two of her three reasons for refusal were delusional.[28] A Massachusetts court found a woman to be competent to refuse the amputation of her gangrenous leg even though her train of thought sometimes wandered, her conception of time was distorted, and she was confused on some matters.[29] The fact that her decision was medically irrational and would lead to her death did not demonstrate incompetence. The court believed she understood the alternatives and the consequences of her decision.

The determination of patient competence is not necessarily the function of psychiatrists. It usually is a practical assessment that should be made by the physician or other health professional who obtains the consent or accepts the refusal. When it is difficult to assess competence, consultation is advisable. If there is suspicion of underlying mental retardation, mental illness, or disorders that affect brain function, consultation with a psychiatrist or other appropriate specialist may be advisable.

Incompetent Adults

The guardian or, if there is no guardian, the representative of the incompetent adult makes decisions concerning that patient's care. Because of the obligations of representatives to the patients, they have a narrower range of permissible choices than they would have concerning their own care. In addition, the known wishes of the patient should be considered.

When a court rules that a person is incompetent, it designates another person as guardian, who then has the legal authority to make most of the decisions regarding the incompetent individual's care.

Some patients who actually are incompetent have never been determined to be incompetent by a court, so they do not have guardians. When decisions must be made concerning their care, it is common practice to seek approvals from the next of kin or others who have assumed supervision of the patient. In many states, laws or court decisions support this practice.[30] In other states, the decision whether to proceed without a guardian depends on an assessment of state law, but guardianship probably is not necessary in most circumstances unless the procedure is elective and the patient opposes it.

If the incompetence is temporary, the procedure should be postponed until the patient is competent and can make the decision unless the delay presents a substantial risk to the person's life or health.

When patients express their wishes concerning treatment before becoming incompetent, those wishes should be considered seriously in deciding on treatment. When patients knew their condition and available treatment when their wishes were expressed, the wishes usually should be followed. When there is a significant unanticipated change in the patient's condition or in available treatments, there is more latitude for the representative or guardian to reach a decision different from the patient's wishes. (The living will and other directives concerning the care of the terminally ill are discussed in Chapter 10.)

Minors

Parental or guardian consent should be obtained before treatment is given to a minor unless it is: (1) an emergency, (2) one of the situations where the consent of the minor is sufficient, or (3) a court order or other legal authorization is obtained.

Emergency Care

As with adults, consent is implied in medical emergencies when there is an immediate threat to life or health unless the provider has reason to believe that consent would be refused by the parent or guardian. When there is reason to so believe, the procedures for seeking court authorization should be followed whenever treatment is necessary.

Emancipated Minors

Emancipated minors may consent to their own medical care. Minors are emancipated when they no longer are subject to parental control or regulation and are not supported by their parents. The specific factors necessary to establish emancipation vary from state to state. Some states require that the parent and child agree on the emancipation, so that a minor cannot become emancipated in those states simply by running away from home.

Mature Minors

Mature minors may consent to some medical care under common-law and constitutional principles and under the statutes of some states. Many states have statutes empowering older minors to consent to medical treatment. The age limits and scope of treatments vary from state to state. Many states have special laws concerning minor consent to venereal disease and substance abuse treatment that have no age limits. In states that do not have an appliable minor consent statute, the risk associated with providing necessary treatment to mature minors with only their consent is minimal.

The oldest minor who underwent a procedure with his personal consent and won a reported lawsuit based on lack of parental consent was age 15.[31] That 1941 case involved a procedure that was not necessary for the minor. It was the removal of some skin for a donation to another person for a skin graft operation. The right of privacy in the Constitution restricts the state's authority to mandate parental involvement in certain reproductive decisions, such as pregnancy termination. (Reproductive issues are discussed in Chapter 12.)

When treating any minor, it is prudent to urge that the minor involve the parents. When a mature minor refuses to do so, necessary care can be provided without substantial risk unless (1) institutional policy requires parental involvement or (2) there is likelihood of harm to the minor or others that requires parental involvement to avoid. When there is likelihood of such harm, parents usually should be involved unless state law or institutional policy forbids their being notified.

Parental or Guardian Consent

Either parent can give legally effective consent except when there is legal separation or divorce. While it is not necessary to determine the wishes of the other parent, when it is known that the other parent objects, either the procedure should not be done or other legal authorization should be obtained. For example, in 1941 a New York court authorized surgical correction of a child's deformity when the parents disagreed.[32] When the parents are legally separated or divorced, the consent of the custodial parent usually must be obtained.

LIMITS ON THE AUTHORITY TO CONSENT

There are limits to what an adult or mature minor can authorize a provider to do. Persons making decisions on behalf of incompetent adults and other minors have a narrower range of permissible choices than persons making decisions for themselves because of their duty to act in the best interests of the incompetent adult or minor.

Mayhem

Intentional maiming or disfiguring of a person without justification, such as intended medical benefit, is the ancient crime of mayhem, which now is sometimes called willful injury. Consent or even request of the victim is not a defense when there is no medical justification. In 1961, a North Carolina court convicted a physician of aiding and abetting mayhem because, at the victim's request, he anesthetized the victim's fingers so they could later be removed by the victim's brother.[33]

Suicide

Aiding and abetting suicide is a crime in most states. Consent and even request of the victim is not a defense. However, as discussed in Chapter 10, courts have recognized that withholding and withdrawing treatment from the terminally ill is not suicide.

Statutory Prohibitions

The federal government through the Food and Drug Administration (FDA) has restricted the use of new drugs and devices until their safety and efficacy are proved. These drugs and devices cannot be used outside of approved testing projects until the FDA approves such use, regardless of a patient's desires, unless they are not subject to the agency's control by not being involved in interstate commerce. Even after drugs are approved for general distribution, many can be used only with a prescription. A physician or other authorized health professional can write a prescription only for appropriate medical uses. Inappropriate prescriptions can subject the professional to discipline by the licensure board and to criminal prosecution. Consent of the patient to the prescription is irrelevant.

Insistence on Inappropriate Treatment

Professionals generally have an obligation to refuse to provide clearly inappropriate treatment despite insistence by the patient. Some courts in the nineteenth century ruled that the patient's insistence after being informed of the inappropriateness could insulate a physician from liability.[34] It is very unlikely that courts would rule in favor of professionals in such circumstances today.

Limits on Consent for Incompetent Adults or Minors

Any person acting on behalf of an incompetent adult or a minor has a responsibility to do so in the patient's best interests. There are two procedures—organ donation and sterilization—that courts have ruled that decisionmakers cannot authorize for incompetent adults or minors without prior court approval. Courts in a few states will not approve kidney donations by minors and incompetents,[35] but courts in other states have authorized them.[36] The courts that have approved kidney donations usually have done so on the basis of the close relationship between the donor and the proposed recipient and the emotional injury to the donor if the recipient were to die without the attempt. (Sterilization of minors and incompetent adults is discussed in Chapter 12.)

THE RIGHT TO REFUSE

Generally the right to consent implies a right to refuse. The right to refuse continues to apply even after consent is given. Patients or their representatives generally can withdraw their consent by, for example, objecting to continuation of treatment. When nurses become aware that consent has been withdrawn, they should discontinue the procedure as expeditiously as possible without endangering the patient and promptly inform the physician or other responsible practitioner of the situation. A reasonable effort to convince the patient to continue to accept treatment is appropriate before discontinuing it. In some situations, withdrawal in the middle of a sequence of procedures poses too great a danger to the patient to permit consent to be withdrawn. For example, after an operation the immediate postoperative procedures necessary to assure a safe transition from an anesthetized state cannot be refused. However, when oriented and readapted to room air, most patients can refuse continued care unless other factors are present.

Most courts have found that since a competent adult has the right to refuse, those making decisions on behalf of incompetent adults and minors must have a right to refuse on their behalf in appropriate situations. However, in certain situations courts have found that the state's interests outweigh those of the patient and have ordered treatment. When the patient's right to refuse is honored, the patient may have to forego other benefits.

There are three legal bases for the right to refuse treatment: (1) the common law right to freedom from nonconsensual invasion of bodily integrity, embodied in the informed consent doctrine and the law of battery; (2) the constitutional right of privacy; and (3) the constitutional right to freedom of religion.

Common Law Bodily Integrity

The common law has long recognized the strong interest of all people to be free from nonconsensual invasion of their bodily integrity. One element of this is the right to make decisions concerning health care. Health care without express or implied authority is a battery. The common law requirement of informed consent has developed to assure that adequate information is made available to provide an opportunity for a knowledgeable decision even when there is not a battery. Courts have recognized that the right to make decisions concerning health care includes the right to decline health care. For example, in 1981 the highest court of New York recognized the right of a comatose patient through his guardian to decline respiratory support based on these principles.[37]

Right of Privacy

The second basis for the right to refuse medical care is the constitutional right of privacy. Unwanted infringements of bodily integrity have been recognized to violate the right of privacy unless state interests outweigh the right. For example, the Florida courts recognized the constitutional right of a competent 73-year-old man with amyotrophic lateral sclerosis (Lou Gehrig's disease) to discontinue the use of a respirator.[38] The right of privacy also was recognized as a basis for refusal in *Quinlan,* even though Karen Ann Quinlan was unable to express her wishes because she was irreversibly comatose.[39] The right of privacy has been the basis for accepting refusals in situations where the patient is neither terminally ill nor comatose. Based on the right of privacy, a Massachusetts court honored a 77-year-old woman's refusal to have her gangrenous leg amputated.[40]

Freedom of Religion

The freedom of religion is another basis for refusal in a few situations. However, this applies primarily to freedom of belief, not freedom of action, so the state may restrain religious conduct. A second reason that freedom of religion seldom has an important role in medical decisions is that few religions command adherents to refuse treatment. Most religions merely permit refusal, so legally required treatment does not violate their religious tenets. The only cases in which freedom of religion has been significant have involved Jehovah's Witnesses refusing blood transfusions or Christian Scientists refusing all treatment. Many courts have upheld the right of adherents to these religions to refuse the care that violates their religion.[41]

Minors and Incompetent Adults

The courts have tended to find that since a competent adult has the right to refuse, those making decisions on behalf of minors and incompetent adults have a right to refuse on their behalf in some situations. However, because the decision-makers have an obligation to act in the best interests of the minor or incompetent adult, they must provide necessary treatment. Their discretion to decline treatment is limited to situations where the treatment is elective or not likely to be beneficial. The duty to provide necessary treatment to minors is reinforced in all states by legislation concerning abused or neglected minors that facilitates state intervention to provide needed assistance. Legislation concerning abused or neglected adults has been enacted in a few states.

Courts generally have permitted the refusal of extraordinary care for terminally ill or irreversibly comatose minors and incompetent adults. For example, the New Jersey Supreme Court permitted the father of an irreversibly comatose adult daughter to authorize the withdrawal of respiratory support.[42] The Massachusetts Supreme Judicial Court agreed that no resuscitative efforts need be attempted in the event of cardiac or respiratory arrest of a child less than one year of age who was terminally ill.[43]

Courts have declined to override parental refusals in several situations where the benefit did not clearly outweigh the risk. For example, the Washington Supreme Court refused to authorize the amputation of an 11-year-old girl's arm that was so abnormally large it was useless and interfered with her association with other people.[44] The Pennsylvania Supreme Court refused to authorize blood transfusions for the 16-year-old son of a Jehovah's Witness so that an operation could be conducted to correct severe spinal curvature.[45]

Courts generally decline to intervene when the parents or guardian are following the advice of a licensed physician in good standing, even if the advice is unorthodox. The highest court of New York refused to authorize chemotherapy for a child with leukemia because the parents were following the advice of a physician who had prescribed laetrile, even though laetrile was not proved to be effective.[46]

Another factor that sometimes has led courts not to intervene has been the wishes of the minor. The highest court of New York declined to authorize surgery to repair the harelip and cleft palate of a 14-year-old boy when told both the father and son opposed the surgery.[47]

Consequences of Refusal

Patients who refuse often must accept consequences beyond those involving health. Payment may be denied or reduced in claims concerning the underlying illness if the refused procedure would help diagnose or reduce the injury. For example, the Iowa Supreme Court affirmed the denial of payment to a policeman for his continuing medical expenses because he refused to submit to coronary arteriography that was necessary to diagnose his condition.[48]

LIMITS ON REFUSAL

State Interests

The state asserts five interests as the basis for overriding a patient's right to refuse: (1) preservation of life when the patient's condition is curable; (2) protection of the patient's dependents, especially minor children; (3) prevention of irrational self-destruction; (4) preservation of the ethical integrity of health care providers; and (5) protection of the public health and other interests. In cases involving minors and incompetent adults, the state asserts its general interest in protecting their welfare.

Preservation of Life

The preservation of life is the most basic of the state interests that have been asserted to outweigh the right to refuse medical care. Courts have ruled uniformly that this interest does not outweigh the right of the terminally ill patient to refuse treatment. The *Quinlan* decision held that the state's interest in preserving life decreases as the prognosis dims and the degree of bodily invasion of the proposed procedure increases. The Massachusetts Supreme Judicial Court stated in a decision that authorized withholding chemotherapy from a patient with leukemia: "The value of life as so perceived is lessened not by a decision to refuse treatment, but by the failure to allow a competent human being the right of choice."[49] Even when the patient is not terminally ill, courts have declined to order treatment when the intervention is major, such as the amputation of a gangrenous limb.

When the patient is a minor or incompetent, courts tend to authorize even major interventions that are necessary to save the person's life unless the individual is terminally ill or irreversibly comatose.

Courts will authorize some treatments for pregnant women to preserve the life of the fetus, especially immediately before and during birth. The New Jersey Supreme Court authorized transfusions for a woman if necessary to save the life of either the fetus or herself.[50] However, other courts have limited their authorizations to transfusions necessary to save the life of the fetus.[51] The Georgia Supreme Court authorized a Caesarean section operation because it was told there was a near certainty the fetus would not survive a vaginal delivery.[52]

Dependents

The state also asserts an interest in protecting minor children and other dependents from the emotional and financial damage of the patient's refusal. This interest has been discussed in cases in which Jehovah's Witness patients refuse blood transfusions. A Massachusetts court authorized transfusions for a Jehovah's Witness man because he was the father of three minor children and his life was threatened by massive gastrointestinal bleeding.[53] However, a District of Columbia court refused to authorize a transfusion for a father of two minor children because he had made adequate arrangements for their future well-being.[54] These cases involved patients who probably could be restored to normal functioning by appropriate therapy. It is doubtful whether dependents will be a determinative issue in cases involving the terminally ill or irreversibly comatose because emotional and financial damage will seldom be increased by discontinuing treatment.

Irrational Self-Destruction

The prevention of irrational self-destruction is a third state interest. A Pennsylvania court authorized transfusions for a male 25-year-old Jehovah's Witness for a bleeding ulcer to prevent self-destruction.[55] Many other courts have refused to consider refusal by Jehovah's Witness adults to be irrational self-destruction.[56] Courts also have recognized that there can be a competent, rational decision to refuse treatment when the treatment involves substantial risks or when death is imminent.

Ethical Integrity of Providers

Several courts have discussed whether they should recognize a state interest in maintaining the ethical integrity of health professions and allowing hospitals the opportunity to care for patients who have been admitted. The courts have concluded that it is not a countervailing interest. Some have found that the right of privacy is superior to these professional and institutional considerations. Others have concluded that honoring the wishes of the patient (or representative) is consistent with medical ethics, at least in the cases in which the issue has been raised, so there is no conflict.

Public Health and Other Interests

The power of the state to require individuals to submit to medical care when the refusal presents a threat to the community at large has been recognized by the courts longer than the other state interests. In 1905, the Supreme Court upheld the right of the state to require an adult to submit to vaccination to help prevent the spread of disease.[57] In 1973, a federal court in Denver upheld a Denver ordinance that required prostitutes to accept treatment for venereal disease.[58]

In unusual individual cases, courts have based authorizations of medical procedures on other state interests. For example, the Massachusetts Supreme Judicial Court authorized dialysis for a prisoner because he attempted to manipulate his prison placement by refusing dialysis until he was moved.[59] Although prisoners ordinarily have the same rights as others to decline treatment, the state's interest in orderly prison administration was found to outweigh those rights.

Some interventions have been authorized on the basis of the state's interest in obtaining evidence of crimes. These are discussed later in this chapter in the section on law enforcement.

Competent Adults

Under the state interests just described, competent adult patients have been required to accept treatment despite their refusal in the following groups of cases:

(1) public health, (2) pregnancy, (3) religious refusal, (4) civil commitment involving treatment for mental illness or substance abuse, and (5) law enforcement and prison. The first two groups have been discussed and the last two groups are discussed later in this chapter. The third group has been addressed to some extent but is expanded on further here. Disoriented patients also are addressed.

Religious Refusals

Jehovah's Witnesses refuse blood transfusions based on a literal interpretation of the Biblical prohibition against eating blood. In many cases, courts have refused to authorize treatment of competent adults. In a few cases, involuntary transfusions have been authorized for adults with a minor dependent or fetus. Some courts have refused to authorize transfusions even when there are minor children. Nearly all of the other court authorizations involving Jehovah's Witness adults have applied to patients who said they would not resist the transfusion if ordered. Thus, the authorization was designed to protect the patient from fellow adherents, not to override the patient's wishes. Changes in the position of the church have eliminated the protective effect of court authorizations, so these cases are much less frequent.

There now is an artificial blood substitute, Fluosol, that is still being studied and is only available in a few medical centers.[60] Until it is approved for wider distribution, it probably will be necessary in all cases involving Jehovah's Witnesses to arrange transfer to a participating center or rule out the possibility of transfer before a court will authorize a transfusion.

Disoriented Patients

The situation involving a temporarily disoriented patient is different from cases involving those who are oriented. Disoriented patients are frequently temporarily restrained. Health professionals and hospitals have the authority under common law to temporarily detain and even restrain temporarily disoriented medical and surgical patients without court involvement. This authority derives from the hospital's duty to use such reasonable care as the patient's known mental and physical condition require.

Hospitals have been found liable for injuries to patients because they were not restrained during temporary disorientation. This common law authority usually does not apply when the patient is being detained for treatment for mental illness or substance abuse. The statutory commitment procedures should be followed for these patients. This common law authority also does not apply when the patient is fully oriented, although custody can be maintained temporarily while the person's status is determined. Institutional policies concerning disoriented patients also should be followed.

Incompetent Adults and Minors

In addition to the types of treatment ordered for competent adults, various other types of treatment have been authorized for incompetent adults and minors, including major surgery and chemotherapy. Courts also have taken a different view of religious refusals involving minors than they have with adults.

Religious Refusals

Courts have taken the position that the state should give minors an opportunity to mature and make their own decisions concerning their religious beliefs. Thus, courts have authorized blood transfusions for minors in every reported case in which they had life-threatening conditions and were not terminally ill. For example, a Florida court authorized transfusions for premature twins whose lives were threatened.[61] In nearly all cases where the condition was not life threatening, the courts have authorized transfusions. The highest court of New York authorized blood transfusions so a 15-year-old boy could undergo surgical correction of his deformed face and neck.[62] There are a few exceptions in which courts have declined to issue an order.[63]

Major Surgery

Courts have authorized the amputation of gangrenous limbs of incompetent adults. A Tennessee court did so when it determined the patient was unable to understand that her life was endangered by her refusal.[64] She was not terminally ill but would have died if her leg was not amputated. Courts have authorized major surgery for minors when it is likely to be beneficial. An Oregon court approved surgical treatment of an infant's hydrocephalus to prevent mental retardation even though her life was not in immediate danger.[65]

Chemotherapy and Other Medication

When parents are not following reputable medical advice, courts authorize treatment that is likely to be beneficial for life-threatening conditions. In 1979, the highest court of Massachusetts authorized chemotherapy for a child with leukemia despite parental insistence on laetrile treatment.[66] The federal courts had previously refused to intervene.[67] Courts will also authorize necessary medications for incompetent adults. A Pennsylvania court approved diabetes medication for an incompetent adult.[68]

Hospitalization

Some states have laws that authorize certain health care providers to hold and treat minors in emergencies. Iowa authorizes a physician to take custody of a child without a court order when there is imminent danger to the child's life or health and not enough time to obtain an order.[69] However, the statute does not authorize treatment of the child, so application must be made to the court to treat. If there is not time to obtain court authorization, apparently the common law emergency exception to the consent requirement must be relied on, notwithstanding a parent's refusal. North Carolina authorizes the physician, with the concurrence of another physician, to provide necessary care when the parents refuse and there is no time to obtain a court order.[70] Familiarity with local law is essential so proper procedures can be followed promptly when these situations arise.

CIVIL COMMITMENT

Most states have laws that establish procedures for involuntarily committing persons to institutions for treatment for mental illness or substance abuse. In 1975, the Supreme Court ruled that the Constitution was not violated when mentally ill persons were confined involuntarily, but that they must be treated if their confinement is not based on dangerousness.[71]

The procedures for obtaining a commitment order vary from state to state, so local law must be checked. For adults, a judicial hearing generally is required, after which the judicial officer decides whether there is sufficient evidence to justify commitment. Many states do not permit involuntary commitment unless the person is found to be dangerous to self or others. Most states permit adults to be held temporarily on an emergency basis until the judicial officer can act.

The Supreme Court ruled in 1979 that states could permit parents to admit their minor children involuntarily for mental treatment without court authorization if there was a requirement that the admission be approved as necessary by a qualified physician after adequate inquiry.[72] However, many states require judicial involvement in commitment of minors.

Commitment is not the same as a court determination of incompetency. A person who has been committed involuntarily still is competent to be involved in some or all medical decisions unless the courts have determined otherwise. Generally, commitment laws authorize involuntary treatment that is necessary to preserve the patient's life or to avoid permanent injury to that person or others. However, there is variation in the extent to which these laws authorize the use of antipsychotic drugs or electroconvulsive therapy for purposes of nonemergency treatment of a patient's mental illness. Thus, familiarity with local law is important.

However, several courts have ruled that the constitutional rights to privacy and due process are violated if medications or electroconvulsive therapy are given involuntarily without a judicial finding of incompetency, except in an emergency.[73] Some states have resolved this issue by requiring that the judicial officer find the person unable to make treatment decisions as part of the commitment process.[74] In states that have laws that authorize involuntary treatment of committed patients without a judicial determination of inability to make treatment decisions, consideration should be given to this evolving standard in developing treatment policies.

A few courts have even required a judicial determination of the need for antipsychotic medications when a patient who has been adjudicated incompetent refuses the medications in a nonemergency situation.[75]

LAW ENFORCEMENT

Law enforcement officers call upon medical personnel, particularly those based in hospitals, to perform procedures on criminal suspects for the purpose of gathering evidence. These procedures include examining the patient, taking blood samples, pumping stomachs, removing bullets, and other interventions. Tests performed at the request of law enforcement authorities without the consent of the subject raise two legal questions. The first is whether the medical personnel performing the test or the institution in which it is conducted are subject to civil liability for battery or violation of the subject's civil rights. The second is whether the information obtained is admissible as evidence in a criminal action involving the person. The second issue leads to the most litigation but is of little interest to the health care provider.

In 1951, the Supreme Court ruled that a police order for pumping a suspect's stomach "shocks the conscience," so the contents of the stomach could not be admitted into evidence.[76] In 1957, the Court ruled that blood drawn from an unconscious person following a traffic accident could be admitted into evidence if this was done after a proper arrest with probable cause to believe the individual was intoxicated while driving.[77] In 1966, the Supreme Court ruled that blood drawn from an objecting defendant without a search warrant can be admitted into evidence if five conditions are satisfied: (1) formal arrest, (2) a likelihood the blood will produce evidence for the criminal prosecution, (3) a delay would lead to destruction of the evidence, (4) the test is reasonable and not medically contraindicated, and (5) the test is performed in a reasonable manner.[78]

If these conditions are present and properly documented, hospital personnel can safely cooperate in drawing blood for law enforcement officers to the extent authorized by state law. To maximize the applicability of immunity provisions under state law, hospital staff should comply with all additional state requirements concerning who may withdraw blood involuntarily, how, and when. However, in most states, the hospital or health professional has no legal duty to perform the test requested by the law enforcement officer.

In jurisdictions where the providers who perform the tests may be required to testify at the criminal trial of the subjects, many health care professionals decline to become involved to avoid the disruption of their clinical schedules. When the subject physically resists the test, it also is prudent to decline to avoid injury to the individual and the involved health personnel.

Several cases have involved requests for court authorization of the removal of a bullet from a suspect. In 1976, a federal appellate court approved an order authorizing removal of a bullet from the forearm of a suspect.[79] The court based its order on the likelihood the operation would produce useful information, the minimal risk of permanent injury because of the minor nature of the operation, and the procedural opportunities the suspect and his attorney had been provided prior to the final order. The court refused to order the removal of another bullet in the suspect's thigh because it would involve greater risk.

In 1977, the Missouri Supreme Court ruled that a bullet extracted pursuant to a court order could not be used as evidence because the court order did not include a finding of minimal risk.[80] The court order had delegated the assessment of risk to the surgeon. Thus, health personnel should insist that the court order include a finding of minimal risk before performing the surgery. With an appropriate court order that includes a finding of minimal risk, health personnel should be exposed to minimal risk in removing bullets.

RESEARCH

Ordinarily, a patient who accepts treatment expects the use of the drugs and procedures customarily used for the condition. When experimental methods are used or established procedures are used for purposes of research, the investigator must disclose this to the subject and obtain the consent of the subject or the subject's representative. Governmental regulations specify the procedures to review many types of research and the disclosures that must be made to obtain informed consent to such research.

All research supported by the Department of Health and Human Services must comply with its regulations for the protection of human subjects.[81] These regulations require that an institutional review board (IRB) approve the research before HHS will agree to support the research. The IRB must determine that the followng requirements are met before approving the research:

1. Risks to the subjects are minimized.
2. Risks to subjects are reasonable in relation to anticipated benefits, if any, to subjects, and the importance of the knowledge that may reasonably be expected to result.
3. Selection of subjects is equitable.
4. Informed consent will be sought from each prospective subject or the subject's legally authorized representative.
5. Informed consent will be appropriately documented.

6. Where appropriate, the research plan makes adequate provision for monitoring the data collected to insure the safety of the subjects.
7. Where appropriate, there are adequate provisions to protect the privacy of subjects and to maintain the confidentiality of data.
8. Where some or all of the subjects are likely to be vulnerable to coercion or undue influence, such as persons with acute or severe physical or mental illness, or persons who are economically or educationally disadvantaged, appropriate additional safeguards have been included in the study to protect the rights and welfare of these subjects.[82]

The general requirements for informed consent include that it be sought "only under circumstances that provide the prospective subject or the representative sufficient opportunity to consider whether or not to participate and that minimize the possibility of coercion or undue influence." The information must be in a language understandable to the subject or representative. Exculpatory wording cannot be included in the information given. The basic elements of information that must be included are:

1. A statement that the study involves research, an explanation of the purposes of the research and the expected duration of the subject's participation, a description of the procedures to be followed, and identification of any procedures which are experimental;
2. A description of any reasonably foreseeable risks or discomforts to the subject;
3. A description of any benefits to the subject or to others which may reasonably be expected from the research;
4. A disclosure of appropriate alternative procedures or courses of treatment, if any, that may be advantageous to the subject;
5. A statement describing the extent, if any, to which confidentiality of records identifying the subject will be maintained;
6. For research involving more than minimal risk, an explanation as to whether any compensation and an explanation as to whether any medical treatments are available if injury occurs and, if so, what they consist of, or where further information may be obtained;
7. An explanation of whom to contact for answers to pertinent questions about the research and research subjects' rights, and whom to contact in the event of a research-related injury to the subject; and
8. A statement that participation is voluntary, refusal to participate will involve no penalty or loss of benefits to which the subject is otherwise entitled, and the subject may discontinue participation at any time without penalty or loss of benefits to which the subject is otherwise entitled.[83]

Additional elements that should be included as appropriate include (1) the potential for unforeseeable risks, (2) circumstances under which the subject's participation may be terminated, (3) additional costs to the subject, (4) consequences of a decision to withdraw from the study, (5) a statement that significant new findings will be disclosed to the subject, and (6) the number of subjects involved in the study.

Several kinds of studies are exempted from these regulations, such as the "collection or study of existing data, documents, records, pathological specimens, or diagnostic specimens, if these sources are publicly available or if the information is recorded by the investigator in such a manner that subjects cannot be identified. . . ."[84] Expedited review is authorized for categories of research that HHS determines involve no more than minimal risk.[85] The initial list of categories approved for expedited review includes, for example, collection of small amounts of blood by venipuncture from certain adults and moderate exercise by healthy volunteers.[86]

Each institution must submit an acceptable assurance to HHS that it will fulfill its responsibilities under the regulations before HHS will accept the decisions of its IRB. The HHS regulations do not preempt other applicable federal, state, or local laws or regulations. Thus, proposals involving investigational new drugs or devices also must satisfy the regulations of the Food and Drug Administration.[87] State and local law must be reviewed because several states have enacted laws regulating research with human subjects.[88]

Researchers and institutions should take appropriate steps to review research involving human subjects regardless of the sponsorship of the research to protect their patients and avoid liability.

NOTES

1. *Truman v. Thomas,* 27 Cal. 3d 285, 611 P.2d 902 (1980).

2. *O'Brien v. Cunard S.S. Co.,* 28 N.E. 266 (Mass. 1981).

3. *Jacovach v. Yocum,* 212 Iowa, 914, 237 N.W. 444 (1931).

4. *E.g., Sullivan v. Montgomery,* 155 Misc. 448, 279 N.Y.S. 575 (N.Y. City Ct. 1935) [Pain sufficient justification]; *Cunningham v. Yankton Clinic,* 262 N.W. 2d 508 (S.D. 1978) [Pain not sufficient justification].

5. *E.g., Kennedy v. Parrott,* 243 N.C. 355, 90 S.E.2d 754 (1956).

6. *E.g., Natanson v. Kline,* 186 Kan. 393, 350 P.2d 1093 (1960).

7. *Canterbury v. Spence,* 464 F.2d 772, 787 (D.C. Cir. 1972).

8. *Cowman v. Hornaday,* 329 N.W.2d 422 (Iowa 1983).

9. *Hales v. Pitman,* 118 Ariz. 305, 576 P.2d 493 (1978).

10. *E.g., Canterbury v. Spence,* 464 F.2d 772 (D.C. Cir. 1972).

11. *E.g., Wilkinson v. Vesey,* 295 A.2d 676 (R.I. 1972).

12. *E.g., Crouch v. Most,* 432 P.2d 250 (N.M. 1967).

13. *E.g., Lester v. Aetna Casualty and Sur. Co.*, 240 F.2d 676 (5th Cir. 1957), *cert. denied* 354 U.S. 923 (1957).

14. *Nishi v. Hartwell*, 473 P.2d 116 (Hawaii 1970).

15. *E.g., Putenson v. Clay Adams, Inc.*, 12 Cal. App.3d 1062, 91 Cal. Rptr. 319 (1970).

16. Georgia Code § 31-9-4 (1981).

17. *Hyles v. Cockrill*, 312 S.E.2d 124 (Ga. App. 1983); *Young v. Yarn*, 136 Ga. App. 737, 222 S.E.2d 113 (1975).

18. *E.g., Fiorentino v. Wenger*, 19 N.Y.2d 407, 227 N.E.2d 296 (1967); Ohio Rev. Code Ann. § 2317.54 (Page 1981).

19. *Magana v. Elie*, 439 N.E.2d 1319 (Ill. App. Ct. 1982).

20. *Schloendorff v. Society of N.Y. Hosp.*, 211 N.Y. 125, 105 N.E. 92 (1914).

21. For an article advocating increased nurse and hospital responsibility for informed consent, see Greenlaw, "Should hospitals be responsible for informed consent?" 11 *Law, Med., & Health Care* 174 (1983); For an article advocating maintaining the physician's responsibility, see Cushing "Informed Consent: An MD Responsibility? 84 *Am. J. Nursing* 437 (April 1984).

22. *Roberson v. Menorah Medical Center*, 588 S.W.2d 134 (Mo. Ct. App. 1979); *see also Cooper v. Curry*, 92 N.M. 417, 589 P.2d 201 (N.M. Ct. App. 1978) [Hospital not liable for admission clerk's failure to obtain informed consent].

23. Joint Commission on Accreditation of Hospitals, Accreditation Manual for Hospitals, 1984 ed., p. 81.

24. *E.g., Rogers v. Lumbermen's Mut. Casualty Co.*, 119 So.2d 649 (La. Ct. App. 1960).

25. *E.g.*, Kaufer, Steinberg, and Toney, *Revising Medical Consent Forms: An Empirical Model and Test*, 11 *Law, Med., & Health Care* 155 (1983).

26. *Tatham v. Hoke*, 469 F.Supp. 914 (W.D.N.C. 1979).

27. *E.g.*, Nev. Rev. Stat. § 41A.110 (1981) [Conclusive evidence]; Iowa Code § 147.137 (1983) [Presumption].

28. *In re Yetter*, 62 Pa. D. & C. 2d 619 (Pa. C. Pl., Northampton Co. 1973).

29. *Lane v. Candura*, 6 Mass. App. 377, 376 N.E.2d 1232 (1978).

30. *E.g.*, Miss. Code Ann. §§ 41-41-3 and 41-41-5 (1972); *Farber v. Olkon*, 40 Cal. 2d 503, 254 P.2d 520 (1953).

31. *Bonner v. Moran*, 126 F.2d 121 (D.C. Cir. 1941).

32. *In re Rotkowitz*, 25 N.Y.S.2d 624 (Dom. Rel. Ct. 1941).

33. *State v. Bass*, 255 N.C. 42, 120 S.E.2d 580 (1961).

34. *E.g., Gramm v. Boener*, 56 Ind. 497 (1877).

35. *E.g., In re Guardianship of Pescinski*, 67 Wis. 2d 4, 226 N.W.2d 180 (1975) [Incompetent adult]; *In re Richardson*, 284 So. 2d 185 (La. Ct. App. 1973) [Minor].

36. *E.g., Strunk v. Strunk*, 445 S.W.2d 145 (Ky. 1969) [Incompetent adult]; *Hart v. Brown*, 29 Conn.Super. 368, 289 A.2d 386 (1972) [Minor].

37. *In re Storar*, 52 N.Y.2d 363, 420 N.E.2d 64 (1981).

38. *Satz v. Perlmutter*, 379 So. 2d 359 (Fla. 1980), *approving* 362 So. 2d 160 (Fla. Dist. Ct. App. 1978).

39. 70 N.J. 10, 355 A.2d 647 (1976).

40. *Lane v. Candura*, 6 Mass. App. 377, 376 N.E.2d 1232 (1978).

41. *E.g., In re Osborne*, 294 A.2d 372 (App. D.C. 1972).

42. *In re Quinlan*, 70 N.J. 10, 355 A.2d 647 (1976).

43. *Custody of a Minor*, 434 N.E.2d 601 (Mass. 1982).

44. *In re Hudson*, 13 Wash. 2d 673, 126 P.2d 765 (1942).

45. *In re Green*, 448 Pa. 338, 292 A.2d 387 (1972).

46. *Matter of Hofbauer*, 47 N.Y.2d 648, 393 N.E.2d 1009 (1979).

47. *In re Seifert*, 309 N.Y. 80, 127 N.E.2d 820 (1955).

48. *McQuillan v. City if Sioux City*, 306 N.W.2d 789 (Iowa 1981).

49. *Superintendent of Belchertown v. Saikewicz*, 373 Mass. 728, 370 N.E.2d 417, 426 (1977).

50. *Raleigh Fitkin-Paul Morgan Memorial Hosp. v. Anderson*, 42 N.J. 421, 201 A.2d 537 (1964), *cert. denied* 377 U.S. 985 (1964).

51. *E.g., In the Matter of Bentley*, Misc. No. 65–74 (D.C. Super. April 25, 1974).

52. *Jefferson v. Griffin Spalding County Hosp. Auth.*, 247 Ga. 86, 274 S.E.2d 457 (1981).

53. *In re September Caine, Marion Caine, Jonathan Caine*, No. 83164–N (Juv. Ct., Mass. November 5, 1983): *see also Application of President and Directors of Georgetown College, Inc.* 331 F.2d 1000 (D.C.Cir. 1964), *reh'g denied* 331 F.2d 1010 (D.C. Cir. 1964), *cert. denied* 377 U.S. 978 (1964) [Transfusions ordered for woman with 7-month-old child].

54. *In re Osborne*, 294 A.2d 372 (App. D.C. 1972).

55. *In re Dell*, 1 Pa. D. & C.3d 655 (Pa. C. Pl. Allegheny Co. 1975).

56. *E.g., In re Brooks Estate*, 32 Ill. 2d 361, 205 N.E.2d 435 (1965); *Matter of Melideo*, 390 N.Y.S.2d 523 (N.Y. Sup. Ct. 1976).

57. *Jacobson v. Massachusetts*, 197 U.S. 11 (1905).

58. *Reynolds v. McNichols*, 488 F.2d 1378 (10th Cir. 1973).

59. *Commissioner of Corrections v. Myers*, 399 N.E.2d 452 (Mass. 1979).

60. "FDA Committee Questions Fluosol Efficacy; US Approval Not Imminent," 250 *J.A.M.A.* 2585 (Nov. 18, 1983).

61. *In the Interest of Ivey*, 319 So. 2d 53 (Fla. Dist. Ct. App. 1975).

62. *In re Sampson*, 278 N.E.2d 918 (N.Y. 1972).

63. *E.g., In re Green*, 448 Pa. 338, 292 A.2d 387 (1972).

64. *State Dep't of Human Servs. v. Northern*, 563 S.W.2d 197 (Tenn. Ct. App. 1978).

65. *Matter of Jensen*, 633 P.2d 1302 (Or. Ct. App. 1981).

66. *Custody of a Minor*, 393 N.E.2d 836 (Mass. 1979).

67. *Green v. Truman*, 459 F.Supp. 342 (D.Mass. 1978).

68. *In re Edward A. Edmundson*, 15 Lebanon Co.J. 34 (Pa. C. Pl. 1973).

69. IOWA CODE § 232.79 (1983).

70. N.C. GEN. STAT. §§ 90–21.1 through 90–21.3 (1981).

71. *O'Conner v. Donaldson*, 422 U.S. 563 (1975).

72. *Parham v. J.L. and J.R.*, 442 U.S. 584 (1979); *Secretary of Public Welfare v. Institutionalized Juveniles*, 442 U.S. 640 (1979).

73. *E.g., In re K.K.B.*, 609 P.2d 747 (Okla. 1980); *Rogers v. Commissioner*, 390 Mass. 489 (Mass. Nov. 29, 1983).

74. *E.g.*, IOWA CODE § 229.1(2) (1983).

75. *E.g., Guardianship of Roe*, 421 N.E.2d 40 (Mass. 1981).

76. *Rochin v. California*, 342 U.S. 1165 (1951).

77. *Breithaupt v. Adams,* 352 U.S. 432 (1957).

78. *Schmerber v. California,* 384 U.S. 757 (1966).

79. *United States v. Crowder,* 543 F.2d 312 (D.C. Cir. 1976), *cert. denied* 429 U.S. 1062 (1977).

80. *State v. Overstreet,* 551 S.W.2d 621 (Mo. 1977); *see also Lee v. Winston,* No. 82–6762 (4th Cir. September 14, 1983) [Injunction prohibiting removal of bullet from chest because too intrusive].

81. 45 C.F.R. pt. 46.

82. 45 C.F.R. § 46.111.

83. 45 C.F.R. § 46.116.

84. 45 C.F.R. § 46.101(b).

85. 45 C.F.R. § 46.110.

86. 46 Fed. Reg. 8392 (Jan. 26, 1981).

87. 21 C.F.R. pts. 50, 56, 312, 314, and 812 (1982).

88. *E.g.,* N.Y. Pub. Health Law §§ 2440–2446 (1977).

BIBLIOGRAPHY

Creighton, Helen. "The Right of Informed Refusal." *Nursing Management* 13, no. 9 (September 1982):48.

Cushing, Maureen. "Informed Consent: An MD Responsibility?" *American Journal of Nursing* 84, no. 4 (April 1984):437.

Greenlaw, Jane. "Should Hospitals Be Responsible for Informed Consent?" *Law, Medicine, and Health Care* 11, no. 4 (September 1983):173.

Trandel-Korenchuk, Darlene, and Trandel-Korenchuk, Keith. "Legal Forum: Informed Consent and Mental Incompetency." *Nursing Administration Quarterly* 8, no. 1 (Fall 1983):76.

Chapter 10

Withholding and Withdrawing Treatment from the Dying

Nurses regularly become involved in situations involving withholding or withdrawing treatment from dying patients. Increasing attention is being focused on the dying process because of achievements in modern medical care that make it possible to sustain life, several widely publicized legal cases, and the increasing openness of discussions concerning death. A clear understanding of the legal aspects of the dying process is essential to deal humanely with this crisis in the lives of patients and their family and friends, while complying with the law.

Physicians, nurses, other involved professionals, and the hospital have legally recognized duties to all patients. These legal duties have always been shaped by: (1) the needs and wishes of patients and their representatives, (2) professional practices, (3) the capacities of medical science and the individual professionals and hospital involved, and (4) societal expectations and norms. Professional practice has long reflected the different needs of terminally ill and irreversibly comatose patients. The famous New Jersey Supreme Court decision concerning the care of Karen Ann Quinlan, who was irreversibly comatose, states the difference as follows:

> We glean from the record here that physicians distinguish between curing the ill and comforting and easing the dying; that they refuse to treat the curable as if they were dying or ought to be; and that they have sometimes refused to treat the hopeless and dying as if they were curable.[1]

The law also has recognized this difference.

CLASSIFICATION OF PATIENTS

Physicians must identify which patients are to be treated differently because they are dying. Some institutions have developed formal classification systems; although these can be helpful, they are not required.

230

There is no widely accepted definition of terminal illness; it remains a diagnosis based on medical judgment. Clearly, one element is that no available course of therapy offers a reasonable expectation of remission or cure of the condition. Another element is that death is imminent but there is no consensus on the time period; this results largely from the fact that it is not possible to predict a time of death precisely. Some courts have accepted patients as terminally ill with predicted lives of one and five years.[2]

Thus, the range of medical opinion concerning terminal illness appears to be legally acceptable. Hospitals generally avoid establishing a specific time period. The most widely publicized institutional classification systems have not included a definition of terminal illness but instead have focused on the nature of the appropriate therapeutic effort.[3] The institutional classification systems have focused on the decision-making process and documentation of decisions concerning withholding resuscitative efforts and withholding other extraordinary care.

'DO NOT RESUSCITATE' ORDERS

The term cardiopulmonary resuscitation (CPR) describes a series of steps developed over the last two decades to reestablish breathing and heartbeat after cardiac or respiratory arrest. The most basic form of CPR, which is being taught to large numbers of the public, involves recognizing the indications for intervention, opening an airway, initiating mouth-to-mouth breathing, and compressing the chest externally to establish artificial circulation. In hospitals and in some emergency transport vehicles, CPR also can include the administration of oxygen under pressure to the lungs, the use of intravenous medications, the injection of stimulants into the heart through catheters or long needles, electric shocks to the heart, insertion of a pacemaker, and open heart massage. Some of these procedures are highly intrusive and even violent in nature. They all are medically justified and indicated for patients whose condition is not yet diagnosed or for those who have a hopeful prognosis. The purpose of CPR is the prevention of sudden, unexpected death. However, it is not indicated in certain situations, such as in cases of terminal irreversible illness where death is not unexpected.

To ensure that CPR is not initiated where it is not indicated, it is important for the physician to write "Do Not Resuscitate" (DNR) or "No CPR" in the orders concerning the treatment of the patient. Many institutions call the CPR team by announcing "Code Blue," so the order might read "No Code Blue." A written DNR order documents the fact that a decision has been made and by whom; it ensures that the decision is communicated to nurses and other staff so that inappropriate CPR is not initiated. When CPR clearly is not part of the planned care, nurses can act in accordance with the decisions without concern that they misunderstood them or later will be thought to have neglected the patient. Written orders reflect that these decisions are an appropriate part of medical practice and have been made after careful deliberation.

Some physicians still are reluctant to write DNR orders because they fear legal liability even though numerous courts have recognized the practice. In 1978 a Massachusetts court ruled that prior court authorization is not necessary for a DNR order.[4] The risk of legal liability from a failure to resuscitate is much less when there is a written order or explanation than when no order is in the record.

The patient or the patient's representative should be involved in the decision and concur in the DNR order. The nature of the care to be withheld should be explained by the physician before obtaining the concurrence. A DNR order was challenged in a 1981 Minnesota case and the court was not convinced the patient's parents knew what they were declining. Therefore, the court ordered that the DNR order be cancelled until the patient's parents gave "knowledgeable approval" to reinstate it.[5]

NO EXTRAORDINARY CARE

Theologians and ethicists have long recognized a distinction between ordinary and extraordinary medical care. They have maintained that humans have a moral and ethical responsibility to seek and accept ordinary medical care to save their lives but that extraordinary medical care may be declined. However, the law generally has recognized a legal right to refuse even ordinary care. Most physicians and nurses, while often deeply troubled by refusals of ordinary care by nonterminal patients, have accepted this legal principle. They find it easier to accede to the wishes of the terminally ill patients and their families who decline extraordinary care, however, and may even recommend that such treatment not be pursued in some instances.

A precise definition of which care is ordinary and which is extraordinary is not possible. One of the most widely quoted definitions is by a Roman Catholic ethicist, Gerald Kelly:

> Ordinary means all medicines, treatments, and operations which offer a reasonable hope of benefit and which can be obtained and used without excessive pain, or other inconvenience. Extraordinary means are all medicines, treatments, and operations which cannot be obtained or used without excessive expense, pain, or other inconvenience, or if used, would not offer a reasonable hope of benefit.[6]

It is clear that it is not possible to create a list of "extraordinary" procedures. The circumstances of the individual situation and the judgment of those involved determine whether a procedure is extraordinary.

The courts are recognizing and accepting the decision to withhold or withdraw extraordinary care. The majority of decisions have addressed the use of respirators. The court in the *Quinlan* case, for example, discussed the distinction between ordinary and extraordinary care at length, citing religious and medical sources. It concluded that it would be extraordinary care to use a respirator for a comatose young woman in a chronic, persistent, vegetative state with no reasonable possibility of emerging to a cognitive, sapient state. Therefore, the court authorized discontinuance of the respiratory assistance.[7]

Other cases have addressed several other treatments. The highest court of Massachusetts discussed the distinction between extraordinary and ordinary care in a 1977 case and stated that its decision was intended to be consistent with this "medical ethos." Thus, it implicitly concluded that chemotherapy could be extraordinary care when it approved withholding such treatment from a profoundly mentally retarded 67-year-old man with leukemia.[8] In a case involving the same court a few years later, the court did not use the extraordinary-ordinary terminology but reached a similar differentiation based on the "magnitude of the invasion." It concluded that it is appropriate to discontinue dialysis for a 78-year-old man with irreversible kidney failure and chronic organic brain syndrome but it was not appropriate to discontinue "supportive oral or intravenous medications."[9]

In a 1980 case, a Delaware court discussed the ordinary-extraordinary distinction and concluded that nearly all treatment is extraordinary for a 55-year-old woman in a irreversible coma since none can return her to a sentient and sapient state. Thus, the court authorized withholding respirators, antibiotics, feeding tubes, CPR, and all other drugs and medicines except for those normally used to preserve bodily hygiene, particularly those related to constipation or diarrhea.[10] Many physicians would consider some of these treatments ordinary care despite their inability to restore the patient's mental functioning. For example, the neurosurgeon in a 1979 District of Columbia case discontinued "heroic measures," including the respirator and drugs to reduce the pressure in the comatose patient's head, but would have continued feeding the patient and preventing pneumonia if the patient had lived.[11]

Maintenance of Supportive Care

Even when terminally ill patients are not receiving extraordinary care, physicians and hospitals have duties to them. While some patients, such as Karen Ann Quinlan, appropriately can be transferred to nursing homes, others require continued hospitalization. Ordinary supportive care must be continued—the "comforting and easing the dying" to which the *Quinlan* decision referred. It is clear that this includes appropriate medications for pain.[12]

There is a difference of opinion concerning supportive care—for example, whether special mechanisms for feeding are required.[13] The trend appears to be toward accepting decisions not to use artificial feeding mechanisms in selected cases. A committee of physicians in early 1984 issued recommendations concerning care of terminally ill patients that supported selective decisions not to use special feeding mechanisms.[14] The Delaware court in the 1980 case did not require special mechanisms for feeding, in accord with the strongly held views the patient had expressed before she became comatose.[15] In 1984 a New York court ruled that a nursing home had neither the right nor responsibility to force nourishment on a competent 85-year-old patient, especially when the force feeding could be accomplished only through the surgical insertion of a gastric feeding tube. The patient's family supported his decision.[16]

However, New York's highest court ruled in 1981 that a mother could not refuse special feeding and transfusions for her terminally ill incompetent adult son.[17] Similarly, a New Jersey court in 1983 refused to permit the guardian to have the nasogastric tube removed from an 84-year-old woman with severe organic brain syndrome and other serious ailments. The court ruled that nutriments and water could not be withheld when the woman was not comatose, not facing imminent death, and not able to speak for herself.[18]

Thus, some courts may not accept withholding feeding unless it is pursuant to the wishes of the patient. If the patient is not terminally ill or comatose, it is unlikely courts will order withholding feeding in an institution even at the patient's request. A California court ruled in 1983 that while a competent adult woman with cystic fibrosis could refuse feeding, she could not do so in a hospital. The court refused to order the hospital not to force-feed her.[19]

In the only prosecution of physicians for withholding hydration and intravenous feeding from a terminally ill patient, a California court ruled that the physician's conduct did not violate the criminal law. The court ruled that artificial means of feeding are treatment, not natural functions, so there is no duty to continue the treatment when it becomes ineffective. The physicians could not be criminally liable for their professional decision made in concert with the patient's family when the individual was incompetent and terminally ill, with virtually no hope of significant improvement.[20]

Limits to the Patient's Choices

Occasionally, terminally ill patients or their families seek therapies that are outside the accepted range or seek hospitalization beyond the time necessary. These are normal responses to an extremely stressful situation. Reliance must be placed primarily on patience and tactful communications to give these patients and their families the time, information, and support to accept the limitations. Sometimes they are not able to accept the limitations, however, so other approaches become necessary.

Patients do not have a right to insist on treatment outside the accepted range of therapies. Physicians have the responsibility and authority to refuse to provide illegal or inappropriate therapies. In 1979, the Supreme Court ruled that the terminally ill have no special right to treatment that the government has declared illegal.[21] A physician who provided a legal, but inappropriate, treatment might be liable for malpractice notwithstanding the patient's consent to such treatment.[22]

If there is a difference of opinion among reputable physicians regarding the appropriateness of a legal treatment, reasonable efforts should be made to transfer the care of the patient to a physician who concurs with the patient. Sometimes, if the inappropriate treatment desired is neither illegal nor dangerous, the most prudent course may be to acquiesce, as long as the patient is willing to continue accepted therapy simultaneously.

Patients do not have a right to stay in a hospital when hospitalization no longer is required. Hospitals have responsibilities to other patients who may need the beds. This is becoming more of a concern as the number of available beds is reduced to meet planning goals and as unnecessary hospitalizations are identified through utilization review, with attendant financial sanctions. Occasionally, terminally ill patients and their families refuse to arrange for transfers to nursing homes or other facilities when hospitalization no longer is required. They should, of course, be given a reasonable time to make arrangements; if they do not then do so, other remedies, including an injunction, may be sought. An injunction was sought in 1976 to transfer a teenager who had been comatose for 18 months from a Florida hospital bed to a nursing home but the patient died before the final hearing.[23]

COMMON LAW AND CONSTITUTIONAL RIGHT TO REFUSE TREATMENT

Competent adults have the right to refuse treatment unless state interests outweigh that right. The right to refuse is based on: (1) the common law right to freedom from nonconsensual invasion of bodily integrity, reflected in the informed consent doctrine and the law of battery; (2) the constitutional right of privacy; and (3) the constitutional right to freedom of religion. The possible state interests that have been advanced include: (1) preserving life; (2) protecting third parties, especially minor dependents; (3) preventing irrational self-destruction; (4) maintaining the ethical integrity of health care professionals and institutions; and (5) protecting the public health and other interests. These rights and state interests and the determination of adulthood and competence are discussed in more detail in Chapter 9 on authorization of treatment. There are few situations in which the state's interests will outweigh the right of a competent, terminally ill adult to refuse treatment. These include cases where there is a threat to the public health or when significant harm to minor dependents can be avoided.

Loss of Competence

Like virtually all adults, those who were competent when they first expressed their desire to have certain treatments withheld or withdrawn generally become incompetent before they die. The refusal of medical care must apply through the period of incompetence, or their right to make decisions regarding their own care is vitiated. Some states have attempted to address this situation through statutes (discussed later in this chapter). In most situations, however, either there is no applicable statute or the statutory procedures have not been followed. Therefore, it is necessary to act according to the underlying common law and constitutional principles.

A distinction often is made between (1) a decision made when the person knows of the terminal condition and (2) a decision made when the person is considering future care without reference to a specific known condition. The first generally is respected while the second may be subjected to more scrutiny because less information was available at the time the decision was made. When the circumstances are substantially different from those the person anticipated in reaching the decision, there must be more latitude to act contrary to the stated wishes.

The expression of the patient's wishes does not have to be in writing. In both the Delaware and New York cases described earlier in this chapter, the courts authorized carrying out the patient's oral wishes.[24] Documentary evidence of the wishes should certainly be given great weight. The growing practice of preparing living wills helps communicate those wishes clearly. Only one court has ruled that a living will is not a sufficient basis for carrying out the wishes of a terminally ill patient. The Florida Supreme Court ruled that permission of close family members or a guardian must be obtained before the wishes of an incompetent terminally ill person may be followed.[25] When proceeding without court involvement, the situation should be considered carefully to ensure that the actual circumstances are not substantially different from those the patient intended to be covered. This is not a problem with most of the widely distributed versions of the living will because they generally are clearly addressed to one condition, irreversible mental incapacity, rather than to specific procedures.

When a competent patient still is able to communicate or when there is a reasonable likelihood that the patient will again be competent and able to communicate, reliance usually should not be placed on directives made before the condition was known. The patient should be given an opportunity to recover the ability to communicate and express present wishes. The major exception applies to directives based on religious or other strongly held views that are intended to transcend individual conditions.

Incompetents

Some terminally ill patients who have never expressed their wishes regarding treatment become irreversibly incompetent and unable to communicate. Others have never had an opportunity to express their wishes because of youth or mental retardation. The courts that have been confronted with such cases have concluded that, since competent adults have the right to refuse treatment, there must be a means for the same right to be exercised on behalf of incompetent patients.

The *Quinlan* decision stated that all patients have a right of choice in this situation, but for the incompetent, "The only practical way to prevent destruction of the right is to permit the guardian and family of Karen to render their best judgment, subject to the qualifications hereinafter stated, as to whether she would exercise it in these circumstances."[26] The qualifications were concurrence by the attending physicians and by a hospital ethics committee or like body regarding the hopelessness of the prognosis. The highest court of Massachusetts reached the same conclusion, i.e., there is "a general right in all persons to refuse medical treatment in appropriate circumstances." The court added: "The recognition of that right must extend to the case of an incompetent, as well as a competent, patient because the value of human dignity extends to both."[27]

When patients have not expressed their wishes and are unable to do so, some individual or group must be able to make decisions for them. Obviously the physicians and other professionals involved in the care of the patient have an important role and are relatively easy to identify. It sometimes is more difficult to identify the proper person to represent the patient in the decision making. When there is a guardian, there usually is no problem because the guardian can make decisions on the patient's behalf. Occasionally, however, close family members disagree with the guardian; in such instances, guidance from a court may be needed.

When there is no guardian, it generally is accepted that the spouse or next of kin of the incompetent patient may make decisions that cannot be deferred until the patient is competent.[28] All the court decisions on the treatment of the terminally ill involve guardians because their appointment is the procedural mechanism available for the courts to effectuate their judgments.

Most courts have not yet directly addressed whether the incompetent patient's representative must be a legal guardian to have the authority to refuse treatment. The Washington Supreme Court ruled that the person refusing must be appointed guardian first,[29] while the Florida Supreme Court ruled that close family members could make these decisions without being appointed guardian.[30] However, in other states, consistent with the general recognition of the role of the spouse or next of kin, the implication is that they may make these decisions without being legally designated guardians. While it is unlikely that the courts will preclude the traditional familial decision-making role, careful analysis of specific precedents in each state is warranted to determine whether this role has been explicitly curtailed.

The family's decision-making role is limited by the physician's diagnostic role and responsibility to the patient. The family can decide to withhold or withdraw treatment without court involvement only when the physician determines that the patient is terminally ill or irreversibly comatose and accepts the family's decision.

When the physician and family concur in withholding or withdrawing treatment in such cases, the risk associated with carrying out the decision is minimal.

A nurse who has concerns about a decision regarding care of a patient, or becomes aware that a patient or family member has concerns that the physician has not addressed, should discuss the concerns with the responsible physician. In situations when this does not result in a satisfactory explanation or response, the nurse must decide whether the concerns are caused by possible deviations from institutional protocols or generally accepted nursing practice or by the nurse's personal beliefs. When the concerns are based on personal beliefs, the nurse should seek to be relieved from responsibility for care of the patient just as a physician should ask to be replaced when personal beliefs do not permit the carrying out of the lawful wishes of patients and their families.

When the concerns result from possible deviations from accepted protocols and practices, the nurse should follow the usual institutional procedures for clarifying apparently erroneous orders, unless the institution has a special procedure for handling questions concerning withholding or withdrawing care. These protocols usually involve notifying the nurse's supervisor and, in some situations, institutional administrators. When in doubt whether to notify supervisors or administrators, the nurse should do so. It is better to convince the physician to consult with administrators but when the physician declines to do so, most administrators would prefer to have an opportunity to become involved in potentially controversial decisions before irreversible action is taken. The administrators may decide that the proposed decision is appropriate, so no intervention is warranted. However, the patient, nurse and the whole patient care team still benefit from the additional review and the clear institutional support for the decision. In other cases, whether invited by the physician or the nurse, administrators may become involved by advising staff, facilitating communication, and assisting if legal clarification needs to be sought. However, administrative intervention is not required in most decisions of this type, especially when the institution has established procedures for these decisions and they are followed.

Severely Deformed or Impaired Newborns

An especially perplexing case concerns the newborn infant with severe deformities that are inconsistent with prolonged or sapient life. It has been accepted practice in many medical centers, upon the concurrence of the parents and the treatment team, to provide only ordinary care to these infants so that their suffering is not prolonged through extraordinary efforts. If the parents wish heroic measures, they are attempted. If the parents refuse treatment when the attending physician believes treatment provides a reasonable likelihood of benefit, the child neglect laws are invoked to obtain court authorization for treatment.

Health care professionals disagree as to which conditions are sufficiently severe that treatment offers no reasonable likelihood of benefit. Although there is general acceptance of withholding treatment when the condition is anencephaly (the absence of the higher brain) or another condition that precludes the development of sapient life or is inconsistent with prolonged life,[31] there is no such agreement in regard to the surgical repair of problems associated with spina bifida. At one time, surgical treatment frequently was withheld. With improvements in treatments and outcomes, however, most physicians now believe that surgery should not be withheld except perhaps in the most severe cases. For example, in 1979 a New York hospital sought and obtained a court order authorizing surgical repair of a newborn with several of the complications associated with spina bifida.[32]

Neither mental retardation, if it is at a sapient level, nor physical deformities, if they are consistent with prolonged survival, are considered to justify withholding treatment from newborns. This is illustrated by the refusal of a Massachusetts probate court in 1978 to approve parental rejection of respiratory support and cardiac surgery, although there was some degree of mental retardation and multiple medical problems, because the condition was not terminal and the degree of mental retardation had not been established.[33]

The Department of Health and Human Services (HHS) began in 1982 to seek to force aggressive treatment of virtually all severely deformed newborns. In May 1982, HHS sent a letter to many hospitals threatening to withhold federal funding from any hospital that permitted medically indicated treatment to be withheld from a handicapped newborn.[34] This letter was a reaction to a widely publicized case in Indiana in which an infant with Down's syndrome (which usually results in mental retardation) was permitted to starve to death when relatively minor surgery would have permitted the newborn to live. A court order was sought to authorize the surgery but the Indiana courts refused to intervene.[35]

In March 1983, HHS published rules creating a hotline in Washington, D.C., where persons could call anonymously concerning suspected violations.[36] Each hospital was required to post a notice advising people of the hotline. HHS created a team to intervene in hospitals when calls were received. The rules were enjoined by a federal court, so hospitals did not have to leave the notices posted.[37] However, the hotline and team continued to operate. HHS reported saving three babies through the functioning of the team. However, several hospitals reported that the team had interfered with the care of babies it was investigating and of other infants in the hospital.[38]

The President's Commission for the Study of Ethical Problems in Medicine and Biomedical and Behavioral Research criticized the federal intervention and recommended hospital review procedures involving medical consultation to confirm the diagnosis in clear cases and committee review in other cases.[39] The American Nurses' Association and the Committee on Bioethics of the American Academy of Pediatrics have supported the development of review committees.[40] HHS published revised rules in January 1984 that continued the hotline, required notices to be posted, and recommended creation of institutional ethics committees.[41] The revised rules were declared invalid by a federal district court in May 1984.[42]

In one widely publicized case in October 1983, New York's highest court upheld the decision of the parents of a newborn with spina bifida and hydrocephalus to decline corrective surgery. The federal government sought access to the child's medical records to determine whether she had been discriminated against because she was handicapped. The parents and the hospital refused to grant access. The federal government then sought a court order, but a federal court of appeals denied access and ruled that the federal government did not have the authority under the existing handicapped rights laws to investigate this type of case.[43]

Even though it appears that HHS does not have the legal authority to deny federal funding to hospitals that honor parents' wishes not to aggressively treat severely deformed newborns, the agency's efforts are another significant indication that withholding treatment is acceptable only when the deformities are inconsistent with prolonged or sapient life. It seldom is justifiable to withhold ordinary care, such as feeding.

These decisions will continue to be controversial but the real exposure to potential legal sanctions is minimal if the practice is carefully limited to appropriate cases. Nurses should contribute to developing appropriate intrainstitutional protocols for dealing with these cases. Physicians should obtain consultations regarding the diagnosis, prognosis, and treatment decisions. Documenting the reasons for the decisions and the decision-making process helps ensure that the decision makers give principled consideration to all relevant information.

When nurses have concerns regarding these decisions, it is recommended that they pursue all internal channels before considering seeking outside intervention. The previous section on ''Incompetents'' discusses some of these channels. Governmental intervention is a disruptive process that should be reserved for the rare cases when other approaches do not provide adequate review.

Other Minors

Minors generally are treated as incompetents for purposes of medical care decisions. When they are able to participate in the decision, however, their wishes should be given substantial weight. This presents no difficulty when the minor and the parents or guardian agree, such as when the minor initiates the idea of withholding treatment and the parents concur. The case is more complex when there is irreconcilable disagreement. If the minor is immature and either the minor or a parent or a guardian want to treat, treatment should be pursued, even though court authorization is required if only the minor wants the treatment. If the minor is mature, court resolution of the conflict usually should be pursued.

Role of the Courts

In most states, it is not necessary to involve courts in decisions concerning withholding or withdrawing treatment for terminally ill patients. Courts need to be involved only when there is disagreement among those involved in the decision making. However, not all disagreements require court resolution. When a competent adult is refusing certain treatment and the physician disagrees, the proper resolution often is to transfer the care of the patient to another physician who will accept the refusal.

The Florida Supreme Court ruled in 1984 that courts do not have to be involved in these decisions in most circumstances.[44] Some of the earlier court decisions, such as those from Massachusetts and New York, appeared to require court involvement.[45] This has been clarified by subsequent decisions.[46] The highest court of Massachusetts clarified its earlier decision, by writing:

> Neither the present case nor the *Saikewicz* case involved the legality of action taken without judicial authority, and our opinions should not be taken to establish any requirement of prior judicial approval that would not otherwise exist. . . . Action taken without judicial approval might be the subject of either criminal or civil liability. Little need to be said about criminal liability: there is precious little precedent, and what there is suggests that the doctor will be protected if he acts on a good faith judgment that is not grievously unreasonable by medical standards. . . .

> Whenever a physician in good faith decides that a particular treatment is not called for, there is a risk that in some subsequent litigation the omission will be found to have been negligent. But the standard for determining whether the treatment was called for is the same after the event as before; negligence cannot be based solely on failure to obtain prior court approval, if the approval would have been given.

> Consent of the patient will not always immunize the physician from a charge of negligence. Immunity afforded by court authorization would seem to be subject to similar limitation, for example, if the physician is negligent in implementing the court order. Thus absence of court approval does not result in automatic civil liability for withholding treatment; court approval may serve the useful purpose of resolving a doubtful or disputed question of law or fact, but it does not eliminate all risk of liability.[47]

However, a few states have required some court involvement in these decisions. The Washington Supreme Court ruled in 1983 that a court must be involved to the extent of appointing a guardian whenever the patient has not signed a directive that satisfies the Washington Natural Death Act.[48] However, the Washington courts do not have to approve the decision of the guardian.

Civil Statutes and Regulations on Refusal

Before the evolution of the judicial consensus regarding the rights of the terminally ill, many physicians and hospitals were reluctant to respect the wishes of such patients and their families that treatments be limited. A substantial minority of physicians still do not accept refusals of care because of either their personal ethics or their concerns regarding legal risks. To facilitate carrying out the wishes of the patient and others and to relieve the concerns of the physicians, several states have enacted laws or promulgated regulations that explicitly authorize health care personnel to honor these wishes.

Natural Death Acts

Several states have enacted laws, starting with California,[49] providing that a patient's wishes may be followed with some degree of immunity if the patient has executed a special directive regarding treatment of terminal illness. Recognizing that, in some instances, the physician may be unwilling to follow such a directive, several of these laws require reasonable efforts to transfer the patient to the care of another physician who will abide by these wishes.

These special directives are special types of living wills. In some states, the widely distributed versions of the living will can serve as the special directive if there are sufficient witnesses. In other states, special forms must be used for the Natural Death Act to apply.

The acts vary concerning who may sign, the content and execution of the directive, the sanctions and immunities, and the effect of the absence of a directive. Most of the natural death acts authorize only competent adults to sign directives. Thus, most of these laws do not cover a large part of the population, such as minors and incompetent adults who have not previously executed a directive.

Each of the laws specifies the precise wording of the directive or the elements that must be included. In states that specify the wording, the patient who wants to express more detailed or different wishes must forego the benefit of the statute and rely on common law and constitutional principles. Furthermore, the physician must have the wording checked carefully to determine that it satisfies the statute's requirements. There can be problems with individualized documents, however, because the intent may not be clear.

Each of the natural death acts specifies the formality with which the directive must be executed. All the acts require witnesses, and some disqualify certain people from being witnesses. Some states require that the directive be notarized.

Most acts specify the means to revoke a directive. Regardless of the technicalities, it is best not to carry out a directive if there is any reason to believe the patient has had a change of mind.

The effect of the directive also varies among states. In some, the directive appears to be binding but no sanction is specified for physicians who do not follow it. In several others, it is binding and there are sanctions for not following it if the person was diagnosed as terminally ill before the directive was signed. In most states, the directive is not binding if signed before diagnosis, so it is only to be given weight in the decisions regarding care. When the directive is binding, the physician who does not wish to follow it has a duty to arrange a transfer to another physician. The specified sanction for failure to arrange this transfer is medical licensing discipline for unprofessional conduct.

All of the natural death acts provide some immunity for those who act or refrain from acting in accordance with a directive that complies with the act. In most states, however, it is questionable whether the immunity provisions offer substantially more protection than common-law and constitutional principles. The primary issue in most controversies will be the diagnosis of terminal illness. Since this diagnosis is viewed as a professional responsibility for which physicians should be accountable, none of the statutes provide any protection from liability that arises from negligent diagnosis. Of course, immunity by statute is easier to establish than immunity under common law or constitutional law principles. Thus, when practical, it is best to attempt to comply with the statutory requirements.

Most natural death acts specify that they do not affect other rights to refuse treatment. The Arkansas statute[50] could be interpreted to supersede nonstatutory approaches because it is comprehensive and does not specifically preserve other approaches. Thus, with the possible exception of cases in Arkansas, it is reasonable to follow the wishes of the patient and/or family in accord with common law and constitutional principles whenever there is no valid statutory directive.[51]

Hospices

Some terminally ill patients elect to forego treatment for their illness but still require nursing care and pain medication in their home or in an institution. Special facilities, called hospices, are being established to provide this limited type of care along with maximal personal support to help the patient and the family cope with the dying process. Home hospice programs have been developed to provide support in the home.

Congress recognized and encouraged this trend by authorizing Medicare reimbursement for hospice services.[52] Several states regulate hospices, indicating their recognition of this practice.[53] The Medicare reimbursement criteria and some of the state licensing regulations limit coverage to persons with a life expectancy of six months or less. This use of a six-month time limit as an administrative convenience to control expenditure of funds and utilization of facilities should not be misinterpreted as an indiction that persons with longer life expectancies must accept aggressive treatment.

Civil Liability

Because of a fear of civil or criminal liability, physicians and hospitals sometimes have been reluctant to honor the wishes of terminally ill patients or their families. While theoretically there is a possibility of liability, it is no more likely that physicians and other health care providers will be held liable for withholding or withdrawing treatment in these cases than for the many other decisions and actions they must make every day.

Civil liability for withholding or withdrawing medical treatment would have to be based on negligent or deliberate failure to act in accordance with some duty to the patient. That duty is shaped by the patient's condition, and there is no duty to treat the terminally ill as if they are curable. In addition, explicit refusal by the terminally ill patient relieves the physician of further duty to provide the refused treatment. If refused treatment is given, liability for battery is possible. The same principles generally apply to refusal by the incompetent patient's representative.

There is always the possibility that a medical decision will be questioned in subsequent litigation and be found to have been negligent. The risk for decisions regarding the care of the terminally ill is no greater than that for the care of other patients. Liability is even possible when physicians act pursuant to a court order if they are negligent in implementing the order. Limited statutory immunity has been granted in some circumstances by natural death acts, but even those provisions have broad exceptions that preserve accountability.

The best indication of the limited exposure to civil liability is the apparent absence of lawsuits brought against physicians for withholding or withdrawing medical treatment from terminally ill patients with the concurrence of the patient or the family. Liability exposure is likely if there is misdiagnosis of terminal illness or unjustifiable failure to obtain the concurrence of the patient or the family, but there are no reported liability cases addressing those issues.

Exposure to civil liability may be greater from refusing to honor the wishes of the patient and the family. Several suits have been brought against providers who continued treatment for a prolonged time after refusal. After a patient won a court order for the Veterans Administration to remove him from a respirator, the administrator of his estate sought payment for his suffering from the prolonged treatment and for the legal expenses in obtaining the order. A federal district court denied the claim and legal expenses for the plaintiff. The administrator appealed the denial of legal expenses. The appellate court upheld the denial because it believed the Veterans Administration was justified in forcing the patient to obtain a court order, since the question had not been decided by the federal court previously.[54] As the question becomes more settled, federal defendants may be required to pay the patients' legal expenses.

The only case that has resulted in payment arose in Massachusetts. After the highest court there decided that a 78-year-old man with chronic organic brain syndrome could discontinue dialysis,[55] his wife sued the health care institution that had forced the matter to be taken to court. A jury award her $2.58 million. The court later ruled that she could be awarded payment only for the breach of contract claim and reduced the award to $100,000.[56] Another case was filed in Ohio.[57] These cases illustrate that extended delay and pursuit of a court order does not always minimize exposure to liability.

Criminal Liability

In some decisions involving the terminally ill, the courts have discussed the potential criminal liability for withholding or withdrawing medical treatment with proper authorization. In the *Quinlan* decision, after observing that termination of treatment would accelerate death, the court concluded that "there would be no criminal homicide but rather expiration from existing natural causes." It added as a second reason, "even if it were to be regarded as homicide, it would not be unlawful. . . . The termination of treatment pursuant to the right of privacy is, within the limits of this case, *ipso facto* lawful." It then discussed the constitutional dimensions:

> Furthermore, the exercise of a constitutional right such as we have here found is protected from criminal prosecution. We do not question the State's undoubted power to punish the taking of human life, but that power does not encompass individuals terminating medical treatment pursuant to their right of privacy. The constitutional protection extends to third parties whose action is necessary to effectuate the exercise of that right where the individuals themselves would not be subject to prosecution or the third parties are charged as accessories to an act which could not be a crime.[58]

Thus, there is little risk of criminal liability for these actions.

The only prosecutions of physicians in the United States for the deaths of terminally ill patients that have resulted in trials have involved alleged injections of substances to hasten death. In all four cases that have gone to trial, the jury acquitted the physician. The results of these cases illustrate the difficulty in obtaining convictions when the patient is terminally ill, even in cases alleging active euthanasia. This is one of the reasons prosecutors do not pursue cases that involve withholding or withdrawing treatment from the terminally ill. The other reason is that it would be difficult to establish a duty to provide the withheld or withdrawn treatment.

One case that did not go to trial supports this position. In 1983, two California physicians were charged with murder for terminating all life support, including intravenous feeding, of an irreversibly comatose patient upon the written request of the family. A California appellate court ordered that the charges be dismissed because there was no legal duty to continue life-sustaining treatment when futile. Since there was no unlawful failure to perform a legal duty, the court ruled the actions could not be considered murder.[59]

Some investigations into the deaths of terminally ill patients have resulted in the prosecution of nurses. Two nurses were accused of poisoning 11 patients at the Ann Arbor Veterans Administration Hospital by injecting a muscle relaxant into their intravenous tubes. They were convicted on several of the counts in 1977, but when the court ordered a new trial their indictments were subsequently dismissed.[60] A Maryland nurse was accused of unilaterally disconnecting three patients' respirators and turning down the oxygen flow to a fourth. Tried for one of the disconnection cases, she surrendered her license before the trial. The jury deadlocked over the issue of whether the patient was already dead when the disconnection occurred, so she was not convicted. All charges were then dropped.[61]

A Nevada nurse was indicted for the death of a patient in an intensive care unit. She was accused of turning down the oxygen on his ventilator. The court dismissed the indictment because of insufficient evidence.[62] A Massachusetts nurse was charged with giving 195 milligrams of morphine every seven hours on the night of the death of a patient terminally ill with cancer and severe heart and lung disease. The physician testified he had ordered the morphine be limited to 45 milligrams, but the nurse testified his orders were to give any amount necessary to ease the pain. The jury acquitted the nurse, but she was dismissed from her job.[63]

A California nurse was charged with the deaths of 12 patients in two hospitals from overdoses of lidocaine. The nurse was convicted of murdering the 12 and sentenced to death.[64] A Texas nurse was indicted in 1983 for the death of one toddler and injuries to seven others by injections of succinylcholine, a muscle relaxant. The nurse was convicted of murder and sentenced to 99 years in prison.[65]

These cases demonstrate the importance of proper documentation of the circumstances under which medical treatment may be withheld or withdrawn so that authorized actions can be distinguished from unauthorized actions. Nurses and other hospital personnel should seek appropriate documentation of decisions by the physician and patient or family before withholding or withdrawing medical treatment to assure appropriate care and to avoid the significant risk of investigation or prosecution in the absence of documented medical authorization of the actions.

The minimum documentation necessary should be an order or note in the medical record specifying the treatment to be withheld or withdrawn and an indication of the concurrence of the patient and/or family (or the reasons they were not involved, such as unavailability or incapacity). It would be wise to document the prognosis and any other rationale for the decision. Obviously, just as with other actions for which written orders are required, it must be recognized that emergency situations may arise in which oral orders are appropriate. However, oral orders must be written or countersigned within a reasonable period, such as 24 hours.

NOTES

1. *In re Quinlan,* 70 N.J. 10, 355 A.2d 647, 677 (1976).

2. *E.g., Matter of Dinnerstein,* 6 Mass. App. 466, 380 N.E.2d 134, 135 (1978) [one year]; *Satz v. Perlmutter,* 362 So. 2d 160, 161 (Fla. Dist. Ct. App. 1978), *aff'd.* 379 So. 2d 359 (Fla. 1980); *Matter of Spring,* 405 N.E.2d 115, 118 (Mass. 1980) [five years].

3. Wanzer et al., *The Physician's Responsibility Toward Hopelessly Ill Patients,* 310 *New Eng. J. Med.* 955 (April 12, 1984); *see also, Optimal Care for Hopelessly Ill Patients,* 295 *New Eng. J. Med.* 362 (1976); Grenvik et al., *Cessation of Therapy in Terminal Illness and Brain Death, Critical Care Med.* 284 (1978).

4. *Matter of Dinnerstein,* 6 Mass. App. 466, 380 N.E.2d 134 (1978).

5. *Hoyt v. St. Mary's Rehabilitation Center,* No. 774555 (Minn. Dist. Ct., Hennepin County, February 13, 1981).

6. *Eichner v. Dillon,* 73 A.D.2d 431, 426 N.Y.S.2d 517, 527 (1980).

7. *In re Quinlan,* 70 N.J. 10, 355 A.2d 647 (1976).

8. *Superintendent of Belchertown v. Saikewicz,* 373 Mass. 728, 370 N.E.2d 417 (1977).

9. *Matter of Spring,* 405 N.E.2d 115 (Mass. 1980); *see also Application of Lydia E. Hall Hosp.,* 116 Misc. 2d 477, 455 N.Y.S.2d 706 (N.Y. Sup. Ct. 1982) [Dialysis is extraordinary care for a terminally ill renal disease patient].

10. *In re Severns,* 425 A.2d 156 (Del. Ch. Ct. 1980).

11. *Matter of J. N.,* 406 A.2d 1275 (App. D.C. 1979).

12. McGivney and Crooks, eds., *The Care of Patients with Severe Chronic Pain in Terminal Illness,* 251 J.A.M.A. 1182 (March 2, 1984).

13. Cushing, *The Implications of Withdrawing Nutritional Devices,* 84 AM. J. NURSING 191 (February, 1984); Bernstein, *A Patient's Right to Die by Starvation,* HOSPITALS 75 (May 16, 1984).

14. Wanzer et al., *The Physician's Responsibility Toward Hopelessly Ill Patients,* 310 NEW ENG. J. MED. 955 (April 12, 1984).

15. *In re Severns,* 425 A.2d 156 (Del. Ch. Ct. 1980).

16. *Application of Plaza Health and Rehabiliation Center* (N.Y. Sup. Ct., Onondaga Cty. February 2, 1984); New York Times, February 3, 1984, at Al.

17. *Matter of Storar,* 52 N.Y.2d 363, 420 N.E.2d 64 (1981).

18. *In re Conroy,* 190 N.J. Super. 453, 464 A.2d 303 (N.J. Super. Ct. App. Div. 1983).

19. *Bouvia v. County of Riverside*, No. 159780 (Cal. Super. Ct., Riverside Cty. Dec. 16, 1983); New York Times, Dec. 21, 1983, at 16; subsequently, court ordered patient to accept feeding or to be force-fed, Miami Herald, Dec. 23, 1983, at 15A.

20. *Barber v. Superior Court*, 147 Cal. App. 3d 1006 (1983).

21. *United States v. Rutherford*, 442 U.S. 544 (1979).

22. *E.g., King v. Solomon*, 323 Mass. 326, 81 N.E.2d 838 (1948).

23. Cedar Rapids Gazette (Associated Press article), November 10, 1976.

24. *In re Severns*, 425 A.2d 156 (Del. Ch. Ct. 1980); *Matter of Storar*, 52, N.Y.2d 363, 420 N.E.2d 64 (1981).

25. *John F. Kennedy Memorial Hosp. v. Bludworth*, 452 So.2d 921 (Fla. 1984). Note that a 1984 Florida Statute (H.B. 127) modifies this to permit honoring certain patient directives without family permission.

26. *In re Quinlan*, 70 N.J. 10, 355 A.2d 647, 664 (1976).

27. *Superintendent of Belchertown v. Saikewicz*, 373 Mass. 728, 370 N.E.2d 417, 427 (1977).

28. *E.g., Farber v. Olkon*, 40 Cal. 2d 503, 254 P.2d 520 (1953).

29. *Matter of Welfare of Coyer*, 660 P.2d 738 (Wash. 1983).

30. *John F. Kennedy Memorial Hosp. v. Bludworth*, 452 So.2d 921 (Fla. 1984).

31. *E.g., Guardianship of Barry*, 445 So.2d 365 (Fla. Dist. Ct. App. 1984), *approved John F. Kennedy Memorial Hosp. v. Bludworth*, 452 So.2d 921 (Fla. 1984) [Approval of termination of ventilatory support of infant who had only minimal brain stem function. Court indicated judicial review is not required in such cases when diagnosis is confirmed by two physicians].

32. *Application of Cicero*, 421 N.Y.S.2d 965 (N.Y. Sup. Ct. 1979); *see also* "Selective Treatment," 84 *Am. J. Nursing* 309 (March, 1984).

33. *In re McNulty*, 4 FAM. L. RPTR. 2255 (Mass. Prob. Ct., Essex County, February 15, 1978); see also "The Rights of Infants with Down's Syndrome," 251 *J.A.M.A* 229 (Jan. 13, 1984).

34. *The Hastings Center Report*, August 1982, p. 6; 34 *Baylor L. Rev.* 715 (1982).

35. *In re Infant Doe*, No. GU 8204-00 (Cir. Ct., Monroe County, Ind. April 12, 1982), *writ of mandamus dismissed sub. nom. State ex rel. Infant Doe v. Baker*, No. 482 S 140 (Ind. Sup. Ct. May 27, 1982). Medical status of Infant Doe is detailed in letter to the editor, 309 *New Eng. J. Med.* 664 (September 15, 1983).

36. 48 Fed. Reg. 9630 (March 7, 1983).

37. *American Academy of Pediatrics v. Heckler*, 561 F.Supp. 395 (D.D.C. 1983).

38. *The Blue Sheet*, July 6, 1983, p. 8; "AHA Files 'Baby Doe' Comments; Criticizes Proposed Rule," 6 *Health Law Vigil* 19, 1–2 (September 16, 1983); "Court Strikes Down 'Baby Doe' Rule, but That Doesn't Stop Investigations," *Modern Healthcare* (May 1983), p. 34.

39. President's Commission for the Study of Ethical Problems in Medical and Biomedical and Behavioral Research, DECIDING TO FOREGO LIFE-SUSTAINING TREATMENT, March 1983, p. 227.

40. "New Baby Doe Regs Out; Debate Goes On," 83 *Am. J. Nursing* 1270 (September, 1983); "Treatment of Critically Ill Newborns," 72 *Pediatrics* 565 (October 1983).

41. 49 Fed. Reg. 1622 (Jan. 12, 1984).

42. *American Hosp. Assn. v. Heckler*, 83 Civ. 2638 (CLB), 84 Cir. 1724 (CLB) (S.D. N.Y. May 23, 1984).

43. *U.S. v. University Hosp.*, 729 F.2d 144 (2nd Cir. 1984). *Weber v. Stony Brook Hosp.*, 469 N.Y. S.2d 63 (N.Y. Ct. App. 1983). Parents subsequently authorized limited surgery that was performed to make child more comfortable. N.Y. Times, April 7, 1984, p. 12.

44. *John F. Kennedy Memorial Hosp. v. Bludworth*, 452 So.2d 921 (Fla. 1984).

45. *Superintendent of Belchertown v. Saikewicz*, 373 Mass. 728, 370 N.E.2d. 471 (1977); *Eichner v. Dillon*, 73 A.D.2d 431, 426 N.Y.S.2d 517 (1980).

46. *Matter of Spring*, 405 N.E.2d 115 (Mass. 1980); *Matter of Storar*, 52 N.Y.2d 363, 420 N.E.2d 64 (1981).

47. *Matter of Spring*, 405 N.E.2d 115, 120–122 (Mass. 1980).

48. *Matter of Welfare of Coyer*, 660 P.2d 738 (Wash. 1983).

49. CAL. HEALTH & SAFETY CODE §§ 7185–7193 (West Supp. 1982).

50. ARK. STAT. ANN. §§ 82–3801—82–3804 (Supp. 1981).

51. *Matter of Welfare of Coyer*, 660 P.2d 738 (Wash. 1983). Applicable common law principles in Washington require involvement of a court-appointed guardian.

52. Pub. L. No. 97–248, § 122 (1982).

53. *E.g.*, FLA. STAT. §§ 400.601–400.614 (1983).

54. *Foster v. Tourtellotte*, 704 F.2d 1109 (9th Cir. 1983).

55. *Matter of Spring*, 405 N.E.2d 115 (Mass. 1980).

56. *Spring v. Geriatric Authority of Holyoke*, No. 14833 (Franklin Super. Ct., Mass., December 10, 1982).

57. *Estate of Leach v. Shapiro*, No. 11238 (Ohio Ct. App. May 2, 1984) [Appellate court reversed trial court's dismissal and remanded for trial. Suit filed by husband after *Leach v. Akron Gen. Medical Center*, 426 N.E.2d 809 (Ohio Com. Pl. Ct. 1980) authorized removal of wife's respirator.]

58. *In re Quinlan*, 70 N.J. 10, 355 A.2d 647, 669–670 (1976).

59. *Barber v. Superior Court of Cal.*, 147 Cal. App. 3d 1006 (1983).

60. *U.S. v. Narcisco*, 446 F.Supp. 252 (E.D. Mich. 1977); "Liability for Death: Nine Nurses' Legal Ordeals," 11 *Nursing 81* 34 (September 1981).

61. 11 *Nursing 81* 37 (September 1981); 20 *Medical World News* (9) 48 (April 30, 1979).

62. 11 *Nursing 81* 40 (September 1981); 19 *Nursing Forum* (3) 212 (1980).

63. 11 *Nursing 81* 41 (September 1981).

64. New York Times, March 30, 1984, at 9; The Post (Palm Beach, Fl.), April 12, 1984, at A11. 11 *Nursing 81* 42 (September 1981).

65. New York Times, April 11, 1984, at 13; New York Times, November 22, 1983, at 8; "Death Shift," *Texas Monthly* (August 1983). 106.

BIBLIOGRAPHY

Cohn, Sarah. "The Living Will from the Nurse's Perspective." *Law, Medicine, and Health Care* 11, no. 3 (June 1983):121.

Dunn, Lee. "The *Eichner/Storer* Decision: A Year's Perspective." *Law, Medicine, and Health Care* 10, no. 3 (June 1982):117.

Eisendrath, Stuart, and Jonsen, Albert. "The Living Will: Help or Hindrance?" *Journal of the American Medical Association* 249, no. 15 (April 15, 1983): 2054.

Greenlaw, Jane. "Orders Not to Resuscitate: A Dilemma for Acute Care as Well as Long-Term Care Facilities." *Law, Medicine, and Health Care* 10, no. 1 (February 1982):29.

Horan, Dennis. "Legally Speaking: The Intolerable Nursing Burden of 'Don't Feed' Orders." *RN* 45, no. 1 (January 1982):75.

Taub, Sheila. "Withholding Treatment from Defective Newborns." *Law, Medicine, and Health Care* 10, no. 1 (February 1982):4.

Wanzer, et al. "The Physician's Responsibility Toward Hopelessly Ill Patients." *New England Journal of Medicine* 310, no. 15 (April 12, 1984):955.

Chapter 11

Collection and Disclosure of Patient Information

Hospitals and health professionals must collect a large amount of sensitive information about patients to provide appropriate diagnosis, treatment, and care. This chapter discusses the recording of patient information and its uses, as well as the law concerning confidentiality and the circumstances in which disclosure is prohibited, permitted, or mandated.

HEALTH CARE RECORDS

Accurate and complete health care records and a functioning records library are required by both governmental and nongovernmental agencies. The licensing laws and regulations of many states include specific requirements with which hospitals must comply. In addition, nongovernmental agencies, such as the Joint Commission on Accreditation of Hospitals (JCAH), establish high standards for the maintenance of records.

The primary purpose of these records is for diagnosis, treatment, and care of the patient. The recording of the data provides a communication link among the team members caring for the patient. Records also document what was found and what was done so patient care can be evaluated, billing and collections can be made, and other administrative and legal matters can be addressed. Health care records also are of value in hospital educational and research programs.

Contents

A variety of statutes and regulations require hospitals to maintain health care records. Hospitals that participate in the Medicare program must comply with minimum content requirements.[1] State hospital licensing laws and regulations addressing health care records can be divided into three groups: (1) those detailing the information required, (2) those specifying the broad areas of information required, and (3) those stating simply that the health care record shall be adequate, accurate or complete. In some cities, municipal codes require certain information not otherwise specified by state law or regulation.[2]

The JCAH also specifies standards concerning health care records that hospitals must meet to be accredited. Standard II in the Medical Records chapter of the *Accreditation Manual for Hospitals* (1984 edition), lists specific items to include. They are designed to assure the patient is identified, the diagnosis is supported, the treatment is justified, and the results are documented accurately. While many of the items apply only to inpatients, the general standards apply to all, including ambulatory care patients, emergency cases, and those served in a hospital-administered home care program.

Certain basic information usually should be recorded for each patient. The health care record consists of three types of data: (1) personal, (2) financial, and (3) medical. Personal information, usually obtained upon admission, includes name, date of birth, sex, marital status, occupation, other items of identification, and the next-of-kin or other person to contact in the event of emergencies. Financial data usually include the name of the patient's employer, health insurance company, type of insurance and policy number, and other information that will enable the hospital to bill for its services. Medical data form the clinical record, a continuously maintained history of the patient's condition and the treatment provided in the hospital: the results of physical examinations, medical history, treatment administered, progress reports, physicians' orders, clinical laboratory reports, radiological reports, consultation reports, anesthesia records, operation records, signed consent forms, nurses' notes, and discharge summaries. Some hospitals also collect social data concerning family status, community activities, and other information related to the patient's position in society.

Accuracy and Timely Completion

Accurate and timely completed records are essential to comply with governmental and accreditation requirements and to minimize liability exposure.

State hospital licensing statutes and regulations and JCAH standards require accurate records. An inaccurate record may increase the hospital's exposure to liability by destroying the credibility of the entire record. In a 1974 case[3] the court found that a clear discrepancy between what the health care record stated and what actually happened to the patient could justify a jury finding that, if the record was erroneous in part, it could be erroneous in other parts as well and thus be considered generally invalid.

Complete records include notations of observations that the patient's condition has or has not changed; if that is lacking, many courts permit the jury to infer that no observation was made. In one case the court was presented with a case involving a patient who had been admitted to the hospital for a broken leg that, while in traction, suffered irreversible ischemia, requiring amputation.[4] The physician had ordered the nurse to observe the patient's toes and the health care record indicated hourly observations during the first day of hospitalization. There was no documentation of observations during the seven hours prior to finding the foot cold and without sensation. Although the nurse may have observed the foot during that period, the court ruled that the jury could conclude that there were no observations, which was a breach of the nurse's duty. The hospital, as employer, could be liable for the resulting injuries.

Complete records can protect the hospital and staff in many situations. In a 1961 Kentucky case a hospital was found not to be liable for the death of a patient 13 hours after surgery because the health care record included documentation of proper periodic observation by the nursing staff, contacts with the physician concerning management of the patient, and compliance with the physician's directions.[5] As discussed in Chapter 7, compliance with the physician's directions does not protect the hospital and its staff when the directions are clearly improper. However, when they are within the ambit of acceptable professional practice, compliance, and documentation of compliance, provides substantial protection from liability.

Record entries usually should be made when the treatment is given or the observations made. Entries made several days or weeks later have less credibility than those made during or immediately after hospitalization. Medicare conditions of participation require completion of hospital records within 15 days following the patient's discharge.[6] JCAH accreditation standards require the hospital's medical staff regulations to state a time limit for completion of the record after discharge. Persistent failure to conform to a medical staff rule requiring the physician to complete records promptly was held in one case to provide a basis for suspension of the staff member.[7]

In some situations, inaccurate records can be a crime. In 1978 a New York court ruled that a nurse and surgeon could properly be charged with the crime of falsifying business records when they failed to enter in the operating room log the fact that an unlicensed salesman had assisted in the surgical implantation of a total hip prosthesis.[8]

Corrections and Alterations

Hospitals should give attention to the method by which their staffs correct errors in health care records. Improper alterations can reduce the credibility of the record, exposing the hospital to an increased risk of liability.

Generally, there are two types of errors made in health care records: (1) minor ones in transcription, spelling, and the like, and (2) more significant ones involving important test data, physician medication orders, inadvertently omitted progress notes, and similar substantive entries. Persons authorized by hospital policy to make record entries may correct minor errors in these entries when errors are discovered soon after the original entry is made. Only a physician or administrative or nursing staff supervisor should correct substantive errors and those discovered some time after the original entry. If the original entry is likely to have been read by others who could be misled by the error, the physicians, nurses, and others likely to be relying on it should be notified of the change.

The person correcting the error should place a single line through the incorrect entry, enter the correct information, initial or sign it, and enter the time and date. Mistakes in the record should not be erased or obliterated, since such changes can create suspicion in the minds of jurors concerning the original entry.

After a claim has been made or a lawsuit has been threatened or filed against the hospital or a staff member, changes should not be made in the records without first consulting defense counsel. In a 1979 New York case, after physicians had won a malpractice case, it was discovered that a page of the record had been replaced not long before the beginning of the suit, so the court ordered a new trial.[9]

Altering or falsifying a health care record for purposes of wrongfully obtaining reimbursement is a crime. In some states, a practitioner who improperly alters a record is subject to licensure revocation or other discipline for unprofessional conduct.

Some patients request modification of records. Since the records are the best evidence of what occurred and were relied on in making decisions concerning the care provided, hospitals usually should not modify records except to update the identity of patients whose names are changed. If a patient disagrees with an entry there are two approaches to modifications: (1) Some hospitals permit the physician or nurse supervisor to make amendments in the same manner as corrections of substantive errors, if the physician concurs in the appropriateness of the change. The amendment should include a note that it is being made at the request of the patient, so that the patient will be responsible for explaining the change if it is questioned later. (2) Some hospitals, instead of changing the original, permit the patient to add a letter of explanation to the record. If the staff concurs with the statement, that can be noted on the letter. This approach clearly documents the source of the change.

Retention of Records

Since the facility's record is maintained primarily for the use of the institution and its staff in providing better patient care, the decision concerning the length of time it shall be retained should be made on the basis of sound hospital and professional practice. However, the decision as to the retention period cannot be made on this basis alone. In several states, regulations specify the minimum length of time all records must be retained; in others, these provisions apply to certain records only, for example, x-rays and clinical lab test reports. Medicare requires records to be kept for the longer of five years after the filing of the hospital's cost report or the period in which suits may be filed. Several states insist that records be kept permanently, but more now are requiring that they be retained for the period in which suits may be filed for breach of contract or personal injuries. Several states provide that records cannot be destroyed without the approval of a regulatory agency.

Where there are no controlling regulations, the retention time after records are not needed for medical and administrative purposes should be determined by the hospital administration with the advice of legal counsel. The factors taken into account should include whether or not microfilming is feasible or practical, storage space, future need for the records, and the legal considerations of having them available in the event a patient sues the hospital or a third party. Hospitals in which extensive research is conducted may prefer a longer retention period to facilitate retrospective studies.

Destruction of Records

The issue of destruction of records can arise when the retention period specified by hospital policy has passed or when the patient requests destruction before expiration of that period.

Some state regulations specify the method by which records may be destroyed. Several states permit burning but the Environmental Protection Agency recommends shredding and recycling. Regardless of the method used, it should protect confidentiality of information and assure complete destruction. The hospital should retain certificates of destruction permanently as evidence of record disposal. Some states require hospitals to create a permanent abstract of the record prior to destruction.

Some patients request premature destruction of records. Some state statutes forbid this on an individual basis.[10] In states without specific statutes, it still is prudent not to destroy records unless ordered to do so by a court—and courts generally have refused to do so. In a New York case the court ruled that records could be ordered sealed, but not destroyed.[11] In an exception to this rule, a Pennsylvania court ordered the destruction of the records of a mental patient who had been hospitalized illegally.[12]

Charting Tips

The health care record is used as evidence in a variety of legal actions, including Workers' Compensation, personal injury actions, and will contests. Generally, nurses are most concerned about the use of records in negligence actions.

The record, including the nurses' notes, is a critical piece of evidence in the determination of the standard of care provided. The notes should reflect, accurately and completely, the patient's condition, progress, and nursing activities for the period the charting covers. Nurses should keep in mind that charts can be a defense against a negligence allegation and that good charting can protect them from liability.

Nurses should be familiar with the hospital policy on charting. The hospital should review each element of the policy periodically to assure that its requirements are realistically designed to promote accuracy and efficiency. It may be advisable to use graphic sheets or charts that summarize numerical and objective data to facilitate ease and completeness of charting. In addition to saving time, a well-designed flow sheet can make it easy to find information and identify trends and changes in patients' conditions.

Specific recommendations for charting include:

1. Charting must be done as soon as possible after the events occur. The notes must include the time events occurred. If charting is done routinely at the end of the shift, notes should be made during the shift to form the basis of entries. It is not advisable to do all charting at once, as details, times, and incidents are likely to be omitted.
2. Observations charted should lead to nursing diagnosis and describe the patient's behavior, appearance, and symptoms. Patient quotes and statements should be used. Conclusions should not be charted without supporting objective data.
3. An error in charting should not be obliterated; rather, the entry should be crossed out and "error" written about it. An obliterated entry could be construed as a cover-up or as an error that injured the patient. Other nurses' notes should not be recopied if an error is made. If a treatment or medication is discontinued, the entry should be crossed out and "D/C" or "discontinued" written in.
4. A late entry is better than no entry. The date and time that the note is made should be charted with a notation that it is a late entry. A note should not be squeezed into a small space or the margin of the page.
5. Chart entries should be clear and correct grammar and spelling should be used. It is not always necessary to use complete sentences, but nurses should not expect an attorney or jury to fill in the gaps left by "shorthand charting."
6. The writing must be legible; abbreviations that could be misunderstood should not be used.
7. It is not necessary to describe everything as "appears" or "seems." Every nurse is capable of documenting observations without these qualifiers. The

only time it may be advisable to use "appears" is when the patient appears to be sleeping.

8. Once is enough: it is not necessary to repeat data that can be found elsewhere in the chart, such as intake and output, medications, or activity, unless it is indicative of a change in the patient's condition.

9. Changes in the patient's status, especially signs that indicate deterioration, should be documented with extra care, along with the steps taken by the nursing staff to respond to the change.

10. "Routine" checks of a patient's status should be charted, including the assessment and the results, even if they are "normal." Failure to enter normal data can lead to the inference that the patient was not checked at all.

11. Inaccuracies are totally impermissible in charting. If discovered, they can cast doubt on the credibility of the record and the nurse.

12. It is imperative to document steps taken to respond to changes in a patient's condition, such as "M.D. notified. Order for oxygen obtained. Patient placed in 40% oxygen." The results of the intervention also must be charted.

13. Diagnostic tests and treatments, who performed them, and the patient's response all should be charted.

14. The writer should be identified by name and title at the conclusion of each chart entry.

15. Charts must not be destroyed or recopied.

A clear, factual account of the patient's condition and care can protect the nursing staff from liability for negligence. Nurses should keep in mind that the charting should reflect compliance with the appropriate standard of care for that patient.

Ownership

The hospital owns the records. They are the hospital's business record. The hospital's ownership is stated explicitly in the statutes and regulations of some states. Courts have recognized the hospital's ownership.[13] If the physician maintains separate records, they are the property of the physician; however, the physician still has a responsibility to maintain complete hospital records.

The health care record is an unusual type of property because physically it belongs to the hospital, which must exercise considerable control over access, but patients and others have an interest in the information it contains. One way of viewing this is that the hospital owns the paper or other material on which the information is recorded but is just a custodian of the information. Thus, patients and others have a right of access to the information in many circumstances but not to possession of the original records.[14] In a 1935 Michigan case, the court ruled that the patient did not have a right to x-ray negatives.[15] The patient does not purchase a picture; the patient purchases the professional service of interpreting the x-ray. Thus, the patient could not use the physician's retention of the x-ray as a defense to a physician's suit to collect his professional fee.

Computers

Taking advantage of automated data processing techniques, hospitals have developed new methods for handling health care record information. Several legal questions are raised by these new techniques. In states that require physicians' signatures as authentication of their entries and orders, some accommodation will be necessary, since a completely automated system provides no conventional written record for the physician to sign or initial. In states requiring retention of the original record for a period of time, that produced in an automated system may not suffice. In some states there may be a question of court admissibility of information generated by the system.

Questions of confidentiality may arise because of the potential access to information by a larger number of people. However, a properly designed computer access security system may provide more confidentiality protection than the traditional hospital record because (1) there are few points of access to the computer, (2) it is possible to restrict each person's access to a limited scope of information, and (3) it is possible to monitor continuously or selectively the information being sought using individual access codes, making misuse easier to detect. Of course, the security system depends in part on educating staff members that disclosure of their personal access codes is equivalent to disclosure of confidential health care information, and thus subject to the same sanctions by the hospital.

CONFIDENTIALITY

The primary rationale for confidentiality is to encourage candor by patients and their associates to optimize diagnosis and treatment. Confidentiality also respects patient privacy; people should not have to broadcast details of their bodily condition to obtain health care. Confidentiality also can promote candor by those caring for the patient.

People outside the hospital seek to obtain this information. There is much interest in the health condition of individuals and the care they receive. Family members are interested in the condition of relatives. Some patients can have a significant effect on affairs of business and state, so their condition is valuable information. There also is a general interest in unusual health conditions and the condition of those involved in public events, so media attention focuses on health information. The health condition is an important element of many insurance coverage determinations and legal proceedings, criminal and civil.

The tension between access and secrecy has existed since the beginning of medicine. Most health professions in addressing the issue have incorporated confidentiality mandates in their ethical standards. For example, the Hippocratic Oath of physicians states: "And whatsover I shall see or hear in the course of my profession, as well as outside my profession in my intercourse with men, if it be what should not be published abroad, I will never divulge, holding such things to be holy secrets."[16] These codes led to tensions as legal requirements of disclosure evolved. For example, some physicians challenged early laws requiring reporting of births and deaths.

Most modern codes recognize that professionals have an obligation to comply with legal mandates regarding disclosure. The American Medical Association code as amended in 1980 states: "A physician . . . shall safeguard patient confidences within the constraints of the law."[17] Nursing has adopted a similar balanced standard. The American Nurses' Association *Code for Nurses* states: "The nurse safeguards the client's right to privacy by judiciously protecting information of a confidential nature."[18]

ACCESS FOR INTRAHOSPITAL USE

There are many needs for access to information within the hospital, including direct patient care, administrative uses, and research.

Patient Care

Those involved in patient care must have timely access to the records, or the communication function of the record is defeated to the detriment of proper treatment. Records must be located where they are readily accessible for patient care, even though this may increase the risk of unauthorized access by others, for treatment of the present condition and for future care. Although confidentiality is an important goal that hospitals and health professionals should strive to achieve, unauthorized access results in less exposure to liability than does improper patient care because of unavailable records.

Administrative Uses

Medical records also are key elements of the business records of the hospital. Many staff members must have access to operate the hospital. Hospitals have the authority to permit internal access by professional, technical, and administrative personnel who have need to do so for such functions as auditing, filing, billing, replying to inquiries, and defending potential litigation.

These administrative uses are so widely understood that they seldom have been addressed in reported court decisions. The few cases have been decided in favor of administrative access. In one case, the court authorized a trustee to examine records of patients involved in a controversial research project.[19] The court observed: "Actually, the supposed strict secrecy does not really exist as to qualified persons since these records have been seen, read and copied by numerous staff members and employees of the hospital and cooperating institutions."[20]

Courts have upheld the authority of hospitals to review records for quality assurance purposes[21] and to permit their insurers and lawyers to have access to prepare to deal with patient claims.[22]

Research

Research uses are the other major type of intrahospital access. Many important medical discoveries have been made through researching health care records.[23] A few commentators still question research uses of records without patient consent but the practice generally is recognized as appropriate and permissible. The general practice is to permit staff members to use the records for bona fide research. Research by nonstaff members should be subject to a review and approval process, including assurances against redisclosure of individually identifiable information. The Department of Health and Human Services recognizes this practice by making some federally funded research involving only records eligible for either exemption from institutional review or expedited review.[24]

PATIENT AUTHORIZATION

One of the clearest sources of authority to release information to nonhospital personnel is the authorization of a competent patient.

Patient Access

Competent patients generally can authorize their own access to records concerning their care. Some states have statutes that establish patients' rights to access to records on their own care and establish procedures for doing so.[25] A common-law right of access has been recognized by several courts. In cases over the past two decades patients generally have been held to have a right of access.[26] Courts also have said that, if a patient wants a copy of the record, the hospital may require that a reasonable charge be paid for it.[27]

Access by Others

When patients may authorize their own access, they may authorize access by others. In an Oklahoma case the court ruled that insurers of the patient have a right to copy the hospital's records upon proper authorization of the patient.[28] The court found the hospital's refusal to provide a copy to be unlawful interference with the insurer's business.

There is implied consent to keep the immediate family informed of the patient's progress unless the person expressly directs that no information be released or a statutory prohibition applies, such as the federal substance abuse confidentiality rules discussed later in this chapter. In a 1963 Louisiana case the court found that the husband had a right of access to information concerning his wife's care even though they were separated and he was pursuing a divorce.[29] It is doubtful whether many courts would extend the right of access that far today. Thus, the most prudent practice would be to require express patient consent or court authorization before releasing information when estrangement is known.

In a 1982 New York case the court stated that a spouse should not be told psychiatric information even where there is no estrangement unless the patient authorizes the disclosure or there is a danger to the patient, spouse, or another person that can be reduced by disclosure.[30] Some statutes authorize the disclosure of psychiatric information to the spouse in other circumstances.[31] Thus, release of psychiatric information is subject to special restrictions in some jurisdictions.

Exceptions

Some courts have recognized exceptions to the general rule in favor of access. They recognize there may be situations when the release of information would be against the best interests of the patient's health. However, as illustrated by a 1979 case, the courts generally have insisted that medically contraindicated information be made available to the patient's representative, frequently an outside professional acting on behalf of the patient.[32]

This case addressed the withholding of information from patients preparing for hearings challenging their transfer to facilities that provide a lower level of care. The court ruled that it was not enough for the state to offer to release the information to a representative when the patient did not have a representative. The state was permitted to withhold medically contraindicated information from the patient only when the person actually had a representative, provided by the state if necessary. In a 1965 case the court stated that records that would be adverse to the patient's health could be withheld from insurance companies.[33] It is doubtful whether this rule would be applied today, given the widespread understanding of third party payment.

Suggested Hospital Policies

It is recommended that hospitals give patients and their representatives access to health care records upon authorization of the patient. In some situations, when the patient is unable to authorize access, approval of the representative should be accepted (as discussed in the next section). Since records contain technical information and many abbreviations and specialized terms, the hospital protocol should offer the patient and representative an opportunity to review the record with someone who can explain it.

The American Hospital Association (AHA) has recommended that the attending physician be notified before records are released, and many hospitals follow the practice. Some medical staffs rely on the hospital to determine which releases can be made without notification, which require notification, and which require physician review before release. Other medical staffs and hospitals agree on guidelines concerning which releases fall in each category. There should be medical staff understanding and acceptance of whatever approach is followed.

However, physicians should not be given a veto over release of hospital records. If the physician has substantial reasons for believing release to a patient is contraindicated, then arrangements should be made for release to someone acting on the patient's behalf. In some situations, especially psychiatric records that contain sensitive information about other members of the family, the person acting on the patient's behalf may need to be from outside the family.

The AHA's Patient's Bill of Rights focuses on release of information by the physician rather than by the hospital.[34] It states that patients should be able to obtain complete information from their physician except when disclosure is not medically advisable, and then the information should be given to an appropriate person on the patient's behalf. When patients will accept information from their physician, this approach is preferable to having the person read the health care record. Thus, physicians should be encouraged to provide information to their patients.

However, in many situations, patients still wish to see the record. Access is recommended because in many situations, patient curiosity and concerns will be satisfied, dispelling any appearance of a cover-up and avoiding the need for the patient to hire an attorney or file suit to obtain the records. A 1980 study that analyzed patient reactions found:

1. One-third of the patients who read their charts had self-induced or factitious illness and were angry to have been uncovered.
2. One-third had believed their physicians to be unsympathetic to their symptoms and some found their suspicions confirmed, while others gained renewed confidence.
3. One-third were worried about their prognosis, fearing the physician was not telling them the severity of their illness, and all these patients were reassured.[35]

Another good reason to provide prompt access is that in some cases courts have ruled that the period from the request until the release does not count toward exhausting the statute of limitations period in which suits must be brought if that span is unreasonably long.[36] Thus, resistance to disclosure can reduce the protection of the statute of limitations.

AUTHORIZATION BY PATIENT'S REPRESENTATIVE

When the patient is unable to authorize access because of incompetency, minority, or death, someone else must be able to authorize access.

Mentally Incompetent Patients

In general, guardians of mentally incompetent patients are entitled to access to records to which the patients would have access, if competent. However, some courts have stated they will suppress portions of the record upon a determination they contain family confidences or information that may upset the patient severely.[37]

When a mentally incompetent patient does not have a guardian, the hospital probably is safe in relying on the authorization of the next-of-kin or other responsible person who is authorizing medical treatment, especially for access by the responsible person or by others for continuity of patient care or payment of charges. When the mental incompetence is temporary and release of the information can reasonably wait, it usually is most prudent to wait for the patient's authorization.

Minors

The scope of parent and guardian access to records of minors is less clear. Some state statutes specify that information regarding certain types of treatment, such as venereal disease and substance abuse, may not be disclosed without the minor's consent. Some states specify by statute that parents must be informed before minors may obtain certain kinds of services. For example, Utah requires parents to be informed of abortions. In a 1981 Supreme Court case, the Court found the Utah reporting law not to violate the Constitution but declined to rule on whether the law would be constitutional if it were applied to mature minors.[38]

When minors are permitted under state law to consent to their own care, it is likely that parents would not have a right to information concerning the treatment. If the minor fails to pay for the care and relies on the parents, they may be entitled to more information. However, providers can release information concerning immature minors to parents without substantial risk of liability, unless state statutes expressly prohibit it. When a mature minor wants information withheld from parents, the provider must make a professional judgment except in the few circumstances where the law is settled, such as when a statute requires or forbids notification. A circumstance that clearly permits disclosure is when there is likelihood of harm to the minor or others, such as a contagious disease, that requires parental involvement to avoid.

Deceased Patients

After the death of a patient, if there is an executor of the estate, authorization by that source usually should be sought. If there is no executor, authorization should be obtained from the next-of-kin, such as a surviving spouse[39] or child.[40] If there is known conflict among next-of-kin, it is most prudent to obtain the authorization of all of the nearest kin available. In such cases, a surviving spouse could authorize release alone but, if there is no spouse, the authorization of all of the available children should be obtained.

In a few states the legal responsibility to maintain confidentiality ends with the death of the patient. However, it still is prudent to insist on appropriate authorization to avoid compromising the interests of the surviving family.

ACCESS BY LAW

Even if the patient or representative opposes release of information, the law requires hospitals and health care professionals to permit access in many circumstances. The law grants parties in lawsuits access through subpoenas and other mechanisms to discover evidence. The law requires health care providers to report a variety of patient conditions to law enforcement or public health authorities or to give certain persons access if they request the information.

Subpoenas and Other Discovery Mechanisms

In lawsuits and many administrative proceedings, the court or agency has the authority to issue orders to assist one side to gain access to information that is in the control of others. Lawyers call this the discovery process. The most frequent discovery orders are called subpoenas, which require a person to appear at a specific place on or before a certain time, frequently bringing certain documents. Other discovery orders can require a person to submit to a physical or mental examination or to permit someone to inspect land, buildings or other property.

Health Care Records

A subpoena may order that health care records (or copies) be provided to the court or to the other side in a suit. A subpoena may order a person to submit to formal questioning under oath prior to the trial. This question-and-answer session is called a deposition and often is used as testimony if the person cannot be at the trial. If the person is at the trial and gives different testimony, the deposition can be used to cast doubt on what is said at trial.

Under the current liberal discovery practices, health care records nearly always can be subpoenaed if the mental or physical condition of the party is possibly relevant to the suit. When records can be subpoenaed, those who provided the health care usually can be ordered to give depositions.

In most circumstances, courts will not permit the discovery of information concerning the care of persons who are not parties. Some attorneys have sought the information to establish what happened when similar treatment was given to other patients. Providers have resisted these attempts on the basis that it invades the patient's privacy, violates the physician-patient privilege (discussed in the section on limitations on disclosures), and is not relevant because of the uniqueness of the condition and reaction of each patient.

The only widely accepted exceptions to the general rule not permitting discovery have been in cases involving billing fraud by, or professional discipline of, the health care provider. However, in recent years, some courts have permitted access to records of nonparties in malpractice suits but have required all "identifiers" to be deleted.[41] There is no clear trend because several courts have reaffirmed the traditional rule and declined to order access.[42]

Patient Names

Some attorneys have attempted to bypass the rule on nondisclosure of nonparty records by seeking the names of nonparty patients and obtaining their permission to get the records. Providers have resisted these attempts for reasons similar to those for resisting discovery of their records. Most courts have not permitted the discovery of the names of nonparties.

For example, in a 1964 case, the court ruled that the names of patients were protected by the physician-patient privilege.[43] However, in 1976, the court held that that privilege does not protect patients' names in Arizona but still refused to order release of other names because it did not consider them relevant to the case.[44] Thus, there is a risk that records obtained without identifiers could be linked later to patient names through another exception.

Committee Reports

Many states' statutes protect quality assurance-related activities and committee reports from discovery or admission into evidence. These laws are designed to permit the candor necessary for effective peer review to improve quality and reduce morbidity and mortality. Courts have found these laws to be constitutional.[45]

Some courts have interpreted statutory protections strictly, reducing their effectiveness. For example, in a 1975 case, the court refused to apply the statutory protection for utilization review committees to related committees such as medical records and audit, tissue, and infection control.[46] On the other hand, some courts have interpreted statutory protections broadly. A Minnesota court in 1980 held that a complications conference report was protected under a statute that protected "the proceedings and records of a review organization."[47]

Some courts have recognized a common-law qualified privilege on the basis of the public interest in peer review activities. In a 1970 District of Columbia case, the court refused to order release of information concerning a peer review committee's activities.[48] However, other courts have refused to recognize such a privilege for peer review.[49]

Because the status of many committee reports still is an open question in many states, they should be carefully written so that, if they must be released, they will not inappropriately increase the exposure to liability.

Responses to Subpoenas and Other Orders

In most situations the proper response to a valid subpoena or other discovery order is compliance. However, prompt legal guidance should be sought because some orders are not valid and others should be resisted. In some states the physician-patient privilege is not automatically waived by the patient's filing of a personal injury claim, so the records custodian has a duty to refuse to respond to some subpoenas. A discovery order never should be ignored.

Subpoenas from state courts in other states usually are not valid unless they are given to the person being subpoenaed while that individual is in the state of the issuing court. However, subpoenas from federal courts in other states usually are valid. Courts in some states have authority to issue subpoenas to persons in only a limited area. Most states have a procedure for obtaining a valid subpoena from a local court to require releasing information for trial in a distant court that does not have the authority to issue such a subpoena.

Sometimes challenges to subpoenas are successful. In a New Jersey case the court refused to order a woman or her psychiatrist to answer questions concerning nonfinancial matters in a marriage separation case because the husband had failed to demonstrate relevance or good cause for the order.[50] When judges are not certain whether to order a release, they sometimes will order that the information be presented to them for their review before ruling on the matter.

In some situations the only way to obtain prompt appellate review of an apparently inappropriate discovery order is to risk being found in contempt of court. In one case a physician challenged a grand jury subpoena of the records of 63 women he had treated in an abortion clinic.[51] The trial court had found him to be in contempt of court for failing to comply. The Illinois Supreme Court held that he must release the records of the one patient who had waived her physician-patient privilege but reversed the contempt finding on the 62 other records. The court ruled that they were protected by the physician-patient privilege in Illinois until there was a showing that a criminal action relating to malpractice or abortion was involved.

Valid subpoenas should never be ignored or challenged except on advice of an attorney. An Illinois court affirmed a $1,000 fine for contempt against an orthopedic surgeon for ignoring a subpoena and refusing to appear at a trial involving a patient he had treated.[52] In a Kansas case the court affirmed the commitment to jail of a treating physician who refused to testify until he was paid an expert fee.[53]

Statutory Duty to Disclose: Reporting Laws

The law compels disclosure of health care information in many contexts other than discovery or testimony. A variety of reporting laws have been enacted that require many kinds of information to be reported to governmental agencies: vital statistics, communicable disease, child abuse and wound reporting. Familiarity with these and other reporting laws is important to assure compliance and to avoid making the report to the wrong agency. Reports to the wrong agency may not be legally protected, resulting in potential liability for breach of confidentiality.

Vital Statistics

All states require the reporting of births and deaths. Courts have ruled as far back as 1882 that these laws are a valid exercise of the state's police power.[54] Many states also require the reporting of some fetal deaths and abortions. In a 1976 Missouri case, the Supreme Court upheld some abortion reporting requirements.[55]

Public Health

Most states require the reporting of venereal and other communicable diseases. In a California case the court observed that in addition to the criminal penalties for not reporting there is a possibility of civil liability in a suit by persons who become diseased but might have avoided the disease if it had been reported properly.[56] Some states have expanded the reporting requirement to encompass cancer and selected other diseases. A few states require reports to the state driver licensing agency of conditions such as seizures that could lead to loss of license.

Child Abuse

Most states require the reporting of suspected cases of child abuse or neglect. Some professionals, including nurses, are required to make reports, and thus are called mandatory reporters. Usually anyone who is not a mandatory reporter may make a report as a permissive reporter. Any report arising out of diagnosis or treatment of a child in an institution usually must be made through the administration. Most child abuse reporting laws extend some degree of immunity from liability for mandatory or permissive reporters who make their reports through proper channels.

There usually are criminal penalties for mandatory reporters who do not make required reports, but there have been few prosecutions. A mandatory reporter who fails to report child abuse is at greater risk of civil liability. Some state statutes specify that a mandatory reporter who fails to make a required report is civilly liable for future injuries to the child that could have been avoided if a report had been made.[57] In one case the California Supreme Court ruled that there could be civil liability under the common law when the statute did not address whether there should be civil liability.[58] A few states have enacted similar adult abuse reporting laws.

Wounds

Many states require the reporting of certain wounds. Some states specify that all wounds of certain types must be reported—in New York, wounds inflicted by sharp instruments that may result in death and all gunshot wounds.[59] Other states limit the reporting requirement to wounds caused under certain circumstances—in Iowa for wounds that apparently resulted from a criminal act, so those that clearly are accidental or self-inflicted do not have to be reported there.[60]

Other Reporting Laws

Some states require the reporting of other types of information, such as industrial accidents, so it is important to be familiar with the requirements of local law. Several national reporting laws apply to hospitals involved in manufacturing, testing, or using certain substances and devices. For example, fatalities from blood transfusions must be reported to the Food and Drug Administration.[61] Sponsors of investigational medical devices must report to the FDA when their use produces unanticipated adverse effects.[62]

Statutory Duty to Disclose: Access Laws

A second type of statute does not mandate reporting but authorizes access on request to certain individuals or organizations or to the general public without the permission of the patient.

Workers' Compensation

Some state statutes specify that all parties to a Workers' Compensation claim have access to all relevant health care information after a claim has been made.[63] In states that do not authorize access by statute, health care records should not be released unless patients or their representatives so authorize or the records are legally subpoenaed by an administrative agency or court. One exception is in states where the courts have ruled that filing a Workers' Compensation claim is a waiver under the common law of the right to confidentiality of relevant health care information.[64]

Freedom of Information Act (FOIA)

The federal Freedom of Information Act (FOIA)[65] applies only to federal agencies. A hospital does not become a federal agency by receiving federal funds. Thus, the act applies to few hospitals outside of the Veterans Administration and Defense Department. When it does apply, health care information is exempted from disclosure only when that would "constitute a clearly unwarranted invasion of personal privacy." Thus, there is only limited protection of the confidentiality of health care information in the possession of federal agencies.

State Public Records Laws

Many states have public records laws that apply to public hospitals. Some statutes explicitly exempt hospital and medical records from disclosure.[66] In a 1974 case Colorado's law was interpreted as not permitting a publisher to routinely obtain all birth and death reports.[67] However, in a 1978 Ohio case, the state law was interpreted to require access to the names of all persons admitted to a public hospital and the dates of admission and discharge.[68] In states that follow the Ohio rule it is especially important to resist discovery of nonparty records because removal of "identifiers" does not offer much protection since dates in the record can make it possible to identify the patient by comparison with the admission list. It is important for those associated with public hospitals to be familiar with local law on records access.

Other Access Laws

Some federal and state statutes give specified governmental agencies access to certain records on request or through administrative subpoena. For example, Utilization and Quality Control Peer Review Organizations (PROs) have access to all health care records pertinent to their federal review functions on request. A federal court has ruled that Medicare surveyors have the right to access to records of non-Medicare as well as Medicare patients.[69] Hospital licensing laws in many states grant state licensing inspectors access without subpoena for audit and inspection purposes.

Common-Law Duty to Disclose

In addition to these statutory requirements, the common law has recognized a duty to disclose health care information in several circumstances. Persons who could have avoided injury if the information had been disclosed have won civil suits against providers who failed to disclose the information.

Contagious Diseases

There is a duty to warn persons at risk of the presence of contagious disease. Hospital staff, family members, and others caring for the patient must be warned. In a 1928 case the court ruled that a physician could be liable for the death of a neighbor who contracted smallpox while assisting in the care of the physician's patient who had smallpox because the physician failed to warn the neighbor of the contagious nature of the disease.[70] However, there is no duty to warn all members of the public individually, although in a California case the court observed that liability to the general public might result from failure to make a required report to public health authorities.[71]

Threats to an Identified Person

The courts of a few states have ruled that there is a duty to warn an identified person whom a patient has made a credible threat to kill. The first time this duty was imposed was in a 1976 case in which the parents of a murder victim sued the California Board of Regents for the death of their daughter.[72] The court found the employer of a psychiatrist liable for his failure to warn the daughter that his patient had threatened to kill her. The court ruled that he should have either warned the victim or advised others likely to apprise the victim of the danger.

Four years later the court clarified the scope of this duty in California by ruling that only threats to readily identified individuals create a duty to warn.[73] There is no duty to warn a threatened group. Some courts have declined to establish a duty to warn even readily identified individuals.[74] The more prudent practice today is to warn identified individuals of credible threats when the patient is not detained.

Other Duties

Courts have recognized other situations when there is a duty to disclose. One example is the duty of referral specialists to communicate their findings to the referring physician.[75] A competent patient can waive this duty by directing the referral specialist not to communicate with the referring physician.

LIMITATIONS ON DISCLOSURE

Several statutory and common law limitations on disclosure have evolved that help preserve confidentiality and impose sanctions for some violations.

Health Care Professional-Patient Privilege

Many states' laws prohibit certain health care professionals from testifying as witnesses concerning certain information gained in the professional relationship with a patient. Health care professionals did not have a privilege from testimonial disclosure under English common law. Nearly all American courts also have adopted this position, so with few exceptions the privilege exists only in states that have enacted privilege statutes. One exception is Alaska, which established a common law psychotherapist-patient privilege for criminal cases.[76]

Approximately two-thirds of the states have enacted a statutory physician-patient privilege and a few have nurse-patient privilege. Privilege statutes address only situations where the professional is being compelled to testify, such as in a deposition, an administrative hearing, or a trial. There is a widespread misperception that privilege statutes apply to other disclosures, but in most states this is not true. The duty to maintain confidentiality outside of testimonial contexts is grounded on other legal principles (discussed in the later section on common-law limitations). Thus, privilege statutes usually are of concern only when responding to legal compulsion.

The privilege applies only when there is a bona fide professional-patient relationship. Thus, for example, it usually does not apply to court-ordered examinations or others solely for the benefit of third parties, such as insurance companies.

The scope of the privilege varies among the states. For example, Pennsylvania limits the privilege to communications that tend to blacken the character of the patient,[77] while Kansas extends it to all communications and observations;[78] Michigan limits it to physicians,[79] New York extends it to dentists and nurses.[80]

When a nurse is present during a confidential communication between physician and patient, some states extend the physician's privilege to the nurse, while others rule that the communication no longer is privileged for the physician. Generally the privilege extends to otherwise privileged information in the hospital record.[81] However, information required to be reported to public authorities generally has been held not to be privileged, unless those authorities also are privileged not to disclose it.

Waiver

The patient may waive the privilege, permitting the professional to testify. In nearly all states, the privilege can be waived by contract, such as in an insurance contract. A variety of other actions constitute implied waiver. If a patient introduces evidence disclosing details of a health condition or fails to object to testimony by a professional, most courts find these actions to be an implied waiver.

Most courts also have ruled that authorization of disclosure outside the testimonial context does not waive the privilege.[82] Thus, the patient could authorize other parties to have access to health care records outside of court and still successfully object to having them introduced into evidence unless other actions had waived the privilege. A few courts have adopted the opposite position, so in those states authorization of any disclosure to opposing parties waives the privilege.[83]

Waiver of the privilege usually permits only formal discovery and testimony, not informal interview. This rule requires express patient consent before informal interviews are permitted.[84] However, other courts have permitted informal interviews based on waiver.[85] The most prudent practice is for providers to limit disclosures to formal channels unless there is express patient consent.

Other Limitations on Disclosure

Some federal and state statutes, such as federal substance abuse confidentiality laws and state licensing and confidentiality laws, limit access to health care information.

Substance Abuse Confidentiality

Special federal rules cover the confidentiality of information concerning patients treated or referred for treatment for alcoholism or drug abuse.[86] The rules apply to any facility receiving federal funds for any purpose, including Medicare or Medicaid reimbursement. The regulations explicitly preempt any state law that purports to authorize disclosures contrary to the regulations but do permit states to impose tighter confidentiality requirements. The rules apply to any disclosure, even acknowledgment of the patient's presence in the facility. Information may be released with the patient's consent if the consent is in writing and contains all of the following elements:

1. the name of the program to make the disclosure
2. the name or title of the person or organization to receive the information
3. the name of the patient
4. the purpose of need for the disclosure
5. the extent or nature of the information to be disclosed
6. a statement that the consent may be revoked and when it will expire automatically
7. the date signed
8. the patient's signature.

A court order, including a subpoena, does not permit release of information unless all the requirements of the regulations have been met. The regulations require a court hearing and finding that the purpose for which the order is sought is more important than the purposes for which Congress mandated confidentiality. Fortunately, the regulations have been interpreted to permit hospitals or other providers to tell the court why they cannot comply with the order until after a hearing.

After a hearing, courts have ordered disclosures to assist probation revocation and child abuse proceedings. In a 1981 case the court ordered disclosure to assist an Internal Revenue Service investigation of a surgeon.[87] Courts have declined to order disclosure when the information was sought to challenge the credibility of witnesses or to assist in determining the rehabilitation potential of a convicted person for purposes of sentencing.

It is important that staff members be oriented to rules involving substance abuse records. In one case a nurse successfully challenged her discharge for failure to report a fellow employee's theft of health care records by establishing the reasonableness of her belief (which actually was erroneous) that these federal regulations prohibited the report.[88]

Professionals and Hospital Licensing Laws

Professional licensing laws or regulations frequently specify that breach of confidentiality is unprofessional conduct and grounds for discipline by the licensing board.[89] Hospital licensing laws and regulations frequently require that confidentiality of records be maintained.[90]

Other State Confidentiality Laws

Some state statutes establish a general responsibility to maintain confidentiality of records[91] while some address only records of treatment for certain conditions. For example, Chapter 140 of the Iowa Code specifies the confidentiality of information concerning venereal disease.[92] Thus, it is important to be familiar with local statutes and regulations.

Accreditation Standards

The JCAH medical records standards specify that hospitals have the responsibility of protecting the record and the information it contains "against loss, defacement, and tampering, and from use by unauthorized individuals."[93] If a hospital accepts this responsibility through its own rules in order to become accredited, many courts will require the facility to follow those rules and impose liability for injuries that result from violations.

Common-Law Limitations

As discussed in the prior section on professional-patient privilege, common law does not provide any protection from disclosure in testimonial contexts except in a few states such as Alaska. Courts have uniformly refused to impose liability for testimonial disclosures.[94] Health care professionals and hospitals are not obligated to risk contempt of court to protect confidences (except for substance abuse records), although they may choose to do so.

In nontestimonial contexts, courts have found limitations on permissible disclosure based on the implied promise of confidentiality in the professional patient relationship, violation of the right of privacy, and violation of professional licensing standards. For example, in a 1977 New York case, the court permanently enjoined a psychoanalyst from circulating a book that included detailed information concerning a patient.[95] The patient was identifiable to friends despite the psychoanalyst's efforts to disguise her identity. The court ruled that the book violated the implied covenant of confidentiality and the right of privacy. The court awarded $20,000 to the plaintiff for the 220 copies that had been sold before the injunction.

Courts have ruled in favor of physicians in cases where the disclosure was intended to prevent the spread of contagious disease.[96] As discussed in the section on "Common-Law Duty to Disclose" information, there could be liability in some circumstances for failing to disclose a contagious disease.

Disclosures to a patient's employer or insurance company have resulted in several suits. In one case the court ruled that disclosures to the employer without authorization violated the implied promise of confidentiality and could result in liability.[97] However, in another case the court held that when a patient authorized incomplete disclosure to his employer, the physician was not liable for giving a complete disclosure.[98] It is questionable whether other courts would rule this way so the prudent practice is to refuse to release any information when only a misleading partial release is authorized.

Some courts have found implied authorization to release information to an insurance company based on actions of the patient. In a Colorado case, submission to a health examination at an insurance company's request was considered implied authorization.[99] However, it is prudent practice to obtain written authorization from the patient. Most insurance companies do so. There have been cases in which courts have ruled that insurance companies may be sued for inducing a physician to divulge confidential information.[100]

A frequent basis for suits for disclosures of confidential information has been defamation. In most cases involving physicians the courts have found a qualified privilege to make specific disclosures. The few cases where liability has been found involved misdiagnosis and disclosure of an embarrassing condition that the patient actually did not have, such as venereal disease, in a manner that sufficiently demonstrated malice so that the qualified privilege provided no protection.[101]

PHOTOGRAPHY

In general, physicians may take and use photographs of patients for the medical record or for professional educational purposes unless the patient expressly forbids them. In a 1969 Massachusetts case, the court enjoined public showing of a film of inmates of an institution for insane persons charged with crimes or delinquency but permitted continued showings to audiences of a specialized or professional character with a serious interest in rehabilitation.[102] The court observed that the public interest in having these people informed outweighs the rights of the inmates to privacy. In another case the court ruled that when the patient had expressly objected to being photographed there could be liability for doing so even if it was solely for the health care record.[103]

The most prudent approach is to obtain express consent for taking and using photographs, but there is little likelihood of liability without express consent if the patient does not object and uses are appropriately restricted. Of course, public or commercial showing without consent can lead to liability, as illustrated by a case involving the public showing of a film of a Caesarean section delivery.[104]

DISCIPLINE OF STAFF MEMBERS

Hospital staff members have been discharged for unauthorized disclosure of health care records. However, courts and arbitration panels tend to reinstate them unless there has been a consistent pattern of enforcement. For example, a Royal Commission that investigated the confidentiality of medical records in Ontario found many unauthorized disclosures. One of the persons responsible for these was a nurse who had given records to her husband who was an attorney representing patients' opponents in legal proceedings. She was fired but the arbitration board ordered her reinstatement with the sanction of suspension without pay up to the time of the ruling.[105] The board accepted her position that, since no one else had been disciplined, she was the scapegoat for the hospital's embarrassment concerning the Royal Commission's findings.

Thus, a consistent pattern of enforcement is important both to communicate the importance of confidentiality to the staff and to increase the likelihood that disciplinary actions will be sustained if challenged.

NOTES

1. 42 C.F.R. § 405.1026(g) (1983).
2. *E.g.*, CHICAGO MUN. CODE § 137-14.
3. *Hiatt v. Groce*, 215 Kan. 14, 523 P.2d 320 (1974).
4. *Collins v. Westlake Community Hosp.*, 57 Ill. 2d 388, 312 N.E.2d 614 (1974).
5. *Engle v. Clarke*, 346 S.W.2d 13 (Ky. 1961).

6. 42 C.F.R. § 405.1026(j) (1983).

7. *Board of Trustees of Memorial Hosp. v. Pratt*, 72 Wyo. 120, 262 P.2d 682 (1953).

8. *People v. Smithtown Gen. Hosp.*, 93 Misc. 2d 736, 402 N.Y.S.2d 318 (N.Y. Sup. Ct. 1978).

9. *Kaplan v. Central Medical Group of Brooklyn*, 419 N.Y.S.2d 750 (N.Y. App. Div. 1979).

10. *E.g.*, TENN. CODE ANN. § 53-1323(c).

11. *Palmer v. New York State Dep't of Mental Hygiene*, 44 N.Y.2d 958, 380 N.E.2d 154 (1978).

12. *Wolfe v. Beal*, 477 Pa. 477, 384 A.2d 1187 (1978).

13. *E.g., Pyramid Life Ins. Co. v. Masonic Hosp. Ass'n*, 191 F.Supp. 51 (W.D. Okla. 1961).

14. *Connell v. Medical & Surgical Clinic*, 21 Ill. App. 3d 383, 315 N.E.2d 278 (1974).

15. *McGarry v. J. A. Mercier Co.*, 272 Mich. 501, 262 N.W. 296 (Mich. 1935).

16. Reiser, Dyck, and Curran, ETHICS IN MEDICINE (1977).

17. American Medical Association, PRINCIPLES OF MEDICAL ETHICS (August 1980).

18. American Nurses' Association, CODE FOR NURSES, Sec. 2.5 (1976).

19. *Hyman v. Jewish Chronic Disease Hosp.*, 15 N.Y.2d 317, 258 N.Y.S.2d 397 (1965).

20. *Id.* at 399.

21. *Klinge v. Lutheran Medical Center of St. Louis*, 518 S.W.2d 157 (Mo. App. 1975).

22. *Re General Accident Assurance Co. of Canada and Sunnybrook Hosp.* (1979) 23 O.R.(2d) 513 (Ont. High Ct. of Justice).

23. Gordis and Gold, "Privacy, Confidentiality, and the Use of Medical Records in Research," 207 *Science* 153 (January 11, 1980).

24. 45 C.F.R. § 46.101(b)(5) and 46 Fed. Reg. 8392 (January 26, 1981).

25. *E.g.*, ILL. REV. STAT. ch. 51, § 71.

26. *E.g., Wallace v. University Hosps. of Cleveland*, 170 N.E.2d 261 (Ohio App. 1960) and *Hutchins v. Texas Rehabilitation Comm'n*, 544 S.W.2d 802 (Tex. Civ. App. 1976).

27. *Rabens v. Jackson Park Hosp. Found.*, 40 Ill. App. 3d 113, 351 N.E.2d 276 (1976).

28. *Pyramid Life Ins. Co. v. Masonic Hosp. Ass'n*, 191 F.Supp. 51 (W.D. Okla. 1961).

29. *Pennison v. Provident Life & Accident Ins. Co.*, 154 So. 2d 617 (La. App. 1963), *writ refused* 156 So. 2d 226 (La. 1963).

30. *McDonald v. Clinger*, 84 A.D.2d 482, 446 N.Y.S.2d 801 (1982).

31. *E.g.*, IOWA CODE § 229.25 (1983).

32. *Yaretsky v. Blum*, 592 F.2d 65 (2d Cir. 1979).

33. *Bishop Clarkson Memorial Hosp. v. Reserve Life Ins. Co.*, 350 F.2d 1006 (8th Cir. 1965).

34. American Hospital Association, *Statement on a Patient's Bill of Rights*, Affirmed by the Board of Trustees, November 17, 1972.

35. Altman, "Patients Who Read Their Hospital Charts," 302 *New Eng. J. Med.* 169 (January 17, 1980).

36. *E.g., Emmett v. Eastern Dispensary & Casualty Hosp.*, 396 F.2d 931 (App. D.C. 1967).

37. *Gaertner v. State*, 385 Mich. 49, 187 N.W.2d 429 (1971).

38. *H.L. v. Matheson*, 450 U.S. 398 (1981).

39. *Claim of Gurkin*, 434 N.Y.S. 2d 607 (N.Y. Sup. Ct. 1980).

40. *Emmett v. Eastern Dispensary & Casualty Hosp.*, 396 F.2d 931 (App. D.C. 1967).

41. *Community Hosp. Ass'n v. District Court*, 570 P.2d 243 (Colo. 1977).

42. *E.g., Teperson v. Donato*, 371 So.2d 703 (Fla. Dist. Ct. App. 1979).

43. *Schechet v. Kesten*, 126 N.W.2d 718 (Mich. 1964).

44. *Banta v. Superior Court of Maricopa County*, 544 P.2d 653 (Ariz. 1976).

45. *E.g., City of Edmond v. Parr*, 587 P.2d 56 (Okla. 1978).

46. *Young v. King*, 344 A.2d 792 (N.J. Super. 1975).

47. *Warrick v. Giron*, 290 N.W.2d 166 (Minn. 1980).

48. *Bredice v. Doctors Hosp., Inc.*, 50 F.R.D. 249 (D.D.C. 1970).

49. *Davison v. St. Paul Fire & Marine Ins. Co.*, 75 Wis. 2d 190, 248 N.W.2d 433 (1977).

50. *Ritt v. Ritt*, 52 N.J. 177, 244 A.2d 497 (1968).

51. *People v. Bickham*, 431 N.E.2d 365 (Ill. 1982).

52. *People v. Miller*, 61 Ill. App. 3d 64 (1978).

53. *Swope v. State*, 145 Kan. 928, 67 P.2d 416 (1937).

54. *E.g., Robinson v. Hamilton*, 60 Iowa 134, 14 N.W. 202 (1882).

55. *Planned Parenthood of Cent. Mo. v. Danforth*, 428 U.S. 52 (1976).

56. *Derrick v. Ontario Community Hosp.*, 47 Cal. App. 3d 154, 120 Cal. Rptr. 566 (1975).

57. *E.g.*, Iowa Code § 232.75 (1983).

58. *Landeros v. Flood*, 17 Cal. 3d 399, 551 P.2d 389 (1976).

59. N.Y. Penal Law § 266.25 (McKinney, 1980).

60. Iowa Code § 147.111 (1983).

61. 21 C.F.R. § 606.170(b) (1983).

62. 21 C.F.R. § 812.150(b) (1983).

63. *E.g.*, Iowa Code § 85.27 (1983).

64. *E.g., Acosta v. Cary*, 365 So. 2d 4 (La. App. 1978).

65. 5 U.S.C. § 552 (1976 & Supp. V 1981).

66. *E.g.*, Iowa Code § 68A.7(2) (1983).

67. *Eugene Cervi & Co. v. Russell*, 184 Colo. 282, 519 P.2d 1189 (1974).

68. *Wooster Republican Printing Co. v. City of Wooster*, 56 Ohio St. 2d 126, 383 N.W.2d 124 (1978).

69. *O'Hare v. Harris*, No. 80-457-D (D.N.H. March 12, 1981) (Medicare and Medicaid Guide (CCH) ¶ 31,054).

70. *Jones v. Stanko*, 118 Ohio St. 147, 160 N.E. 456 (1928).

71. *Derrick v. Ontario Community Hosp.*, 47 Cal. App. 3d 154, 120 Cal. Rptr. 566 (1975).

72. *Tarasoff v. Board of Regents*, 17 Cal. 3d 425, 551 P.2d 334 (1976).

73. *Thompson v. County of Alameda*, 27 Cal. 3d 741, 614 P.2d 728 (1980).

74. *Shaw v. Glickman*, 45 Md. App. 718, 415 A.2d 625 (1980).

75. *Thornburg v. Long*, 178 N.C. 589, 101 S.E. 99 (1919).

76. *Allred v. State*, 554 P.2d 411 (Alaska 1976).

77. Pa. Stat. Ann., tit. 42, § 5929 (Purdon 1982).

78. Kan. Stat. Ann. § 60-427 (1976).

79. Mich. Comp. Laws § 27A.2157 (1979).

80. N.Y. Civ. Prac. Law § 4504 (McKinney Supp. 1982-83).

81. *New York City Council v. Goldwater*, 284 N.Y.296, 31 N.E.2d 31 (1940).

82. *Cartwright v. Macabees Mutual Life Ins. Co.*, 65 Mich. App. 670, 238 N.W.2d 368 (1975).

83. *Willis v. Order of R.R. Telegraphers,* 139 Neb. 46, 296 N.W. 443 (1941).

84. *Wenninger v. Muesing,* 307 Minn. 405, 240 N.W.2d 333 (1976).

85. *Transworld Invs. v. Drobny,* 554 P.2d 1148 (Alaska 1976).

86. 42 C.F.R. pt. 2 (1983).

87. *U.S. v. Providence Hosp.,* 507 F.Supp. 519 (E.D. Mich. 1981).

88. *Heng v. Foster,* 379 N.E.2d 688 (Ill. App. 1978).

89. *E.g.,* IOWA ADMIN. CODE §§ 590-1.2(d)(6)(1980)[nurses] and 470-135.401(10) (1979)[physicians].

90. *E.g.,* KAN. ADMIN. REGS. § 28-34-9(b) (1974).

91. *E.g.,* CAL. CIV. CODE §§ 56-56.32 (West 1982).

92. IOWA CODE § 140.3 (1983).

93. Joint Commission on Accreditation of Hospitals, ACCREDITATION MANUAL FOR HOSPITALS, 1984 ed.

94. *E.g., Boyd v. Wynn,* 150 S.W.2d 648 (Ky. 1941).

95. *Doe v. Roe,* 400 N.Y.S.2d 668 (N.Y. Sup. Ct. 1977).

96. *E.g., Simonsen v. Swenson,* 104 Neb. 224, 177 N.W. 831 (1920).

97. *Horne v. Patton,* 291 Ala. 701, 287 So. 2d 824 (1973).

98. *Clark v. Geraci,* 208 N.Y.S.2d 564 (N.Y. Sup. Ct. 1960).

99. *Conyers v. Massa,* 512 P.2d 283 (Colo. Ct. App. 1973).

100. *Hammonds v. Aetna Casualty & Surety Co.,* 243 F.Supp. 793 (N.D. Ohio 1965).

101. *E.g., Beatty v. Baston,* 130 Ohio L. Abs. 481 (Ohio App. 1932).

102. *Commonwealth v. Wiseman,* 356 Mass. 251, 249 N.E.2d 610 (1969).

103. *Estate of Berthraume v. Pratt,* 365 A.2d 792 (Me. 1976).

104. *Feeny v. Young,* 181 N.Y.S. 481 (N.Y. App. Div. 1920).

105. *In re Metropolitan Gen. Hosp. and Ontario Nurses' Ass'n,* 22 L.A.C. 2d 243 (Ontario Labor Arbitration 1979).

BIBLIOGRAPHY

Bernstein, Arthur. "Confidential Records: Piercing the Protective Veil." *Hospitals* 56, no. 7 (August 1, 1982):48.

Eggland, E.T. "Charting: How and Why to Document Your Care Daily and Fully." *Nursing 80* 80, no. 2 (February 1980):39.

Greenlaw, Jane. "Documentation of Patient Care: An Often Underestimated Responsibility." *Law, Medicine, and Health Care* 10, no. 4 (September 1982):172.

Horsley, Jack. "Legally Speaking." *RN* 46, no. 7 (July 1983):16.

———. "Legally Speaking." *RN* 46, no. 9 (September 1983):23.

O'Sullivan, A. "Privileged Communication." *American Journal of Nursing* 80, no. 5 (May 1980):947.

Regan, William. "Legally Speaking." *RN* 46, no. 2 (February 1983):79.

Chapter 12

Reproductive Issues

The reproductive issues of contraception, conception, and abortion are sensitive both because of their effect on the individuals involved and because of the intense political, social, and religious controversies they engender. They have been recognized by the courts as a fundamental aspect of individuals' right of privacy. This chapter discusses these issues as well as prenatal testing, genetic screening, and liability for the birth of children after negligent sterilizations or failure to inform of genetic risks. Nurses in a variety of settings need to be aware of the status of the law on these issues, because of the implications for nursing practice and patient counseling.

CONTRACEPTION

Contraception includes the various drugs, devices, and procedures designed to avoid pregnancy.

Contraceptive Drugs and Devices

Numerous drugs and devices are available to reduce the probability of pregnancy. In the past some states passed laws restricting their sale or use. In the first case to address the constitutionality of such provisions, the United States Supreme Court in 1965 declared a Connecticut law forbidding the use of contraceptives by married persons to be an unconstitutional violation of the right of privacy.[1] In a 1972 case, the Court voided a Massachusetts law forbidding the sale or use of contraceptives by unmarried persons.[2] The Court ruled that whatever the rights of adults to access to contraceptives may be, they are the same for married and unmarried persons. The Court said: "If the right to privacy means anything, it is the right of the individual, married or single, to be free from unwarranted governmental intrusion into matters so fundamentally affecting a person as the decision whether to bear or beget a child."[3]

It is clear from these two cases that a state may not prohibit the use of contraceptives by its adult population. Many states, however, have continued to regulate the sale and distribution of contraceptives to some extent. In a 1977 case, the Supreme Court limited the extent to which a state may restrict the sale and distribution of contraceptives by holding that a provision in a New York statute prohibiting the distribution of nonprescription contraceptives to persons over 16 by anyone other than licensed pharmacists was an undue burden on an individual's right to decide whether to bear a child.[4] The Court invalidated the prohibition on advertising and display of prescription as well as nonprescription contraceptives, at least when the advertising is done by persons licensed to sell such products.

Thus, few legal barriers confront adults who seek to obtain contraceptives. For presumed safety reasons, prescription contraceptives or those requiring fitted insertion must be obtained through a physician. Nonprescription birth control devices can be purchased legally in drug stores, vending machines, or through mail-order services.

Minors

While it now is relatively easy for adults to obtain contraceptives, minors still face many obstacles. The Supreme Court's first comment on a minor's right of access to birth control came in the New York case. Four members of the Court agreed that "the right to privacy in connection with decisions affecting procreation extends to minors as well as to adults . . . and since a state may not impose a blanket prohibition or even a blanket requirement of parental consent on the choice of a minor to terminate her pregnancy, the constitutionality of a blanket prohibition on the distribution of contraceptives is *a fortiori* foreclosed."[5] The four justices also held that allowing a minor to obtain contraceptives only from a physician gave the doctor absolute and possibly arbitrary discretion over the privacy rights of a minor and that such power was impermissible. Three other members of the Court concurred in the result of the case, but for other reasons. These three and the two dissenting justices did not agree that the right of privacy in decisions affecting procreation extends to minors.

In a 1980 case, a court ruled that minors have a right to contraceptive devices from a county-run family planning center without parental notification or consent.[6] In another case, a court ruled that federally funded family planning centers could not require parental notice or consent as a condition to the providing of services.[7] The court based its ruling on its interpretation of the federal statute authorizing the program, not on constitutional principles.

Section 931 of Public Law 97–35 enacted in 1981 added a requirement that federally funded family planning projects "encourage family participation" in counseling and decisions about services.[8] In the February 22, 1982, *Federal*

Register, the Department of Health and Human Services (HHS) proposed rules that would interpret this to require parental notification for all minors under 18 unless (1) specific acts such as marriage or parenthood make them emancipated under state law or (2) the project director determines that notification will result in physical harm to the minor by the parents or guardian. The proposed rules would require compliance with all state laws concerning notification or consent.[9]

The rules never took effect because they were blocked by permanent injunctions.[10] The courts ruled that Congress had intended to encourage, not require, parental involvement, so the rules exceeded statutory authority.

This leaves many questions yet to be answered and a possibility that states still will be able to regulate minors' access to contraceptives more strictly than adults'.

While the most prudent practice is to encourage minors to involve their parents in the decisionmaking, it must be recognized that many minors cannot or will not do so. Physicians then must decide whether or not to prescribe contraceptives in the absence of parental involvement. Physicians who choose to prescribe contraceptives to unemancipated minors face a theoretical possibility of civil liability for battery or malpractice in some states. Several states explicitly authorize minors to consent to these services.

In actuality, even in states without a minor consent statute, the legal risk is small, especially when the minor is mature. The most likely difficulty for the physician will be in collecting payment because the parents probably will not be responsible. The nurse has an important role in ensuring that minors have adequate information on which to base their decisions and that they are aware of their rights and the availability of information on contraception.

Liability for Side Effects

Both oral contraceptives and intrauterine devices are known to have harmful side effects in a few instances. Litigation has resulted in the most serious of these situations, much of it against the manufacturer and based on product liability or inadequate warnings of the risks involved in taking birth control pills or using certain devices. It appears that physicians will not be held liable in the absence of negligence or intentional misconduct. However, they will be held liable for injuries to their patients if they do not provide adequate information as to potential side effects or the risks of continuing the use of the contraceptive after adverse reactions.

VOLUNTARY STERILIZATION

Sterilization involves termination of the ability to produce offspring. Sterilization may be the desired result of a surgical operation or may be the incidental consequence of an operation to remove a diseased reproductive organ or to cure a particular malfunction of such an organ. Where the reproductive organs are not diseased, most sterilizations are effected by vasectomy in males and tubal ligation in females.

In the past there were concerns about the legality of voluntary sterilizations of competent adults. States recognized a distinction between therapeutic sterilizations to protect a woman who was at risk of impairment of life or health if she became pregnant and contraceptive sterilizations for which there was no therapeutic reason. Some states permitted therapeutic, but not contraceptive, sterilizations. However, these restrictions have been eliminated so that no state now prohibits voluntary consensual sterilization of a competent adult regardless of the purpose.

Federal regulations require the signing of a special consent form at least 30 days prior to sterilizations funded by Medicaid.[11] Exceptions are made for some therapeutic cases. Some states, such as California, impose similar requirements on all sterilizations performed in the state.[12] A California court upheld the constitutionality of the state requirements in a 1981 case.[13]

The specific wording of the federal consent forms and the 30-day wait requirement do not apply to other patients unless required by state law. However, the consent of the person who is to be sterilized or subjected to an operation that may incidentally destroy the reproductive function should be obtained first. In the absence of consent, even if an operation is medically necessary, a sterilization almost always constitutes a battery. Courts are less likely to find that there is implied consent to a sterilization than to other extensions of surgical procedures.

When it may be predicted that an operation necessary to cure a condition will incidentally destroy the ability to procreate, the consequences to the reproductive function should be clearly brought to the attention of the patient. Where sterilization is to be performed in conjunction with another procedure, specific reference should be made to the sterilization. The use of a specific consent form that clearly indicates the effect upon the reproductive process is recommended. It is important that the risk that the sterilization will be unsuccessful also be disclosed in addition to the disclosure that reproduction probably will not be possible. Failure to inform of the small risk of future reproductive ability can expose the provider to liability (as discussed later in this chapter).

Ordinarily, the patient's consent alone is sufficient authorization for any operation. But since sterilization affects the legally sensitive procreative function, some hospitals and physicians have a policy of requiring that the spouse's consent also be obtained when the patient is married. It is doubtful whether public hospitals can enforce such policies. In several cases, courts have declared such a public hospital policy to be an unconstitutional violation of the right of privacy.[14]

In a 1973 case, a court ruled that a governmental hospital may not impose greater restrictions upon sterilization procedures than upon other procedures that are medically indistinguishable from sterilization with regard to risk to the patient or demand on staff or facilities. The hospital was enjoined from enforcing its policy against all contraceptive sterilization procedures.[15] However, private hospitals can forbid contraceptive sterilizations or require spousal consent. For example, a 1976 case held that federal courts do not have jurisdiction to order a private hospital to end its policy of requiring spousal consent to sterilization since state action was not involved.[16]

In the past, several states had laws requiring spousal consent to sterilizations but when these laws have been challenged federal courts consistently have declared them unconstitutional and enjoined their enforcement.

It is prudent to encourage spousal involvement in the decision, especially when the two are not estranged. Individual physicians may have a personal practice of not performing sterilizations without spousal consent in any hospital if the practice is not required by institutional policy. In one case, the court found no violation of the Constitution in a physician's personal policy to condition treatment of pregnant indigent patients on their involuntary submission to sterilization following the delivery of their third living child.[17] The fact that the doctor served Medicaid patients did not make his actions "state action." He applied his policy to all his patients and notified them of his practice early in their relationship so they were free to go elsewhere for care.

There is little legal risk from performing a sterilization procedure without spousal consent. There are a few modern cases in which a spouse has sued a physician for performing a sterilization procedure without spousal consent. In Oklahoma, the court dismissed the suit because the husband had no right to a child-bearing wife as an incident to marriage so he had not been legally harmed by the procedure.[18]

Voluntary contraceptive sterilization of unmarried minor patients presents special problems, so local laws concerning minor consent should be observed carefully. Some states' statutes authorize such sterilizations if the parent or guardian also consents,[19] others forbid sterilization of unmarried minors.[20] As discussed in the following section, it is well established that parents or guardians alone cannot authorize sterilizations. Patient consent is essential unless court authorization is obtained. Unless there is a medical reason for the sterilization and unless the consent of the minor and the parent is clearly voluntary, informed, and not equivocal, prudent providers should be reluctant to sterilize minors without a court order.

Some states have enacted legislation stating that hospitals are not required to permit the performance of sterilization procedures and that physicians and hospital personnel may not be required to participate in such procedures or discriminated against for refusal to so participate.[21] Such legislation, more frequently found with regard to abortion procedures, often is referred to as a "conscience clause" and was not found objectionable by the Supreme Court in its decision striking down most state abortion laws.

In Montana a nurse-anesthetist was awarded payment from a hospital that violated the state's conscience clause by dismissing her for refusing to participate in a tubal ligation.[22] However, it is doubtful that this legislation could constitutionally be interpreted to authorize governmental hospitals to forbid sterilizations by willing physicians and staff.

INVOLUNTARY STERILIZATION

Statutes and courts in some states have authorized involuntary sterilization of two groups of people: (1) those believed to transmit hereditary defects to succeeding generations; (2) those who are severely retarded, sexually active, unable to use other forms of contraception, and unable to care properly for their offspring.

In the first half of this century, many states enacted eugenic sterilization laws authorizing the sterilization of those with presumed hereditary defects against their will. The Supreme Court upheld such laws in a 1927 case.[23] However, many states have repealed their eugenic sterilization laws. As for the second group, several states have enacted involuntary sterilization laws authorizing the sterilization of individuals a court determines meet all such criteria. The primary focus of these laws is in the best interest of the patient and potential future offspring, rather than genetics.

These modern laws have been upheld by the courts. For example, North Carolina's statute[24] was upheld by the North Carolina Supreme Court,[25] and by the federal courts.[26] That statute does not allow the patient's next of kin or guardian to initiate sterilization proceedings, restricting the role to the director of a state institution or the county director of social services. The key elements of a constitutional statute appear to be (1) identification of an appropriate class of persons subject to the law without discrimination or arbitrary bias and (2) guarantees of procedural due process, including notice, hearing, right to appeal, and assurance that decisions will be supported by qualified medical opinion.

It is well established by court decisions that parents or guardians do not have the authority to consent to sterilization of retarded children or wards without a valid court authorization.[27]

Several courts have been presented with applications for orders authorizing involuntary sterilizations in states that do not have statutes specifically granting them authority to issue such orders. Thus, the courts have had to decide whether they have authority to do so under their general jurisdiction concerning the welfare of incompetents.

Prior to 1978, most state courts ruled that they did not have the authority and refused to issue sterilizations orders. Their primary reasons were the decisions in 1971 and 1977 cases that judicial immunity did not protect judges who issued sterilizations order without specific statutory authority because they were not acting within their jurisdiction.[28] These courts permitted civil rights suits against the judges and the involved health care providers.

However, one of the cases was reversed and the Supreme Court ruled that a court of broad general jurisdiction is entitled to consider a petition for sterilization of a minor unless statutes or case law in the state circumscribe the jurisdiction to foreclose consideration of such petitions.[29] Thus, the judge was protected by judicial immunity. In another case, the court ruled that the private individuals who had sought the petition and carried out the order could not be sued for federal civil rights violations because there was not a showing of a conspiracy between them and state officials.[30]

Since the Supreme Court's 1978 decision that a court of general jurisdiction could consider a petition for sterilization of a minor, several state courts have ruled that they have authority to authorize involuntary sterilization of incompetents in appropriate cases. These decisions have set forth procedures to be followed and criteria that must be met.[31] These procedures and criteria generally are similar to those specified in modern involuntary sterilization statutes. However, one court ruled that Alabama courts do not have such authority.[32] In a 1981 Wisconsin case, the court adopted the unusual position that state courts have the authority but should not exercise it.[33] The Wisconsin Supreme Court, under its power to regulate the lower courts in the state, ordered them not to issue authorizations. The court called upon the legislature to pass appropriate legislation and said that, if it did not do so, the court might in the future permit lower courts to issue authorizations.

Hospitals and physicians should participate in involuntary sterilizations only when court authorization has been obtained following procedures and criteria established by statute or by the highest court in the state. The procedures should include notice, a hearing, and an opportunity to appeal.

CONCEPTION

When couples who desire children cannot become pregnant, they often seek medical assistance. Techniques such as artificial insemination, surrogate mothers, and in vitro fertilization (literally, in glass, such as a test tube) have been attempted when other approaches fail.

Artificial Insemination

When the woman can conceive but the man either cannot deliver the semen or cannot produce effective semen, artificial insemination may be attempted. In the former situation, the artificial insemination is achieved through injection of the husband's semen, while in the latter situation donor semen is used. There are few legal problems with artificial insemination with the husband's semen (AIH).

Artificial insemination with donor semen (AID) presents several legal issues, including whether the resulting child is legitimate and who is responsible for support. Some state statutes specify (1) the child is legitimate when the husband consents to the AID and (2) the donor is not responsible for child support.[34] In states without statutes, the courts have ruled that the consenting husband of the impregnated woman is responsible for child support.[35] However, those courts disagree on whether the child is legitimate under the common law.

Sound hospital policy would be to allow performance of AID procedures only for married women and only with the written consent of the woman and her husband, including an acknowledgment of paternity and an acceptance of child-support responsibilities. If a statute or decision of the highest court of the state protects the donor, the hospital, and its staff from child-support responsibilities in other situations, then consideration can prudently be given to performing AID procedures in those situations.

Surrogate Mothers

When a man has viable semen but the woman cannot conceive, some couples seek a surrogate mother to bear a child after artificial insemination with the man's semen. The artificial insemination is legal in most states but the agreement by the surrogate mother to give the child to the couple after delivery probably is not enforceable and may be illegal in some states. The Michigan Circuit Court in Wayne County has ruled against enforceability in two cases.[36] The most prudent policy for hospitals is not to permit artificial insemination of surrogate mothers on hospital premises. If the hospital decides to permit the practice, it should not become involved in the agreement that the child be given to the couple.

In Vitro Fertilization

Some couples produce viable reproductive cells but conception is not possible naturally or through artificial insemination. For some of these couples the experimental procedure called in vitro fertilization is available. The reproductive cells of the couple are combined outside the woman's body, are allowed to begin growing there, and later are implanted in the woman's womb. In 1979, the then Department of Health, Education, and Welfare Ethics Advisory Board approved experimental use of in vitro fertilization.[37] Several "test tube" babies have been born as the result of this procedure.

In the only lawsuit arising from in vitro fertilization, John and Doris Del Zio were awarded $50,000 by a federal jury in New York on August 18, 1978, for their emotional distress following intentional destruction of a cell culture containing their reproductive cells. This illustrates the importance of establishing clear procedures that are understood by all involved, including the subjects, before attempting in vitro fertilization.

ABORTION

Medically, an abortion may be defined as the premature expulsion from the uterus of the products of conception. An abortion may be classified as spontaneous or induced. An induced abortion can be for the purpose of saving the life of the fetus, saving the life or health of the mother, or terminating the pregnancy to preclude the birth of a child. The attention of the law has focused on the induced abortions that are not intended to result in a live birth.

Historically, the common law did not prohibit induced abortions prior to the first fetal movements. Many states by statute made induced abortions a crime, whether before or after fetal movements began, unless performed to preserve the life of the mother. These laws were amended in the 1960s and early 1970s to permit induced abortions when there were threats to the physical or mental health of the mother, the child was at risk of severe congenital defects, or the pregnancy resulted from rape or incest. A few states such as New York permitted induced abortions on request up to a designated stage of pregnancy if performed by a licensed physician in a licensed hospital.

Roe v. Wade and Doe v. Bolton

In January 1973, the United States Supreme Court in *Roe* v. *Wade*[38] held that the Texas criminal abortion law was unconstitutional, stating: "A state criminal abortion statute . . . that excepts from criminality only a *life saving* procedure on behalf of the mother, without regard to pregnancy stage and without recognition of the other interests involved, is violative of the Due Process Clause of the Fourteenth Amendment."[39]

The court discussed the three stages of pregnancy, concluding that the right of privacy of the patient and her physician precluded most state regulation during the first trimester but that the state's interest in protecting the patient's health and the potential life of the fetus permitted some forms of regulation in the later stages. In the companion decision, *Doe* v. *Bolton*,[40] the court declared a Georgia abortion statute to be unconstitutional and further defined the types of state regulations that are not permitted.

The First Stage

During the first stage or trimester of pregnancy, the state is virtually without power to restrict or regulate the abortion procedure; the decision is between the woman and her physician. A state may require only that abortions be performed by a physician licensed pursuant to its laws. However, a woman does not possess an unqualified right to an abortion since the decision to perform the procedure must be left to the medical judgment of her attending physician. Any woman has the right in the first three months to seek out a physician willing to perform an abortion and to have the abortion performed free from intervention by the state. The state has no "compelling interest" at this stage of pregnancy that would permit it to override the woman's right to privacy by legislation. The state may require that all abortions be performed by licensed physicians but cannot require them to be performed in a hospital.

The Second Stage

In *Roe* v. *Wade,* the Supreme Court stated that: "For the stage subsequent to approximately the end of the first trimester, the State, in promoting its interest in the health of the mother, may, if it chooses, regulate the abortion procedure in ways that are reasonably related to maternal health."[41]

Thus, during approximately the fourth to sixth month of pregnancy, the state may regulate the medical conditions under which the procedure is performed. The constitutional test of any legislation concerning abortion during this period would be its relevance to the objective of protecting maternal health.

The Third Stage

By the time the final stage of pregnancy has been reached, the Supreme Court reasoned that the state had acquired a compelling interest in the fetus that could override the woman's right to privacy and could justify stringent regulation, even to the extent of prohibiting abortions. The court formulated its ruling as to the last stage in the following words: "For the stage subsequent to viability the State, in promoting its interest in the potentiality of human life, may, if it chooses, regulate, and even proscribe abortion except where it is necessary, in appropriate medical judgment, for the preservation of the life or health of the mother."[42]

Thus, during the final stage of pregnancy a state may prohibit all abortions except those deemed necessary to protect maternal life or health. The state's legislative powers over the performance of abortions increase as the pregnancy progresses toward term.

Specific Requirements

In *Doe* v. *Bolton,* further restrictions were placed on state regulation of the procedure. The provision of the Georgia statute that established residency requirements for women seeking abortions and that required the procedure to be performed in a hospital accredited by the Joint Commission on Accreditation of Hospitals (JCAH) was declared constitutionally invalid. The Supreme Court, in considering legislative provisions establishing medical staff approval as a prerequisite to the abortion procedure decided that ". . . interposition of the hospital abortion committee is unduly restrictive of the patient's rights and needs that . . .

have already been medically delineated and substantiated by her personal physician. To ask more serves neither the hospital nor the State."[43]

The Court thus was unable to find any constitutionally sufficient reason for the statutory requirement of advance approval by the abortion committee of the hospital's medical staff. It found no rational connection between a requirement of acquiescence by two copractitioners and the patient's needs. Furthermore, it found the requirement unduly infringed on the physician's right to practice. Thus, by using the test of the relationship to patient needs, the Court struck down several preabortion procedural requirements commonly imposed by state statutes concerning (1) residency, (2) performance of the abortion in a hospital accredited by JCAH, (3) approval by a committee of the hospital's medical staff, and (4) consultations.

Status of State and Local Regulation

The effect of the Supreme Court's decisions has been to invalidate all or parts of almost every one of the state abortion statutes in existence prior to 1973. State and local governments have enacted a variety of new laws designed to regulate abortions. Court decisions resulting from challenges to their constitutionality have helped to define the limits within which state and local governments may regulate abortions. Some of the requirements have concerned informed consent, paternal approval and notification when the woman is married, parental approval and notification when the woman is a minor, when the procedure must be performed in a hospital, the type of procedure, reporting of abortions, and zoning restrictions.

Informed Consent

Reasonable requirements concerning informed consent were upheld in a 1975 Pennsylvania case.[44] A 1983 Supreme Court decision addressed several issues involving informed consent.[45] At issue were several city ordinances in Akron, Ohio, that required that the physician made certain specific statements to the patient as part of an informed consent and imposed a 24-hour waiting period between the time the consent form was signed and the abortion was performed. The ordinance required that the woman must be informed of the status of her pregnancy, development of the fetus, date of viability, the physical and emotional consequences that may result, and the availability of agencies to provide information and assistance with respect to birth control, childbirth, and adoption.

The Supreme Court noted that the validity of an informed consent requirement is based on the state's interest in protecting the health of the pregnant woman and that this interest does not justify attempts to influence her choice. Under that standard the Court ruled that much of the information required was designed not to inform the woman's consent but rather to persuade her to withhold it. The ordinance also required that the physician inform the woman that "the unborn child is a human life from the moment of conception." The court found that this was an intrusion upon the discretion of the pregnant woman's physician. The court also ruled that the 24-hour waiting period was "arbitrary and inflexible."

Paternal Approval and Notification

In a 1976 case,[46] the Supreme Court ruled that states could not require paternal approval of abortions. However, one federal circuit court has ruled that the state may require a married woman to notify her husband prior to the abortion when the pregnancy was jointly conceived.[47] It returned the case to the District Court to make findings concerning notification for pregnancies not jointly conceived.

Parental Approval and Notification

In a 1979 case, the Supreme Court ruled that a state could require parental approval before a minor has an abortion if the state provides an appropriate and timely alternate procedure for (1) mature, informed minors and (2) other minors whose best interests indicate that parents should not be involved.[48] In 1981, the Supreme Court ruled that a state could require the notification of a parent before a minor has an abortion but declined to rule on the constitutionality of enforcing the law when the minor is mature or when the disclosure would not be in the best interests of the minor.[49]

There is no requirement of parental approval or notification unless the state has enacted such a law. In Nebraska, a reasonable good-faith belief that a minor is an adult is not a defense to a charge of performing an abortion without notifying a parent or guardian.[50] However, it is prudent for providers to encourage minors to involve their parents or other adult relatives in the decision-making process. In a 1972 case, the court ruled that parents do not have authority to give effective consent for an abortion unless the minor also consents.[51]

The Supreme Court in 1983 overturned the Akron ordinance discussed above that also required notification of and consent by parents before an abortion could be performed on an unmarried minor.[52] The Court said the ordinance failed because it did not provide for case-by-case evaluation of pregnant minors but was a blanket provision. The Court upheld a Missouri statute because it authorized juvenile courts to allow a pregnant adolescent to demonstrate that she was sufficiently mature to make the decision to have an abortion or that an abortion was in her best interest.[53]

Hospitalization

In 1976, the Supreme Court declared it an unconstitutional interference with the right of privacy in the physician-patient relationship to require that first trimester abortions be performed in a hospital.[54] In the Akron case, the Supreme Court also struck down a requirement that all abortions after the first trimester be performed in a hospital.[55] The Court said regulation of second trimester abortions must reasonably relate to the preservation and protection of maternal health and that present medical knowledge indicated that a blanket requirement that all second trimester abortions be performed in a hospital was unjustified. In the Missouri case above, the Court also ruled that a similar state law provision was unconstitutional.[56]

Procedure

In *Planned Parenthood of Central Missouri v. Danforth,* the Supreme Court invalidated a Missouri law that prohibited the saline method of abortion.

Reporting

In the same case the Court ruled that states could require recordkeeping and reporting that is reasonably directed to the preservation of maternal health and that respects the patient's confidentiality and privacy.

Zoning

In two cases decided in 1977, courts enjoined zoning rules that precluded abortion clinics from locating in a community.[57] However, in another case the court refused to enjoin a zoning rule that prohibited abortion clinics in some areas, but not the entire community.[58]

Funding of Abortions

Under the Constitution there is no obligation to provide public funding for abortions but several state constitutions have been interpreted to require it. In 1980, the Supreme Court ruled that the Congress could constitutionally forbid the use of federal funds to pay for abortions.[59] The court said that the prohibition:

> . . . places no governmental obstacle in the path of a woman who chooses to terminate her pregnancy, but rather, by means of unequal subsidization of abortion and other medical services, encourages alternative activity deemed in the public interest . . . Although government may not place obstacles in the path of a woman's exercise of her freedom of choice, it need not remove those not of its own creation. Indigency falls in the latter category.[60]

In a companion case, the Court ruled that similar state funding restrictions do not violate the Constitution.[61] However, several state courts have held that state constitutional provisions restrict the state's latitude. For example, in a 1981 Massachusetts case, the highest court in the commonwealth ruled that the Massachusetts constitution prohibits the state from restricting Medicaid payments for abortions in cases where the mother's life is endangered.[62]

Hospital Restrictions on Abortions

The *Wade* and *Bolton* decisions left open the question of how far a hospital may proceed in placing restrictions and prerequisites on those seeking abortions. Both decisions focused on state regulations of the procedures.

Lower federal courts have ruled that public hospitals may not forbid the use of their facilities for the performing of abortions. For example, in a 1982 case the court ruled that a city hospital commission could not constitutionally prohibit nontherapeutic abortions in a public hospital.[63] In a 1977 case, the Supreme Court ruled that St. Louis did not have to provide publicly funded abortions in a city hospital. However, the Court did not address the use of the city hospital facilities for privately funded abortions.[64]

Lower federal courts have ruled that there is no state action when private hospitals forbid or restrict the use of their facilities for abortions, so there is no violation of the Constitution. For example, a court found no state action when a private hospital prohibited abortions in its facilities, even when the two other private hospitals in the community had the same policy.[65] Lower federal courts found state action in a few cases in the 1970s but it is doubtful whether these decisions will be followed in future cases because, as discussed in Chapter 3, courts now apply stricter standards in determining whether there is state action.

State courts in some states may limit the discretion of some private hospitals based on state law. The New Jersey Supreme Court decided in 1976 that a private nonprofit, nonsectarian hospital could not deny the use of its facilities for elective first trimester abortions when it permits therapeutic abortions, has staff and facilities available, and is the only general hospital in its community.[66] The opinion was based on the common-law responsibilities of "quasi-public" hospitals in New Jersey.

Conscience Clause

Several states have enacted "conscience clauses" that prohibit discrimination against physicians and hospital personnel who refuse to participate in abortions. These clauses were found to be constitutional in 1973. In a 1980 New Jersey case, the court ruled that it was not discrimination to transfer a refusing nurse from the maternity to the medical-surgical nursing staff when there was no change in seniority, pay, or shift.[67] Thus, in some jurisdictions it may be possible to transfer staff to areas where they are not involved with the procedure without violating their right to refuse.

Trespass

Some opponents of abortion have tried to disrupt the operation of facilities providing the service. When their actions have gone beyond picketing to actual harassment and disruption, the courts have issued injunctions and enforced trespass convictions. In a 1980 case, the court upheld an injunction against harassment of staff and patients by demonstrators.[68] In another case a year later, a court affirmed the trespass convictions of several demonstrators for their sit-in in a facility.[69]

Of course, these sanctions can apply to anyone who enters a restricted area of a health care facility or disrupts the operations of the facility. In another case, a court upheld the trespass convictions of a group of women who violated hospital rules concerning entrance to the postpartum area even though they said they were conducting a "consumer inspection."[70]

PRENATAL TESTING AND GENETIC SCREENING

It is possible through certain tests during pregnancy and soon after birth to detect numerous disorders.

One of the most common genetic tests during pregnancy is amniocentesis. It involves withdrawing through a long needle a small amount of the amniotic fluid that surrounds the fetus. The fetal cells in the fluid are cultured for several weeks, then studied for genetic defects. More than 100 genetic conditions can be detected this way. These tests can help the parents to decide whether to have the child.

However, the tests actually reduce the number of abortions. By family genetic history it often is possible to identify parents at risk of having children with defects and many such parents have elected abortions even when the risk is one-fourth or lower. Most frequently, though, amniocentesis identifies that the fetus does not have the feared genetic disorder, so the parents decide to have the child.

The major legal issues concerning amniocentesis involve consent and disclosure. In 1982, a Utah court ruled that the mother's consent to amniocentesis was sufficient and there was no obligation to obtain the father's consent.[71] In obtaining consent, it is important to disclose the risks. There is a small risk of damage to, or even death of, the fetus. Thus, amniocentesis usually is not performed unless there is known risk of genetic defects because of family history or maternal age.

It is important to offer the option of amniocentesis to any woman who is known to be at an increased risk of a child with genetic defects that could be detected by this process. Failure to do so can lead to the liability discussed in the next section.

A second major type of genetic screening is the blood test within a few days after birth to detect metabolic disorders such as phenylketonuria (PKU). Some states have encouraged or required that these tests be performed on all newborns. If these conditions are detected early, special diets and other treatment can be given that preclude the severe mental retardation caused if the condition is not treated. Hospitals need to be familiar with local legal requirements. When not required by local law, it still is important to offer the tests to every family and explain the consequences of refusal. Liability for the complications from not detecting the condition is possible if the test is not offered.

WRONGFUL LIFE AND OTHER ACTIONS

Parents have sued physicians and hospitals for the wrongful conception or wrongful birth of children they did not want or deformed children they would have aborted had they known of the deformity. Deformed children have sued for their alleged wrongful life, claiming they were injured by being born. Courts have struggled with these suits to determine when there should be liability and what the basis for calculating the payment by the defendants should be.

Wrongful Conception and Wrongful Birth

The term *wrongful conception* is used, whether or not birth results, (1) when an unwanted pregnancy results from medical negligence or (2) when a fetus with a genetic defect is conceived after the parents were not informed or were misinformed of the risk of the genetic condition. The term *wrongful birth* is used (1) when a birth results from a wrongful conception or (2) when a birth follows medical negligence after conception that denies the mother the opportunity to make a timely informed decision whether to have an abortion. Parents have made six basic types of wrongful conception or wrongful birth claims. Three types concern unsuccessful sterilization and abortion procedures, and the three others involve genetic counseling and testing.

The three types arising from unsuccessful sterilization and abortion procedures include parents' claims that (1) they were not informed of the risk of the procedure's not being successful, (2) they were promised the procedure would be successful, or (3) the procedure was performed negligently. The first type is based on lack of informed consent, the second on breach of contract warranty, the third on malpractice.

Since there is a known risk of pregnancy even after a properly performed procedure, the mere fact that pregnancy occurs is not sufficient to establish that the procedure was performed negligently. Since it usually is difficult to establish negligence in performing the procedure, claims tend to be of the first two types.

However, a well-written consent form can make those types difficult to pursue. For example, in 1975, a Colorado court affirmed the dismissal of a suit by parents because the consent form included a statement that no guarantee had been made concerning the result of the treatment.[72]

The three other types of claims arise when an abnormal child is born whom the parents would have aborted if they had known of abnormality. The parents' claims parallel those of negligent sterilizations, either (1) they were not advised of the possibility of the condition and the availability of tests, (2) they were told there was no risk of the particular abnormality, or (3) the tests were performed negligently and the abnormality was not discovered. Thus, when there is reason to suspect that an abnormality is likely, it is prudent to advise the parents and offer them available tests.

Courts generally have awarded parents some payment when they are able to prove one or more of the six claims. There is disagreement on what the basis for the payment should be. The most significant difference concerns whether the defendants must pay for the cost of raising the child to adulthood. A few courts have permitted parents to collect the entire cost of raising the child.[73] Several courts have permitted parents to collect the cost of rearing the child, reduced by the amount the jury believes they are benefited by the joy and other benefits of parenthood.[74]

However, most courts have refused to permit the parents to collect the cost of rearing the child, especially if the child is healthy.[75] These courts have based their refusal on public policy considerations. They have been reluctant to label as an injury the presence of an additional child in a family. They have been concerned about the implications of the general rule that those who are injured must take steps to reduce their injuries, which could mean the parents would have to have an abortion or put the child up for adoption to reduce their injuries. However, some of the courts that have permitted payment for child-rearing costs have addressed this rule by stating that the parents do not have to reduce their injuries.

Wrongful Life

Some deformed children have sued physicians and hospitals claiming they were injured by being born. They have based their suits on the same claims their parents have made. All courts, except in California, have refused to allow such suits. In one of the earliest cases addressing this issue, the court observed that compensation ordinarily is computed by "comparing the condition plaintiff would have been in, had the defendants not been negligent, with plaintiff's impaired condition as a result of the negligence."[76] The condition of the child had the defendants not been negligent would have been the "utter void of nonexistence." The decision said that courts could not affix a price tag to nonlife, so it would be impossible to compute the amount to award.

In a 1982 California case, the court adopted the unusual position of permitting a child to collect for the extraordinary expenses of living with deafness from a genetic defect, even though there was no way the child could have been born without the deafness.[77] From the perspective of the defendant's actual liability, the decision does not appear as unusual. The court permitted the child to collect the same amount the parents could have collected in several other states if the suit had been in their name.

NOTES

1. *Griswold v. Connecticut*, 381 U.S. 479 (1965).

2. *Eisenstadt v. Baird*, 405 U.S. 438 (1972).

3. 405 U.S. 438, at 453.

4. *Carey v. Population Servs. Int'l.*, 431 U.S. 678 (1977).

5. 431 U.S. 678 at 693–694.

6. *Doe v Irving*, 615 F.2d 1162 (6th Cir. 1980).

7. *Doe v. Pickett*, 480 F.Supp. 1218 (S.D.W.Va. 1979).

8. 42 U.S.C.A. § 300(a) (West 1982).

9. 47 Fed. Reg. 7699–7701 (February 22, 1982).

10. *State of N.Y. v. Heckler*, Nos. 83–6073 and 83–6075 (2d Cir. October 7, 1983) [Permanent injunction].

11. 42 C.F.R. §§ 441.250–441.259 (1983).

12. *E.g.*, CAL. ADMIN. CODE. tit. 22, 70707.1–70707.8 R. (1977).

13. *California Medical Ass'n v. Lachner*, 124 Cal. App.3d 28, 177 Cal. Rptr. 188 (1981).

14. *See, e.g., Sims v. University of Ark. Medical Center*, No. LR 76–C–67 (E.D. Ark. March 4, 1977).

15. *Hathaway v. Worcester City Hosp.*, 475 F.2d 701 (1st Cir. 1973).

16. *Taylor v. St. Vincent Hosp.*, 523 F.2d 75 (9th Cir. 1975), *cert. denied*, 424 U.S. 948 (1976).

17. *Walker v. Pierce*, 522 P.2d 302 (4th Cir. 1977).

18. *Murray v. Vandevander*, 522 P.2d 302 (Okla. Ct. App. 1974).

19. *E.g.*, COLO REV. STAT. ANN. §§ 25–6–101, 25–6–102 (1982).

20. *E.g.*, GA. CODE ANN. § 84–932 (1979).

21. *E.g.*, KAN. STAT. ANN. § 65–446, 65–447 (1980).

22. *Swanson v. St. John's Lutheran Hosp.*, 615 P.2d 883 (Mont. 1980).

23. *Buck v. Bell*, 275 U.S. 200 (1927).

24. N.C. GEN. STAT. §§ 35–36—35–50 (1976 & Supp. 1981).

25. *In re Sterilization of Moore*, 221 S.E.2d 307 (N.C. 1976).

26. *North Carolina Ass'n of Retarded Children v. North Carolina*, 420 F.Supp. 451 (M.D.N.C. 1976).

27. *See, e.g., In re Grady*, 426 A.2d 467 (N.J. 1981).

28. *Wade v. Bethesda Hosp.*, 337 F.Supp. 671 (S.D. Ohio 1971); 356 F.Supp. 380 (S.C. Ohio 1973), and *Sparkman v. McFarlin*, 552 F.2d 172 (7th Cir. 1977).

29. *Stump v. Sparkman*, 435 U.S. 349 (1978).

30. *Sparkman v. McFarlin*, 601 F.2d 261 (7th Cir. 1979).

31. *See, e.g., In re Guardianship of Hayes*, 608 P.2d 635 (Wash. 1980).

32. *Hudson v. Hudson*, 373 So. 2d 310 (Ala. 1979).

33. *In re Guardianship of Eberhardy*, 307 N.W.2d 881 (Wis. 1981).

34. *E.g.*, OKLA. STAT., tit. 10, §§ 551–553 (West Supp. 1982–1983).

35. *People v. Sorenson*, 437 P.2d 495 (Ca. 1968).

36. *Doe v. Kelly*, 6 FAM.L.RPTR. (BNA) 3011 (January 28, 1980), *aff'd.* 307 N.E.2d 438 (Mich. App. 1981); *Syrkowski v. Appleyard*, 8 FAM.L.RPTR. (BNA) 2139 (November 25, 1981).

37. 44 Fed. Reg. 35033–58 (June 18, 1979).

38. 410 U.S. 113 (1973).

39. 410 U.S. 113, 164 (1973).

40. 410 U.S. 179 (1973).

41. 410 U.S. 113, 164 (1973).

42. 410 U.S. 113, 164 (1973).

43. *Doe v. Bolton*, 410 U.S. 179, 198 (1973).

44. *Planned Parenthood Ass'n v. Fitzpatrick*, 401 F.Supp. 554, (E.D.Pa. 1975) *aff'd, mem., sub. nom. Franklin v. Fitzpatrick*, 428 U.S. 901 (1976).

45. *City of Akron v. Akron Center for Reproductive Health*, ___ U.S. ___, 76 L.Ed.2d 687 (1983).

46. *Planned Parenthood of Cent. Mo. v. Danforth*, 428 U.S. 52 (1976).

47. *Sheinberg v. Smith*, 659 F.2d 476 (5th Cir. 1981).

48. *Belloti v. Baird*, 443 U.S. 622 (1979).

49. *H.L. v. Matheson*, 450 U.S. 398 (1981).

50. *Orr v. Knowles*, 337 N.W.2d. 699 (Neb. 1983).

51. *In re Smith*, 295 A.2d 238 (Md. App. 1972).

52. *City of Akron v. Akron Center for Reproductive Health*, ___ U.S. ___, 76 L.Ed.2d 687 (1983).

53. *Planned Parenthood v. Ashcroft*, ___ U.S. ___, 76 L.Ed.2d 733 (1983).

54. *Arnold v. Sendak*, 416 F.Supp. 22 (S.D. Ind. 1976), *aff'd sub. nom. Sendak v. Arnold*, 429 U.S. 968 (1977).

55. *City of Akron v. Akron Center for Reproductive Health*, ___ U.S. ___, 76 L.Ed. 687 (1983).

56. *Planned Parenthood v. Ashcroft*, ___ U.S. ___, 76 L.Ed. 733 (1983).

57. *Framingham Clinic, Inc., v. Board of Selectmen of Southborough*, 367 N.E.2d 606 (Mass. 1977); *Planned Parenthood of Minn. Inc., v. Citizens for Community Action*, 558 F.2d 861 (8th Cir. 1977).

58. *West Side Women's Servs. Inc. v. City of Cleveland*, 450 F.Supp. 796 (N.D. Ohio 1978) *aff'd mem.*, 582 F.2d 1281 (6th Cir. 1978), *cert. denied*, 439 U.S. 983 (1978).

59. *Harris v. McRae*, 448 U.S. 297 (1980).

60. 448 U.S. 297, 315–16 (1980).

61. *Williams v. Zbaraz*, 448 U.S. 358 (1980).

62. *Moe v. Secretary of Admin. of Fin.*, 417 N.E.2d 388 (Mass. 1981).

63. *Nyberg v. City of Virginia*, 667 F.2d 754 (8th Cir. 1982).

64. *Poelker v. Doe*, 432 U.S. 519 (1977).

65. *Doe v. Bellin Memorial Hosp.*, 479 F.2d 756 (7th Cir. 1973).

66. *Bridgeton Hosp. Ass'n v. Doe*, 366 A.2d 641 (N.J. 1976), *cert. denied*, 433 U.S. 914 (1977).

67. *Jeczalik v. Valley Hosp.*, No. C–2312–78 (N.J. Super., Bergen County, January 8, 1980).

68. *Northern Va. Women's Medical Center v. Balch & Horam*, No. 78–1673 (4th Cir. March 14, 1980).

69. *Cleveland v. Anchorage*, No. 4956 (Alaska, July 24, 1981).

70. *Donner v. State*, 375 So. 2d 840 (Fla. 1979).

71. *Reisner v. Lohner*, 641 P.2d 93 (Utah 1982).

72. *Herrara v. Roessing*, 533 P.2d 60 (Colo. App. 1975).

73. *See, e.g., Ochs v. Borelli*, 445 A.2d 883 (Conn. 1982).

74. *See, e.g., Sherlock v. Stillwater Clinic*, 260 N.W.2d 169 (Minn. 1977).

75. *See, e.g., Kingsbury v. Smith*, 442 A.2d 1003 (N.H. 1983).

76. *Gleitman v. Cosgrove*, 227 A.2d 689 (N.J. 1967).

77. *Turpin v. Sortini*, 643 P.2d 954 (Cal. 1982).

BIBLIOGRAPHY

Amato, John. "Legal Issues in Donor Selection for Artificial Insemination." *Health Matrix* 1, no. 2 (Summer 1983):57.

Regan, William. "Legally Speaking: Assisting at Abortions." *RN* 45, no. 6 (June 1982):71.

Chapter 13

Legal Aspects of Death

The definition of death is once again relatively settled but its application requires great care. The law regarding handling dead bodies also is settled and must be followed strictly because of the important societal and individual interests affected. Thus, it is important for nurses to be familiar with the law concerning the determination of death and the handling of bodies so they can fulfill their responsibilities and not inadvertently interfere with other staff members who are carrying out other duties.

DEFINITION OF DEATH

The question of the definition of death is distinct from the questions concerning treatment of the living. Once the patient is legally dead, there no longer is a patient. Patient care should be discontinued. The institution becomes the custodian of a dead body with the responsibilities discussed later in this chapter.

Because of the capacity of modern technology to sustain vegetative functions of persons with irreversible cessation of brain function and the development of modern transplant surgery, such irreversible cessation has been accepted as the definition of death when a patient's vital signs are being maintained artificially. The traditional definition still is applicable in all other situations.

Medical Definition of Death

For more than a century, the traditional definition of death has been the cessation of respiration, heartbeat, and certain indications of central nervous system activity, e.g., responsiveness to pain and reaction of pupils to light.

Advances in technology in the 1950s and 1960s produced cardiac pumps and respirators that can maintain the first two traditional indicators of life for indefinite periods, well beyond the irreversible cessation of all detectable brain activity; thus, medical science was forced to decide whether such an individual was alive or dead when the first two traditional life indicators were being maintained artificially.

It was concluded that such individuals were dead and that the use of machines should be discontinued. In 1974, the House of Delegates of the American Medical Association (AMA) recognized that "permanent and irreversible cessation of function of the brain constitutes one of the various criteria which can be used in the medical diagnosis of death."

It is accepted in the medical profession that death occurs when there is irreversible cessation of all brain functions, including the brain stem. While it may be appropriate to discontinue certain treatments for patients with only brain stem functioning, it is not appropriate to declare them dead until the brain stem also irreversibly ceases to function.

There still is some debate regarding optimal diagnostic criteria. The first widely publicized criteria were announced in 1968 by the Ad Hoc Committee of the Harvard Medical School to Examine the Definition of Brain Death. The lack of consensus at that time is reflected in the cautiously worded title of its report, *A Definition of Irreversible Coma*.[1] This title is unfortunate because it has led some to believe that the criteria can be used to assess only higher brain function, when in fact they can also be used to assess brain stem activity. Thus, despite the title, the Harvard criteria do apply to irreversible cessation of total brain function.

The report set forth the following criteria:

1. "unreceptivity and unresponsivity" to "externally applied stimuli and inner need;"
2. absence of spontaneous muscular movements or spontaneous respiration; and
3. absence of any elicitable reflexes.

A flat (isoelectric) electroencephalogram (EEG) was mentioned as having "great confirmatory value" in the diagnosis. There also was a warning that either hypothermia (low body temperature) or central nervous system depressants could cause the criteria to be met, so an assessment in the presence of either would not be valid. The report also specified that all of the criteria had to be met again at least 24 hours later.

The EEG is not a mandatory adjunct to the diagnosis but it is helpful. If appropriate EEG machines, trained operators, and trained interpreters are available in the hospital, it may be difficult to explain a failure to use them since some of the public unfortunately has identified brain death with the flat line on the EEG tracing. However, if all of the listed criteria are present, it is permissible to diagnose brain death without the EEG.

While the Harvard criteria still are widely used, various organizations have proposed modifications. In addition, the President's Commission for the Study of Ethical Problems in Medicine and Biomedical and Behavioral Research released in 1981 a set of guidelines developed by its medical consultants on the diagnosis of death.[2] Although the commission presented these solely as advisory guidelines, they can be expected to receive increasing recognition.

Some of the modifications include: (1) focus on the importance of the cause of the condition, (2) changes in the length of time for the diagnosis, (3) use of other tests, and (4) other matters. The Harvard criteria focused not on cause but entirely on the patient's present condition. The only reference to cause in the Harvard criteria is the statement that, if there is evidence of drug intoxication, time should be allowed for elimination of the intoxicating agent before the diagnosis is made.

The commission guidelines emphasize the importance of determining cause but recognize that it is not necessary in all cases. The commission urged caution when: (1) diseases or drugs that may cause total paralysis are involved, (2) metabolic abnormalities may be present, or (3) the patient is in shock. The Harvard criteria addressed the length of time for diagnosis by specifying that all tests must be repeated after at least 24 hours. It now is recognized that, in some cases (for example, when the cause clearly is massive head trauma), a much shorter period may be appropriate. There is some acceptance of a 12-hour or even six-hour period in cases in which drug intoxication is not suspected.

Some institutions use other tests to measure blood flow in the brain directly. If there is no blood flow, then the brain is dead, and no second test is required. These tests are particularly helpful to confirm the diagnosis when drug levels preclude reliance on the other tests. The Harvard criteria also did not address the age of the patient. The criteria are not so reliable in infants and young children because their recuperative potential is much greater. Great caution must be used in evaluating a child's clinical condition and in interpreting supplemental tests, including the EEG.

The Legal Definition of Death

The common-law definition of death includes brain death as determined in accordance with usual medical standards. In the first years that followed the medical recognition of brain death, some lower courts had difficulty accepting brain death in suits involving organ donations for heart transplants. One California trial court refused to accept brain death as death, acquitting the person who had been charged with manslaughter in the death of the donor. Such trial court cases now are historical anomalies.

The statutory recognition of brain death not only has superseded these decisions in their jurisdictions but also has resolved the question in more than half of the states. The common-law definition now also clearly includes brain death. Every appellate court that has ruled on the question has recognized brain death as legal death. Since 1977, the highest courts of Arizona, Colorado, Indiana, Massachusetts, Nebraska, and Washington all have adopted the brain death standard.[3]

Laws that include brain death in the definition were passed in an effort to avoid the case-by-case approach of the common law. The early contradictory trial court decisions added impetus to the statutory trend. Many of these cases involved organs removed from victims of apparent homicides. Some persons accused of homicide argued that they were not responsible for the death of the victim whose organs were transplanted.

To avoid this issue, many centers did not accept organ donations from victims of apparent homicide. An important factor in the passage of the statutes was that they facilitated organ donations from such victims, increasing the number of organs available to treat others and frequently helping the bereaved family to find some solace in helping others.

The details in the brain death laws vary from state to state, so physicians and nurses must be familiar with local law to assure compliance, especially with consultation and documentation requirements. Several groups have developed model legislation in an effort to achieve more uniformity. In 1980, several of the major groups involved in this effort agreed on the following model: "An individual who has sustained either (1) irreversible cessation of circulatory and respiratory functions, or (2) irreversible cessation of all functions of the entire brain, including the brain stem, is dead. A determination of death must be made in accordance with accepted medical standards."[4]

DEAD BODIES

This section discusses the duties of institutions and health care professionals in handling dead bodies and communicating with the family and legal authorities. Autopsies and anatomical donations are discussed in the following sections.

Communications with the Family

The hospital or health care institution in which a patient dies has a duty to inform an appropriate member of the family of a death. This is necessary not only ethically but also legally to permit arrangements to be made for disposition of the body. Information regarding deaths should be confirmed before being communicated. Erroneous notification will be upsetting to the family and may cause them to make expenditures for funeral arrangements—or even file a lawsuit. The hospital could be liable for the emotional harm and expenses.

Failure to make reasonable efforts to notify the appropriate member of the family within a reasonable time also can result in liability. In most institutions it is the responsibility of the physician to make the notification. However, in some institutions or circumstances, nurses may be expected to assist. Nurses should be familiar with their responsibilities so they can make appropriate communications—and refrain from them when others are doing so.

The method by which the family is informed also is important. In 1977 a New Jersey court ruled that a hospital could be sued for the method in which a mother had been informed of the death of her baby.[5] While still in the hospital where the birth occurred, the mother had been telephoned by a person from the hospital to which her baby had been transferred for specialized care. The caller, who was otherwise unidentified, told her the baby was dead, and the mother became hysterical.

In addition to the potential liability issues, this case illustrates the humanitarian reasons for thoughtful communications with the family. If it can be avoided, members should not be informed of unexpected deaths by telephone unless someone is with them to provide support. Obviously, when death is anticipated, there may be less need for immediate support.

Medical Examiner's Cases

All states have laws providing for legal investigation of certain suspicious deaths by a legal officer, such as a medical examiner or coroner. Most of the laws require a physician in attendance at a death known or suspected to be of the type requiring investigation to report it to the medical examiner. One typical example is the Iowa requirement that physicians report any "death which affects the public interest," which is defined to include:

1. Violent death, including homicidal, suicidal, or accidental death.
2. Death caused by thermal, chemical, electrical, or radiation injury.
3. Death caused by criminal abortion, including self-induced, or by sexual abuse.
4. Death related to disease thought to be virulent or contagious that may constitute a public hazard.
5. Death that has occurred unexpectedly or from an unexplained cause.
6. Death of a person confined in a prison, jail, or correctional institution.
7. Death of a person if a physician was not in attendance within 36 hours preceding death, excluding prediagnosed terminal or bedfast cases for which the time period is extended to 20 days.
8. Death of a person if the body is not claimed by a relative or friend.
9. Death of a person if the identity of the deceased is unknown.
10. Death of a child under the age of 2 years if death results from an unknown cause or if the circumstances surrounding the death indicate that sudden infant syndrome may be the cause of death.[6]

Each state's list is somewhat different so it is helpful for nurses to be familiar with their state's so the body is not mishandled inadvertently.

Physicians who are not sure whether to report should be encouraged to do so. The medical examiner then can decide whether further investigation is warranted. When it clearly is not a medical examiner's case, however, a report is inappropriate. When it is determined that the death is in fact a medical examiner's case, all health care providers have a duty to cooperate with the investigation.

The first requirement is not to move the body without the permission of the medical examiner, except as authorized by law. Some states authorize moving bodies, if necessary, to preserve the body from loss or destruction, to permit travel on highways or other public transportation, or to prevent immediate danger to the life, safety, or health of others. Not all states have the same exceptions, so nurses should become familiar with the laws of their own states.

Release of the Body

Upon the death of a patient, the hospital or other health care institution in which the person dies becomes the temporary custodian of the body. The institution is responsible for releasing the body to the proper recipient in the proper condition in accordance with state law. Thus, nurses and other institutional staff members should be familiar with the laws in their state that apply to handling and releasing dead bodies.

In general, the proper recipient of the body has a right to its prompt release in the condition at death unless the deceased has directed otherwise or the body is being retained or examined in accordance with law. Thus, the major issues are: (1) scope of the deceased's authority, (2) the authority of others to act in the absence of binding directions by the decedent, (3) the timing of the release of the body, and (4) the condition of the body when it is released.

Deceased's Authority

Some state statutes give individuals broad authority to direct the disposition of their remains.[7] All states now have enacted a version of the Uniform Anatomical Gift Act[8] so individuals can donate their body or certain organs for various purposes. When the situation is not covered by statute and the person entitled to dispose of the body is not willing to carry out the decedent's wishes, the common law determines whether the individual's wishes can be enforced.

Most courts have recognized a right to direct the disposition of the body by will but have recognized exceptions. Courts have taken other types of documents and statements into account in deciding how bodies shall be disposed of, but have recognized many more exceptions. Courts have been more likely to defer to such directions when they are in a will or a document authorized by statute. The one direction that the common law generally enforces is an autopsy authorization.

Authority of Others to Control Disposition

In the absence of binding directions by the deceased, the surviving spouse is recognized as the person who controls the disposition of the remains. However, in some states, if the surviving spouse has abandoned and is living apart from the deceased, the right is waived. If there is no surviving spouse or if that person fails to act or waives the right, then control passes to the next of kin. Unless statute or common-law precedent in the jurisdiction establishes a different order of kinship, the priority generally is recognized to be adult child, parent, and adult sibling. If the person with the highest priority either fails to act or waives the right, the next priority level becomes the highest priority level and has control.

Timing of Release of the Body

The person who is entitled to control of the body for disposition is entitled to have it released promptly, i.e., as soon as the person can show entitlement to the body and has satisfied any legal requirements, including permits. The hospital can retain the body long enough to transport it from the place of death to the usual place for releasing bodies and long enough to confirm that the person claiming control has the highest priority of those able and willing to do so. Refusal to release the body, even of a stillborn, can result in liability. Delay in delivery of the proper body also can result in liability.

Condition of the Body

The person who is entitled to control of the body is entitled to have it in the condition at the time of death. The change in condition that most frequently has led to litigation has resulted from an autopsy. An autopsy that is done without proper consent or other lawful authority can result in liability for violation of the right to the body in the condition at the time of death.

Burial or Other Disposition

The ultimate disposition of the remains is seldom the direct responsibility of the institution or the health care professional, either because others assume responsibility or because arrangements are made for a mortician to handle the disposition. In a few situations, however, state law may permit the institution to dispose of certain bodies directly. For example, in some states, hospitals may dispose of a stillborn when the parents elect such a disposition.

Unclaimed Dead Bodies

When there are no known relatives or friends to claim the body, the institution must dispose of the body in accordance with applicable laws. Some states require that unclaimed bodies be buried at public expense, and a public official is assigned to make arrangements. Most states provide that such bodies may be delivered to certain types of institutions or individuals for educational and scientific purposes. The institution should notify the appropriate public official when it has an unclaimed dead body in its possession so the official can make arrangements for either type of disposal. Before notifying the public official, there should be a reasonable attempt to locate and contact relatives so they can claim the body.[9]

AUTOPSIES

Autopsies are the most frequent cause of litigation involving dead bodies and health care providers. This section outlines the legal prerequisites to autopsies and the potential sources of liability involving them.

Autopsies are performed primarily to determine the cause of death. This finding can be crucial in detecting crime or ruling out transmittable diseases that may be a threat to the public health. More frequently, the cause of death can affect whether death benefits are payable under insurance policies, Workers' Compensation laws, and other programs. Autopsies help to advance medical science by permitting the correlation of anatomical changes with other signs and symptoms of disease. At the same time, they can be educational for those involved in them.

Community mores and religious beliefs have long dictated respectful handling of dead bodies. Societal views now have evolved to the point that a substantial portion of the population recognizes the benefit of autopsies. Out of respect to those who continue to find autopsies unacceptable, the law requires appropriate consent before one can be performed, except when it is needed to determine the cause of death for public policy purposes.

Authorization by Decedent

The statutes of many states permit people to authorize an autopsy to be performed on their bodies after death. In states that do not explicitly address authorization before death, the anatomical gift act can be used. The person can donate the body for the purpose of autopsy, with such conditions as are desired, by following the rules for executing an anatomical gift. Even when there clearly is valid authorization from the decedent, hospitals and physicians may decide in some cases to decline to perform an autopsy—for example, when it is contrary to the strongly held wishes of the family.

Authorization by Family or Others

When the patient has not given legal authorization for an autopsy, authorization may be obtained from someone else. Many states have statutes that specify who may authorize an autopsy. Some specify a priority ordering; the available person with the highest priority may give the authorization.[10] Others specify that the person assuming responsibility for disposal of the body may consent to the autopsy.[11] This second type of statute does not specify a priority so common-law principles must be followed to determine that point. In a few states, autopsy authorization statutes do not establish priority but rather specify the priority of the duty to assume custody for disposal.[12] In such cases, the courts look to the duty of disposal statutes to establish the priority. In the absence of either an autopsy authorization or duty-of-disposal statute, the common-law priority is followed.

The general common-law rule is that the surviving spouse has the highest priority and duty to arrange for disposal and, thus, is the proper person to authorize an autopsy. If there is no surviving spouse or the spouse's right is waived, the next of kin has the responsibility. The most common order is child, parent, sibling, then other next of kin. Most statutes disqualify any on the list who are not adults.

Under most of the statutes, the authorization of the highest priority person who can be located with reasonable efforts is sufficient unless there is actual knowledge of the objections of a person of the same or a higher priority, or of the deceased. In these states, objections by persons of lower priority have no legal effect. However, a few states permit persons of lower priority to veto an authorization[13] so familiarity with state law is essential.

Most of the authorization statutes specify others who may authorize an autopsy when there is no spouse or next of kin available. In most states, the final priority rests with whoever assumes responsibility for disposal of the remains. A few states permit a physician to perform an autopsy without authorization when there is neither knowledge of any objection nor anyone assuming responsibility for disposal after due inquiry.[14]

Scope of Authorization

The general rule is that whoever authorizes the autopsy may limit its scope by imposing conditions. If these conditions are not met, then the autopsy is not authorized. If the conditions are unacceptable, however, the physician who is to perform the autopsy may decline to do so. Examples of conditions include limits on the areas to be examined, restrictions on retention of parts of the body, and requirements that certain observers be present. Unless the authorization specifically includes permission to retain parts of the body, an autopsy authorization usually is interpreted not to permit retention.

Form of Authorization

A few states require that an autopsy be authorized in writing. Many states include telegrams and recorded telephone permissions as acceptable forms of authorization. Common law does not require that the authorization be documented in a particular way. A written authorization or recorded telephone authorization obviously is easier to prove.[15]

Medical Examiner or Other Legal Officials

There are many circumstances in which authorization of the deceased, a family member, or friend is not required. Determination of the cause of death is so important in some cases that statutory authority has been granted to certain public officials to order an autopsy. In addition, courts have the authority to issue an order.

All states have a state or county officer, usually called a medical examiner or coroner, who is authorized to investigate certain deaths. In most states, the medical examiner has the authority to perform an autopsy when it is necessary for the investigation. In some of the states, other officials also are given the power.

Liability for Unauthorized Autopsies

Under general principles of liability, the hospital can be liable for unauthorized autopsies by its employees and agents. Hospitals are not the insurers of the safety of dead bodies so they are not generally liable for unauthorized autopsies by persons not acting on the institution's behalf but they must take reasonable steps to protect the body from an unauthorized autopsy.[16]

DONATION OF BODIES

Prior to 1969, the uncertainty surrounding the authority of persons to make binding anatomical donations prior to death and of others to make such donations after death limited the availability of organs for transplantation. The Uniform Anatomical Gift Act was developed as a model to resolve the uncertainty.[17] It was approved by the National Conference of Commissioners on Uniform State Laws and the American Bar Association in August 1968. Laws substantially equivalent to the model were enacted in all of the states by the end of 1971. Every state now has statutory authority and procedures for anatomical gifts, so the uncertainty has been removed.

The Uniform Anatomical Gift Act specifies who may donate and who may receive anatomical gifts. It specifies the documentation required, the permitted uses of the anatomical gift, and how a gift may be revoked. It also provides some limitations on liability.[18] Many of the states modified the act before enactment or by subsequent amendment. For example, the age requirements for donation and the liability limitation provisions vary. The act is subject to all laws regarding autopsies. It gives the medical examiner's responsibilities and duties a higher public priority than anatomical donations.

NOTES

1. 205 J.A.M.A. 337 (1968).
2. President's Commission for the Study of Ethical Problems in Medicine and Biomedical and Behavioral Research, DEFINING DEATH (July 1981).
3. *State v. Fierro*, 603 P.2d 74 (Ariz. 1979); *Lovato v. District Court*, 601 P.2d 1072 (Colo. 1979); *Swafford v. State*, 421 N.E.2d 596 (Ind. 1981); *Commonwealth v. Golston*, 366 N.E.2d 744 (Mass. 1977); *cert. denied* 434 U.S. 1039 (1978); *State v. Meints*, 322 N.W.2d 809 (Neb. 1982); *In re Welfare of Bowman*, 617 P.2d 731 (Wash. 1980).
4. Horan, "Definition of Death: An Emerging Consensus," 12 *Trial* 22, 25-26 (1980).
5. *Muniz v. United Hosps. Medical Center Presbyterian Hospital*, 153 N.J. Super. 72, 379 A.2d 57 (N.J. Super. Ct. App. Div. 1977).
6. IOWA CODE § 331.802 (1983).
7. *E.g.*, CAL. HEALTH & SAFETY CODE § 7100.
8. 8 U.L.A. 15 (1972).
9. *E.g.*, *Burke v. New York U.*, 188 N.Y.S. 123 (N.Y. App. Div. 1921).
10. *E.g.*, IOWA CODE § 144.56 (1983).
11. *E.g.*, COLO. REV. STAT. ANN. § 12-36-133 (1978 Repl. Vol.)
12. *E.g.*, ARIZ. REV. STAT. ANN. § 36-831 (1980-81 Supp.).
13. *E.g.*, MINN. STAT. ANN. § 145.161 (1970).
14. *E.g.*, N.Y. PUB. HEALTH LAW § 4214 (1971).
15. *E.g.*, *Lashbrook v. Barnes*, 437 S.W.2d 502 (Ky. 1969).
16. *E.g.*, *Grawunder v. Beth Israel Hosp. Ass'n*, 266 N.Y. 605, 195 N.E. 221 (1935).
17. 8 U.L.A. 15 (1972).
18. *Williams v. Hofmann*, 223 N.W.2d 844 (Wis. 1974) [Liability limitation constitutional but not · applicable to treatment of donor prior to death].

BIBLIOGRAPHY

Cushing, Maureen. "Treatment Beyond Death?" *American Journal of Nursing* 81, no. 8 (August 1981):1527.

Glossary of Legal Terms

Abortion: The termination of pregnancy or inducement of miscarriage with intent to destroy a fetus.

Administrative agency: An arm of government that administers or carries out legislation; for example, the Workers' Compensation Commission.

Admissibility (of evidence): Worthiness of evidence that meets the legal rules of evidence and will be allowed to be presented to the jury.

Affidavit: A voluntary sworn statement of facts, or a voluntary declaration in writing of facts, that a person swears to be true before an official authorized to administer an oath.

Agency: The relationship in which one person acts for or represents another; for example, employer and employee.

Allegation: A statement that a person expects to be able to prove.

Amicus curiae: "Friend of the court;" a brief filed in a lawsuit on behalf of one side, usually by an expert who provides information on a matter before the court.

Appellant: The party who appeals the decision of a lower court to a higher jurisdiction.

Appellee: The party against whom an appeal to a higher court is taken.

Assault: An intentional act designed to make the victim fearful and that produces reasonable apprehension of harm.

Assignment: A transfer of rights or property.

Attestation: An indication by a witness that the documents of procedures required by law have been signed.

Battery: The touching of one person by another without permission.

Best evidence rule: The legal doctrine requiring that primary evidence of a fact (such as an original document) be introduced, or at least explained, before a copy can be introduced or testimony given concerning the fact.

Bona fide: In good faith; openly, honestly, or innocently; without knowledge or intent of fraud.

Borrowed servant: An employee temporarily under the control of another. The traditional example is a nurse employed by a hospital who is "borrowed" by a surgeon in the operating room. The temporary employer of the borrowed servant will be held responsible for the act of the borrowed servant under the doctrine of *respondeat superior*.

"Captain of the ship" doctrine: Doctrine by which the physician, as "captain," is held liable for the actions of all members of the health care team.

Civil law: The law of countries such as Germany and France that follow the Roman system of jurisprudence in which all law is enacted. It also is the portion of American law that does not deal with crimes.

Closed shop contract: A labor-management agreement that provides that only members of a particular union may be hired.

Common law: The legal traditions of England and the United States where part of the law is developed by means of court decisions.

Comparative negligence: Doctrine by which the negligence of the parties is compared and recovery permitted when the negligence of the plaintiff is less than that of the defendant.

Concurring opinion: *See* Opinion of the court.

Confidential information: *See* Privileged communication.

Consent: A voluntary act by which one person agrees to allow someone else to do something. For medical liability purposes, consents should be in writing with an explanation of the procedures to be performed.

Counterclaim: A defendant's claim against a plaintiff.

Crime: An act against society in violation of the law. Crimes are prosecuted by and in the name of the state.

Criminal law: The division of the law dealing with crime and punishment.

Decedent: A deceased person.

Defamation: The injury of a person's reputation or character by willful and malicious statements made to a third person. Defamation includes both libel and slander.

Defendant: In a criminal case, the person accused of committing a crime; in a civil suit, the party against whom suit is brought demanding compensation to the other party.

Deposition: A witness's sworn statement, made out of court, that may be admitted into evidence if it is impossible for the witness to attend in person.

Directed verdict: The verdict returned by a jury when the judge directs it to do so in favor of one party because the evidence or law is so clearly in favor of that party that it is pointless for the trial to proceed.

Discovery: Pretrial activities of attorneys to determine what evidence the opposing side will present if the case comes to trial. Discovery prevents attorneys from being surprised during a trial and facilitates out-of-court settlement (*see* Interrogatories).

Dissenting opinion: *See* Opinion of the court.

Emergency: A sudden, unexpected occurrence or event causing a threat to life or health.

Employee: One who works for another in return for pay.

Employer: A person or firm that selects employees, pays their salaries or wages, retains the power of dismissal, and can control their conduct during working hours.

Expert witness: One who has special training, experience, skills, and knowledge in a relevant area and who is allowed to offer an opinion as testimony in court.

False imprisonment: The unlawful restriction of a person's freedom by holding the person against his/her will without legal justification; an intentional tort.

Federal question: A legal question involving the United States Constitution or a statute enacted by Congress.

Felony: A crime of a serious nature usually punishable by imprisonment for a period of longer than one year or by death.

Good Samaritan law: A legal doctrine designed to protect those who stop to render aid in an emergency.

Grand jury: A jury called to determine whether there is sufficient evidence that a crime has been committed to justify bringing a case to trial. It is not the jury before which the case is tried to determine guilt or innocence.

Gross negligence: The intentional failure to perform a duty in reckless disregard of the consequences; willful or wanton conduct.

Harm or injury: Any wrong or damage done to another, either to a person or to the person's rights or property.

Hearsay rule: A rule of evidence that restricts the admissibility of evidence that is not the personal knowledge of the witness. Hearsay evidence is admissible only under strict rules.

Holographic will: A will handwritten by the testator.

In loco parentis: The legal doctrine providing that under certain circumstances the courts may assign a person to stand in the place of parents and possess their legal rights, duties, and responsibilities toward a child.

Independent contractor: One who agrees to undertake work without being under the direct control or direction of an employer.

Indictment: A formal written accusation of crime brought by a prosecuting attorney against one charged with criminal conduct.

Injunction: A court order requiring one to do or not to do a certain act.

Interrogatories: A list of questions sent from one party in a lawsuit to the other party to be answered before trial (*see* Discovery).

Judge: An officer who guides court proceedings to ensure impartiality and enforce the rules of evidence. The trial judge determines the applicable law and states it to the jury. The appellate judge hears appeals and renders decisions concerning the correctness of actions of the trial judge, the law of the case, and the sufficiency of the evidence.

Jurisprudence: The philosophy or science of law upon which a particular legal system is built.

Jury: A certain number of persons selected and sworn to hear the evidence and determine the facts in the case.

Larceny: The taking of another person's property without consent and with intent to deprive the owner of its use and ownership.

Liability: An obligation one has incurred or might incur through any act or failure to act.

Liability insurance: A contract to have someone else pay for any liability or loss thereby in return for the payment of premiums.

Libel: A false or malicious writing that is intended to defame or dishonor another person and is published so that someone besides the one defamed will observe it.

License: A permit from the state allowing certain acts to be performed, usually for a specific period of time.

Litigation: A trial in court to determine legal issues, rights, and duties between the parties to the litigation.

Malpractice: Professional misconduct, improper discharge of professional duties, or failure to meet the standard of care of a professional, that resulted in harm to another.

Mayhem: The crime of intentionally disfiguring or dismembering another.

Misdemeanor: An unlawful act of a less serious nature than a felony, usually punishable by fine or imprisonment for a term of less than one year.

Negligence: Carelessness, failure to act as an ordinary prudent person, or action contrary to the conduct of a reasonable person.

Next of kin: Those persons who by the law of descent would be adjudged the closest blood relatives of a decedent, patient, or person.

Non compos mentis: ''Not of sound mind;'' suffering from some form of mental defect.

Notary public: A public official who administers oaths and certifies the validity of documents.

Opinion of the court: In an appellate court decision, the reasons for the decision. One judge writes the opinion for the majority of the court. Judges who agree with the result but for different reasons may write concurring opinions explaining their reasons. Judges who disagree with the majority may write dissenting opinions.

Ordinance: A law passed by a municipal legislative body.

Perjury: The willful act of giving false testimony under oath.

Plaintiff: The party to a civil suit who brings the suit seeking damages and other relief.

Police power: The power of the state to protect the health, safety, morals, and general welfare of its citizens.

Privileged communication: A statement made to an attorney, physician, spouse, or anyone else in a position of trust. Because of the confidential nature of such information, the law protects it from being revealed, even in court. The term is applied in two distinct situations: (1) the communications between certain persons, such as physician and patient, cannot be divulged without the consent of the patient; (2) in some situations the law provides an exemption from liability for disclosing information where there is a higher duty to speak, such as statutory reporting requirements.

Probate: The judicial proceeding that determines the existence and validity of a will.

Probate Court: A court with jurisdiction over wills. Its powers range from deciding the validity of a will to distributing property.

Proximate: In immediate relation with something else. In negligence cases, the careless act must be the proximate (immediate) cause of injury.

Punitive damages: An amount awarded to a plaintiff, over and above actual damages, to punish the negligent party.

Real evidence: Evidence furnished by tangible things such as weapons, bullets, and equipment.

Rebuttal: The giving of evidence to contradict the effect of evidence introduced by the opposing party.

Regulatory agency: An arm of the government that enforces legislation regulating an act or activity in a particular area; for example, the Federal Food and Drug Administration.

Release: A statement signed by one person relinquishing a right or claim against another person, usually for a valuable consideration.

Res gestae: All of the surrounding events that become part of an incident. If the statements are made as part of the incident they are admissible in court as *res gestae,* as an exception to the hearsay rule.

Res ipsa loquitur: "The thing speaks for itself." A doctrine of law applicable to cases where the defendant had exclusive control of the thing that caused the harm and where the harm ordinarily could not have occurred without negligent conduct.

Respondeat superior: "Let the master answer." The legal doctrine that holds the employer responsible for the legal consequences of the acts of the servant, or employee, while acting within the scope of employment.

Slander: An oral statement made with intent to dishonor or defame another person when made in the presence of a third person.

Standard of care: Acts performed or omitted that an ordinary prudent person would have performed or omitted. It is a measure against which a defendant's conduct is compared.

Stare decisis: "Let the decision stand." The legal principle indicating courts should apply previous decisions to subsequent cases involving similar facts and questions.

State statute, statutory law: A declaration of the legislative branch of government having the force of law.

Statute of limitations: A legal limit on the time allowed for filing suit in civil matters, usually measured from the time of the wrong or from the time when a reasonable person would have discovered the wrong.

Subpoena: A court order requiring one to appear in court to give testimony.

Subpoena duces tecum: A subpoena that commands a person to come to court and to produce whatever documents are named in order.

Subrogation: The substitution of one person for another in reference to a lawful claim or right.

Suit: A court proceeding in which one person seeks damages or other legal remedies from another. The term is not usually used in criminal cases.

Summons: A court order that directs a sheriff (or other appropriate officer) to notify the defendant in a civil suit that has been filed and when and where to appear.

Testimony: The oral statement of a witness given under oath at a trial.

Tort: A civil wrong. Torts may be intentional or unintentional.

Tortfeasor: One who commits a tort.

Trial court: The court in which evidence is presented to a judge or jury for decision.

Ultra vires: An act beyond the scope of the power of a corporation.

Uniform act: A model act concerning a particular area of the law created by a nonlegal body in the hope that it will be enacted in all states to achieve uniformity in that area of law.

Union shop contract: A labor-management agreement making continued employment contingent upon joining a union.

Verdict: The formal declaration of a jury's findings of fact, signed by the jury foreman and presented to the court.

Waiver: The intentional giving up of a right, such as allowing another person to testify to information that ordinarily would be protected as a privileged communication.

Will: A legal declaration of the intentions a person wishes to have carried out after death concerning property, children, and estate.

Witness: One who is called to give testimony in a court of law.

Written authorization: A consent given in writing specifically empowering someone to do something.

Introduction to
Index of Cases

Cases decided by courts are reported through a regional reporting system. The numbers and letters after each case name tell where to find the decision and opinion of the court. For example, in *Tuma* v. *Board of Nursing*, 593 P.2d 711 (Idaho 1979), the first number, 593, is the volume. It is followed by the abbreviation for the reporter system; "P.2d" means *Pacific Reporter, Second Series*. The next number, 711, is the page on which the case begins. The name of the court and the date of the decision are given in parentheses following the citation, namely the Idaho Supreme Court, and 1979. Sometimes a case is reported in more than one reporter system, so there will be another set of numbers and letters before the parentheses. If the other reporter system includes only cases from one court, the name of the court is not repeated in the parentheses.

When there is another set of numbers and letters after the parentheses, they refer to another court's decision concerning the same case. If the second one is a higher court, it will be preceded by letters such as *aff'd, rev'd.* or *cert. denied,* indicating that the court affirmed, reversed, or declined to review the lower court's decision. In some situations the order of the references is reversed, so that the higher court is listed first. In those situations the abbreviations will be *aff'ing* or *rev'ing,* indicating whether the higher court is affirming or reversing the lower court.

Major abbreviations include the following:

U.S.	*United States Reports* contains United States Supreme Court cases.
S. Ct.	*Supreme Court Reporter,* also United States Supreme Court cases.
U.S.L.W.	*United States Law Week,* also United States Supreme Court cases.
F.	Federal Reporter, contains cases decided by federal courts.
F.2d	*Federal Reporter, Second Series*, additional federal court cases.
F.Supp.	*Federal Supplement,* still further federal cases.
C.F.R.	*Code of Federal Regulations*
U.S.C.	*United States Code*
Fed. Reg.	*Federal Register*

Index of Cases

C

Subject Index

U

V

About the Authors

Ann Marie Rhodes, R.N., M.A., J.D., is a graduate of the College of St. Teresa and received both her masters degree in nursing and her law degree from the University of Iowa. Over the course of her career Ms. Rhodes has served as a pediatric nurse, shift supervisor, and clinical nursing specialist in charge of the University Hospital's 160-bed pediatric nursing division. In her current capacity as assistant to the director of the University of Iowa's hospitals and clinics, she brings to bear a wealth of both personal experience and professional nursing and legal expertise.

Robert D. Miller, J.D., M.S. Hyg., is a graduate of Iowa State University, the Yale University Law School, and the University of Pittsburgh Health Law Training Program. He is currently practicing law with the firm of Shutts and Bowen in West Palm Beach and Miami, Florida. In addition to lecturing frequently to nursing groups, Mr. Miller is the author of Aspen's *Problems in Hospital Law, Fourth Edition, 1983* and a contributor to Aspen's *Hospital Law Manual.*